Contemporary Asian American Communities

In the series

Asian American History and Culture
edited by Sucheng Chan, David Palumbo-Liu, and Michael Omi

Contemporary Asian American Communities

Intersections and Divergences

Edited by Linda Trinh Võ and Rick Bonus

TEMPLE UNIVERSITY PRESS

PHILADELPHIA

Temple University Press, Philadelphia 19122
Copyright © 2002 by Temple University
All rights reserved
Published 2002
Printed in the United States of America

Library of Congress Cataloging-in-Publication Data

Contemporary Asian American communities : intersections and divergences /
edited by Linda Trinh Võ and Rick Bonus.
    p. cm. — (Asian American history and culture)
    Includes bibliographical references and index.
    ISBN 1-56639-937-8 (alk. paper) : ISBN 1-56639-938-6 (pbk. : alk. paper)
    1. Asian Americans—Social conditions.   2. Asian Americans—Ethnic identity.
3. Ethnic neighborhoods—United States.   4. Asia—Emigration and immigration—
Social aspects.   5. United States—Emigration and immigration—Social aspects.
I. Võ, Linda Trinh, 1964–   II. Bonus, Rick, 1962–   III. Series.
E184.O6 C666 2002
305.895073—dc21

                                                                    2001052506

To my supportive parents, Thuy Hanlon and Robert Joseph Hanlon. And to my loving partner Bill Ross and our marvelous children Aisha and Kian. —LTV

To my mother, Miren, for her love.
And to my families here and abroad, for their sustenance. —RB

We also dedicate this book to Asian American community workers whose passionate devotion and tireless efforts have benefited us all.

Contents

Acknowledgments

Our collaboration on this book has been a journey. One of us was born in Vietnam, the other in the Philippines. Our working as co-editors of this collection with these personal beginnings speaks to the dynamic and growing field of Asian American studies. Our migrations eventually brought us to the University of California, San Diego, where as graduate students we shared mentors and taught in the Summer Bridge Program and Ethnic Studies Department. In particular, we thank Yen Le Espiritu, Lisa Lowe, and George Lipsitz for sharing their intellectual passion with us. We were allowed to nurture our interest in Asian American studies, and this fostered a friendship that has been strengthened while working on this endeavor.

Our journey spans several other institutions of which we have been part: Oberlin College; the University of California, Berkeley; the University of California, Irvine; the University of Washington; and Washington State University. We are thankful to the College of Liberal Arts at Washington State University for providing an Initiation/Completion Grant that gave us the opportunity to review the proposals. Our appreciation also goes to Susan Jeffords, divisional dean of social sciences in the College of Arts and Sciences at the University of Washington, for making available valuable funding support for the completion of the book. We thank the numerous students, staff, faculty, and administrators at these institutions for their collegiality, encouragement, and guidance. Along the way, we have been engaged in community formations inside and outside of the academy and have learned many enduring lessons about building communities in these environments. We thank all those who were patient and generous enough to teach us and would like to believe that we have come away wiser.

Some of the essays in this anthology were contributed by scholars who participated in a Contemporary Asian Pacific American Communities Conference at the University of Southern California on 11 April 1998. The conference was designed specifically to discuss the themes and issues we present. We thank our institutional sponsors, the Center for Multiethnic and Transnational Studies, the Department of Sociology, and the Asian American Studies Program—all based at the University of Southern California—and our generous co-organizer, Edward Park, for making that conference possible. We also acknowledge the presenters and senior discussants—Shirley Hune, Russell Leong, John Liu, and Paul Spickard—for their important participation and rigorous analysis. Mariam Beevi, Shilpa Davé, Antoinette Charfauros McDaniel, Viet Thanh Nguyen, and Okiyoshi Takeda also deserve acknowledgment for their contribution to the conference.

We deeply appreciate Janet Francendese of Temple University Press and Michael Omi, a series coeditor, for their confidence in and support of our project, and we are grateful to our anonymous reviewer for providing us with important critiques of our manuscript. We thank Michael Tuncap, David G. Palaita, and Caroline Tamayo for their valuable research assistance. We are the auspicious beneficiaries of Martin Manalansan's wisdom about traversing the sometimes harrowing world of editing an anthology. We have also been privileged to work with superb contributors who have made this volume finer than we ever imagined.

Along our journey, we have been fortunate to have the support of our devoted families and we dedicate this book to them. Thank you all for sustaining us.

Rick Bonus and Linda Trinh Võ

On Intersections and Divergences

During a recent conference of the Association for Asian American Studies, we attended a dinner banquet at a restaurant in the Chinatown section of Philadelphia. When our server came, he gave chopsticks to all but one person, who is half Japanese, a quarter Danish, and a quarter Czech, and has reddish hair and freckles. To her, he gave a fork. When she pointed this out, we laughed and decided that, in solidarity, we would all ask for forks. When we did, the server was puzzled. He looked at our friend and said, "She's American, isn't she?" We understood what he meant, but somehow the implication that the rest of us were not "American," an all-too-common experience for many, had a peculiar sting, even if it was expressed by someone of Chinese ancestry.[1]

Our friend is Yonsei, a fourth-generation Japanese American. This "American" studied Japanese in college; attended summer school in Tokyo; and traveled in rural Japan. Ironically, a person sitting next to her was also a Yonsei but had never been to Japan; spoke only English but was learning Spanish; and had spent a couple of years hitchhiking around Europe. Our group varied in ethnic origin. We lived in different parts of the country. Some were immigrants. Some were monolingual, while others were multilingual. The list of common and varying attributes is long. And over dinner, this one small and seemingly inconsequential gesture mushroomed into discussions and debates about who Asian Americans are, how we define ourselves, what others think about us, and, perhaps more provocative, what others still do not know about us. On the surface, it seems amusing that people can make assumptions about tableware preferences based on one's physical features. But more seriously, this is yet another instance of the persistence of racial stereotypes in which assumptions about who counts as "Asian," what "Asians" use to eat, and what "Asian American" means are brought into question. The year before this conference was held, questions about the status and quality of Filipino American presence within the association's institutional arrangements and political practices had been heatedly debated. And in several communities within and outside academe, parallel questions are constantly being raised: Who are the Iu Mien? What does "1.5" generation mean? Should we count as Asian American those who spend more time outside the United States than in it? What about those who are multiracial, the *hapas*? Can we form a group on the Internet and call it an Asian American community? Which strategies are most effective for collectively challenging the model-minority myth that affects most, if not all, Asian American groups?

The impetus for this "community" collection originally came from questions derived during our graduate-student days, when we were both doing ethnographic research projects on Asian American groups in Southern California.[2] Our aim is to advance the practice of applying multidisciplinary approaches to similar objects of study in order to open a broader, more complex, and richer set of conversations among scholars from different fields, such as history, literature, cultural studies, sociology, anthropology, urban studies, and legal studies.[3] The contributors to this collection grapple with ideas and practices of community formation from empirical, literary, and theoretical perspectives, exploring, revealing, and expanding the themes of both shared histories and diverse experiences of Asian American communities.

This anthology presents a collection of original essays on the dynamics of contemporary Asian American communities; taken as a whole, the volume engages the intersections and divergences of community formations and considers whether these formative elements persist or are transformed. Most of the available sources on this subject emphasize the historical development of these communities (e.g., Chan 1991; Daniels 1988; Okihiro 1994; Takaki 1989). With the influx of post-1965 immigrants and refugees and the generational growth and spread of pre-1965 communities, Asian Americans are transforming the demographics of the American population, and Asian American communities are altering the nature of the American landscape (Barkan 1992; Chan 1991; Hing 1993; Kitano and Daniels 1995; Ong et al. 1994; Zia 2000). In addition, the historical legacies and unique present-day environments created by globalization and transnational movements have complicated individual and collective Asian American identities in ways that connect the local with the regional and the global.[4] These conditions call for new ways to analyze how we think about Asian Americans, how we think about Americans, and how we think about "community" formations.[5]

Asian Americans, because of the increasing heterogeneity of their subpopulation groups, raise questions not only about the assumed stability of such a categorical identification but also about the persistent articulation of U.S. race relations solely through a black–white framework. Viewed through the local and global contexts of their influx and presence in the United States more than through their sheer numbers, Asian Americans also prompt a critical rethinking of social norms regarding nationhood, visibility, and power. Who can be considered American? Who can belong? And on whose and what terms? Likewise, the need to understand race as a central social and political force in Asian Americans' lives and as a category of experience that interlocks with gender, class, and sexuality suggests new questions about how Asian Americans perceive themselves, interact with others, and locate themselves in various contexts. We address these issues by considering the centrality of ideas and practices of "community" as they are formed and transformed within Asian America.

In the parts that follow, we will provide such explanatory contexts and identify each of our authors' contributions to the discussions of specific themes in this collection. We focus on three themes:

Communities in Transition: Spaces and Practices discusses the concepts and processes of forging aggregations that relate to physical settlements, situational spaces, and social sites.

Communities in Transformation: Identities and Generations examines elements of change within Asian American community identities, specifically in light of their generational composition and the way these compositions intersect with ethnic and racial factors, class configurations, and gender distribution.

Communities of Alternatives: Representations and Politics highlights nontraditional modes of evoking "community" with respect to cultural representation and activist political organizing.

By no means do we argue that these three themes exhaust all the formations of community that can be identified as Asian American. Rather, we employ these thematic perspectives to make explicit the contours and complexities of contemporary Asian American community configurations. The essays in this collection demonstrate how, over the past twenty years or more, Asian American social spaces and practices have been in transition; internal group compositions and identities have been undergoing transformations; and group initiatives have been positing alternative constructions of cultural representations and political interests. Hence, we can consider these works as proposals that offer multiple avenues for understanding "community." Although we assigned each of the chapters to only one theme, we wish to make it clear that the thematic groupings do not disallow overlaps and cross-connections. The themes we have laid out are more fluid and intersecting than they appear to be. For these reasons, our discussion of the parts will include not only the primary essays grouped under the themes but also other essays in the volume that may be relevant.

We begin our scrutiny of these changing configurations by locating such population transformations within local and global historical contexts of capitalism, immigration legislation, and race relations as they affect Asian American group identification. These histories—some of them shared, some of them inherited—continue to impinge significantly on fundamental sociopolitical issues: in the ways we think about American society and its communities as fraught with consensus and contestation; in the continuation, emergence, or reformulation of communities that are not bound solely by geography, ethnicity, or racial identification; and in the recognition of the heterogeneous composition and multiple identifications of Asian American communities that include, among others, youths, mixed-race people, sexually marginalized groups, and transnationals. Our collective perspective therefore envisions communities as both territorial sites or geographically delineated formations *and* socially constructed entities; as such, these communities are based on relations of similarities and differences and on relations that extend to multiple networks *across* locations and interests. Taken together, the essays in this collection address how Asian Americans are reconceiving and reshaping their own communities, and examines the representations, expressions, practices, and cultures of Asian Americans located within and beyond homes, families, and formal organizations.

Capitalism, Immigration, and Race

Transnational capitalism, historically and currently, exerts direct influence on the Asian American experience as one of labor. Before 1965, Asian Americans, particularly in the West Coast states and in Hawai'i, were used as a cheap labor source in the service of American expansionism and internationalization (Cheng and Bonacich 1984). Asians were recruited as contract laborers to build and maintain the national infrastructure, to develop and sustain massive agricultural production, and to assist in domestic work. As a result of the 1965 Immigration Act, Asians have been able to come to the United States mainly through the act's family-reunification and employment-specific provisions. Immigrants from diverse backgrounds have entered low-end service-sector jobs by working as cooks, janitors, or maids, or have taken low end manufacturing jobs as factory assemblers or seamstresses in the garment industry. Others have entered high-end sectors as well-educated, skilled professionals (Barkan 1992; Kitano and Daniels 1995).

Many from these immigrant populations still provide the low-income labor that is crucial to local industrial production and manufacturing (Lowe 1996; Ong et al. 1994). After 1975, refugees and immigrants from Vietnam, Cambodia, and Laos came to the United States to escape the chaos created by the aftermath of the Vietnam War. Although they did not initially enter as a laboring class, they, too, have been used to fulfill U.S. industrial and service-sector employment needs (Gold 1992; Kibria 1993). Thus, Asian immigrants and refugees and those who are American-born of Asian descent are fulfilling the demands of the dual labor market that requires both workers who are highly educated and skilled and workers who are unskilled or semiskilled with minimal formal education (Espiritu 1997; Lowe 1996). The global restructuring of capitalism, whose expansion and contraction require and depend on different forms of exploitation, benefits from more liberalized policies of immigration to perpetuate the recruiting of Asian labor.

Today, about half of all immigrants to the United States come from Asia. As a result, the Asian American population has increased dramatically, becoming significantly more foreign-born as well as more ethnically, economically, politically, and socially diverse. For example, past legislation ensured that Asian immigrants were mainly single men in their prime working years with limited formal schooling (Chan 1991). Now, the immigration of multi-generational families, women and children, highly skilled and unskilled individuals, and refugees is changing the internal composition of this population. Moreover, many of these individuals are twice or thrice immigrants. Some migrated internally within their homelands, and others resided briefly, or for generations, in neighboring Asian countries or in Africa, Europe, the Middle East, Latin America, or Canada prior to their arrival in America (Kitano and Daniels 1995). These paths of migration to the United States, facilitated largely by immigration legislation, U.S. participation in the global restructuring of capitalism, political and economic crises in Asia, and the ideological persistence of the so-called American dream fueled by the U.S. presence abroad, have influenced the ways in which Asian Americans are reconceiving and reshaping their communities.

Finally, and most important, the history of U.S. race relations has fundamentally shaped the course of Asian American experience over the years. U.S. imperialism in Asia in the form of militarization, colonialization, and "democratizing" projects shapes the lives of Asians even before they arrive in America. Upon their arrival, Asians have been subjected to both de jure and de facto discriminatory treatment. As a racialized group, they have been singled out in immigration-exclusion acts, barred from citizenship and property ownership, interned in concentration camps during a period of war, exploited on the job, and greatly disfranchised in civil society. Many suffered violence and dehumanization borne out of racial and gender prejudice that was expressed openly as the "Yellow Peril" and other forms of Orientalism. Yet many of them have found ways to circumvent barriers or escape hostility by forming self-sufficient, semi-autonomous enclaves; by appealing to the local or national justice system; or by forging political alliances among themselves and with other groups (Aguilar-San Juan 1994; Chan 1991). Asian American groups that participated in the Civil Rights Movement and the anti-imperialist movements of the late 1960s provide evidence of this history of struggle and proactive engagement against racial injustice (Espiritu 1997; Wei 1993).

One cannot conclude, however, that antidiscrimination legislation passed during and in the aftermath of the Civil Rights and Asian American movements has erased all forms of racism. We contend, rather, that both pre-1965 and post-1965 Asian Americans currently experience racism in more complex ways. Sometimes this racism is expressed overtly in the form of hate crimes, but often it is covert and subtle, taking the form of "glass ceilings" and other hidden barriers to positions of power or of persistent stereotyping as exemplified by the chopsticks incident mentioned earlier and even "model minority" characterizations. Even as new Asian groups inherit a long legacy of Orientalized stereotyping, new forms of racism arise in the name of fairness for all individuals. Those who argue against affirmative action programs often articulate an opposition to "group preferential treatment." They portray white groups also as victims of discrimination because they assume all groups are similarly situated, disregarding uneven forms of access and power. Oppositionists regard antiracist programs as unnecessary even in the face of persistent underrepresentation of particular Asian American groups in the educational system (Hirabayashi 1998; Wang 1993).

Communities in Transition: Spaces and Practices

The term "community" has several definitions. The most conventional and prevalent one refers to a collection of people situated in a geographical space and grouped together out of shared histories, experiences, and values (Marshall 1994). Traditionally, the word is used to denote territorial units, as in ethnic communities or villages, ethnic neighborhoods, ethnic pockets, or ethnic enclaves (Breton 1964). In contrast, a community does not necessarily have to be a spatially defined territory; rather, it may be based on an array of interpersonal networks defined (although not exclusively) out of a sense of belonging, a body of shared values, a system of social organization or interdependency (Webber et al. 1964: 108–9; Wellman 1979). An example might be a community of doctors, a religious community, a working-class community, or a community of women.

Disputes have arisen in the social sciences about adequate and appropriate definitions and understandings of community, but certain models and constructs have persisted. They include the conceptualizing of community as constitutive of a "set of social relationships based on something which the participants have in common—usually, a common sense of identity" (Marshall 1994). More broadly speaking, communities can be conceived of as social groups in which an aggregate of individuals interact with one another. Models for types or kinds of community, as elaborated by Ferdinand Tonnies (1963 [1922]), include *Gemeinshaft* and *Gesellschaft* (intimate communal and large-scale associative social relations) and, in the scholarship of Emile Durkheim (1915), mechanical versus organic solidarities. In many community studies, these models enable specific descriptive and analytical perspectives that explain ideal-typical societies as well as external factors that cause change in the nature and extent of community life.

In this book, we do not intend to dispute these definitions and models per se. Rather, we have gathered essays together to propose a less territory-centered orientation of community sites, a more unstable or fluid rendition of the nature and scope of communities, and an understanding of communities that goes beyond the dualisms dictated by traditional scholarship. Although the principal theories do not address Asian American communities explicitly, we can think about them as foundational constructs whose meanings persist or change according to context, and from which we can draw larger questions about community, given particular material conditions and literary productions associated with Asian Americans. As with other groups of color, Asian Americans' experiences of group formation cannot simply be generalized as instances of ideal-typical societal arrangements. Their experiences may be far more complex and nuanced than, and qualitatively different from, the experiences of more dominant groups to fit neatly into any of the specific binary categories. In this instance, we agree with Gary Okihiro's contention that "a simpleminded assertion of race or ethnicity [as a central phenomenon of Asian American communities] is no longer adequate, nor will an 'instinctual' basis for ethnic solidarity and identity suffice" (1988: 181).

We also do not intend to reconceptualize mainstream notions of community in order to substitute arbitrary definitions or even to do away with any definition of community. Instead, we aim to propose definitions of communities of Asian Americans that are grounded in specific conditions that are both external and internal to these communities. Challenging mainstream definitions of "community" opens new avenues of thinking beyond the strictures of distinct territories and closed boundaries; at the same time, there is risk in moving too far from such definitions (so that they seem totally disconnected and unrecognizable) or appearing random or arbitrary (as in, "anything goes"). We do recognize these dangers, and we offer this collection of essays as a testament to the ways in which we test, grapple with, and navigate through such challenges. Indeed, we claim that in examining new and alternative perspectives regarding Asian American communities, we also recognize that there are connections and continuities across definitions and formations. These are, as we discussed earlier, the shared historical and contemporary experiences of capitalist, immigrant, and racialized processes among Asian Americans.

In regard to particular Asian American communities as communities in transition, we propose to illustrate connections as well as disconnections between the traditional enclave-defined incarnations of community and the changes associated with broader conceptions of communities as "sites." Territorially defined communities are usually understood to have been formed by structural forces. Restrictive U.S. immigration policies limited the number of Asians, particularly women and children, and initially deterred the formation of permanent settlements. Naturalization laws prohibited Asians from obtaining citizenship; as "aliens ineligible for citizenship," they were prevented from purchasing property, which was later reinforced by restrictive covenants on housing. These and other discriminatory policies led to the segregation of Asian Americans in ethnic enclaves in urban areas and in clusters in rural settings. Hysteria against Asian Americans, led by the white working class, who targeted them as economic competitors, resulted in anti-Asian riots that included the murdering of Asian Americans and the firebombing and destruction of their physical communities. Threats of violence kept Chinese, Japanese, Koreans, Filipinos, and Asian Indians from establishing more stable and permanent roots. The internment of Japanese Americans during World War II shattered the spatial communities they had occupied in urban and rural areas. But while these factors curbed the development of their early residential and business communities, they did not prevent them altogether.[6]

Asian American ethnic concentrations were once perceived as unsavory slums marked by vice, disease, degradation, co-ethnic exploitation, and disorganization. As a result, these areas by the late 1960s were prime targets for replacement through gentrification projects. Community studies focused on how ethnic and racial communities have, will, or should assimilate economically, politically, and socially into the American mainstream, leading to the dissipation of ethnic communities (Bonacich and Modell 1980). Although some locations became extinct because of residential dispersion or evictions; others survived because their residents struggled to preserve them. More important, the influx of Asian newcomers after 1965 rejuvenated dwindling ethnic enclaves and helped to create new ethnic communities; it also brought an infusion of domestic and international financial investment that led to a revitalization of urban spaces and a re-energizing of local economies (Fong 1998; Horton 1995; Saito 1998). Although some Asian American communities are still condemned for their insalubrious components, others are celebrated for their positive contributions to American society.

Chain migration and occupational opportunities are still the primary reasons that Asian Americans choose to settle in particular areas and help to explain the dispersal of Asians across the nation, even though many of them are still concentrated in urban and suburban locations. In the chain-migration process, Asian immigrants tend to settle in areas with established ethnic communities where they can rely on the resources and support of relatives and friends. Some groups do not use social networks as extensively as others when selecting a settlement site, because occupational considerations are primary elements in their limited choices. As a result of their association with the military, for example, Filipinos tend to choose locations near military bases, where many remain even after retirement (Bonus 2000; Espiritu 1995). Asian professionals who immigrated using the occupational provisions of the 1965 legislation found work at hospitals, universities, and research companies, many of which were located in the Midwest or South or on the East Coast. This explains the growth of this group in these regions in the post-1965 period.

Given such patterns of spatial concentration, Asian American communities have been historically studied as ethnic enclaves that display common elements: mostly homogeneous, self-sufficient, and isolated from the rest of society. Regarding them as such produced works that have depicted enclaves as places where collective immigrant narratives of success (or failure) are played out.[7] In recent years, however, scholars have questioned the presumed accuracy of mainstream definitions of community as having fixed borders. They have instead introduced alternative perspectives of communities that are more porous, interdependent, and transspatial.[8] The work of Tarry Hum in Chapter 1 is emblematic of this scholarship. Using a case study of the neighborhood of Sunset Park in Brooklyn, Hum demonstrates how traditional perspectives on immigrant communities fail to account for contemporary communities that are directly linked to global assembly lines, racially diverse, and transnationally configured. This work is crucial not only because it gives us a better understanding of global interconnections within which Asian American communities play critical roles (whether as centers of capital or as providers of labor), but also because it provides us with expansive tools that can situate contemporary Asian American realities beyond the isolationist and internally self-sufficient models of community formations.

Since Asian Americans were denied U.S. citizenship, they had an incentive to remain in close contact with their homelands. With most of their family still in Asia, many were involved in homeland politics, with some assisting abroad in the nationalist and anticolonialist movements in their home countries. Since World War II and afterward, when U.S. citizenship became available to them, Asians were able to choose the kinds of connections they wanted to maintain with their homelands. With the ease of air travel today, those who can afford to can shuttle between countries and maintain residences and businesses in both or multiple continents. Connections to "homelands" and ethnic cultures vary depending on when one immigrated and, particularly, where one was socialized into adulthood. The tension and uncertainty that might accompany these connections are the central theme of Eileen Chia-Ching Fung's essay (Chapter 2). Fung analyzes the works of the filmmakers Ang Lee and Nien-Jen Wu, showing how the histories of Taiwan, China, and the United States find their way into the complex conditions faced by Taiwanese Chinese Americans; these conditions, in turn, inform filmic narratives of fragmentation, colonialism, and "homelessness" that may well characterize transnational and diasporic elements of this particular Asian American community. Again, these factors bring to light the porous boundaries of many Asian American communities and the situational parameters from which we can understand their composition.

Connections within and among communities may not be solely ethnically or racially determined. In Russell Jeung's essay (Chapter 3), we can clearly infer that "homeland" connections among a community of Southeast Asian American youth are neither absolutely unidirectional nor predictably sharp and singular. For his participants, primarily Khmer and Iu Mien youth, collective identities are dynamically forged among relationships revolving around concepts of tradition and Americanness. For these youths, living in the inner city of Oakland, California, constructions of community and ethnicity are intertwined with their experiences of poverty, racism, gang violence, and struggles for panethnic partnerships.

When we come to understand that territorially defined communities can often exceed their physical boundaries and have overlapping elements located within and outside neighborhoods, we can extend the theme of *Communities in Transition* to include communities that are organized around sexualized spaces and virtual arrangements. Eric C. Wat (Chapter 4) focuses on interactions between a community composed of individuals who identify as Asian American and gay and the larger and more dominant community of mostly white gay men. It is difficult to determine how the post-1965 immigration flows have transformed the character of the queer Asian American communities. Because historical sources and studies are lacking, the transitions are too intricate to demarcate. Scholars of history are only beginning to speculate on the freedom available to gay Asian American men, most of whom lived in racially segregated, predominantly male communities unrestricted by the traditions of their homelands and the scrutiny of their families. On some level, it would seem that contemporary immigration to America allows gay men, lesbians, bisexuals, and transgendered individuals the opportunity to escape the traditional expectations of their families in their homelands. The gay rights movement of the 1960s and 1970s improved the situation for gays and lesbians, even though white racism limited the inclusion of people of color in their political agendas.

The increased immigration from Asia has allowed substantial numbers of Asians to choose potential partners and seek validation for their life experiences. This has led to the creation of queer spaces, such as Asian gay bars, and the allocation of resources to organize formal support groups. For many Asian American gays and lesbians today, however, ethnic-bound communities are not sanctuaries but stifling sites of exclusion where homophobia persists and where they are remarginalized (Eng and Hom 1998). Based on historical and fieldwork research conducted primarily in two Asian gay bars in Los Angeles, Wat's chapter elucidates these tensions in the lives of gay Asian American men who have been involved in forging panethnic coalitions among the L.A. gay communities and in developing personal sexual relationships among specific Asian American gay men in the area. His study is illustrative of the uneven and often conflictual processes of community formation.

One relatively recent phenomenon is the rise of cyberspace-mediated communication in the late twentieth century. In this anthology, we scrutinize its current use and potential for expressing and explaining communities in transition by way of an essay written by Emily Noelle Ignacio (Chapter 5). Ignacio's chapter looks at how a particular Internet-based newsgroup or discussion list became a global electronic site for conversations about identities for its Filipino participants; hence, the interrogative *"Pilipino ka ba?"* ("Are You Pilipino?"). This "community" was configured as a virtual connection to its participants' homeland and, even though its community boundaries were only electronically fixed (they were available only to those who have access to the technology), the Internet exchanges posed more expansive ways to construct "Filipinoness" (especially in relation to "Americanness"), as exemplified by the 'Netters' debates on language use.

Communities in Transformation: Identities and Generations

This part highlights the major transformations affecting the composition of Asian American groups and analyzes how these factors shape relations within these socially constructed communities. With the 1965 Immigration Act, ethnic groups already present in the United States such as the Chinese, Asian Indians, Koreans, and Filipinos expanded and new groups formed with the influx of populations from Vietnam, Laos, Kampuchea, Thailand, Indonesia, Sri Lanka, and other parts of Asia. The numbers of biracial and multiracial Asian Americans have also increased in recent decades and are changing the contours of these communities. The educational and occupational mobility of established Asian Americans, along with the arrival of newcomers, has led to a socioeconomically diverse population. The increasing numbers of women and children have made possible the establishment of multigenerational Asian American families. These transformations have greatly reconfigured group boundaries and interactions.

The expansion of some ethnic groups and the emergence of new ones have accentuated internal differences in Asian America. The ethnic Chinese American population is a clear representation of a community reshaping itself. As the largest ethnic group, it incorporates people of Chinese ancestry from the Americas, Australia, New Zealand, the South Pacific, Europe, Africa, and throughout Asia (Pan 1998), creating new subgroups in the United States. Taiwanese Americans, an emerging group, are attempting to define their distinctive social and political history, using various means by which their members contend with their positions within the triangle of America, Taiwan, and mainland China, as Eileen Chia-Ching Fung points out in Chapter 2. Their substantial numbers have enabled them to organize their own language schools, professional organizations, and cultural events. Filipinos are another example of a group with varying regional and linguistic differences, especially as a result of the post-1965 immigrant waves. These affiliations create internal divisions among immigrant communities that go largely unnoticed by outsiders. Their legacy of Spanish colonization has led to their being considered a mixed-race population as well as one shaped by Spanish language and culture and by Catholicism. This aspect of Filipino history has led many to question their positioning within Asian America rather than with Latinos.

Before 1975, the few Southeast Asians living in the United States were mainly international students, military trainees, or war brides. Arriving here after the Vietnam War, refugees and immigrants from Vietnam, Laos, and Kampuchea (formerly Cambodia) were lumped together as "Southeast Asians" or "Indochinese," even though stark ethnic, historical, religious, cultural, and linguistic differences separated these groups. Their diversity and status as involuntary immigrants gives them perhaps stronger commonalities with refugees from Central America, Africa, and Europe, but they have been principally included in the Asian American category. The fit has not always been comfortable for them.

Like "Southeast Asian," the "South Asian" label conveniently incorporates diverse ethnic groups and faces the same challenges of inclusion in the Asian American classification. Asian Indians have a long history in the United States; the population of other "South Asians," from Bangladesh, Bhutan, Nepal, Pakistan, and Sri Lanka, however, has increased substantially since 1965. Although historically linked to Chinese, Filipinos, Japanese, and Koreans, Asian Indians were officially included in the Asian American category only in the 1980 census (Chan 1991; Takaki 1989). Once a predominantly laboring class from the Punjab region of India and mainly of Sikh faith, contemporary immigrants are from diverse class backgrounds, come from varying regions in India (some are twice immigrants from Africa, Europe, and the Caribbean), and represent a wide spectrum of religious faiths and political affiliations (Mathew and Prashad 1999–2000). Such differences obviously affect their ability to come together as a cohesive community (Prashad 2000; see also Margaret Abraham's essay [Chapter 12] in this volume).

Although there has been little open debate about grouping Asians and Pacific Islanders together, the alliance between these groups has never been easy. Although it is a misnomer imposed by outsiders, the term "Asian Pacific American" is widely used in educational programs and courses and by political, social, and economic organizers. As Debbie Hippolite Wright and Paul Spickard argue in Chapter 6, however, Pacific Islanders' experiences are culturally distinct from Asians', and their historical markers differ from those of the Asian immigrant experience. Hawaiians, for example, are U.S. citizens by birth and are socialized with English; having lived in what is now known as the American territory since A.D. 500, they cannot be considered immigrants. In fact, because of the annexation of their lands and their continuing struggle for sovereignty, they may have more in common with Native Americans than with other Asian groups.

As Wright and Spickard show, the label "Pacific Islander" includes diverse groups (Chamorros, Fijians, Hawaiians, Maoris, Northern Mariana Islanders, Palauans, Samoans, Tahitians, Tongans, etc.) who have varying ethnic experiences depending on their place of birth, where they were socialized, and how their family life was structured. Their association with other Asian Americans raises contentious problems for a number of scholars, including the editors of this volume, who continue to grapple particularly with the negative impact this forced, artificial, and seemingly irrational grouping with Asian Americans has had on specific groups of Pacific Islanders. This also raises complicated questions about, for example, the commonalties that exist in the colonization and militarization of populations in the Pacific, and about the colonial histories of the Philippines, Vietnam, and India, and the continuing military presence in Korea, Japan, and other Asian countries. On the mainland, how does the process of racialization affect Asians and Pacific Islanders and their ability to contend collectively with hate crimes, poverty, social services, juvenile delinquency, and police mistreatment? While some argue that this grouping has largely done a disservice to both groups, others contend that these communities have been geographically situated together. And as neighbors in America, they have had close, daily interactions that have led to a sharing of life experiences beyond governmental classifications. Nevertheless, the alliance is becoming more precarious, especially because the 2000 U.S. Census disaggregated the two groups, affecting whether these communities will go their separate ways or choose to strengthen their connections, however they opt to define them.

Although not openly discussed, the ethnic and racial boundaries of the Asian American community have always been porous because of the presence of multiracial populations. Because earlier immigration laws restricted the number of female co-ethnics, Asian American men had sexual relations with—and in some instances, married—Alaskan Native, Hawaiian, Native American, Black, and Latino women. Although anti-miscegenation laws and social pressure prevented relationships between Asians and whites, some mixed-race couples formed. As a result of these unions, interracial Asian children changed the composition of the population. Their numbers have increased with more contact between racial groups and the lessening (to a certain extent) of social stigma attached to these relationships in the contemporary period. The children of war brides and their American husbands, many of them of non-Asian ancestry, have also contributed to the multiracial composition of the community. Furthermore, Filipino immigrants, many of them of mixed-race ancestry, have been a large part of continuing immigration flows to the United States.

Intra-racial relationships and marriages are reported to be more commonplace, so children who are biethnic (Japanese and Filipino, Chinese and Japanese, etc.) are also prevalent in many Asian American communities (Shinagawa and Pang 1996). The Japanese American community, which has the highest rate of out-marriage, is contending with this mixed-race population, and their experience can be instructive for all Asian American groups that are also likely to become more ethnically and racially diverse. In Chapter 7, Rebecca Chiyoko King examines two pastimes, beauty pageants and basketball leagues, to analyze how the Japanese American community uses the transracial ethnic strategy to justify the inclusion of multiethnic and multiracial people of Japanese ancestry in these activities and, in so doing, constructs a community that moves beyond the assimilationist or panethnic models. The 2000 Census's inclusion of a "mixed racial heritage" category will clearly reconfigure Asian American communities in unpredictable ways.

Class disparities among Asian Americans have become more pronounced in the past couple of decades. Once a population made up primarily of common laborers living in low-income neighborhoods, Asian Americans now also work in the most privileged professions and claim some of the most exclusive addresses in the country. More of the new immigrants are well-educated professionals from metropolitan areas in Asia, and their material and cultural capital ease their adjustment in this country. Pensri Ho's essay (Chapter 8) addresses the growth of affluent Asian Americans who are interested in economic integration and in advancing within mainstream professions, while simultaneously identifying with their ethnicity and forging a deterritorialized Asian American community. Their attempts to form a professional organization raise questions about how we might redefine activism in the post-Civil Rights era and how this contrasts with efforts by Asian American factory and service workers to organize unions.

While Cambodians, Hmong, and Laotians have the highest rate of those living in poverty, Chinese, Filipinos and Asian Indians can be found in the higher income brackets as well as in the lowest ones. Some members of these communities insist that Asian Americans are the "model minority." The myth of successful immigrants and citizens who contribute to the economic growth in America is the one they want to project of their communities, even when they are confronted with realities that contradict this image, as Abraham notes in Chapter 12. Others argue that many Asian Americans still live in dire poverty and that there is a need to continue the struggle for adequate social services for this population (see Andrew Leong's essay [Chapter 15]). Class divisions, along with other differences, affect Asian Americans' opinions on issues such as affirmative action, unionization, welfare reform, partisan politics, and race relations.

The new immigration has balanced the generational composition of the population. Whereas families and children once were rare, they are now commonplace. In this section, we define generational differences, first, to mean age, and second, to mean period of immigration. We group these together because they are often related, with groups of immigrants of similar age arriving at the same time. The 1990 Census found that Asian Americans had a median age of 30 years, younger than the national median of 33 years (U.S. Bureau of the Census 1993). The Asian American population has undergone several generational transitions. During the 1970s, primarily first-generation immigrants gave way to a mainly U.S.-born group; that trend was reversed in the 1980s, as Asian Americans went back to being a primarily foreign-born, first-generation population. With continuing immigration, Asian newcomers are joining co-ethnic old-timers who are several generations removed from the initial immigration experience.

The post-1965 immigration waves have included multi-generational families whose experiences of adaptation vary widely. Although social scientists have used "first," "second," "third," and so on to designate generations, we find these terms inexact. More recently, the term "1.5" has been commonly used to describe the experiences of those who were born abroad and immigrated with their families, including those who came as toddlers, teenagers, or young adults. In Chapter 9, Mary Yu Danico captures the distinctions among the 1.5 generation—who are bicultural and bilingual—contrasting them to the first and second generation and raising new possibilities for how we discuss multi-generational communities. The 1.5-generation children, for example, have recast what it means to be "Korean" in Hawai'i, mediating their position and identity in American society in relation to other Koreans and in relation to the larger sociopolitical context. The ideological outlook of Korean Americans, like that of most Asian American groups, is affected by generational factors, along with language ability, socialization, class position, and familiarity with the structure of American society, as Edward J. W. Park discusses in Chapter 13. The younger generation also may have access to different tools to construct their identity—notably, access to Internet technology to connect to co-ethnics (see Chapter 5).

It is almost a cliché to discuss how Asian American children experience a clash between traditional ethnic practices at home and the Americanized values and norms promoted in the schools and through the popular media. Such cultural and identity clashes occur primarily during the first-generation stages. Asian Americans have tried to maintain their cultural and linguistic practices in a variety of ways. Reacting to the racialization process that lumps Asian Americans together, for instance, Southeast Asian youths who were born or largely socialized in the United States and reside in low-income, multiracial neighborhoods are forging their own sense of a specific youth culture. As children of refugee parents, they are affected by their parents' experiences and ideologies, but they are also distanced from them, making the relationship among generations difficult, as Russell Jeung notes in Chapter 3. As with all ethnic groups, connections to "homelands" and ethnic cultures vary depending on when one immigrated and particularly where one was socialized into adulthood.

Although Asian Americans are praised for their entrepreneurial acumen, this often overlooks the fact that many immigrants are able to achieve the "American dream" only because their small family businesses are sustained by the invisible labor of their children. Lisa Sun-Hee Park's case study of immigrant entrepreneurial families (Chapter 10) focuses on the lives of Chinese and Korean children who grew up in such businesses, showing how their experiences have led to a reorganization of their family life, as well as to a reconstruction of their sense of identity and community. These children often take on adult responsibilities and tasks at an early age, helping their families eke out a living and functioning as translators for their immigrant parents. Although many of them manage to adapt, others do not fare as well, choosing to rebel against their families and the establishment, as a result earning the classification of "juvenile delinquents." Many immigrants turn to entrepreneurship because they lack educational and occupational skills. However, others find that educational degrees from their homelands are not recognized here. This, combined with their lack of fluency in English and prevailing racial discrimination, can force them into self-employment. As a result, Asian Americans are over-represented in the total U.S. population as small-business owners, and many of them barely make a profit or go bankrupt. The costs that this exacts on youths and families in the community are just beginning to be considered.

The shifts in the ethnic, racial, gender, class, and generational composition of the Asian American population since 1965 have created new internal tensions and fissures in Asian American communities. As a result, they are realigning and rearranging themselves, a dialectic process that is determined largely by interactions among individuals and groups.

Communities of Alternatives: Representations and Politics

We hope to open discussions of more expanded and fluid notions of Asian American communities by exposing the intersections of race, class, gender, and sexuality in such formations. Ethnicity and racial identification cannot be the only means for defining the boundaries and composition of community. Asian Americans, in addition to their ethnic or racial identification, can be strategically identified and positioned as women, gays, lesbians, immigrants, seniors, mixed-race, transnationals, biculturals, or poor. These added perspectives enable scholars to recognize the processes of community identification whether they are internally or externally defined.

In the 1970s, for example, when Asian American studies were being defined, a great deal of emphasis was placed on thinking about "Asia" within "America." As the proportion of foreign-born immigrants increases, questions about the meanings of "America" and their relationship to "Asia" can no longer be assessed and contained within strict national boundaries and distinct, racialized identities. To be sure, cultural constructions of Asian Americans have always been complicated and shaped by connections to "homelands," race relations, and imperialism. And it is in the sites of cultural production that we observe a dialectic process that involves exchanges among groups on local, national, and global levels. Such exchanges have had enormous consequences not only for how communities have been formed and reformulated, but also for how they have been represented.[9]

To a large degree, new communication technology and the globalization of culture in the mass media have transformed our understanding of space and place. Capitalist expansion has led to interconnections among individuals separated by national boundaries. Mobile telephones, fax machines, and computers have facilitated instantaneous communication among individuals and groups; Internet communications via e-mail chat rooms now allow co-ethnics residing in various parts of the world to maintain constant contact, and these dialogue exchanges help shape a variety of self-perceptions and encourage a reconfiguration of spatial communities (see Chapter 5). Many young people are more adept than their elders at manipulating the new technology to create and sustain complex social relationships, changing the process by which culture and identity are transmitted from one generation to the next. The emerging processes affect Asian American cultural representations, expressions, and practices in multiple spaces, including language schools, religious performances, beauty pageants, video stores, *karaoke* clubs, community parades, and ethnic presses. Given these conditions, how do we think about Asian American communities in their generalities and particularities? How do we understand the ways in which cultures are created, changed, sustained, and reformulated?

In Chapter 11, Karen Har-Yen Chow interrogates what may be one of the most pressing concerns of communities bound by historical tracings of presumed common identities and current manifestations of diversity by discussing Asian American panethnicity and its representation in fiction. Through Yen Le Espiritu's (1992) scholarship on that subject, we learn that panethnicity is created by external and internal dynamics. Chow adds another twist to that argument by peering through the work of Maxine Hong Kingston and reading it as a social text whose elements emblematize and embody a particular notion of Asian American panethnicity. To a large degree, Chow challenges us to explore the boundaries and interstices of history and fiction as places where we encounter ideas about how ideology and consciousness work and about how the permeable borders between them can be made less obscure in order to examine alternative community formations.

The remaining four essays delve into organizational and institutional forms of political activism. Earlier, we said that the changing internal composition of many Asian American communities along the lines of gender, sexuality, and class suggests a reconsideration of traditional emphases on the centrality of race and ethnicity in alliance formation and maintenance. Likewise, the larger dynamics of social, political, and economic relationships in American society have become more complex due to globalized capitalism, changing population demographics, and the emergence of neoconservative racism. These circumstances pose challenges and alternatives to the ways politics have been played out among specific Asian American groups and their relationships with other local and national communities. In Chapter 12, Margaret Abraham places the changing dynamics of South Asian community identities in the United States within the larger historical and contemporary debates over the concepts of model minority (as applied particularly to Asian immigrants) and the persistence of cultures of patriarchy in many ethnic groups. A key context to her analysis is the dramatic rise in the immigration of women and families in the post-1965 years. Women are immigrating with their partners, their families, and, in some instances, on their own as college students and as professionals. Filipinas and South Asian women, for example, have qualified to immigrate because of their professional skills, fulfilling some of the occupational provisions of the 1965 Immigration Act. They have also sponsored family members along the way. With the presence of more women in the communities, otherwise hidden or unmentioned problems of sexism and patriarchy begin to surface. Abraham's chapter targets domestic violence as a primary concern for women in her study and examines the formation of South Asian women's organizations as a proactive effort in this instance.[10]

We recognize in Abraham's essay that the problem of violence against women is not simply interpersonal; it reveals multiple dynamics of race relations and internal group politics. In fighting against domestic violence, South Asian women in the United States are not only contesting the mainstream treatment of this social problem, for example, they are also challenging sexism among their male co-ethnics. Put another way and from a larger perspective, these women (and the men who fight alongside them) are challenging the patriarchal systems within both Asian and mainstream American society. But choosing gender politics over a politics of ethnic nationalism brings risks, such as ostracism, marginalization, and exposure to other forms of social punishment. Traditionalists lament that many anti-patriarchy movements have led to a breakdown of "comfortable" gender relations and, ultimately, of community life. For others, however, these struggles have created new opportunities to curtail gender oppression. As they come of age, some young Asian American women are attempting to find their own voices in a society that still holds gendered expectations for girls and that stereotypes Asian women as secondary to men (see also Chapter 3). As some of them have become independent women, they have exercised more choices and greater freedom to pursue partners and careers than women had a generation ago. However, many—particularly those with immigrant parents—still face strict obligations to family and community, as Lisa Sun-Hee Park also discusses in Chapter 10. Furthermore, these groups and organizations have to weigh the consequences of publicizing social problems such as domestic violence and juvenile delinquency in an era in which anti-Asian and anti-immigrant sentiments continue to be pervasive.

Contrary to common misperceptions, most Asian Americans have been neither politically passive nor mere victims of their situations. They have worked within the constraints placed on them to contest unfair working conditions, as well as against anti-miscegenation laws, segregation in the schools, biased naturalization laws, and immigration restrictions (Chan 1991; Lowe 1996; Okihiro 1994). In the contemporary period, they have worked within and across Asian American communities against racism, exploitation, imperialism, and marginalization (Aguilar-San Juan 1994; Espiritu 1992). Newcomers bring human and material capital, providing new resources for community building and political mobilization. But they also bring divergent socioeconomic and political agendas. Edward J. W. Park's essay (Chapter 13) addresses how Korean Americans in particular challenge traditionally configured black—white liberal politics in urban settings that do not take the interests, strategies, and political visions of other groups into account. Using comparative models, Park lucidly describes the terrains of urban political struggles involving Korean Americans and their relationships with one another and other racialized groups, particularly African Americans, to map the multiple contexts of intergroup power relations.

The diversity of the Asian American population has increasingly become evident through active attempts to maneuver for social change. The political stance in the United States has moved toward the right, as demonstrated by the passage of propositions, initiatives, acts, and bills that rescind support for social services, affirmative-action programs, and immigrants' rights. However, poverty, educational and occupational discrimination, and anti-immigrant sentiments persist. How Asian Americans approach the quest for racial equality is determined by local race relations and the available political discourses and actors in a specific location. In Chapter 14, Jiannbin Lee Shiao directs our attention to the ideological, institutional, and social contexts of particular Asian American communities so that we can better understand parallels and discontinuities of civic participation among such communities. In his chapter, he frames two case studies of city-based philanthropic foundations, one in the San Francisco Bay area and the other in Cleveland, along two differing tropes of race discourse—race defined in terms of inequality and race defined in terms of diversity—to derive the lessons from past, current, and future initiatives in political inclusion of Asian American communities. Ultimately, Shiao's chapter may well be read as an invitation to examine the prospects of moving beyond the strict boundaries of ethnic-specific community interests and ethnic organizations, as he argues that Asian Americans need to direct themselves toward the larger, more complex interactions among social movements and philanthropic actors, institutions, and policies.

As individuals and in various collectivities, Asian Americans have made significant gains in electoral politics, as shown in their efforts to win seats in public office.
This is not to say that numbers and presence are enough or that they guarantee that
meaningful political participation has been fully achieved. Like other ethnic groups,
Asian Americans are beset with conflicts between conservatives and progressives,
while others choose to remain apolitical or complacent. Diversity makes strategizing,
politicizing, and organizing around common sets of interests and agendas particularly difficult. In Chapter 15, Andrew Leong examines the parameters of these difficulties and the prospects by which differences can be managed or transcended within specific conditions. His snapshots of group cleavages as well as alliances
demonstrate the advantages of having Asian Americans recognize, tolerate, and work
with differences within their communities in moments that particular issues, such as
welfare reform and immigration, provide opportunities for unity and solidarity. As
the composition of the population and the sociopolitical contexts are being altered,
Asian Americans increasingly need to re-examine how we define activism and resistance, especially in relation to promoting transgressive politics. As this collection's final
essay, Leong's chapter offers what we consider a key set of arguments for addressing intersections and divergences in contemporary Asian American communities.

Over the years, racist policies led to the forcible social and physical segregation of Asian
Americans from mainstream society. The geographically bound sites they occupied—
the Chinatowns, Japantowns, and Manilatowns—were safe havens where they were
temporarily protected from the discrimination of outsiders and from taunts about how
they looked, what they wore, what they ate, and what language they spoke. These were
places of refuge that enabled them to maintain their dignity and form voluntary social
networks among co-ethnics that helped them find housing, employment, and other
assistance—essential services because of the transitory life they lived as migrant or
transnational laborers. Thus, their spatial ghettoization and occupational status reinforced the cohesiveness of their social communities. For many contemporary Asian
Americans, geographic communities and social networks continue to provide a symbolic and material place for escape, solace, belonging, acceptance, and protection.

However, such communities can also be fraught with conflict and tension. And they
can be places of entrapment and danger. The term "community" has often been associated with the comforts of home, but the familiarity and security of a haven can be
an illusion. As transnational immigrants, as queers, as monolingual speakers, as
women, or as multiracials, we may feel abandoned, displaced, or disconnected from
our so-called communities. All of us at some moments in our lives are "othered" by
our "own" communities and, in some cases, even exploited by them.

Some may argue that the concept or praxis of contemporary community is elusive.
We do not. We concur with Chandra Mohanty, who writes about "home not as a comfortable, stable, inherited and familiar space, but instead as an imaginative, politically
charged space where the familiarity and sense of affection and commitment lay in
shared collective analysis of social injustice, as well as a vision of radical transformation" (1993: 353). For us, Asian American communities manifest themselves in

everyday spaces, geographic and social, where Asians reside, work, and carry out their social and political activities. They are evident in the relationships and interactions Asian Americans have with one another and with people of all ethnic and racial backgrounds. And their constant reformulations suggest different spaces and visions that attempt to braid local experiences with connections that extend into the regional, the global, and the transnational.[11] This does not mean that community formations, geographic or social, are based only on congenial relations. They are marked by contestation, negotiation, and compromise. The Asian American population is fluid and flexible. Thus, we want this collection to reflect the non-static, non-essentialized nature of contemporary Asian American communities.

We felt a need to redefine and reconstruct our understanding of various possibilities under which such competing or consensual formations of communities occur, paying particular attention to the larger structural and historical forces transfiguring these formations. Immigration policies determined by both economics and politics; the changing racial dynamics of the U.S. population that mark the numerical decrease in the white population; the emphasis foreign-policy makers place on Latin American and Pacific Rim markets and investments; the de-industrialization of America in the global economy, along with the expansion of the service sector; the reactionary stance the American polity holds toward issues of social and civil rights; and technological advances that supposedly give people instantaneous connections to the world—these factors only begin to speak to the confluence of national and international forces, that affect Asian America. Focusing on the intricacies of Asian America and its contours reflects these broader trends and developments.

We know that this collection does not exhaust the possibilities for the continuation, emergence, and re-formulation of contemporary Asian American communities. We hope, however, that it serves as an introduction to the complexities of the issues, and we expect that it will generate further discussions and debates about such communities as we move into the new century.

Notes

1. The "perpetual foreigner" status continues to stigmatize Americans of Asian ancestry. The events of the Wen Ho Lee case speak to the detrimental impact of this racialized stereotyping. Lee is a naturalized U.S. citizen of Taiwanese ancestry who worked as a nuclear scientist for the University of California Los Alamos National Laboratory in New Mexico for twenty years and was accused of espionage on behalf of mainland China. His defense lawyers, along with active members of the scientific and Asian American communities, claim that he was being unfairly targeted because of his race.

2. See Bonus 2000; and our essays in Manalansan 2000.

3. We also emphasize this aim to distinguish our anthology from other collections and works that employ specific disciplinary approaches, not so much to create distance from them as to offer a complementary view.

4. For an incisive collection of essays on the phenomenon of globalization with respect to Asian Americans, see Hu-DeHart 1999.

5. See Omi 1988 for an engaging discussion of the need for Asian American studies scholars to debate these critical issues.

6. Scholarship on specific Asian American communities since the 1965 Immigration Act includes, among others, Abelmann and Lie 1995; Almirol 1985; Bacon 1996; Bonus 2000; Chan 1994; Chen 1992; Eng and Hom 1998; Fisher 1980; Fong 1994; Fugita and O'Brien 1991; Gold 1992; Horton 1995; Kibria 1993; Kim 1981; Koltyk 1998; Kwong 1996; Lee 1998; Light 1972; Lin 1998; Loo 1998; MacDonald 1997; Montero 1979; Okamura 1998; Park 1997; Rangaswamy 2000; Saito 1998; Smith-Hefner 1999; Takahashi 1997; and Zhou 1992. For scholarship on specific historical communities, see Friday 1994; Ichioka 1988; Jensen 1989; Leonard 1992; Loewen 1988 (1971); Lukes and Okihiro 1985; Lydon 1985; Matsumoto 1993; Miyamoto 1984 (1939); Modell 1977; Nee and Nee 1972; Tamura 1993; and Yung 1995.

7. Chinatowns are the most commonly studied Asian American communities in this regard. Refer to Kwong 1996; Lyman 1986; and Zhou 1992 for examples.

8. Abelmann and Lie 1995; Chen 1992; Hu-DeHart 1999; and Lin 1998 are recent examples of scholarship that places sets of Asian American communities within the context of global economic exchanges.

9. Regarding the relationships across Asian American literature, representation, identity, and nationhood, refer to Hamamoto 1994; Kondo 1997; R. C. Lee 1999; R. G. Lee 1999; Li 1998; Ling 1998; and Marchetti 1993.

10. For a recent discussion of critical issues confronting Asian American women, see Sciachitano and Võ 2000.

11. For an important discussion of the politics of the local and the transnational, see Basch et al. 1994 and Dirlik 1999.

References

Abelmann, Nancy and John Lie. 1995. *Blue Dreams: Korean Americans and the Los Angeles Riots.* Cambridge, Mass.: Harvard University Press.

Aguilar-San Juan, Karin, ed. 1994. *The State of Asian America: Activism and Resistance in the 1990s.* Boston: South End Press.

Almirol, Edwin B. 1985. *Ethnic Identity and Social Negotiation: A Study of a Filipino Community in California.* New York: AMS Press.

Bacon, Jean. 1996. *Life Lines: Community, Family, and Assimilation Among Asian Indian Immigrants.* New York: Oxford University Press.

Barkan, Elliott R. 1992. *Asian and Pacific Islander Migration to the United States: A Model of New Global Patterns.* Westport, Conn.: Greenwood Press.

Basch, Linda, Nina Glick Schiller, and Cristina Szanton Blanc. 1994. *Nations Unbound: Transnational Projects, Postcolonial Predicaments, and Deterrorialized Nation-States.* Langhorme, Penn.: Gordon & Breach.

Bonacich, Edna, and John Modell. 1980. *The Economic Basis of Ethnic Solidarity: Small Business in the Japanese-American Community.* Berkeley: University of California Press.

Bonus, Rick. 2000. *Locating Filipino Americans: Ethnicity and the Cultural Politics of Space.* Philadelphia: Temple University Press.

Breton, Raymond. 1964. "Institutional Completeness of Ethnic Communities and the Personal Relations of Immigrants." *American Journal of Sociology* 70: 193–205.

Chan, Sucheng. 1991. *Asian Americans: An Interpretive History.* Boston: Twayne.

————. 1994. *Hmong Means Free: Life in Laos and America*. Philadelphia: Temple University Press.

Chen, Hsiang-shui. 1992. *Chinatown No More*. Ithaca, N.Y.: Cornell University Press.

Cheng, Lucie, and Edna Bonacich, eds. 1984. *Labor Immigration under Capitalism: Asian Workers in the United States Before World War II*. Berkeley: University of California Press.

Daniels, Roger. 1988. *Asian America: Chinese and Japanese in the United States since 1850*. Seattle: University of Washington Press.

Dirlik, Arif. 1999. "Asians On the Rim: Transnational Capital and Local Community in the Making of Contemporary Asian America." Pp. 29–60 in *Across the Pacific: Asian Americans and Globalization*, ed. Evelyn Hu-DeHart. Philadelphia: Temple University Press.

Durkheim, Emile. 1915. *The Elementary Forms of the Religious Life: A Study in Religious Sociology*, trans. Joseph Ward Swain. London: Allen.

Eng, David L., and Alice Y. Hom, eds. 1998. *Q & A: Queer in Asian America*. Philadelphia: Temple University Press.

Espiritu, Yen Le. 1992. *Asian American Panethnicity: Bridging Institutions and Identities*. Philadelphia: Temple University Press.

————. 1995. *Filipino American Lives*. Philadelphia: Temple University Press.

————. 1997. *Asian American Women and Men: Labor, Laws, and Love*. Thousand Oaks, Calif.: Sage.

Fisher, Maxine P. 1980. *The Indians of New York City: A Study of Immigrants from India*. New Delhi: Heritage.

Fong, Timothy P. 1994. *The First Suburban Chinatown: The Remaking of Monterey Park, California*. Philadelphia: Temple University Press.

————. 1998. *The Contemporary Asian American Experience: Beyond the Model Minority*. Upper Saddle River, N.J.: Prentice Hall.

Friday, Chris. 1994. *Organizing Asian American Labor: The Pacific Coast Canned Salmon Industry, 1870–1942*. Philadelphia: Temple University Press.

Fugita, Stephen S., and David J. O'Brien. 1991. *Japanese American Ethnicity: The Persistence of Community*. Seattle: University of Washington Press.

Gold, Steven J. 1992. *Refugee Communities: A Comparative Field Study*. Newbury Park, Calif.: Sage.

Hamamoto, Darrell Y. 1994. *Monitored Peril: Asian Americans and the Politics of TV Representation*. Minneapolis: University of Minnesota Press.

Hing, Bill Ong. 1993. *Making and Remaking Asian America Through Immigration Policy, 1850–1990*. Stanford, Calif.: Stanford University Press.

Hirabayashi, Lane, ed. 1998. *Teaching Asian America: Diversity and the Problems of Community*. Lanham, Md.: Rowman & Littlefield.

Horton, John. 1995. *The Politics of Diversity: Immigration, Resistance, and Change in Monterey Park, California*. Philadelphia: Temple University Press.

Hu-DeHart, Evelyn, ed. 1999. *Across the Pacific: Asian Americans and Globalization*. Philadelphia: Temple University Press.

Ichioka, Yuji. 1988. *The Issei: The World of the First Generation Japanese Immigrants, 1885–1924*. New York: Free Press.

Jensen, Joan M. 1989. *Passage from India*. New Haven, Conn.: Yale University Press.

Kibria, Nazli. 1993. *Family Tightrope: The Changing Lives of Vietnamese Americans*. Princeton, N.J.: Princeton University Press.

Kim, Illsoo. 1981. *New Urban Immigrants: The Korean Community in New York*. Princeton, N.J.: Princeton University Press.

Kitano, Harry H. L., and Roger Daniels. 1995. *Asian Americans: Emerging Minorities*. 2nd ed. Englewood Cliffs, N.J.: Prentice Hall.

Koltyk, Jo Ann. 1998. *New Pioneers in the Heartland: Hmong Life in Wisconsin*. Boston: Allyn & Bacon.

Kondo, Dorinne. 1997. *About Face: Performing Race in Fashion and Theater*. New York: Routledge.

Kwong, Peter. 1996. *The New Chinatown*. New York: Hill & Wang.

Lee, Jae-Hyup. 1998. *Dynamics of Ethnic Identity: Three Asian American Communities in Philadelphia*. New York: Garland.

Lee, Rachel C. 1999. *The Americas of Asian American Literature: Gendered Fictions of Nation and Transnation*. Princeton, N.J.: Princeton University Press.

Lee, Robert G. 1999. *Orientals: Asian Americans in Popular Culture*. Philadelphia: Temple University Press.

Leonard, Karen I. 1992. *Making Ethnic Choices: California's Punjabi Mexican Americans*. Philadelphia: Temple University Press.

Li, David Leiwei. 1998. *Imagining the Nation: Asian American Literature and Cultural Consent*. Stanford, Calif.: Stanford University Press.

Light, Ivan. 1972. *Ethnic Enterprise in America: Business and Welfare among Chinese, Japanese, and Blacks*. Berkeley: University of California Press.

Lin, Jan. 1998. *Reconstructing Chinatown: Ethnic Enclave, Global Change*. Minneapolis: University of Minnesota Press.

Ling, Jinqi. 1998. *Narrating Nationalisms: Ideology and Form in Asian American Literature*. New York: Oxford University Press.

Loo, Chalsa M. 1998. *Chinese America: Mental Health and Quality of Life in the Inner City*. Thousand Oaks, Calif.: Sage.

Loewen, James W. 1988 (1971). *The Mississippi Chinese: Between Black and White*. Prospect Heights, Ill.: Waveland Press.

Lowe, Lisa. 1996. *Immigrant Acts: On Asian American Cultural Politics*. Durham, N.C.: Duke University Press.

Lukes, Timothy J., and Gary Y. Okihiro. 1985. *Japanese Legacy: Farming and Community Life in California's Santa Clara Valley*, Local History Studies 31. Cupertino, Calif.: California History Center.

Lydon, Sandy. 1985. *Chinese Gold: The Chinese in the Monterey Bay Region*. Capitola, Calif.: Capitola Book Company.

Lyman, Stanford M. 1986. *Chinatown and Little Tokyo: Power, Conflict, and Community among Chinese and Japanese Immigrants in America*. Millwood, N.Y.: Associated Faculty Press.

MacDonald, Jeffrey L. 1997. *Transnational Aspects of Iu-Mien Refugee Identity*. New York: Garland.

Manalansan, Martin F., ed. 2000. *Cultural Compass: Ethnographic Explorations of Asian America*. Philadelphia: Temple University Press.

Marchetti, Gina. 1993. *Romance and the "Yellow Peril": Race, Sex, and Discursive Strategies in Hollywood Fiction*. Berkeley: University of California Press.

Marshall, Gordon. 1994. *The Concise Oxford Dictionary of Sociology*. Oxford: Oxford University Press.

Mathew, Biju, and Vijay Prashad, eds. 1999–2000. "Special issue: Satyagraha in America: The Political Culture of South Asian Americans." *Amerasia Journal* 25, no. 3: ix–xv.

Matsumoto, Valerie J. 1993. *Farming the Home Place: A Japanese American Community in California 1919–1982*. Ithaca, N.Y.: Cornell University Press.

Miyamoto, S. Frank. 1984 (1939). *Social Solidarity among the Japanese in Seattle*. Seattle: University of Washington Press.

Modell, John, 1977. *The Economics and Politics of Racial Accommodation: The Japanese of Los Angeles, 1900–1942*. Urbana: University of Illinois Press.

Mohanty, Chandra. 1993. "Defining Genealogies: Feminist Reflections on Being South Asian in North America." Pp. 351–8 in *Our Feet Walk the Sky: Women of the South Asian Diaspora*, ed. Women of the South Asian Descent Collective. San Francisco: Aunt Lute Books.

Montero, Darrel. 1979. *Vietnamese Americans: Patterns of Resettlement and Adaptation*. Boulder, Colo.: Westview Press.

Nee, Victor G., and Brett Debary Nee. 1972. *Longtime Californ': A Documentary Study of an American Chinatown*. New York: Pantheon.

Okamura, Jonathan Y. 1998. *Imagining the Filipino American Diaspora: Transnational Relations, Identities, and Communities*. New York: Garland.

Okihiro, Gary Y. 1988. "The Idea of Community and a 'Particular Type of History'." Pp. 175–83 in *Reflections on Shattered Windows: Promises and Prospects for Asian American Studies*, ed. Gary Y. Okihiro, Shirley Hune, Arthur A. Hansen, and John M. Liu. Pullman: Washington State University Press.

———. 1994. *Margins and Mainstreams: Asians in American History*. Seattle: University of Washington Press.

Omi, Michael. 1988. "It Just Ain't the Sixties No More: The Contemporary Dilemmas of Asian American Studies." Pp. 31–6 in *Reflections on Shattered Windows: Promises and Prospects for Asian American Studies*, ed. Gary Y. Okihiro, Shirley Hune, Arthur A. Hansen, and John M. Liu. Pullman: Washington State University Press.

Ong, Paul, Edna Bonacich, and Lucie Cheng, eds. 1994. *The New Asian Immigration in Los Angeles and Global Restructuring*. Philadelphia: Temple University Press.

Pan, Lynn, ed. 1998. *The Encyclopedia of the Overseas Chinese*. Cambridge, Mass.: Harvard University Press.

Park, Kyeyoung. 1997. *The Korean American Dream: Immigrant and Small Business in New York City*. Ithaca, N.Y.: Cornell University Press.

Prashad, Vijay. 2000. *The Karma of Brown Folk*. Minneapolis: University of Minnesota Press.

Rangaswamy, Padma. 2000. *Namasté America: Indian Immigrants in an American Metropolis*. University Park: Pennsylvania State University Press.

Saito, Leland. 1998. *Race and Politics: Asian Americans, Latinos, and Whites in a Los Angeles Suburb*. Urbana: University of Illinois Press.

Sciachitano, Marian, and Linda Trinh Võ, eds. 2000. Special Issue on Asian American Women. *Frontiers: A Journal of Women Studies* 21, no. 1/2.

Shinagawa, Larry Hajime, and Gin Yong Pang. 1996. "Asian American Panethnicity and Intermarriage." *Amerasia Journal* 22, no. 2: 127–52.

Smith-Hefner, Nancy J. 1999. *Khmer American: Identity and Moral Education in a Diasporic Community*. Berkeley: University of California Press.

Takahashi, Jere. 1997. *Nisei–Sansei: Shifting Japanese American Identities and Politics*. Philadelphia: Temple University Press.

Takaki, Ronald. 1989. *Strangers from a Different Shore: A History of Asian Americans*. Boston: Little, Brown.

Tamura, Linda. 1993. *The Hood River Issei: An Oral History of Japanese Settlers in Oregon's River Valley*. Urbana: University of Illinois Press.

Tonnies, Ferdinand. 1963 (1922). *Gemeinschaft und Gesellschaft* (Community and Society). Ed. and trans. Charles P. Loomis. New York: Harper & Row.

U.S. Bureau of the Census. 1993. *We the American. . . Asians*. Washington, D.C.: U.S. Government Printing Office.

Wang, L. Ling-chi. 1993. "Trends in Admissions for Asian Americans in Colleges and Universities." Pp. 49–60 in *The State of Asian Pacific America: Policy Issues to the Year 2020*. Los

Angeles: LEAP Asian Pacific American Public Institute and UCLA Asian American Studies Center.

Webber, Melvin M., John W. Dyckman, Donald L. Foley, Albert Z. Guttenberg, William L. C. Wheaton, and Catherine Bauer Wurster. 1964. *Explorations into Urban Structure.* Philadelphia: University of Pennsylvania Press.

Wei, William. 1993. *The Asian American Movement.* Philadelphia: Temple University Press.

Wellman, Barry. 1979. "The Community Question: The Intimate Networks of East New Yorkers." *American Journal of Sociology* 84, no. 5 (March): 1201–31.

Yung, Judy. 1995. *Unbound Feet: A Social History of Chinese Women in San Francisco.* Berkeley: University of California Press.

Zhou, Min. 1992. *Chinatown: The Socioeconomic Potential of an Urban Enclave.* Philadelphia: Temple University Press.

Zia, Helen. 2000. *Asian American Dreams: The Emergence of an American People.* New York: Farrar, Straus, and Giroux.

Part I

Communities in
Transition: Spaces
and Practices

CHAPTER 1

Tarry Hum

Asian and Latino Immigration and the Revitalization of Sunset Park, Brooklyn

A consequence of the most recent period of immigration from the Caribbean, Latin America, and Asia is the rise in multi-racial and multi-ethnic neighborhoods. [1] The transformation of local neighborhoods presents a critical opportunity to examine the enduring and new ways in which race, ethnicity, and nativity shape the spatial and socioeconomic organization of urban life (Muller 1993; Waldinger 1987). Sunset Park, Brooklyn, exemplifies the dramatic demographic recomposition of New York City neighborhoods and provides an ideal case study to examine the micro-level processes of post-1965 immigrant settlement and neighborhood change. More important, Sunset Park shows the need for new epistemological approaches to immigrant neighborhoods that integrate a restructuring urban economy, racial and ethnic diversity, and the role of the state and related institutions in mediating immigrant trajectories and struggles in defining and building communities.

The geographic boundaries of Sunset Park encompass "multiple publics." The neighborhood is simultaneously called a "satellite" Chinatown, reflecting its status as the third-largest concentration of Chinese in the New York metropolitan area after Manhattan's Chinatown and Flushing, Queens (Lin 1998; Matthews 1997; Oser 1996), and a "full" Latino neighborhood, a status it shares with Washington Heights in Manhattan and Hunts Point in the Bronx.[2] Sunset Park is frequently cited in both the scholarly and popular press as an exemplar of immigrant-driven neighborhood revitalization (Kadet 2000; Oser 1996; Winnick 1990, 1991). Immigrants' capital and sweat equity has pumped new life into a "dying neighborhood"[3] and, in the process, has transformed decaying urban spaces into vibrant marketplaces and streetscapes.

Defying simplistic characterizations of an immigrant enclave, Sunset Park offers an important venue to study the integral role of multiethnic, multiracial neighborhoods in advanced urban economies. Rather than emphasizing Sunset Park's revitalization as a stage in the historic process of immigrant ethnic succession and neighborhood change (McKenzie 1925; Winnick 1990, 1991),[4] I propose that Sunset Park's transformation signifies new social, spatial, and economic configurations of a "post-industrial" urbanization (Mollenkopf and Castells 1991). Sunset Park illustrates how contemporary immigrant community formations represent a break from the historical trajectory of ecological succession, and exemplifies the need for a reformulation of the positivist and assimilationist enclave model.

Placing a study of Sunset Park in a political and economic framework problematizes the proposal of spatial and economic mobility, as well as such attributes of enclaves as protected niche markets, cultural homogeneity, and social insularity. Rather than promote Sunset Park as a platform for immigrant assimilation and mobility, this chapter examines Sunset Park's position in the urban political economy and the new and enduring ways that race and class influence sociospatial patterns, including residential settlement, economic incorporation, and community definition (Mollenkopf and Castells 1991; Sassen 1990). The exemplar value of Sunset Park's transformation is, hence, based less on a projection of immigrant succession than on a much more complex story of structural changes in neighborhood opportunities and the persistence of race and ethnicity in shaping urban inequality.

This study of Sunset Park uses several methodologies and data resources. To document the racial transformation of Sunset Park, I summarize demographic data from the 1980, 1990, and 2000 decennial Census. Because the sample data from the 2000 Census will not be available until June 2002, I rely on the 1990 Census Public Use Microdata Sample (PUMS), which provides a comprehensive analysis of racial and ethnic populations by sub-borough areas that approximate neighborhoods. In addition to household data, I use the 1997 County Business Patterns, an annual subnational economic-data series compiled by the U.S. Census Bureau, to document Sunset Park's neighborhood economy and 1990–97 Immigration and Naturalization Service (INS) data to profile new immigrants settling in New York City neighborhoods. A historical narrative that situates the post-1965 economic and social restructuring of Sunset Park supplements this empirical overview. I also draw on personal interviews and observations, as well on as oral histories,[5] to complete this ethnography of an emerging Asian and Latino neighborhood.

Why Sunset Park?

Sunset Park is located in the southwestern section of Brooklyn; its western border runs along a two- to three-mile stretch of the Brooklyn waterfront facing the East River, with views of lower Manhattan and the Statue of Liberty. A stroll along Eighth Avenue, one of the two main commercial stretches in Sunset Park, confirms the neighborhood's designation as a "Chinatown" to even the most casual observer: Familiar cultural and commercial markers include open produce and fish markets; street vendors selling all types of goods, from phone cards to fried chicken wings; ethnic restaurants; multilingual signs; and ubiquitous traffic and commuter vans. The shared socioeconomic, demographic, and cultural qualities of Sunset Park and Manhattan's Chinatown were recently described as constituting a "community of interest".[6] Through an extensive immigrant economy based on garment factories and small retail businesses, Asians have dramatically revitalized and transformed a significant share of Sunset Park's neighborhood economy and real-estate market (Aloff 1997; Browning 1994; Hays 1993; Matthews 1997; Oser 1996; Robaton 1996). This economic revitalization is evident in the commercial activity that has spilled onto "once-dead commercial strips" (Winnick 1991: 77) between Eighth and Fifth Avenues[7] and in escalating real-estate values that have made the doubling and tripling of families in overcrowded and illegally converted basement apartments a common strategy for affordable housing.[8]

Three blocks south on Fifth Avenue is the Latino section—an equally vibrant streetscape of bodegas, street vendors, bargain furniture, and clothing and toy outlets. Concentrated in the western portion of Sunset Park adjacent to the waterfront, Latinos have endured the upheaval of urban-renewal projects, including the expansion of the Gowanus Expressway, and economic hardship due to declining manufacturing and waterfront-related industries (Sullivan 1993; Winnick 1990). The Latino population in Sunset Park has grown steadily since the 1950s, and Latinos now constitute close to one-half of the population (see Table 1-1). The 1997 election of Angel Rodriguez to the New York City Council has further consolidated Latino political leadership as other key elected representatives for Sunset Park include Congresswoman Nydia Velasquez of the 12th U.S. Congressional District and Assemblyman Felix W. Ortiz of the 51st Assembly District of New York State.

Sunset Park has a long history as a multiethnic immigrant neighborhood. The racial composition of its residents, however, has shifted decidedly from the white ethnic groups—Scandinavian, Irish, Italian, and Polish—of an earlier era. Until the 1980s,

TABLE 1-1.   Racial Composition of Sunset Park

	1980	Population Share	1990	Population Share	2000	Population Share	% Change 1980–90	% Change 1990–00
Total Population	91,181	100%	106,185	100%	127,609	100%	8%	20%
Non-Hispanic White	46,294	47%	34,330	32%	24,449	19%	−26%	−29%
African American	2,154	2%	3,436	3%	3,182	2%	60%	−7%
Latino	43,990	45%	50,375	47%	61,438	48%	15%	22%
Asian Pacific American	5,211	5%	17,516	16%	33,628	26%	236%	92%
Other	532	1%	528	.05%	1,091	1%	−1%	107%
Multi-Race[a]					3,821	3%		

[a]The multi-race category was first introduced in the Census 2000 and permits persons to check more than one of the six race categories.
Sources: U.S. Census 1980, 1990 Summary Tape File 3, 2000 Sumary File 1.

Sunset Park was largely a working-class neighborhood of European immigrants and their descendants (Freeman 2000; Winnick 1990). Today, non-Hispanic whites represent fewer than one in five residents in Sunset Park (Table 1-1). Although Latinos are the largest racial group, this population is increasingly diverse, with growing numbers of Dominicans, Mexicans, and Central Americans joining a majority Puerto Rican population. Asians account for one-quarter of Sunset Park's residents, and although three-quarters are Chinese, South Asians are also a prominent part of the community. Asians, moreover, are the fastest-growing population segment: Their numbers virtually doubled in the 1990s, in contrast to a 22 percent growth rate among Latinos in the same period. These immigration patterns underscore how Asians and Latinos will continue to transform the demographic and cultural landscape of Sunset Park.

Socioeconomic indicators such as educational attainment, English-language ability, labor-force participation, and average 1989 earnings complete the profile of a working-class immigrant neighborhood. Table 1-2 illustrates how racially based socioeconomic disparities differentiate Sunset Park residents. Non-Hispanic whites generally have completed higher levels of education, hold different labor-market positions, and are less likely than Asians and Latinos to be poor. The Asian population in Sunset Park is overwhelmingly foreign-born; subsequently, more than two-fifths do not speak English well or at all. The poverty rate among Latinos is particularly stark at 32 percent.

Although technical, sales, and administrative support occupations are common for all Sunset Park residents in the labor force, more than half of Asian and Latino workers hold service, operator, or laborer jobs, in contrast to fewer than a quarter of non-Hispanic whites. Manufacturing industries and retail trade are central to Asian and Latino workers, whereas non-Hispanic whites concentrate in service and financial, insurance, and real-estate (FIRE) industries. These racial differences in labor-market locations are further reflected in the average annual 1989 earnings of Sunset Park residents, which highlight a significantly higher level of earnings for non-Hispanic whites than for their Asian and Latino counterparts.

Sunset Park's demographic transformation is driven by the influx of post-1965 immigrants. Among the top destination neighborhoods in New York City, Sunset Park received more than 16,000 immigrants during 1990 to 1997.[9] Based on INS data, the two largest immigrant groups settling in Sunset Park are from the People's Republic of China and the Dominican Republic (see Table 1-3). New immigrants settling in Sunset Park also include sizable numbers of Europeans from Poland and the former Soviet Union as well as Filipinos, Mexicans, Central and South Americans, Pakistanis, Bangladeshis, Vietnamese, Guyanese, Trinidadians, and Egyptians. One-half of the newcomers age sixteen or older held a job prior to migration. Although a small percentage (7 percent) did not report their occupation, of the majority who did, the most common occupations were laborers, agricultural workers, or sales and services. Among those immigrants who did not hold a job, approximately one-third were homemakers (36 percent), unemployed or retired (33 percent), or students (31 percent).[10]

There are notable differences between the top two immigrant groups—Chinese and Dominicans—that affect their incorporation into and impact on the neighborhood. Chinese immigrants tend to be older, with an average age of thirty-four, compared

TABLE 1-2.   Detailed 1990 Population Characteristics of Sunset Park

	Asians	Latinos	Non-Hispanic Whites
Total	17,516	50,375	34,330
% of neighborhood population	16%	47%	32%
Top five ethnic groups	Chinese (72%)	Puerto Rican (61%)	Italian (22%)
	Asian Indian (15%)	Dominican (11%)	Irish (20%)
	Filipino (5%)	Mexican (9%)	Polish (9%)
	Vietnamese (3%)	Ecuadorian (5%)	Russian (4%)
	Other (5%)	Other (14%)	German (4%)
Poverty rate	19%	32%	18%
% of foreign-born	85%	27%	21%
Does not speak English well or at all[a]	43%	23%	5%
Highest education level attained[b]			
Less than high school	45%	58%	32%
High-school graduate	23%	21%	30%
College or beyond	32%	21%	38%
In the labor force[c]	65%	60%	55%
Industry			
Retail trade	28%	19%	12%
Manufacturing	25%	21%	9%
Servcies	20%	27%	39%
Financial, insurance, real estate (FIRE)	10%	9%	16%
Wholesale trade	4%	5%	3%
Transportation, communications, utilities	4%	8%	9%
Construction	4%	6%	5%
Public administration	2%	3%	4%
Agricultural/mining	0.2%	0.2%	0.4%
Occupation			
Technical, sales, administrative support	29%	30%	35%
Operators, laborers	25%	25%	9%
Servcies	20%	21%	13%
Executive, managerial, professional specialities	16%	11%	31%
Craft production	8%	12%	11%
Mean wages in 1989[d]	$13,950	$14,494	$22,477
Self-employment rate	3.1%	1.4%	2.7%

[a]Three years and older, [b]25 years and older, [c]16 years and older, [d]16 years and older and in the labor force.

Source: U.S. Census 1990 Public Use Microdata Sample.

with twenty-five for Dominicans. In fact, a third of Dominican immigrants are children younger than sixteen. Among the adults, the majority of Chinese immigrants are married and held jobs prior to migration. Reflecting a younger population overall, only 41 percent of adult Dominicans held a job prior to migration. The occupational composition of both Chinese and Dominican immigrants indicates a largely low-skill labor force. More than two-fifths of the Dominican immigrants who held

TABLE 1-3.   New Immigration to Sunset Park, 1990–97

	Total	Chinese	Dominican
Total number of immigrants	16,698	4,861	3,302
Top contries of origin	People's Republic of China (26%)	People's Republic of China (91%)	
	Dominican Republic (20%)	Hong Kong (8%)	
	Poland (6%)	Taiwan (1%)	
	Ecuador (5%)		
	Philippines (3%)		
Feamale	52%	52%	53%
Average age (years)	29	34	25
Married[a]	64%	68%	52%
Children (younger than 16)	23%	16%	32%
Held a job prior to migration[b]	49%	59%	41%
Occupation			
Laborer	23%	21%	43%
Sales/service	20%	16%	13%
Farming, forest, fishery	16%	34%	12%
Executive, profession, managerial	13%	11%	8%
Precision craft	12%	7%	13%
Administrative/clerical	10%	9%	10%
Health professional	5%	2%	2%
Did not hold a job prior to migration[a]	43%	35%	59%
Homemaker	36%	29%	45%
Unemployed/retired	33%	52%	8%
Student or younger than 16	31%	19%	47%
Occupation unknown[b]	7%	6%	0.2%

[a]Immigrants 16 years and older, [b]Occupation was not reported.
Source: U.S. Department of Justice, Immigration and Naturalization Services, Public Use Files, 1990–97.

a job prior to migration were employed as laborers. Similarly, more than half of the Chinese immigrants who held jobs prior to migration were employed in agricultural work or as laborers. Sunset Park's demographic profile illustrates a racially and ethnically diverse neighborhood of largely low-skill workers in retail trades, services, and nondurable manufacturing. Immigration patterns underscores the centrality of Latinos and Asians in shaping the future landscape of Sunset Park and, moreover, point to the persistence of socioeconomic disparities among its multiple population segments.

Immigrant Enclaves and Ethnic Succession

The spatial organization of urban life and its related dynamic processes of growth and decline were framed by Robert E. Park and his associates at the University of Chicago in pioneering the field of human ecology (Park et al. 1925). Concepts derived from the biological processes of changing ecosystems formed the theoretical foundation for early urban sociology and continues to shape the analysis of contemporary community formation and change. The premise of an urban ecological model is that the dynamic of neighborhood change is facilitated by a process of "invasion and succession" in which one population group replaces another. The key dynamic in neighborhood change is migration. Contemporary scholars have elaborated on this ecological model by noting how supply-side changes such as the out-migration of particular populations groups—namely, non-Hispanic whites—create "vacancies" for new immigrant settlement (Waldinger 1987, 1989).

This ecological model poses neighborhood change as a series of successions that signal the spatial and social assimilation of different population groups. Premised on the assumption of socioeconomic mobility, the "invasion and succession" model proposes a natural and orderly process of neighborhood change that "refreshes urban pluralism even as assimilation draws others into the mainstream" (Macionis and Parrillo 1998: 241). This trajectory of neighborhood change reinforces the commonly held view that immigrant settlements are transitional. Immigrant enclaves serve as "stepping-stone" and "port-of-entry" communities that assist newcomers in their adjustment process. Providing the necessary social, economic, and cultural resources, enclave communities facilitate the integration of new immigrants and subsequent generations (Marcuse 1997; Portes and Bach 1985; Portes and Rumbaut 1990). If not for the continued influx of co-ethnic newcomers, neighborhoods would decline and become prime targets for invasion. Although the term "invasion" has fallen out of favor, implicit assumptions in the succession model still current—that is, a queuing trajectory of neighborhood transition that parallels racial and ethnic mobility and assimilation (Godfrey 1988; Waldinger 1987).

Integral to the ecological model are spatially segregated and socioculturally distinct enclaves that are considered natural elements of urban form and life (Park et al. 1925). The historical and sociological significance of enclaves is particularly salient in the Asian immigrant experience, particularly for the Chinese. Historic Chinatowns formed as a collective response to racism and exclusion (Kwong 1987; Wong 1982). The hostile societal environment contributed to the centrality of Chinatown in ensuring individual and collective livelihood by providing ethnic housing and labor markets, social services, and cultural sustenance (Ong 1984; Wong 1982). Studies on Chinatown emphasize informal ethnic networks, self-governance, insularity, and an institutionally complete neighborhood (Wong 1982; Zhou 1992). Reflecting the various types of racialization of Asian communities, Chinatowns have been depicted as ghettos (Kinkead 1991; Light 1974), impoverished working-poor neighborhoods (Kwong 1987, 1996; Loo 1991), and, more recently, socioeconomic powerhouses (Zhou 1992).

The revitalization of historic Chinatowns and the formation of new "satellite" Chinatowns in the aftermath of the 1965 Immigration and Nationality Act have led some scholars to proclaim enclaves a superior strategy for immigrant economic and social integration (Portes and Zhou 1992; Zhou 1992). In contrast to the transitory nature of immigrant enclaves, the concentration of ethnic residence and economy provides important benefits and opportunities not available in non-enclave communities. The reproduction of enclave communities does not necessarily indicate the persistence of involuntary segregation; rather, it may indicate the capacity of ethnic solidarity and social networks to facilitate economic mobility, community life, and cultural continuity (Portes and Bach 1985; Portes and Zhou 1992; Zhou 1992). In other words, enclave residence is not the sole option for new immigrants, but it can be a superior one, because it provides privileged access to ethnic resources and opportunities (Li 1999; Zhou and Logan 1991).

Studies of satellite enclaves emphasize that new ethnic clusters are distinct from historic enclaves, as reflected in *Chinatown No More*, the title of a book on Flushing, Queens (Chen 1992). Ethnic diversity, class position, and suburban location are qualities that differentiate satellites from historic Chinatown (Chen 1992; Fong 1994; Horton 1995; Li 1999). Notwithstanding these important differences in the institutional, social, and economic arrangements of historic and satellite enclaves, an enduring theme in the sociological and urban studies literature on immigrant communities is that enclaves connote positive outcomes. This proposition is exemplified in a current definition of an enclave as a "spatially concentrated area in which members of a particular population group, self-defined by ethnicity or religion or otherwise, congregate as a means of enhancing their economic, social, political and/or cultural development" (Marcuse 1997: 225).

Based on this definition, the key attributes of an enclave are clear: self-segregation, mutual support and solidarity, and upward mobility. Undoubtedly, Sunset Park's demographic profile and socioeconomic qualities distinguish it as an immigrant enclave neighborhood. However, two aspects of neighborhood life in Sunset Park show the limitations of a succession model of neighborhood change and the positivist qualities of an enclave. A key issue is the evolving configurations of global economic restructuring and whether the subsequent restructuring of local neighborhood economies presents paths of incorporation and mobility for new immigrants that are comparable to those of previous immigrant generations. The types of neighborhood opportunity structures generated by immigrant ethnic economies in a globalized and restructuring New York regional economy need to be investigated.

A second aspect of neighborhood life that points to the need to revisit the epistemological approach to immigrant neighborhoods is the growing significance of multiracial and multiethnic populations. Recent studies on racially diverse neighborhoods have documented and analyzed processes of racial identity construction, struggles over political representation, neighborhood redevelopment, and quality of life; however, these studies have largely focused on middle-class, suburban neighborhoods (Fong 1994; Horton 1995; Saito 1998; Sanjek 1998). A study of Sunset Park illustrates how the opportunities for defining common concerns and interests, and the process of engagement in community-building efforts may differ in working-class and working-poor immigrant neighborhoods.

Although there are undoubtedly other critiques of the assimilationist enclave model, this chapter will examine economic restructuring and multiracial, multiethnic relations as two aspects of neighborhood life in Sunset Park. These aspects challenge the succession trajectory of immigrant neighborhoods and underscore the importance of new research directions in documenting immigrant settlement and community formation.

The Evolution of an Asian–Latino Neighborhood

When Sunset Park is placed in the context of a broader political economic framework, its evolution represents less a narrative of ethnic succession and immigrant mobility than a mapping of how race, ethnicity, and nativity shape the socioeconomic and spatial geography of urban inequality. Drawn by employment opportunities in the developing industrial waterfront, Irish, Scandinavian, Italian, and Polish immigrants settled in Sunset Park in successive waves beginning in the early 1800s. Institutions built by these immigrants, including St. Michael's Church, Our Lady of Perpetual Help, the Norwegian Lutheran Deaconess' Home and Hospital (now Lutheran Medical Center), the Finnish Housing Cooperative, and Greenwood Cemetery, are standing testimonials to the rich community life of this early period. During the 1880s, Sunset Park was the center of Norwegian culture and contained the largest concentration of Norwegians east of Minneapolis (Winnick 1990). The occupational profile of these immigrants as sailors, shipbuilders, dockworkers, construction workers, laborers, cargo handlers, harbor pilots, and maritime officers reflected the prominence of waterfront development and city-building activities.

During the late 1890s, the construction of Bush Terminal, covering almost two miles of shoreline and consisting of a complex of piers, warehouses, and factory lofts linked by a railway, was completed. Bush Terminal was the largest commercial and industrial facility in New York and employed 20,000 workers in manufacturing and shipping industries. Bush Terminal ultimately became a prototype of industrial park development (Sunset Park Waterfront Community Design Workshop 1997). In 1918, the waterfront expanded to include the Brooklyn Army Terminal—a complex of piers, warehouses, railroad yards, administration buildings, and mechanical facilities—which served as a central departing point for soldiers and supplies during World War II.

At its height, Sunset Park's waterfront was a center of industrial production and trade (Freeman 2000). Bush Terminal comprised 150 industrial structures and eight large piers, including shipyards. Combined with the Brooklyn Army Terminal, it provided more than 5 million square feet of workspace interconnected by the fourteen-mile New York Dock Railroad, which linked Brooklyn to the regional economy (Winnick 1990: 76). Large industrial firms such as Bethlehem Steel Shipyard, Colgate-Palmolive-Peet, American Can Company, and American Machine and Foundry, as well as hundreds of small machine shops, repair shops, truckers, waterfront suppliers, and trade services, provided a steady flow of blue-collar manufacturing jobs in Sunset Park.

As with many New York City neighborhoods during the 1940s, Robert Moses's capital-infrastructure projects set the stage for residential displacement and neighborhood destruction (Caro 1974). A central factor in Sunset Park's decline was the construction of the Gowanus Expressway in 1941. Despite community opposition, the Gowanus, which connects the Brooklyn–Battery Tunnel with southern Brooklyn, was routed through Sunset Park along Third Avenue. Once a commercial center, Third Avenue fell into the expressway's dark shadow, and the roadway created a physical barrier separating the waterfront from the rest of Sunset Park, prompting its physical decline. Displacement and destruction occurred again in the late 1950s, when the Gowanus Expressway was widened to accommodate new traffic lanes. By the 1990s, concentrated poverty dominated the area around Third Avenue and the elevated Gowanus Expressway (Sullivan 1993).

Employment in the local industries and the widening of the Gowanus Expressway brought increasing numbers of Puerto Ricans to Sunset Park in the 1950s and 1960s.[11] Unlike earlier immigrant waves who arrived in a period of industrial and urban growth, Puerto Ricans occupied a marginal economic position that steadily worsened. The closing of the Brooklyn Army Terminal and seven of Bush Terminal's eight piers in the 1960s marked the massive deindustrialization of Sunset Park's local economy. The growing number of Puerto Ricans coupled with a shrinking employment base facilitated Sunset Park's racial transformation, as white ethnic groups began to flee to surrounding suburbs (Sullivan 1993; Winnick 1990). The "white flight" and industrial decline brought urban disinvestment and abandonment. Sunset Park was designated a poverty area in the 1970s. Vacant buildings in the underused Bush Terminal symbolized the massive loss of jobs. Although some warehouses, bakeries, and garment factories remained, these firms represented only a shadow of an earlier period of economic vitality. Rather than an orderly succession process, the transformation of Sunset Park was an outcome of the interrelated dynamics of deindustrialization, racism, and urban redevelopment.

By the 1970s, Sunset Park had become a "dying neighborhood, another sad victim of urban blight" (Winnick 1991). Because it offered a vast affordable housing stock, a convenient public-transportation line to Manhattan, and weak organized resistance to newcomers, the neighborhood attracted notable numbers of Asian and Latino immigrants, who made Sunset Park their home starting in the early 1980s. Recognizing potential market opportunities, immigrants with financial and human capital purchased or leased commercial storefronts and established new businesses catering to ethnic consumers (Kadet 2000). Increasingly, the demographic recomposition of Sunset Park was reflected in the small retail and commercial storefronts along the main avenues as well as other public spaces that serve the neighborhood. As Table 1-4 shows, Sunset Park's neighborhood economy is largely based on small businesses in retail trade and services that support the social-reproduction needs of an immigrant population. Manufacturing firms make up an additional one-fifth of all Sunset Park establishments, and more than half of those are garment manufacturers or contractors. Less than two decades ago, according to the 1987 County Business Patterns, manufacturing in Sunset Park included significant numbers of printing and metalmaking firms.

The revitalization of Sunset Park's neighborhood economy is embedded in the economic restructuring of New York City and is instructive on the position of immigrant neighborhoods in the sociospatial organization of advanced urban economies.[12] Once a center of maritime and durable-goods-manufacturing industries (Freeman 2000), Sunset Park has again become a noted site of production, but now this activity is largely based on downgraded manufacturing of non-durable goods—namely, garment production (Lii 1995; Moore 1998). Despite the steady decline of manufacturing jobs, the mass influx of Asian and Latino immigrants has enabled New York to hold on to

TABLE 1-4.   Neighborhood Economy of Sunset Park, 1997

	Total Number of Establishments	Types of Establishments	Fewer than 10 Employees
Total number of establishments	2,278	100%	75%
Retail trade	508	22%	86%
Grocery and food markets	121	24%	
Eating and drinking places	111	22%	
Clothing stores	59	12%	
Services	452	20%	79%
Auto repair, services, parking	86	19%	
Medical services	75	17%	
Individual and family services	44	10%	
Business services	32	7%	
Repair services	31	7%	
Manufacturing	446	20%	57%
Apparel production	249	56%	
Wholesale trade	376	17%	70%
Construction	202	9%	77%
Financial, insurance, real estate (FIRE)	150	7%	83%
Transportation/public utilities	94	4%	66%
Agricultural, forestry, fishing	4	0%	50%
Unclassified	46	20%	100%

ᵃSunset Park comprises the zip codes 11220 and 11232.
Source: U.S. Census Bureau, County Business Patters, Zip Code Data 1997.

several manufacturing industries, including the garment industry (Johnson 1998; Levitan 1998). Although cheap imports and production outsourcing have created conditions of fierce competition, New York City is able to retain a segment of this industry because it offers several competitive advantages. They include its status as a fashion center; an agglomeration of retailers, designers, manufacturers, and contractors; and easy access to a skilled and low-wage workforce.

Sunset Park's neighborhood economy is a critical part of the globalized production process that provides cheap industrial rents, easy access to regional transportation networks, and a largely non-unionized labor supply. The production of standardized garments has essentially moved overseas, but New York City's garment industry has reoriented itself toward specialized niche markets and highly fashion-sensitive products, such as junior clothing and women's outerwear, that require quick turnarounds. Competition among retailers creates tremendous incentives to avoid stockpiling inventory, compounding the instability and unpredictability of the market. This unpredictability is ultimately absorbed by garment contractors and their workers. And because the capital requirements for setting up a garment shop are low, apparel production continues to be a viable strategy for immigrant business ownership. Moreover, access to a vast co-ethnic labor market enables immigrant contractors to squeeze their workers in order to eke out marginal profits.

Conditions in Sunset Park's immigrant garment industry has brought renewed attention to sweatshops.[13] Assemblyman Felix Ortiz sponsored two public hearings on this issue in the late 1990s, and the testimonials were compiled in two mono-graphs, titled, "Behind Closed Doors: A Look into the Underground Sweatshop Indus-try." These booklets detailed frequent violations of basic labor and health standards. Sunset Park's economy illustrates how local neighborhoods are positioned in the spa-tial geography of "the Third World within," as immigrant Asian and Latino women labor in substandard work conditions and in direct competition with overseas coun-terparts in Mexico, the Dominican Republic, and the People's Republic of China.

The decline of Sunset Park's waterfront industries in the 1960s was related to the massive and fundamental shift in New York City's economic base from manufactur-ing to service-related industries (Bluestone and Harrison 1982; Fitch 1993; Mollenkopf and Castells 1991). The reindustrialization of Sunset Park centers on downgraded manufacturing in which the key competitive advantage is cheap domestic labor in the form of risk-taking entrepreneurs and exploited workers (Sassen-Koob 1984). Sun-set Park's neighborhood economy has moved from industrial jobs that provided avenues for worker mobilization and unionization to marginal manufacturing and service industries that are made viable by low-wage immigrant labor. The rejuve-nating qualities of Sunset Park's transformation hence are countered by the repro-duction of inequality. Immigrant-owned businesses may be a key catalyst in revers-ing Sunset Park's economic decline, but this new prosperity is countered by the uneven development that is inherent in advanced urban economies. Immigrant work-ing poverty, the expansion of the informal and sweatshop economy, and the casual-ization of employment relations are also part of the economic life of Sunset Park.

Racially diverse neighborhoods represent a transitional phase in the multistage process of ecological succession that ultimately results in racially homogenous neigh-borhoods brought about by out-migration and voluntary segregation (Aldrich 1975). The transformation of Sunset Park suggests, however, that racial diversity is not tran-sitory and that Asian and Latino relations, in particular, will be critical in negotiating the neighborhood's future community politics and identity. The following excepts from interviews conducted in 1993 by the Brooklyn Historical Society and the Muse-um of Chinese in Americas for the oral-history project "Eighth Avenue, Sunset Park: Brooklyn's Chinatown" illustrates the racial tensions that typically underlie daily interactions in public spaces, schools, and workplaces:[14]

> I resent the characterizations of our community being called Chinatown. To me, it's dis-regarding all the other people who still live in this community. It's saying, we're here and no one else who's been here counts anymore. —Edward Pavez

> All our parents worked on the waterfront or in the factories. But it was also a difficult expe-rience, because the Puerto Ricans were the last ones to arrive, so that there was a lot of prej-udice against Puerto Ricans, and we always found ourselves on the defensive. —Teddy Rodriquez

> We were the first Chinese family to buy a house on this block. The block was mostly Ital-ian, a few Hispanics. Hispanic children my age would throw things at our windows or ring the doorbell and run away. I don't feel bad about it anymore, but at the time (I was eleven or twelve) it was scary. They called us names like "Chinks." —Annie Wong

The urgency to cultivate institutional and community leadership to address systemic inequality and foster a broad and inclusive vision of community building that goes beyond ethnic-specific claims and social-service solutions was brought to a head several years ago by a number of bias-related incidences, including one in which a thirty-two-year-old Chinese man was attacked by two Latino youths with a machete. To fill the leadership void, Sunset United was formed. Sunset United is a coalition of more than twenty community institutions, including the Chinese American Planning Council, Chinese Promise Baptist Church, Hispanic Young People's Alternatives (HYPA), and United Puerto Rican Organization of Sunset Park (UPROSE). The organization's philosophy is encapsulated in its motto, "Real peace is not just the absence of conflict but the presence of justice."[15]

Recognizing the need to cultivate new leadership especially among the youth, the Sunset United Youth Collaborative has organized peace vigils and participated in the Community Conflict Resolution Training and Capacity Building Program at Columbia University's Teachers College. Upon completion of the program, youth leaders will "train the trainers" and set up conflict-resolution workshops for the staff and members of community organizations. Although efforts to build the necessary infrastructure for co-existence are embryonic, awareness is growing that the spatial, economic, and cultural boundaries of daily neighborhood life in Sunset Park are porous and that they are contested in the marketplace, in residential housing patterns, in public spaces, and in neighborhood institutions. There is no doubt that Sunset Park's future depends on cultivating community leadership that promotes a multiracial perspective on community concerns and quality of life.[16]

Race, Ethnicity, and Urbanization in a "Post-Industrial" City

Sunset Park's rich immigrant history provides fertile ground for examining how the settlement and incorporation processes of Asian and Latino immigrants embodies both continuities and discontinuities in historic immigrant experiences. This chapter suggests that post-1965 immigrant settlement patterns and community formation require a new theoretical perspective that integrates the centrality of race and class in the incorporation of immigrants, the mediating role of ethnic economies in facilitating both economic livelihood and marginality, and the fundamental shifts in the local urban political economy that pose opportunities and challenges. Most important, the experience of Sunset Park proposes that the formation of new immigrant settlements as multiethnic, transnational immigrant neighborhoods is integral to advanced urban economies and embodies new arrangements in social, cultural, and economic life that require alternative models and strategies for community studies and community building.

Rather than illustrating a stage in a historic process of ethnic succession, the transformation of Sunset Park tells a story about the socioeconomic and spatial geography of urban inequality. The persistence of Chinatown and the formation of new "Chinatowns" suggests not only that we reconsider the historic assimilationist function of immigrant settlements, but that we examine the implicit assumptions of a hierarchical model of ethnic queuing in neighborhood and social mobility. Sunset Park reflects how race, ethnicity, and class shape post-1970s neighborhood change. Its decline was an outcome of white flight, disinvestment, and racial segmentation in the housing market. The succession model deflects from these social relations of power, marginalization, and resistance in neighborhood transitions.

Increasingly, Asian immigrants' daily lived experiences are no longer centered in homogenous and isolated communities. They are mediated in multiethnic, multiracial contexts. Research on the social impact of Asian immigration on urban neighborhoods has focused on the dynamics between "established" Anglo residents and newcomers (Horton 1995; Smith 1995). The geographic boundaries of Sunset Park embrace multiple publics, including an established Puerto Rican population, which offers important opportunities in and challenges to building community. Asian and Latino relations in Sunset Park will need to reconcile what the sociologist Manuel Castells (1996: 2) has called "urban schizophrenia," defined as the "structural lack of communication between different cultures and different spaces within the same urban system." A central part of this project involves moving beyond racialized conceptions of communities of color as enclaves, ghettos, barrios, or underclasses. Sunset Park suggests that immigrant communities can be conceptualized as "transnational" to represent the multiple ways in which national, cultural, and racial borders are traversed in the local environments of "global cities" and their neighborhoods.

Sunset Park provides information about "post-industrial" urbanization processes that reproduce spatial and social fragmentation and economic polarization in multiple and complex ways. Sunset Park is not a simple model of urban rejuvenation brought about by immigrants' ethnic resources and investments. It is a dynamic representation of the local expressions of post-1970s urban restructuring and reflects the changing needs of capitalist development (Harvey 1978). Sunset Park's transformation provides insight into how local neighborhoods are situated in the decentralization of production sites that produce new patterns of ethnic concentration and segregation (Kwong 1996). The utility of traditional approaches to immigrant settlements such as enclave and neighborhood succession limit our effort to extricate the integral role of immigrant neighborhoods in the emerging systems of production and social organization that define advanced urban societies.

Sunset Park is no isolated and self-sufficient enclave neighborhood; rather, it informs the process of urbanization and the social, spatial, and economic arrangements of a post-industrial New York. Whether Sunset Park will continue to facilitate the ethnic and spatial succession of new immigrant groups is unclear. What is clear is that Sunset Park exemplifies the macro-economic and demographic trends that are fundamentally reshaping urban America.

Notes

1. Recent studies that document neighborhood diversity include Alba et al. 1995; New York City Department of City Planning 1996; Nyden et al. 1997; and Sanjek 1998. See also U.S. Department of Housing and Urban Development 1998.

2. In a study for the Institute for Puerto Rican Policy, Chris Hanson-Sanchez designated "full" Latino neighborhoods as those in which Latinos make up at least 40 percent of the population: see Hanson-Sanchez 1996.

3. Winnick 1991 used this phrase to describe Sunset Park.

4. This view is exemplified a quote from City Councilor Angel Rodriquez: "It's part of the progression—standard operating procedure for immigrants" (cited in Kadet 2000).

5. The oral histories were collected by the Museum of Chinese in Americas and the Brooklyn Historical Society in 1993.

6. The Asian American Legal Defense and Education Fund engaged in a successful effort to keep Sunset Park and Manhattan's Chinatown together in one congressional district by emphasizing the qualities these two neighborhoods share (Hicks 1997; Levy 1997).

7. My research assistants conducted a census of Sunset Park businesses in August 2000 and counted 118 businesses on Sixth and Seventh avenues between 65th and 45th streets, which Winnick 1991 describes as "once dead commercial strips."

8. An article in the Chinese-language *World Journal* newspaper dated 3 September 2000 noted that housing prices in Sunset Park have risen sixfold in the past twenty years.

9. This figure does not include undocumented immigrants.

10. The INS lumps those who were unemployed or retired in their country of origin into one category.

11. Puerto Ricans initially settled in Sunset Park in the early 1900s. Sullivan (1993: 7) discusses how their arrival can be traced to the Marine Tiger Company ships that docked along the waterfront.

12. See Freeman 2000.

13. Jane Lii, a *New York Times* reporter, worked in a garment factory in Sunset Park to research her article, "Week in Sweatshop Reveals Grim Conspiracy of the Poor": see Lii 1995.

14. The names of the oral-history participants are pseudonyms.

15. The information about Sunset United is based on a funding application to the Surdna Foundation prepared by the organization's coordinator/facilitator.

16. Christian 2000 highlights the diversity of Sunset Park and how local Muslim and Jewish relations have been affected by events in the Gaza Strip and West Bank.

References

Alba, Richard D., Nancy A. Denton, Shu-yin J. Leung, and John R. Logan. 1995. "Neighborhood Change Under Conditions of Mass Immigration: The New York City Region, 1970–1990." *International Migration Review* 29, no. 3: 625–55.

Aldrich, Howard. 1975. "Ecological Succession in Racially Changing Neighborhoods." *Urban Affairs Quarterly* 10, no. 3: 327–48.

Aloff, Mindy. 1997. "Where China and Brooklyn Overlap." *New York Times*, February 7.

Bluestone, Barry and Bennett Harrison. 1982. *The Deindustrialization of America*. New York: Basic Books.

Bonacich, Edna, Lucie Cheng, Norma Chinchilla, Nora Hamilton, and Paul Ong. 1994. *Global Production: The Apparel Industry in the Pacific Rim*. Philadelphia: Temple University Press.

Browning, E. S. 1994. "A New Chinatown Grows in Brooklyn." *Wall Street Journal* (31 May).

Caro, Robert. 1974. *The Power Broker: Robert Moses and the Fall of New York*. New York: Alfred A. Knopf.

Castells, Manuel. 1996. "Advanced Information Technology, Low-Income Communities, and the City." Colloquium, Massachusetts Institute of Technology, Department of Urban Studies and Planning, 8 March. Available from <http://web.mit.edu/sap/www/colloquium96/summaries/castells.html>.

Chen, Hsiang-shui. 1992. *Chinatown No More: Taiwan Immigrants in Contemporary New York.* Ithaca, N.Y.: Cornell University Press.

Christian, Nichole M. 2000. "New Hostility in Mideast Echoes in a Brooklyn Neighborhood." *New York Times* (5 October).

Fitch, Robert. 1993. *The Assassination of New York.* London and New York: Verso.

Fong, Timothy. 1994. *The First Suburban Chinatown: The Remaking of Monterey Park, California.* Philadelphia: Temple University Press.

Freeman, Joshua B. 2000. *Working Class New York: Life and Labor Since World War II.* New York: New Press.

Godfrey, B. J. 1988. *Neighborhoods in Transition: The Making of San Francisco's Ethnic and Nonconformist Communities.* Berkeley: University of California Press.

Hanson-Sanchez, Chris. 1996. *Latino Neighborhoods Data Book.* New York: Institute for Puerto Rican Policy.

Harvey, David. 1978. "The Urban Process Under Capitalism: A Framework for Analysis." *International Journal of Urban and Regional Research* 2, no. 1: 101–31.

Hays, Constance L. 1993. "To Markets! To Markets!" *New York Times,* November 28.

Hicks, Jonathan P. 1997. "Albany Charts New Congressional Map." *New York Times* (30 July).

Horton, John. 1995. *The Politics of Diversity: Immigration, Resistance, and Change in Monterey Park, California.* Philadelphia: Temple University Press.

Johnson, Kirk. 1998. "Report Shows a Strong and Diverse Job Growth for New York City." *New York Times* (5 March).

Kadet, Anne. 2000. "New Dawn in Sunset Park." *Brooklyn Bridge* (February–March).

Kinkead, Gwen. 1992. *Chinatown: A Portrait of a Closed Society.* New York: HarperCollins.

Kwong, Peter. 1987. *The New Chinatown.* New York: Hill and Wang.

———. 1996. *Forbidden Workers: Illegal Chinese Immigrants and American Labor.* New York: New Press.

Levitan, Mark. 1998. *Opportunity at Work: The New York City Garment Industry.* New York: Community Service Society of New York.

Levy, Clifford. 1997. "Court Outlaws New York District Drawn Up to Aid Hispanic Voters." *New York Times* (27 February).

Li, Wei. 1999. "Building Ethnoburbia: The Emergence and Manifestation of the Chinese Ethnoburb in Los Angeles' San Gabriel Valley." *Journal of Asian American Studies* 2, no. 1: 1–28.

Light, Ivan. 1974. "From Vice District to Tourist Attraction: The Moral Career of American Chinatowns, 1880-1940." *Pacific Historical Review* 43: 367–94.

Lii, Jane H. 1995. "Special Report: Week in Sweatshop Reveals Grim Conspiracy of the Poor." *New York Times* (12 March).

Lin, Jan. 1998. *Reconstructing Chinatown: Ethnic Enclave, Global Change.* Minneapolis: University of Minnesota Press.

Loo, Chalsa. 1991. *Chinatown: Most Time, Hard Time.* New York: Praeger.

Macionis, John J., and Vincent N. Parrillo. 1998. *Cities and Urban Life.* Upper Saddle River, N.J.: Prentice-Hall.

Marcuse, Peter. 1997. "The Enclave, the Citadel, and the Ghetto: What Has Changed in the Post-Fordist City." *Urban Affairs Review* 33, no. 2: 228–64.

Matthews, Joe. 1997. "The 3 Chinatowns." *The Sun* (Seattle) (7 May).

McKenzie, R. D. 1925. "The Ecological Approach to the Study of the Human Community." Pp. 63–79 in *The City*, ed. Robert E. Park, Ernest W. Burgess, Roderick D. McKenzie. Chicago: University of Chicago Press.

Mollenkopf, John H., and Manuel Castells, eds. 1991. *Dual City: Restructuring New York*. New York: Russell Sage Foundation.

Moore, Eugene (district manager of the Community Board). 1998. Interview with the author, 7 May.

Muller, Thomas. 1993. *Immigrants and the American City*. New York: New York University Press.

New York City Department of City Planning, Population Division. 1996. "The Newest New Yorkers, 1990–1994." Report.

New York State Assembly Subcommittee on Sweatshops. 1997. "Behind Closed Doors: A Look into the Underground Sweatshop Industry." Report.

———. 1999. "Behind Closed Doors II: Another Look into the Underground Sweatshop Industry." Report.

Nyden, Philip, Michael Maly and John Lukehart. 1997. "The Emergence of Stable Racially and Ethnically Diverse Urban Communities: A Case Study of Nine U.S. Cities." *Housing Policy Debate* 8, 2: 491–534.

Ong, Paul. 1984. "Chinatown Unemployment and the Ethnic Labor Market." *Amerasia* 11, no. 1: 35–54.

Oser, Alan S. 1996. "Immigrants Again Renew Sunset Park." *New York Times* (1 December).

Park, Robert E., Eugene W. Burgess, and Robert D. McKenzie. 1925. *The City*. Chicago: University of Chicago Press.

Portes, Alejandro, and Robert Bach. 1985. *Latin Journey: Cuban and Mexican Immigrants in the United States*. Berkeley and Los Angeles: University of California Press.

Portes, Alejandro, and Ruben G. Rumbaut. 1990. *Immigrant America: A Portrait*. Berkeley and Los Angeles: University of California Press.

Portes, Alejandro, and Min Zhou. 1992. "Gaining the Upper Hand: Economic Mobility Among Immigrant and Domestic Minorities." *Ethnic and Racial Studies* 15, no. 4 (October).

Robaton, Anna. 1996. "Chinese Stake Out Sunset Park, Rebuilding Brooklyn Neighborhood." *Crain's New York*, vol. 12, no. 39, 30.

Saito, Leland. 1998. *Race and Politics: Asian Americans, Latinos, and Whites in a Los Angeles Suburb*. Urbana: University of Illinois Press.

Sanjek, Roger. 1998. *The Future of Us All: Race and Neighborhood Politics in New York City*. Ithaca, N.Y.: Cornell University Press.

Sassen-Koob, Saskia. 1984. "The New Labor Demand in Global Cities," Cities in Transformation. Pp. 139–71 in *Cities in Transformation: Class, Capital, and the* State, ed. M. P. Smith. Beverly Hills, Calif.: Sage Publications.

Sassen, Saskia. 1990. "Economic Restructuring and the American City." *Annual Review of Sociology* 16: 465–90.

Smith, Christopher. 1995. "Asian New York: The Geography and Politics of Diversity." *International Migration Review* 29, no. 1: 59–85.

Sullivan, Mercer L. 1993. "Puerto Ricans in Sunset Park, Brooklyn: Poverty Amidst Ethnic and Economic Diversity." Pp. 1–25 in *In the Barrios: Latinos and the Underclass Debate*, ed. Joan Moore. New York: Russell Sage Foundation.

Sunset Park Waterfront Community Design Workshop. 1997. Briefing Book. Co-sponsored by Community Board 7, American Planning Association New York Metro Chapter, Municipal Art Society Planning Center.

U.S. Department of Housing and Urban Development. 1998. "Special Issue: Racially and Ethnically Diverse Urban Neighborhoods." *Cityscape: A Journal of Policy Development and Research* 4, no. 2.

Waldinger, Roger. 1987. "Beyond Nostalgia: The Old Neighborhood Revisited." *New York Affairs,* vol. 10, 1–12.

————. 1989. "Immigration and Urban Change." *Annual Review of Sociology* 15: 211–32.

Winnick, Louis. 1990. *New People in Old Neighborhoods.* New York: Russell Sage Foundation.

————. 1991. "Letter from Sunset Park," *City Journal,* vol. 1, no. 2, 75–9.

Wong, Bernard. 1982. *Chinatown: Economic Adaptation and Ethnic Identity.* New York: Henry Holt.

Zhou, Min. 1992. *Chinatown: The Socioeconomic Potential of an Urban Enclave.* Philadelphia: Temple University Press.

Zhou, Min, and John R. Logan. 1991. "In and Out of Chinatown: Residential Mobility and Segregation of New York City's Chinese." *Social Forces* 70, no. 2: 387–407.

CHAPTER 2

Eileen Chia-Ching Fung

The Politics and Poetics of a Taiwanese Chinese American Identity

Indeed, the yearning for fathers, for past authority and sure knowledge that can no longer be supported, permeates male texts of modernity.

—*Ellen G. Friedman (1997: 159)*

Diasporas are emblems of transnationalism because they embody the question of borders.

— *Khachig Tololyan (1991: 6)*

He Is Not Chiang Kai-shek's Son

In the fall of 1997, Taiwan's major news and media organizations made a shocking announcement: "Chiang Ching-kuo is not Chiang Kai-shek's son." "Lard, wild dog sterilized President Chiang," the media reported. "We must rewrite history." The story told the nation that the revered Chiang Kai-shek and his first son, Chiang Ching-kuo, both of whom became presidents of Taiwan, were not of the same blood. A tape made in the spring of 1994 and discovered in 1997 tells a story about the dubious birth of Chiang Ching-kuo, who inherited the presidency of Taiwan from his father in 1975 and became the country's second beloved president.[1] The rumor was that Chiang Kai-shek had become infertile after he was bitten by a dog at the age of four or five; thus, his first son, Chiang Ching-kuo, was suspected to be the result of his first wife's adultery.[2] This rumor is further compounded by the known fact that, although Chiang Kai-shek was married three other times, he failed to father other children. For months, the Taiwanese politicians cried for "truth"; the historians vowed to rewrite history;

the people remembered their presidents with suspicion and distrust; and the Chiang family remained silent, even when Congress demanded that the widows—the "mothers" and stepmothers of the presidents—present the truth to the nation.

This obsession with bloodlines epitomizes the affinity among communal identity, national sensibility, and paternalism. The interworkings of these ideologies have become the template on which the Chinese in Taiwan play out their anxiety about self-definition. The "scandal" about Chiang Kai-shek and his son brings forth legitimacy and paternal distress as a national crisis, exposing the bodies of founding fathers and promiscuous mothers for the world to judge. The question of Taiwan's legitimacy and its relationship with China is not new to those who are familiar with the Taiwan–China impasse. Taiwan's national crisis has almost always been a public one. Taiwan had to re-establish itself after Japanese colonial rule, rename itself to differentiate it from China, and renegotiate its political footing as China replaced it in the United Nations. Taiwan became a bastard sibling of China after Mao Zedong's takeover of China, the United Nations' disassociation of Taiwan, China's frequent bomb threats against Taiwan, and, finally, Hong Kong's return to China.

The Chiang family and its history had been the basis of Chinese identity in Taiwan for forty years. The dynastic rule of the Chiang family—Chiang Kai-shek and his first son, Chiang Ching-kuo—established Kuomintang (KMT), or Nationalist Party, domination in Taiwan after the Chinese exodus from China in 1949. Chiang Kai-shek's establishment of martial rule and his "Three Principles of the People" ideology are still the core of Taiwan's political and cultural indoctrination.[3] Following his father's path, Chiang Ching-kuo stepped into the presidency with ease, and with majority support. The Chiang family embodied an aura and mythos of royalty that created—or re-created—a "new" nation of China in Taiwan, a temporary home for the true Chinese who would one day reclaim the Old China. Thus, Taiwanese Chinese communal and national identity is often construed intimately with the ideology of paternalism, especially as it concerns the authenticity of their presidents' cultural and even biological purity.

My concern here is not to search for the truth behind Chiang Kai-shek's lineage but, rather, to point out the disturbing subtext of a tenacious identity formation that ties directly to the discourse of paternalism, the myth of legitimacy, and the communal identity of many Chinese in Taiwan—and, later, Taiwanese Chinese in America. After hearing about the possibility of a bastard "prince" of their founding father, the Taiwanese Chinese had to confront once again a long-standing anxiety about national legitimacy—that of being Chinese exiled from mainland China. For the Chinese in Taiwan who exited China some fifty years ago and who perceive themselves to be merely temporarily dislocated ultimately believe that they will return home. Their precarious hold on this clearly defined self-identity as a displaced community is based on the belief that their political leaders will help re-establish legitimate roots by taking them back to China.[4] In effect, their "legitimacy" lies in the bodies of the founding fathers and the continual construction of their legacy; the "bastardization" of the presidents is therefore especially threatening because it further emphasizes the displacement of the Chinese in Taiwan from the authentic national space: China. This anxiety about legitimate paternity and community has given authors, artists, and scholars the impetus to generate narratives about national and personal crises. These narratives, I argue, symbolically reflect the cultural and political concerns of the Taiwanese Chinese in diaspora, creating a distinct literary form that ultimately posits the possibility of a postcolonial and postmodern communal identity.

In exploring this sensibility of postcoloniality and postmodernity in community formation, my goal is to see how local and individual narratives become global informants about nations and communities. In this chapter, I first examine the construction of Taiwanese Chinese Americans' identity politics within the international dimension of Taiwan and its complex relationship with China. My argument demonstrates how the historical and the national and international complication of Taiwan are manifested in works by two filmmakers, Ang Lee and Nien-Jen Wu, who attempt to construct (or deconstruct) local and global identities for Chinese in Taiwan and Taiwanese Chinese in America. Second, I treat these filmmakers' films as narratives of national crisis, in which the image of Taiwanese Chinese national identity becomes one of fragmentation and internalized colonialism. Taiwan, a cultural and sexual hybrid of postmodernity, confronts the impossibility, the uncertainty, and the undefinability of a recognizable national community.

The works of both Lee and Wu struggle to deal with this inevitable fate, giving Taiwan a voice within a semiotic of loss, diaspora, and heterogeneity. Wu's *Buddha Bless America*,[5] for example, deals with the survival of a southern Chinese town and its reaction to the intrusion of the American military in the 1960s; Lee's *The Wedding Banquet* problematize the self-fashioning of Taiwanese and Taiwanese Chinese Americans who must constantly negotiate the contemporary globalization of identities. The works of these two directors contextualize Taiwan within a national duality and a masculine anxiety that help us to understand the issues that Taiwanese Chinese Americans must confront—fragmentation, vagrancy, and diasporas—in thinking about "community." Their works both articulate and challenge the construction of "home" and "origin," a process that is fundamental to other Asian Pacific American communities and their identity politics. Lee's and Wu's works gesture toward the possibilities of renegotiating transcultural, transgender, and transhistorical terrains for the Taiwanese Chinese in diaspora. In their films, we see these processes of fragmentation and hybridization play out in personal and national traumas about the anxiety of individuals' loss, as well as the recuperation of a nation's identity. Their works ultimately offer possibilities for individual and communal identities, I argue, by embracing or deconstructing ideological boundaries of internal colonialism and patriarchy.

Diaspora as Home

Cultural and national instability have long shaped the understanding of community for Taiwanese Chinese in America. Their experience with exile, displacement, marginality, and "doubleness"—that is, their dual identification as Taiwanese and Chinese—is intimately linked to their inability to claim a homeland of origin, a theme that other Asian American writers often construct in their narratives as a source of cultural affirmation and legitimacy. In other words, the process of reproducing Asia as home and origin empowers many Asian Pacific American writers who wield their pens for self-representation in poetry and fiction. Many of these writers, including Carlos Bulosan, Teresa Hak Kyung Cha, Maxine Hong Kingston, Jessica Hagedorn, Sky Lee, Bharati Mukherjee, David Mura, and Myung Mi Kim, project their identities by imagining a complex intimacy with Asia in which displacement and re-territorialization become a major part of self-construction. Most Asian Pacific Americans can claim a clear geographic origin, be it China, Korea, Japan, the Philippines, or Vietnam. Taiwanese Chinese immigrants, however—especially those who were born in Taiwan but grew up in families that still treat mainland China as home—suffer acute geographic displacement of identity. They forever see both China and Taiwan as "home" but only through mis-recognition, for one politically denies them while the other geographically disassociates them from their parents' and grandparents' memories. The Taiwanese Chinese in America, whose displacement as experienced in their immigration is reinforced by their prior history of displacement from China, seem to be left with representing themselves through a system of referentiality between Taiwan and China.

As noted earlier, Taiwan has a long and complex history of self-definition: It has become a cultural locale constructed by constant exodus that defies a unified category and concordant reality, even though the dominating power of the KMT after 1949 set a cultural context for the national image of Taiwan today. Taiwan's turbulent history, not unlike that of other Asian Pacific countries, serves as a significant context for those who have decided to make another exodus to the West. The Taiwanese, who are among the most recent Asian Pacific American immigrant groups to arrive in the United States, have emerged as an independent community in America, despite the long-standing practice of grouping them with the "Chinese" from mainland China and the earliest settlers from Kangtong.[6]

As Taiwan's international involvement and economic success have increased, the Taiwanese Chinese in America have become more vocal and active in searching for a solution to the political and cultural dilemma surrounding their identification as a distinct nationality. In order to understand one of the concerns of Taiwanese Chinese settlers in the United States, one must first examine the construction of Taiwan as a problematic national community in an international context. As a nation whose origin is rooted in another land, Taiwan has struggled with its own identity politics with China for almost fifty years. The issues of national identity and cultural authenticity have symptomatically underpinned both the political debates and literary production of Taiwan and Taiwanese Chinese Americans. Locating and resolving threats to that myth of origin has become an instrument in the process of understanding community and communal identities.

As an emergent group of new (post-1965) arrivals in America, Taiwanese Chinese immigrants face several problems related to how they are identified by others and how they identify themselves. Taiwanese Chinese American literature in English is scarce, and scholarship about Taiwanese Chinese American works and communities is limited. As a result, Taiwanese Americans of Chinese ethnic origin often are both under- and misrepresented.[7] Writers and artists from Taiwan such as Ang Lee, Kenneth Pai, and Eileen Chang are identified as "Chinese" because they choose to write in Chinese, even though they have spent most of their lives in Taiwan and in the United States. Although their own educations and the subjects of their works may be heavily affiliated with China and "Chinese" values, as people or offspring of people who had to flee China to Taiwan they have all matured within, and share with others, diasporic sentiments of displacement. The issues of legitimacy, loss, diaspora, exile, patriarchy, internalized colonialism, and dis-nationalization of Taiwanese and Taiwanese Chinese Americans must be incorporated as one of critical concerns in Asian American, postcolonial, and cultural studies.

For Chinese writers who were exiled to Taiwan and later resettled in America, experiences of displacement, dislocation, and loss have given rise to a language of mourning and nostalgia as they negotiate between Taiwan and China to define a "home" community. That loss becomes significantly visible and fathomable when the nation realizes its lack of historical legitimacy; in the process of recovering an authentic self, the national subject attempts to construct a moment of national origin and proper placement in history. With some predictability, a generation of narratives has emerged that reflects this trauma about authenticity, purity, and nostalgia for a lost and abandoned nation. This serves the nation in two ways. First, the artists repeatedly focus on anxieties about the nation's legitimacy and its boundaries. Second, and paradoxically, they ratify and invoke the nature of a postcolonial nation by embodying and performing the crisis, thus confirming themselves as the "owners" of power. Taiwan is constructed by a postcolonial government that struggles to become an independent nation. The postcolonial Taiwanese Chinese cultural climate generates narratives about national "crisis" in which artists struggle to produce ideal images of "fatherhood."[8] In other words, because Taiwan confronts historical desires and political urgency as a postcolonial nation, its desire for legitimate national origin takes the form of evoking a patriarchal history that ultimately represents the potential for self-destruction. A postcolonial community, as many writers, scholars, and artists would discover, must generate an alternative narrative about identity and community that moves beyond the conventional rhetoric of national and cultural perils.

In the works of both Lee and Wu, the nation's crisis is imagined through the development of crisis. Wu's *Buddha Bless America* articulates an escalation of personal and communal crises through the representation of American military intrusion in a southern town in Taiwan. In Lee's *The Wedding Banquet*, the crisis comes when the father discovers his son's homosexuality—a serious threaten to the national production of masculine lineage. The ways in which both works attempt to achieve resolution demonstrate both anxiety about cultural authenticity and the poetics of redefining identity by embracing fragmentation and denaturalization. The issues of history, national authenticity, and identity politics of Taiwanese Chinese Americans within and beyond the politics of China and America become apparent in both works. Although one of the films is set in Taiwan and describes a village's interaction with American soldiers, and the other is set in the United States and focuses on an immigrant from

Taiwan, both works address the issues of legitimacy and placement of identity among intercultural and intergenerational relationships. And both help to set the stage to discuss the identity politics confronting Taiwanese Chinese immigrants in America.

"Nothing Is at Its Proper Place"

Even before the military intrudes on the small southern Taiwanese town in *Buddha Bless America*, the narrative crisis has begun to develop at an individual level in the film's portrayal of loss, displacement, and rootlessness in a Taiwanese family. The problem of proper placement, which is central to Wu's *Buddha Bless America*, stands for the fragmentation and rootlessness of early Taiwanese history. The public national trauma surrounding dubious birth and the desexualization of the national "father" signal an underpinning anxiety about "proper" paternity, national affiliation, and sexual identity. Wu's film is set in 1960, just a decade after the exodus from China. The story focuses on a family of four, composed of the first brother, a younger brother, the first brother's wife, and their son, and opens with three instances of "improper" conduct. In the first instance, the first brother, whose nickname is "the Brain" because is the only educated and literate person in town, loses his position as the teacher for saying something improper. His emasculation is made clear from the beginning of the film and is reinforced later, when, goaded to prove to his wife that he is a man and can still provide for his family, he steals a large metal ice box from the American military camp, in which the town discovers the dead body of an American soldier. The displaced body becomes a symptom of "improper" placement, and the townspeople's anxiety that the American soldier will not find his way "home" compounds the narrative anxiety about proper placement.

In the second instance, the second brother loses the fingers on his right hand while working at the town's Japanese-owned factory. The fingers become a symbol of inconceivable loss and the impossiblity of recovery. He keeps his fingers in a jar because his brother has told him that only American doctors with "high technology" can save his hand. The recurring phrases "They walk on the moon" and "They can do anything" point to the first brother's firm belief that science—Western science—can provide the answer to social dreams and problems. The fingers also become a symbol for displacement when his wife mistakes them for ginger root and marinates them in vinegar and when the second brother buries them at the end of the film when he realizes that they can never be recovered. Although the wife's mistake and the brother's burial of the fingers are presented humorously, they cannot hide the fact that all is not well with the family, the village, and Taiwan as a nation because, as the wife mumbles, "nothing is at its proper place."

The third, and climactic, instance of "improper" placement comes when the American soldiers arrive to conduct military exercises in the town, and the government builds a "whorehouse" in the middle of the fields. The brothers' misappropriation of the metal ice box containing the dead soldier represents the town's startling realization that the West does not belong here. Although the film never provides a justification for the military occupation, the presence of American soldiers during the early 1960s, roughly a decade after the KMT lost China to the communist government, underscores Taiwan's continual desire to reclaim China through an alliance with the Western military. This longing for a land that is lost can be contrasted with the land that the soldiers are destroying during their military exercises. The representation of the KMT as a group of unsympathetic and deceptive soldiers further demonstrates the anxiety in the film about internal fragmentation among Chinese ethnic groups in Taiwan. Their lack of knowledge about one another's regional dialects, compounded with mistranslations of English, magnify the complete lack of communication and cohesion among the Chinese in Taiwan.

The film ends with a message of bewilderment and displacement: The soldiers kill crops, destroy the town's ancestral grave site, lure the townspeople into committing thievery, and leave sex toys, contraceptives, records, and pornographic magazines in the "whorehouse" for the young boys to find. The last of these represents spreading inappropriate knowledge to a generation of Taiwanese youth and signifies the completion of the miscommunication and disturbing relationship between the Taiwanese-Chinese government and the colonial structures of the West. However, the film does leave the audience with another final image—one of acceptance and survival as the two brothers and the first brother's son visit the ancestral graves and the boy imitates dance steps he has seen Americans do in the dance hall. The possibility of amalgamating different cultural values and elements and adapting them as their own—even if the acts are meaningless— becomes the ultimate strategy in the formation of a postmodern identity as diasporic people.

Wu's film deals with internal colonialism and displacement in ways that visibly mirror the experiences of most Taiwanese Chinese, whose dislocation and oppression began when they started migrating from China three hundred years ago in search of a better life. These Taiwanese Chinese were colonized by the Japanese in the early twentieth century, fled from communist China in the early 1950s, and finally experienced interference by American forces in Taiwan after World War II. The second brother's loss of his fingers in the Japanese factory; the KMT's martial rule, as represented by a Mandarin-speaking general; the miscommunication between the villagers and the American soldiers; and the bewilderment of the boys in the whorehouse set up the context of an internalized colonialist history in which the illiterate, uneducated, and poor villages must suffer fragmentation, insecurity, and disconnection.

Lines in the film such as "The government will take care of us" and "American doctors can fix anything" represent the ultimate in lies and disillusionment. Wu's social commentary constructs a dialogic discourse between filmmakers and scholars. Hou Hisa-hsien's "Taiwan Trilogy"—comprising the films City of Sadness, The Puppetmaster, and Good Men, Good Women—also attempts to construct (or deconstruct) a national identity via the "internationality" of Taiwan's relationships with other territories and nations. And in his introduction to Transnational Chinese Cinemas: Identity, Nationhood, Gender, Sheldon Hsiao-peng Lu (1997) points to Taiwan's past as a rapture that creates its own unique memory, which, I argue, is instrumental in understanding Taiwanese Chinese American identity poetics and politics. Lu writes: "Taiwanese history has its unique memory of the past, a past shaped by the forces of the mainland, ex-colonizer Japan, the Nationalist government, and the West" (1997: 13). This "past" constructs the present and the future that directly address the concerns about "proper" placement in Wu's film. As members of the Chinese diaspora, the Taiwanese Chinese must find both a proper footing in Taiwan and a sense of "appropriateness" in displacement. *Buddha Bless America* ultimately replaces the notion of proper placement with an embracing of change and dislocality. It teaches us that surviving in the postcolonial era is about negotiating change and disorientation.

Dislocation and displacement are also crucial themes in *The Wedding Banquet*, Ang Lee's portrayal of how families in Taiwan and Taiwanese Chinese immigrant families in America struggle with Westernization within the Chinese diaspora. Like Wu's film, which attempts to articulate the problem of diaspora within Taiwanese history and its contact with West, Lee's works provide a locale where one can understand Taiwanese Chinese history and identity politics through the construction of tradition and transformation. The film's story teaches a lesson about accepting fragmentation and diaspora as a survivalist identity. Wu's rigid binary of "proper" and "improper," paradoxically, is both reaffirmed and deconstructed in Wu's film. While Wu offers acceptance, Lee tries to construct an alternative identity through crisis and resolution. His attempt to assert a Taiwanese Chinese immigrant identity, I argue, begins with a crisis of masculine identity and ends with an appropriation of patriarchal lineage and legitimacy.

"The Gao Family Will Thank You"

These are the words that Mr. Gao says to Wei-wei when announces that she will keep the unborn child she has conceived with Wai-tung, the gay Taiwanese American protagonist of *The Wedding Banquet* and Mr. Gao's son. The father's words of gratitude to his "green-card" daughter-in-law mark the film's preoccupation with patriarchal lineage and the maintenance of tradition for Taiwanese Chinese in diaspora. Like *Buddha Bless America*, *The Wedding Banquet* struggles to understand intercultural relationships and national survival. The film explores the "inter-culturation" of a Taiwanese Chinese American gay man and an illegal-immigrant woman from mainland China through a drama of deceit that raises issues of legitimacy and the placement of cultural and sexual identities. Thus, a national crisis is symbolized in a crisis of sexuality. The homosexual orientation of Wai-tung challenges the wishful fantasy and myth of nationhood—its masculinity, purity, legitimacy, and paternal lineage. Lee's film shows that many Taiwanese Chinese immigrants become twice alienated when they immigrate to the West: As immigrants from Taiwan, their state of "double-exile"—from China, then from Taiwan—is played out in the dimension of both gender and sexuality.

Lee himself is marked by shifting transnational identities: Questions have been raised about how he should be labeled as a director—as Taiwanese, Chinese, Chinese American, Asian American, just American, or a New Yorker—and how his films should be classified. These questions are linked intricately with attempts to understand trans-Pacific politics. As a first-generation Taiwanese Chinese American filmmaker, Lee has an intimate association with Taiwan, his native country; at the same time, however, his immigration to and education in the United States give him a different perspective on Taiwanese Chinese identity politics. His films, especially *The Wedding Banquet*, open critical forums for discussing sexual politics in the context of cultural and generational conflicts in Taiwanese Chinese immigrant families who came to the United States after 1965.

Lee's sensitivity to these cultural issues is well coded in his films about children dealing with aging parents and American cultural norms interrupting Chinese traditional values. However, in his effort to articulate dual cultural conflicts, he inadvertently constructs Asia as an imagined community of specific gender and national identifications. He constructs the cultural identities of his protagonists on stereotypes of Asian values, which, as I will illustrate later, are produced on the bodies of the father, who is played in several of the films by the veteran Taiwanese Chinese actor Sihung Lung (who has been associated with Chinese nationalism). In *The Wedding Banquet*, the body politics of the dying but manipulative father provide the language of national identity for the immigrant son.

It is not difficult to understand why Lee's films have received critical attention in the West. The significance of his position as a first-generation Asian director in America whose works are internationally popular and critically acclaimed, and whose artistry has been incorporated into the mainstream Hollywood industry, cannot be overlooked. To many scholars, Lee's films have become a counterhegemonic art, in alliance with the works of other such Asian American directors as Wayne Wang and David Henry Hwang, that combats Orientalist discourse in the West. Since Edward Said's *Orientalism* (1979) opened a critical space for discussing the construction of the Orient in Western philology and history, scholars of both postcolonial and cultural studies have been analyzing the construction of "Asia" in different cultural productions.[9] I caution the literary movement, however, about the problems inherent in using the body of the "father" as a symbol for the history and culture of Asia and the Pacifics. Although it evokes loss and nostalgia, it also reproduces patriarchy in the formulation of Asian American—or more specifically Taiwanese Chinese American—identity. An Asia that is gendered as masculine is no less problematic than the feminized Asia constructed by Western Orientalist traditions.

Lee's first three films, *Pushing Hands*, *The Wedding Banquet*, and *Eat, Drink, Man, Woman*, all of which star Lung Sihung as the father, are known as the "Father Trilogy." This term itself suggests the masculinist tradition around which the films' plots are woven.[10] The "Asia" constructed in the persona of the father figure as a Chinese native defines a masculinist purposiveness that continues to exclude the active participation of Asian women. If these films are concerned with maintaining strict cultural and sexual boundaries through the identification of the fathers as natives, what role does the immigrant woman play? How do the pregnancy of Wai-tung's green-card wife and Mr. Gao's indirect manipulation serve agendas in *The Wedding Banquet*? Most evidently, Wei-wei—an illegal immigrant who speaks no English and a marginal Chinese dialect of Chinese, and who ultimately becomes a single parent—is both atypical and stereotypical to audiences in Asia and to those who are familiar with Asian Pacific American politics. Although the character pleases the liberal-minded and the traditional, Wei-wei nevertheless represents background material that serves only to develop the father's Chinese values in the film. Wei-wei's "Westernized" behavior and sexual aggression at the beginning of the film become simply a foil to the domesticated and traditional role that she is forced to play later. Her decision to keep the child promotes the film's ultimate agendas: First, it challenges the son's homosexuality; and second, it maintains the masculine Asia as represented. The promise of the unborn child signals the completion of Wei-wei's domestication and her compliance in constructing the heterosexual and patriarchical "Asia" imagined throughout the film.

In *The Wedding Banquet*, national identity is based on underlying anxiety about cultural preservation and sexual normalcy, as the film traces the development of cultural identity first through the body of the father, then through his son's sexuality. Mr. Gao, who is also known in the film as General Gao, embodies what is perceived to be the nativistic Chinese elements that drive the major narrative action of the film. The father's position as an "authentic" Chinese native depends on his cultural ties to the Old China. His legitimacy as Chinese is inscribed in his military background, his scholarly training in Chinese calligraphy, and his stubborn insistence on traditions. His role ultimately brings about the conflict, as well as the resolution, for all of the characters in America. For example, viewers learn that the father is ill. His impending death is an ever-present undertone, and it is his desire for both cultural and familial continuance (that is, a grandson) that complicates the romantic triangle among Wai-tung, his Taiwanese Chinese American gay son; Simon, his son's European American gay lover; and Wei-wei, the immigrant wife. Rather than developing the complexity of these relationships, the film seems more concerned about the father's nationalist and traditionalist agendas. The father's desire for a grandson disrupts and challenges his son's homosexual identity and transgressive sexual desire, which signifies the "castration" of the masculine nation—Asia—that the native father hopes to preserve. The end of the film also presents "Asia" in the most traditional sense: Not only does Mr. Gao maintain his status as a loyal, nationalist Chinese, but his gay son is "nativized"—willingly or unwillingly, he has turned "temporarily" heterosexual to consummate his marriage and will also become a father. National continuity and lineage is once again preserved within masculinist rules and conventions.

The fathers in Lee's films carry additional signficance for viewers in Taiwan, the audience for whom Lee's films were originally intended. To the audience at "home," the fathers signify residual national and patriarchal traditions. The political climate between the Nationalist Party and the more recently formed People's Progressive Party is explosive, so the fathers in Lee's films do not appear as marginal to Taiwanese audiences as they may to Americans. Rather, in Taiwan, these dominant father characters play out a cultural history that the older generation of Chinese in Taiwan continues to mourn and hopes to recover; they evoke the center and the hegemonic force in Chinese and Taiwanese culture. It is no accident that Lee's fathers' are veterans of the Chinese Civil War, have only one son, and hope for grandsons: These are deliberate narrative attempts to signify masculinist anxiety about national history, dynastic cycles, and male lineage. The fathers' "Chineseness" is based on a hierarchical national and cultural relationship between China and Taiwan and between northern and southern China. The dialects and cultural references these native fathers use contextualize them as exiled soldiers specifically from northern China—the traditional location of China's capital cities and the least Westernized. Thus, although Lee depicts China only through transitory images and metaphorical references in his films, those images and references are classical and Confucian. His China is transmitted in the dialects in which the main characters speak and in cultural references to calligraphy and martial arts. In a way, the "China" to which Lee refers is the most "originary" and "national," even to Taiwanese audiences. His films elicit memories of a world lost to them. Lee creates experiences and images of China as an authentic "homeland" for the exiled Chinese in Taiwan. As Westernization and immigration increase, nostalgia for a "native land" among immigrants and those whose children have immigrated intensifies. This nostalgia grows daily as they confront gaps that have become more than generational. They are also intercultural and transnational.

Indeed, the memory of Old China and the continual confusion of Chinese-versus-Taiwanese identity inevitably places Taiwanese Chinese Americans in a double layer of "in-betweenness." The origin of home vacillates between Taiwan and China; cultural identity is negotiated between East and West. Unlike Wu's film, which uses symbols of internal displacement and estrangement to articulate Taiwan's internalized colonial mentality, Lee's work focuses on finding a stronger voice of unity and closure in diaspora. He negotiates spaces and values to arrive at an intercultural and international identity for his characters, who live among crises and conflicts that are resolved only if tradition is ultimately maintained.

Lee's attempt to negotiate between crisis and resolution lies in "mimesis," in which literary works attempt to mimic life through processes of exchange, appropriation, and symbolic acquisition among different cultural zones. Clearly, Lee constructs cultural zones and compromises in order to achieve a mimic of life for his immigrant characters in crisis. The green-card wedding between Wei-wei and Wai-tung, the strategic sex scene in which Wei-wei "rapes" Wai-tung, and Wei-wei's ultimate decision to keep the child they have conceived are exchanged for the truth of national legitimacy, Wei-wei's appropriation of her sexuality, and a symbolic acquisition of tradition.

The masculine representation and anxiety about patriarchal continuity in *The Wedding Banquet* underscore the nationalist longing for legitimate and proper cultural identification evident in the scandal over Chiang Kai-shek's "son." The national identity in crisis is a man in crisis. The fantasy of retrieving testimony from the mothers and wives of their men echoes the construction of Wei-wei as a willing "mother" who will serve mainly as a biological reminder of Wai-tung's heterosexuality and the continuity of patriarchy. Her status as an illegitimate citizen leads to her insidious marriage to Wai-tung; her sexual intercourse and, finally, her choice of motherhood are products of appropriation and exchange. Her action as a heterosexual woman provides a subtext of heterosexuality for the gay protagonist. In a way, her sexuality is overly invested to compensate for and affirm the son's masculine ability: Wei-wei's hypersexuality and heterosexuality are shown through camera views of her body—sweaty in her tenement apartment, during preparations for the wedding, in the shower, and, finally, in pregnancy. Her body ultimately serves the Gao family—first sexually, then biologically—in the effort to maintain the traditional male lineage that depicts the Taiwanese Chinese "nation."

Although Lee's films define Taiwanese Chinese immigrant identity in America as crossing sexual and geographical borders, it does so only as long as the borders are ultimately fixed and remapped in another kind of patriarchal fantasy. Lee's female characters continue to confront exclusion and both gender and ethnic boundaries. The works of Lee and Wu address concerns about national and cultural identity through silence, fragmentation, duality, oppositions, alienation, negotiation, and diaspora. Lee, unlike Wu, refuses to accept Taiwan as a diasporic nation and culture that is part of the colonial discourse of the twentieth and twenty-first centuries. He struggles against the symptoms and subversions of internal exile and against the Westernization of Chinese Taiwanese immigrants, showing signs of change only when they conform to the patriarchy. Despite my critique of Lee for being unwilling to let go of nationalist sensibility in his narratives and characters, I must also note that his narratives leave no one unaffected. The Gao family, Wei-wei, and Simon ultimately are forced to live with the consequences of their actions and their newfound knowledge about one another. This brings the narrative close to a new level of understanding about transcultural dilemmas and postmodern possibilities that, if the film delivered it, would challenge and unsettle the film's Hollywood ending.

"We Are Re-creating Kochapogen"

Monarneng, a blind poet in Kochapogan, Taiwan, articulated the poetics of diasporic identity this way:

> I had an icy cold shower under the waterfall this morning. While the water rushed down my face and my body, I felt I was reborn. I prayed immediately to our ancestors. I thanked them for washing away all my sorrows and cleaning away every single bit of my resentment. The voices echoing in the air told me clearly, so clearly, that we had to fight so hard, for the recovery of our identity is meant precisely to give it up once again, it is to set an example for all mankind to give it up. We are re-creating Kochapogen. Yes, what we are really creating is a fairer tomorrow for us all.[11]

For a Taiwanese aborigine, the issue of communal and individual identity is a source of constant struggle and negotiation. Monarneng's words show the contradiction of identity politics clearly: Recovering an identity means simultaneously giving it up. His final declaration that he must "re-create Kochapogen" is self-empowering and performative. An internally consistent "identity" is impossible and false not only for the aborigines who moved into Taiwan's mountains, but also for the Chinese from the southeastern coast of China who first migrated there three hundred years ago, for the northern Chinese who fled from China with the KMT in 1949, and for the Chinese

Taiwanese who have once again found homes elsewhere in the world through immigration or exile.[12] Wu's and Lee's films offer a way to understand issues of cultural nativity, patriarchy, and coloniality for the Chinese in Taiwan and Chinese Taiwanese in America who must locate themselves in a discourse of self-fashioning. Taiwan, an independent nation for almost fifty years, has its own historical and cultural agency from which its people in diaspora may draw inspiration as postmodern subjects. None of us can claim authentic heritage as Chinese away from China and Taiwan; as Taiwanese Chinese, we must deconstruct our origin and reinvent ourselves through continual loss and recovery. As the liminal position of Taiwan continues to affect the experiences of Taiwanese Chinese in America, they confront difficult choices. They may choose either to follow Lee's desire to internalize and embody Chinese tradition as Taiwanese, or they may search for new ground in the context of postmodernity. To view fragmentation and diaspora as possible sources of individual and communal identity is to reject the concepts of nativism and authenticity as one embraces heterogeneity and exile as sources of self-knowledge and acceptance.

Notes

1. Chiang Ching-kuo was unanimously elected chairman of the Central Committee of the Nationalist Party until January 1988, supported lagely by those who had paternalistic loyalty to his father, Chiang Kai-shek. This kind of devotion has helped the Taiwanese to construct imaginary authentic "fathers" upon whom to build their nationalist and nostalgic sentiments as diasporic people who will one day reclaim China, the original homeland.

2. The discovered tape told a shocking story about Chiang Kai-shek's tragic childhood accident. At age five, it said, he accidentally burned his rear and inner thigh, and his mother, who lacked medical knowledge, rubbed lard on the burns. The lard attracted a wild dog, which bit Chiang and ultimately rendered him sterile. This was the main argument used to challenge the paternity of Chiang Ching-kuo. The alleged story is reported in Wong 1997.

3. This political ideology in *Three Principles of the People*, formulated by Sun Yat-Sen, emphasizes nation-building (nationalism), democracy, and economic development (people's livelihoods): see Coppers 1990 for a more comprehensive discussion of the political and cultural formation of Taiwan.

4. The distinction between the Chinese who left China in the 1940s and those who had migrated to Taiwan (also known as Formosa) as early as the seventeenth century should be noted. Further, one must not forget that indigenous people are present on the island. In this paper, I focus on the those Chinese in Taiwan, regardless of when they arrived, who have maintained a cultural affiliation to China and faith in an ultimate return to mainland China.

5. Translations taken from the narrative of *Buddha Bless America* (also known as *Tai Ping Tien Guo*) in this essay are mine.

6. I use the term "Chinese Taiwanese" to refer to the Chinese who emigrated from Taiwan after 1965. My concerns about grouping the Taiwanese with the "Chinese" will also be made clear in the discussion of those who have come from Hong Kong since 1965.

7. The lack of literature from Taiwanese Americans of Chinese ethnic origin can be attributed to the issue of "identification," as well as to the fact that many writers from Taiwan are first-generation immigrants who write and publish only in Chinese. Chinese from Taiwan are

often lumped together with Chinese from mainland China, Hong Kong, and other parts of Asia. Taiwanese national sensibility has begun to surface only in the past couple of decades as a call for Taiwanese independence, initiated by the political group Taidu, has gained momentum in Taiwan. Immigrants from Taiwan were among the last groups to come to the United States, with most Chinese from Taiwan coming after 1965 and the largest wave arriving in the 1980s. Their communities have become increasingly visible as modernization and industrialization have turned Taiwan into a wealthy international port for commercial trade and technological development. The country's affluence has allowed many of its residence to relocate to other parts of the world to take advantage of business and educational opportunities. The Taiwanese Chinese community in America has created its own enclaves, such as Monterey Park in Southern California, whose lifestyle and customs differ from those of other Chinese and Asian groups: see Fong 1994.

8. I find that Taiwan and Singapore, both of which still continue to experience both external and internal colonialization, use many similar political strategies: see Heng and Devan 1992.

9. Said critiques the Western epistemologization of the Orient as a strategy of containment and control. His argument that the relationship between the East and the West is one of power and domination helped to establish, and ultimately led to, a deconstruction of this binary opposition in poststructural and postcolonial scholarship.

10. For a more detailed discussion of Lee's cultural politics, see Dariotis and Fung 1997.

11. Monarneng is quoted in Yen 1995: 144.

12. The incorporation of the native Taiwanese tribal poet is not an act of equating the experience of Taiwanese aborigines with those Taiwanese inhabitants who are originally from China. The native Taiwanese face genocide and internalized colonialization on the island. Thus, their identity crisis takes on another dimension that this paper excludes in order to focus on the diaspora of Chinese in Taiwan and later in America. For more on native Taiwanese aborigines, see Yen 1995.

References

Coppers, John Franklin. 1990. *Nation-State or Province.* Boulder, Colo.: Westview Press.

Dariotis, Wei Ming, and Eileen Fung. 1997. "Breaking the Soy Sauce Jar: Diaspora and Displacement in the Films of Ang Lee." Pp. 187–220 in *Transnational Chinese Cinemas: Identity, Nationhood, Gender,* ed. S. H. Lu. Honolulu: University of Hawaii Press.

Friedman, Ellen G. 1997. "Where Are the Missing Contents? (Post) Modernism, Gender and the Canon." Pp. 159–77 in *Narratives of Nostalgia, Gender, and Nationalism,* ed. J. Pickering and S. Kehde. New York: New York University Press.

Fong, Timothy. 1994. *The First Suburban Chinatown: The Remaking of Monterey Park, California.* Philadelphia: Temple University Press.

Heng, Geraldine, and Janadas Devan. 1992. "State Fatherhood: The Politics of Nationalism, Sexuality, and Race in Singapore." Pp. 343–64 in *Nationalism and Sexuality,* ed. A. Parker, M. Russo, D. Sommer, and P. Yeager. New York: Routledge.

Lu, Sheldon Hsiao-Peng. 1997. "Chinese Cinemas (1896–1996) and Transnational Film Studies." Pp.1–31 in *Transnational Chinese Cinemas: Identity, Nationhood, Gender,* ed. S. H. Lu. Honolulu: University of Hawaii Press.

Said, Edward. 1979. *Orientalism.* New York: Vintage Books.

Tololyan, Khachig. 1991. "The Nation-State and Its Others: In Lieu of a Preface." *Diaspora* 1, no. 1 (Spring): 3.

Wong, Fong. 1997. *Business Weekly* (Taipei), vol. 10, no. 6, 83–110.

Yen, Liang Chin. 1995. "From the Politics of Identity to an Alternative Cultural Politics: On Taiwan's Primordial Inhabitants' A-Systemic Movement." Pp. 120–144 in *Asia/Pacific as Space of Cultural Production*, ed. R. Wilson and A. Dirlik. Durham, N.C.: Duke University Press.

CHAPTER 3

Russell Jeung

Southeast Asians in the House: Multiple Layers of Identity

One hot summer afternoon in East Oakland, I stopped by 2-7, a known hangout for the Oaktown Junior Crips. The name "2-7" stands for 27th Avenue, the street where the house was located. I sat on the front steps with Sharon, a young mom on welfare who was feeding her baby. Nearby, tattooed teenagers dressed in blue stood around their cars, throwing dice and smoking. They had been there all day, because none of them held a job. "What do you'll think you'll do for work when you get old?" I asked one. He just laughed at the thought of getting a good job. "Probably McDonald's," he answered.

Given the stereotypical image of the underclass—welfare moms and inner-city gangs—I would expect these teenagers to be African American. Yet here, the Crips were a panethnic Southeast Asian gang, made up primarily of Khmer (Cambodian) and Mien youth, the latter's parents coming from the highlands of Laos. The gang also included Laotian, Chinese, and Filipino teenagers from the neighborhood.

While lounging on an abandoned couch, a not-so-sober KS[1] suddenly wanted to say something:

KS: Can I say one thing? Fuck the Cambodian Red Shit! All about the Cambodian blue!

JS: We don't want the Khmer Rouge, man!

KS: We don't want no fuckin' Khmer Rouge, man. It destroyed our country. Fuck that red shit!

While the guys were going off on this political discourse, the girls wanted to make sure that I saw their tag names graffitied on the wall:

BB: See (pointing to the wall)? Blacky-B, man!

JS: The Khmer Rouge killed our people, y'know, man? Yeah, the Khmer Rouge, they claim red!

The invectives against the Khmer Rouge and the identification with gang colors demonstrate how these youth integrate their lives in Oakland with their cultural homelands. Perhaps the best way that they could interpret the history of their people is to view it from their gang-life perspective. The Khmer Rouge and their rival factions were seen as opposing gangs. Khmer Rouge claimed the color red, so these teens claim blue. While the boys railed against the Khmer Rouge and the political situation back in Cambodia, the girls wanted to make sure that we saw their colors and names. They brought us back to their current day-to-day reality in the inner city. Little concerned for their homeland, they asserted their newfound identity as gang members with street names.

These Southeast Asian youth announce that they are "in the house" in Oakland, meaning that they are not hapless refugees or temporary exiles in this city but desirous of full acceptance and recognition. The following vignettes, informed and colored by my perspective, are about a community of teenagers who grow up in an American, multiracial, and inner-city setting. Participant observation of their day-to-day lives has led me to challenge current assimilationist perspectives about ethnic identity. Rather than adopting either an "American" or an "ethnic-American" identity, these youths maintain multiple layers of ethnic identity influenced by ethnic symbols, gang subcultures, and racial categories. They possess each of these layers simultaneously, but a particular aspect of their ethnic identity may become more salient given the social context. In the interaction of their traditional cultural identities and their new American identities framed by racial or political constructions, the youth strategically establish self-representations of themselves.

In addition, youths' stories demonstrating the persistence and multiple layers of ethnic identity question our conceptual understanding of assimilation itself. I argue that identificational assimilation as Americans does not entail a decline in ethnic distinction, as Richard Alba and Victor Nee (1997) have defined assimilation. Rather, assimilation into the multiracial American urban centers paradoxically involves a heightened saliency of ethnic identity. Youths' ethnic identities take on three different forms in different contexts. First, the youths' claims to ethnic roots are often more symbolic than substantive, because their ties to their ancestral, traditional roots have loosened. This symbolic ethnic identity is not necessarily an optional, voluntary choice for the youth; it may also arise from categories ascribed to the youth by larger institutional processes. Second, Oakland's class conditions of poverty, the ecological context of gangs and turf violence, and the prevailing ideologies define the lived experiences of the youths. New Southeast Asian youth subcultures that emerge mediate their interpretations of their American environment and their construction of their identities. Third, the racialization of ethnic minorities fosters the development of a panethnic identity for the Southeast Asians as Asian Americans. In Oakland, immigrants and refugees assimilate not in a melting pot but into a racial order where ethnic boundaries are emphasized and promoted. They thus lose sight of their traditional culture but maintain a symbolic ethnic identity, an Americanized ethnic subculture, and an Asian American consciousness.

Reconceptualizing Assimilation: Multiple Layers of Identity

In the sociological literature on the processes and theories of immigrant incorporation, three perspectives approach issues of ethnic identity differently. The first revisits the classical assimilation theories predicting that immigrants will undergo a loss of culture, social networks, and, eventually, ethnic identification (Gordon 1964; Park 1950; Warner and Srole 1945). In an article titled, "The Possibility of a New Racial Hierarchy" (1999), Herbert Gans argues that the United States is transforming into a dual hierarchy of blacks and non-blacks. He suggests that one possible trend may lead to Asian Americans' being perceived and treated "much like whites." In my case, however, the fact that Southeast Asian youth are forming along racial lines and claiming Asian identities for themselves contradicts these expectations of a loss of racial distinctiveness. Instead, a racial identity and a panethnic group affiliation prove useful and protective in the violent, gang-controlled areas of Oakland.

The second perspective, that of multiculturalists, rejects the assimilationist assumption of a unified, mainstream core into which immigrants are incorporated. Instead, they argue, ethnicity and ethnic identity are invented constructs as immigrants incorporate, adapt, and amplify pre-existing ethnic identities (Conzen et al. 1992). As agents of their own identity, immigrants and their children select aspects of original culture that fit with their new real-life context. The gangs' symbolic interpretation of their gang-color identities is an example of this process. One problem with this perspective, however, is that the mechanism of ethnic reconstruction is unclear. Why and how do immigrant youth pick and choose, drop, or retain the cultural patterns and identities that they adopt?

In the third perspective, "segmented assimilation," Alejandro Portes (1995) offers a more differentiated set of paths that immigrant youth may pursue. Immigrants may adapt by assimilating into the white middle class, adopt the oppositional culture of the American poor, or retain strong ethnic identity in order to adapt economically. Each of these paths also correlates with the type of identity and cultural pattern a youth might assume. According to Min Zhou (1997), segmented-assimilation theory focuses on the interaction of structural factors and an ethnic group's social capital, which determines structural assimilation—that is, one's economic incorporation. However, this emphasis on social capital and the cohesion of ethnic networks does not explain fully how ethnic identity develops. Even if a youth does not affiliate with his or her co-ethnics and may seem fully acculturated, he or she may still identify strongly with his or her heritage. Identificational assimilation, then, is a much different process from the acculturation and structural assimilation that these theorists emphasize. These three perspectives on the paths that assimilation may take each fail to account for a multitude of identities that can be adopted in the increasingly multicultural setting of California.

Studies that do specifically examine ethnic identity instead of acculturation or structural assimilation conceptualize it in generally fixed, unitary, and exclusive categories. For example, Ruben Rumbaut (1997) found segmented paths to identity formation in a survey of more than 2,000 children of immigrants conducted in 1992. Their responses to an open-ended question to ascertain ethnic self-identity made four types apparent: 32 percent identified with a national-origin identity (Mexican); 43 percent chose a hyphenated identity (Mexican-American); 3 percent claimed an assimilative American national identity (American); and 16 percent took a panethnic identity (Hispanic). These types constitute the either–or options so that the embracing of a particular identity is "opposition to another identity." Unfortunately, the concepts and methodologies of this type of research assume that youth possess only one discrete identity at a particular point in time.

In contrast, participant observation of Southeast Asian youth in their homes, schools, clubs, and churches gave me an opportunity to understand the fluid, multi-layered, and situational nature of their ethnic identities. Since 1992, I have lived in an East Oakland apartment complex with Cambodian refugee families and have worked with youth here and at Harbor House, a religious neighborhood center. As a mentor to the youth and as a tenant organizer in the complex, I have become intimately involved with the day-to-day lives of these families. Paying attention to the youth in conversation and social interaction has enabled me to examine not only self-reported identities, but also self-represented identities in multiple contexts. Assimilation does not necessarily involve decline in ethnic identification. Furthermore, ethnic identity is not an exclusive, unitary construct. Instead, Southeast Asian youth reconstruct and invent their identities all the time.

Symbolic Ethnicity: The Struggle to Be Different

In Oakland, I found that families maintain many old customs, but the youth are uninterested in their original cultures and hold only superficial understandings of their ethnic heritage. At the same time, they remain proud of who they are as ethnic people and firmly identify themselves as Mien or Khmer. The nature of the youths' ethnicity is symbolic in the sense that they possess subjective feelings of ethnic-group solidarity, but they only intermittently engage in traditional ethnic practices (Gans 1979).

The youth consciously identify themselves as ethnic Mien or Khmer with a clear sense of pride. In the homes, families maintain traditional patterns of behavior and attempt to perpetuate Southeast Asian values and roles. Cambodian parents speak to their children in the Khmer language, shop at Cambodian and Asian markets, and cover their carpets with bamboo mats. During the Cambodian New Year, families do traditional dances in the courtyard of our apartment complex until midnight. Toddlers, teens, parents, and grandparents all form a circle and follow one another in step to the music. The Mien youth report that their parents often engage in sacrificial rites to appease ancestral spirits and for healing. Parents especially want their daughters to remain at home to guard their reputations.

With these influences at home, the youth reported the cultural conflict that the "1.5 generation"—those who were born abroad but came to the United States before adulthood—may face when their parents' worldview and expectations clash with their "American" values and aspirations. I joined a group of Mien high-school boys who had already been meeting regularly for four years for Bible study at Harbor House. One day, as we spoke about the school tests that Dan was stressed about, he exclaimed: "You know what the most pressure I face is? It's to get married! In Mien culture, boys are supposed to marry at eighteen. If you get too old, you might not find someone." When I asked whether he was going to get married soon, since he was already eighteen, he quickly rejected the idea: "No way! I want to go to school!"

For Southeast Asian girls, the maintenance of ethnic culture is even more problematic because Asian patriarchal cultures tend to devalue women and their roles. Girls clearly observe and often reject the traditional gender roles of their parents and grandparents. Sharon, for example, was dressed in a plaid flannel shirt, tight jean shorts, a oversize black jacket, and working boots. She also wore heavy eye make-up and lipstick, although she was only thirteen. As a rebellious young teenager, she spoke often about being "totally free" from rules, the old ways, and people telling her what to do. She chatted unabashedly in her typical, animated manner about these traditional Mien rules:

SS: My parents say the culture is like, if you sleep with a guy, then you ought to marry him. That's their rule; that's not my rule. Whereas I like to get to know them better inside first. My parents say the lady is always the doormat, gets stepped on by the man who does whatever he wants. Hey, that's not my rule! My rule is you treat me with respect and I give the same thing to you. I'll give you what you want as long as you treat me the same way. My parents don't think that.

They think the kids are the slaves or the servants. . . . I mean, I fight with my parents over that a lot because when they're unreasonable. I hardly listen to them 'cause of their old-fashioned ways.

RJ: Are you going to marry a Mien guy?

SS: My parents want me to marry a Mien guy, but they know they can't stop me, because I already told them, you know. They asked me if I was going to marry a Mien guy or not because my Aunt Jennifer—she didn't marry a Mien guy; she married an American guy. I take after her a lot. She's American. She's totally modern American; she's like Madonna! I'm more like her. . . a lot like her actually. And my mother is terrified of that because she's a cousin married to an American guy. But her own daughter?!

A modern Mien woman is more like an American woman. Once we learned the customs of the American ways, then they become more used to than their old customs. The American woman [sic], they're totally free, totally take charge of their own life. They have a husband, but they still have their own freedom, their own strength inside. I guess an American woman is stronger or something.

The Mien youth contrast their views of traditional Mien culture, which deal largely with gender and marriage relations, with their conception of what modern Americans are like. This image of the American is also a social construct mediated by popular culture. According to Sharon, the polar opposite of the traditional Mien woman to be married off is Madonna, who is totally free and can take charge of her own life. "Old-fashioned ways," as Sharon described, can be selectively lost or maintained.

The Mien youth may gradually lose much of their traditional culture because it is not integrated into the material circumstances of their lives. Agricultural practices and rituals used for subsistence farming in the highlands of Laos do not function in Oakland's blue-collar and service-sector economy. The Mien were a preliterate people, without reading and writing. What traditional Mien cultural practice might help students who attend public school six hours a day? One night before a test, John complained that "other students have all the luck. Their parents can help them in school." Unfortunately, refugee parents with little formal education cannot assist their children much in this educational system. It is not only cultural practices that are in conflict here; cultural values are in conflict, as well. The girls especially chafed at the idea of having a traditional Mien marriage at an early age and remaining at home, where they would play subservient roles. Not wanting to be bound by rules, they come to desire autonomy and egalitarianism in relationships with parents and future spouses.

Another time, I directly asked some teenagers what it meant for them to be Mien. Rob barely understands the Mien ethnic customs that his parents practice and the native religion that previously dictated the Mien worldview. I pointed out that he does not dress the way Mien people used to dress; nor doe he believe in the Mien spirits. Yet he steadfastly defended his sense of ethnic identity and concluded that pride in one's heritage is simply about loving oneself:

> I'm all Mien. The way you dress is an adaptation to the environment you live in. Being Mien means loving your own people. ("There you go!" agreed another.) You love your own culture more than anybody else. I love being Mien. I don't care what kind of race you are, I love myself!
>
> Being Mien mean you don't have to know the religion, you don't have to know stuff. All you have to do is know about your people. Like blacks: They love they race more than they love anybody else's, and whites, they love they race more than anybody.

Rob spoke about loving his "culture" even though he knew little about it.

Similarly, seventeen-year-old Helen asserted pride in her ethnicity although she no longer hangs out with many other Mien girls. She has also converted to Christianity, even though her father is a shaman who performs "special sacrifices" for other Mien families. Although religious conversion signals another change from ethnic traditions, Helen remains adamant about identifying with her ethnicity:

> I'll probably get married after college, have two kids, and live happily ever after. I wouldn't raise my kids with the parents arranging the marriage. I don't want to be against others. I wouldn't tell them to marry this or that.... You try to teach your kids the Christian ways. If you teach them early, if you're loving, caring parents, then they won't go bad....
>
> I would keep the Mien language. I wouldn't want them to lose it. I would want them to have a Mien name. I wouldn't want them to have to have an American name. They're

very common, so I wouldn't want that. I just want my children to be different. I want my children to grow up bilingual. Because it's more unique.

Here, Helen expresses herself with distinctly Western, Christian ideology in wanting to "live happily ever after" and to be "loving, caring parents." Both she and Rob expressed pride in the uniqueness of their ethnicity but not necessarily in the values or traditions of their ethnic culture. Their ethnicity, then, makes them special, even though they are not much different in dress, behavior, or aspirations from their American counterparts.

Symbolic ethnicity, in which ethnic values are malleable and identities are based on subjective connections, allows the girls to maintain pride in their heritage while casting off oppressive gender roles that they believe parts of their traditional culture perpetuate. They want to preserve their unique ethnic identity but also to develop a new form of gender relations that will provide greater independence. Today's multicultural ideology enables minority women to assert ethnic difference while also transforming ethnic values that were once patriarchal.

The Mien boys and the Khmer gangsters in Oakland group together along ethnic lines and also stress their pride in their ethnicity. Yet as we have seen, their traditional ethnic cultures no longer serve as a basis for drawing together. The boys do not understand those cultures very well, do not practice many meaningful customs, and do not find those cultures practical or useful to their lives here. Although traditional culture and language do serve as a marker to form ethnic boundaries and ethnic consciousness, structural determinants of class and race, I suggest, primarily shape the Americanized and racialized ethnic subcultures of Southeast Asian youth in Oakland.

Americanized Ethnicity: Competition for Resources and Power

About ten feet outside my bedroom window, all the teenage Khmer boys of our apartment complex play basketball in a parking lot. Although many are flunking in school and have major reports due the next day, they find the urge to be with their friends, play in the sun, and talk about girls irresistible. I, too, go out to shoot hoops. As I walk outside with my basketball, a four-year-old Khmer toddler confronts me and demands, "Gif me da' ball, nigga!" I ignore him and join the teens. With music from a boombox blaring, Chan shouts, "This is for my dead homies!" and he lofts a shot up from the corner. He swishes it and gets the ball back. "This is for dead homies, too!" he yells somberly and shoots again. When I note to Chan that he does not know anybody dead, he laughs, "I have a dead hamster."

If the Southeast Asian youth are not perpetuating old group practices, and if their ethnic identities are more symbolic than substantive, what cultural patterns do they adopt and why do they still band together? As described in the preceding paragraph, they employ the language and practices that are consistent with their neighborhood context of poverty, violence, and racial diversity. Although they live in a distinct and fairly uniform urban youth culture with its own vernacular, dress, and style, they remain segregated along ethnic and racial lines for protection and power. The struggle for respect and resources in America reinforces the formation of ethnic-group communities that have new, American characteristics, as well.

Extreme poverty and increasing ethnic diversity characterize Oakland's population demographics. According to the 1990 U.S. Census, 18 percent of Oakland families fell below the national poverty level of about $12,000. Children younger than eleven made up 29 percent of those in poverty. Within East Oakland, Asians and Pacific Islanders made up 23 percent of the population and 24 percent of the population below the poverty level. The Khmer and Laotian (mostly Mien) populations within this area had poverty rates of 39 percent. As I drove with KS, the OakTown Junior Crips (OJC) member, down East 14th Avenue to his home in the Oakland Housing Authority project, he did not miss the impoverished conditions:

RJ: You think the gang situation is gonna' get better or worse and worse here?

KS: Worse and worse. The way society goes, it'll more and more. Each kid that grows up each day will be in a gang. More and more gangs. Cuz this is the ghetto. You don't see no gangs in rich. . . rich places' houses. This is the ghetto. This is where all the projects and all that drugs, you know.

In the urban settings in which many Southeast Asian families have resettled, African American urban subculture is hegemonic. These Southeast Asian "1.5ers" grow up learning the language, dress, dance styles, and behavioral responses of their African American peers. In a movie-making workshop I held for the teenagers, I showed two videos: *Bright Teens, Dark Days* and *Straight Out of Brooklyn*. Southeast Asian teenagers in San Francisco wrote and directed the first video, while the second was directed and produced by a nineteen-year-old African American. The similarities between the videos were striking. Each video had the same main plot and subplots: A male teenager gets thrown out into the streets, joins a gang, and gets into trouble. The alcoholic father's ability to provide for his family is limited by race, language, and educational or cultural barriers. The mother desperately tries to maintain family ties. Sex and violence are prominent themes in their lives.

At one point in *Straight Out of Brooklyn*, heavy-hitting rap highlights the build-up to a showdown between gangs. All the youth in the room—three African Americans and three Khmer— began singing along. They sat together, entranced by the street images that were so familiar to them, and sang out the in-your-face words of the rap: "Life is too short, would you agree? While I'm livin' my life, don't mess with me." Each of these students used urban images and symbols to construct their own categories and understandings of the environment around them.

The Southeast Asians also develop a sense of marginalization shared by other groups in the schools. At school, they learn about the oppression of African Americans and then want to learn about their own group's history. From 1991 to 1994, Latino high-school students staged an annual walkout day in protest of the lack of Latino studies in their curriculum. The Southeast Asian students have expressed similar complaints about the lack of role models in the schools and a lack of a culturally relevant curriculum (East

Bay Asian Youth Center 1994). Although they are all economically disadvantaged and live in the same neighborhoods, ethnic groups find themselves pitted against one another. The African Americans feel that the Asians are at the top of the socioeconomic order, while the Southeast Asians feel oppressed by the blacks:

SG (*a fourteen-year-old black man*): We're at the bottom of the pole. Everywhere. Because if you got prison, the population that's got the most in there. . . is the blacks. Eighty-nine percent are blacks. Asians? They're on the top, they got all the money. Look at who's on the honor roll. Eighty-five percent of them are Asian. And the rest, you got a couple of blacks, a couple of Hispanics.

SL (*a Mien teen*): A lot of blacks, they dominate at school and everywhere in the city. And if you get a bunch of them together and they see an Asian, they'll jump 'em, they'll most likely get jumped.

Recognizing their marginalized minority status in a violent urban youth culture, the young people band together for protection. Ruben Rumbaut and Kenji Ima predicted that the Khmer refugee youth from Cambodia would not join gangs because of their cultural background. They wrote:

> For the most part, the refugee peer group does not resemble traditional African American and Hispanic gangs which are characterized as having territory, names, symbols, special clothing, and permanence. Aggressive acts are more likely to be found among Vietnamese, Chinese Vietnamese and Lao rather than the Khmer or Hmong. They are less sensitive to loss of face and therefore have to be more severely provoked to respond in kind. (Rumbaut and Ima 1988: 9–10)

However, traditional ethnic values are not always maintained in light of a refugee youth's new neighborhood. At Harbor House, one gang member spoke to a counselor about his adventures the night before:

KS: The problem last night, was my pardner. . . he drunk, right. He walked into this black dude, who pushed him. You know how drunk people is. . . . He just went over and "Pow!" (*swings his arm and fist to demonstrate*). The dude pulled a gun, so I went back to my house, my uncle went back to his house, my cousin go over there to get his gun. I came back with mine. . . .

SL: What were you going to do with your guns?

KS: Get our revenge back. We can't be letting no one shoot us with a gun. Those guys were Rollin' 20s [a black gang], and we don't get along with Rollin' 20s. Last time we shot eight of them. [They] trying to get us back, but they've never had a chance.

SL: Is that any way to solve the problem?

KS: These days, yeah. You just can't say it's cool, yeah. No, that's not how it works no more these days. They the ones that started it, though. So we have to finish it.

SL: But then you or your friends may get hurt. . .

KS: That's the way it goes.

Clearly, the gang members no long behave in the culturally scripted Khmer manner of non-aggression, non-competition, and avoidance of confrontation. Instead, they have established new values, norms, and attitudes adapted to their new environment.

Oakland youth spatially orient themselves along ethnic gang turfs as they quickly learn to recognize where they can hang out in this environment of violence. As KS and his other friends learned that other ethnic groups had banded together to control certain areas and activities, they adjusted to the geography:

KS: One thing I hate about Oakland is the gangs. . . too much gangs. Some want to join the gangs for the fun, but they don't know where the fun is going to end up, you know.

Oakland, this part is cool, right? (KS points as we drive along.) But my part where I live, you can't even walk around there. Oakland, everywhere you go you see gang graffiti. (He points to a wall.) They claim hundreds; 69th Street will be 69 hundred. You have to live there [to claim a turf]. Your turf have to be powerful to survive in Oakland, you know.

We drive farther along, and KS points out where they sell dope and later, down the corner, where he was stabbed in a gang fight.

KS: Daytime looks cool, right? Nighttime, that's when everything's happening. Nighttime, it's a whole new ballgame. . . . Shootings, people sell dope.

Just as Khmer gang youth kick back on their turfs, the Mien youth congregate at certain schoolyards to gamble, play volleyball and basketball, and meet one another.

SC (a Mien teen): If it's a black territory, or something, and you go in there and you're Asian, they gonna' mop on you. (Huh?) Mop on you means a lot of them jumps on you and hits you ten to one.

ML (a Mien teen): We know where to hang out. You just try to avoid where a lot of black people are. You just make sure you don't go to the gang areas. Oakland is made out of turf areas. If you live in it, you adapt to your neighborhood. You be cool.

Even though the boys try to be cool and wary, by the time he reaches high school almost every Asian boy in Oakland has an account of being jumped. In a survey of 500 Oakland Asian teenagers conducted by Asian youth, 63 percent reported having witnessed four or more physical fights in the previous six months. In addition, 68 percent said they knew someone who had been hurt or killed by a gunshot (East Bay Asian Youth Center 1994). The staggering amount of violence the youth see in schools, the streets, and at home fosters a great sense of mistrust among the overall youth population and paranoia among the gang youth.

Adaptation to neighborhood economics, group marginalization, violence, and power struggles leads to organization along ethnic lines for important resources, protection, and social support. The phenomenal rise in Southeast Asian and other Asian ethnic-specific gangs (Chinese and Vietnamese) in Oakland, with total membership ranging from 100 to 200 youths, can be linked to the limited options and racial order of the streets. Many of the Southeast Asian youth whom I have met are involved with street gangs, such as the OakTown Crips (OTC), the OakTown Junior Crips (OJC), the OakTown Mien Boys (OMB), and the Softer Shade of Blue (SSB). In the neighborhood and apartment complex where I live along with several Khmer families, signs of gang culture are ubiquitous: OJC graffiti marks off streets as turfs; teenagers tattoo themselves; and youth dress in all-blue clothing, the color of the Crips. Five-year-olds pretend to be gang members by wearing bandanas and shouting, "OJC! OJC!" Even at this young age, they know which teenagers are members and which are not. In this environment, gangs and even unaffiliated groups of Mien boys who steal car pull-outs (stereos) mobilize on ethnic boundaries for needed protection and economic advantage. Becoming Americanized for these youths involves relying on co-ethnics for very material concerns.

Racialized Ethnicity: Reactive Panethnic Solidarity

Not only do youth of color in East Oakland need one another to confront poverty and marginalization; they also grow up in communities where both racism and multiculturalism promote racial difference. Southeast Asian students complain of racial taunts and being called "Chink," even though they are not Chinese. They also report being misidentified as gang members from other ethnic gangs and then being physically attacked. Beyond these examples of racism and anti-Asian violence, state and local government policies also promote ethnic mobilization along ethnic and panethnic lines (Espiritu 1992). For example, the federal government, schools, social-service agencies, and other public institutions categorize Mien and Khmer together as Asians on the census and on other forms. Social-service agencies, such as the East Bay Asian Youth Center, cater to pan-Asian constituencies to amass larger client populations and obtain more funding. As a result of these forces, Southeast Asian youth also see themselves as new Asian Americans.

While the Southeast Asian youth assert their own individual ethnic identities, others assign the racial identity of "Asian" to the refugee youth. Dan, a Mien teenager, once spoke about a trip he took to Canada. He recounted that he had entered a room by mistake and was rudely told to get out. Dan vehemently claimed, "They treated me that way because I'm Asian! If I was a white boy or something, they wouldn't have done that!" Dan recognized that when white people discriminated against him, they saw him as an Asian, not as a Mien person in particular. Not only did he accept the fact that people saw him as Asian; he identified himself as Asian.

Not just whites but other people of color, including African American and Latino gang members, taunt and categorize the youth as a monolithic Asian race who do not belong here:

PC (*Khmer*): The Mexicans, they prejudiced. Everybody thinks we're Chinese.... They yell at us, "Hey, China!" (*She begins talking about a Japanese exchange student who had been raped and killed recently in San Jose and links that murder with general violence against Asians.)*

ML (*Mien*): I'm used to prejudice—you know how they talk about things, about the way you look, the way you dress, your eyes. (*"Yeah! Your eyes!" others say.*) When they're young, they don't know crap. The only thing they know is Chinks, man. All of them is Chinks. Every single one is Chinks. They beat you up.

Because of this racial conflict and their mistrust of other ethnic groups, the impression that they are on the bottom and disrespected, and their dislike for school, the Khmer students form gangs. They argue that the gangs are necessary for protection and safety against the racial violence. An older OJC member points out an external threat that caused Khmer boys to join together:

> A couple of years ago, we were just homeboys.... We don't know nothing. The old people, they got jumped by the black people. They didn't do nothing. We'd get beat up, too....
>
> See this? (*He points to a nasty scar over his left eyebrow.*) I got jumped by these Mexicans. They hit me with a bat, a steel bat. My cousin, he was knocked cold. Unconscious for ten minutes.
>
> I was a good student then at Roosevelt Junior High. I was just carrying my books, getting all As. The [Mexican gang] thought I was another Cambodian, but we all the same to them. Later, we learned we need to get together, get a name. Now they don't look down on us. They know we got guns. They're scared; we're scared. We're not really a gang.... It's mostly for protection, to hang out.

Reactive solidarity against anti-Asian violence and discrimination creates a common identity that cuts across individual Asian ethnic groups.

Further, multiculturalism in the Bay Area promotes the racialization of youth so that they are aware of racial differences. As the youth interact with the wider society beyond their ethnic enclaves, their sense of race heightens. During the summer, I took four Khmer gang youth with me to watch the filming of a television commercial in Oakland. As we entered a room that had a predominantly white crowd, one boy looked around and noted, "There aren't too many Asians here, huh?" The boy had a heightened awareness of the ethnic make-up of the room and noticed the absence of this group. In addition, he felt out of place in the situation and wanted to leave. In this case, he would have been more at ease if there were people like himself—that is, people who were Asian. In situations in which he did not expect to find many Khmer, possibly because of their small numbers in California, he looked to identify with other Asian Americans, who make up more than 30 percent of the San Francisco–Oakland Bay Area.

To promote positive self-esteem among youth, public and private institutions rehearse multicultural ideology that celebrates ethnicity in their programs and efforts. At Harbor House, youth sing traditional African American spirituals, Indonesian folk songs, and contemporary Christian hymns. A director of Harbor House explained his program's philosophy:

> We're out to promote to the kids that other countries are fun, other cultures are great, and we should be proud and happy that we live in a place where there are different cultures all living together, rather than being suspicious of each other and thinking we all ought to be the same and that we could be both Asian people or black people—we should be happy that we're all from different ethnic backgrounds.

Indeed, even Christian organizations, which once were seen as colonizing ethnic minorities, now encourage ethnic and racial diversity.

During the summers, Harbor House sponsored an "Asian Youth Conference" for immigrant and refugee youth that highlighted racialized and panethnic commonalties. Association with other Asian Americans has enabled girls to see their common experiences as female—as Asian daughters, mothers, and wives—and institutions such as Harbor House has encouraged them to assert their own values. One year, Mien, Laotians, and Chinese Vietnamese girls gave testimonies about their difficulties with their parents. One girl's father actually came to the camp and verbally threatened her in front of the others. After this incident, many of the youth shared stories of abuse and generational conflict. In an interview, sixteen-year-old Helen spoke about her family dynamics:

> RJ: How do you relate to your parents?
> Helen: I'm very close to my mother. And with my father, I don't really have a time of sitting down and talking. It's very typical of Asian families, where the father [and] daughter don't talk—how I feel, what I think of what they're doing is not right. They're really protective of me and not want me to stay out late.
> RJ: Why are you and your mom close?
> Helen: I think she understands me. I can't talk to my father because he goes out more and he's gets angry sometimes. My father, he's the head of the household and he makes all of the decisions. They're [mother and father] very close. But my father would sometimes put my mother down. He's the kind of husband that gets his way.

Helen was able to describe her relationship with her father as a "typical Asian" non-communicative relationship because she has become aware of her common ties with other Asian women.

Southeast Asian youth in Oakland today thus receive contradictory messages: Their native culture is to be respected, but the youth themselves do not belong here. With remarkable insight, Rob observed that "American" means "white," but that Asians will always be outsiders:

> A lot of people when they look at us, or even Chinese people who have been here so long, when they look at us they don't call us American, they just call us Asian. I told you that before. The Irish, the Germans, the Italians, they blend in with the people, with the locals. The Chinese live here as long as them, but when you look at them [the European immigrants], they call them Americans. You look at these descendants, they'll still be Asians. We don't want to be American! We want to be our own culture!

Earlier, Rob asserted pride in his ethnic Mien-ness; here, he alludes to his panethnic Asian-ness. He is both Mien and Asian American, and the recognition that Asians are not considered "American" demonstrates his racialized consciousness. He, like the great majority of the youth I have encountered, sees no contradiction in possessing both an ethnic and a panethnic identity, and he often employs racial categories and references to present himself. To resolve the racial exclusion that he experiences, he employs a discourse of ethnic pride that distinguishes him from Americans.

Conclusion

One afternoon, I watched OTC members greet one another in a billiard room with such phrases as, "What's up, cuz?" "OTC! OTC! In the house!" "In the house!" is a way to announce someone's presence at a party. Settling in Oakland's San Antonio district in large numbers, these Southeast Asian youth are making their presence felt. Traditional culture and language do set Mien and Khmer apart from other Asian and non-Asian groups. The youth band together because they live together and can relate to one another in their native tongue. As they grow up in Oakland, though, they find that their parents' traditional customs and patterns are no longer advantageous. They thus take on the characteristics of those around them and those glorified in popular culture so that their ethnic identities are largely symbolic.

Being poor and non-white does have material consequences, however. Southeast Asian youth affiliate with their respective ethnic groups because they are threatened in the Oakland streets and locked out of the economy. To secure turf, money, or support, they continue to associate with co-ethnics and form gangs. They feel they can belong "in the house" within their neighborhoods, because they find strength in numbers. These new 1.5-generation youth subcultures have their own dress, language, and group symbols, which are distinct from both their parents' communities and other youth subcultures.

These youth also claim a panethnic identity that coincides with their ethnic identity. As Asian Americans, youth from Cambodia, Laos, Thailand, and Vietnam recognize their common family and group experiences here in the United States. Being "in the house" of multicultural Oakland, they have taken racial categories assigned to them and transformed them into identities that they now claim as their own.

Southeast Asian youth are indeed assimilating, but they are assimilating into a house and social environment that is much more differentiated than assumed and has more space for new identity formation. In contrast to the views of the assimilationists and multiculturalists, their identities are not bound by cultural scripts of what Americans or traditional Southeast Asians should be. Neither are their identities bound to the economic paths that they encounter, as segmented assimilationists might argue. Instead, these youths strategically employ a variety of identities and group affiliations in different contexts. Southeast Asian youth are in the house, and they are now reconstructing the house, their own identities, and the communities in which they live.

Note

1. The names of individuals who participated have been changed.

References

Alba, Richard, and Victor Nee. 1997. "Rethinking Assimilation Theory for a New Era of Immigration." *International Migration Review* 31: 120–59.

Conzen, Kathleen Neils, David Gerber, Ewa Morawska, George Pozzetta, and Rudolph Vecoli. 1992. "The Invention of Ethnicity: A Perspective from the U.S.A." *Journal of American Ethnic History* 12: 3–42.

East Bay Asian Youth Center. 1994. *EBAYC Five-Year Strategic Plan.* Oakland, Calif.

Espiritu, Yen Le. 1992. *Asian American Panethnicity.* Philadelphia: Temple University Press.

Gans, Herbert. 1979. "Symbolic Ethnicity: The Future of Ethnic Groups and Cultures in America." *Ethnic and Racial Studies* 2 (January): 1–20.

———. 1999. "The Possibility of a New Racial Hierarchy in the Twenty-First Century United States." In *The Cultural Territories of Race,* ed. M. Lamont. Chicago: University of Chicago Press.

Gordon, Milton. 1964. *Assimilation in American Life.* New York: Oxford University Press.

Park, Robert. 1950. *Race and Culture.* New York: Free Press.

Portes, Alejandro. 1995. "Segmented Assimilation among New Immigrant Youth: A Conceptual Framework." In *California's Immigrant Children: Theory, Research, and Implications for Educational Policy,* ed. R. Rumbaut and W. Cornelius. San Diego: Center for U.S.–Mexican Studies, University of California.

Rumbaut, Ruben. 1997. "Assimilation and Its Discontents: Between Rhetoric and Reality." *International Migration Review* 31: 923–61.

Rumbaut, Ruben, and Kenji Ima. 1988. "The Adaptation of Southeast Asian Youth." Washington, D.C.: U.S. Department of Health and Human Services, Office of Refugee Resettlement.

Warner, W. L., and L. Srole. 1945. *The Social Systems of American Ethnic Groups.* New Haven, Conn.: Yale University Press.

Zhou, Min. 1997. "Segmented Assimilation: Issues, Controversies, and Recent Research on the New Second Generation." *International Migration Review* 31: 975–1009.

CHAPTER 4

Eric C. Wat

Gay Asian Men in Los Angeles
Before the 1980s

Gay bars were once the major site of community formation for gay men in metropolitan American cities. When most gay men had to keep a watchful eye in their own neighborhoods and workplaces, they could not very well form communities where they lived and worked. Bars, many of them lifeless and inconspicuous in broad daylight, became safe (or, at least, safer) havens for men who reserved expressions of their sexuality for the night. As the historian John D'Emilio has written about his experience as a young gay undergraduate at Columbia University in the mid-1960s, "Virtually all of the visual images of gay experience that I can conjure up from those days are shaded in darkness" (1992: xix).

Yet even when homosexual or even homosocial behavior (such as men holding hands or dancing in public) was heavily persecuted and vice cops posed as potential tricks and laid traps like landmines in a brutal war, many patrons frequented these establishments with a mixture of caution and abandon. The darkness in D'Emilio's memories can be accounted for only partly "by nighttime hours looking for... sex?... love?... closeness?... comfort?" (1992: xix). The cover of night was also a metaphorical shield—from an acquaintance or a co-worker who was prone to tattling, from an undercover cop who spoke sweeter words than a one-night stand, or from a gay-basher who had nothing to do on a Saturday night.

The bars, then, were a contradictory space. It is hard to imagine that a community could be formed in spaces where telephone numbers could be as imaginary as the names people exchanged with one another. Granted, there were other sites of socialization for gay men, especially after Stonewall in 1969 and the AIDS epidemic in the mid-'80s. They included churches, organizations, publications, support groups, community centers, even restaurants and other informal networks of friends that developed out of these spaces. Yet gay bars have remained a rite of passage for any man coming out in a city, and for most, a point of entry into the gay community. Not all gay bars are created equal, however. There are enough varieties to accommodate different "tastes" and "specialties." In this chapter, using information gathered from in-depth interviews, I will describe the role of various gay bars in both hindering and facilitating the formation of gay Asian men's community in Los Angeles. It will encompass the years leading to the founding of Asian/Pacific Lesbians and Gays (A/PLG) in 1980, the first formal gay Asian organization in Los Angeles.

I retrieved the names of most of my first narrators from early A/PLG newsletters. Some of them were familiar to me because they had remained active in the queer Asian Pacific Islander community. From my first interviews I collected more contacts. Twenty interviews (not counting follow-ups) were conducted between October 1997 and March 1998. All of the narrators are Asians, except one, who is Caucasian. All lived in Los Angeles during the 1970s or early '80s. Most of them were members of A/PLG or the Gay Asian Rap Group, another gay Asian organization in Los Angeles that was founded in 1984. (It is not the Gay Asian Pacific Support Network, or GAPSN). Five of the nineteen Asian narrators are immigrants; at the time of the interviews, they ranged in age from their late thirties and to the early sixties.

A general theme emerged from their experiences. Before the River Club, which in the mid-1970s became the first of the gay bars in Los Angeles to attract a significant Asian clientele, gay Asians were so scattered in the many gay establishments spread across Los Angeles that it was rare for most of the narrators to find and meet other gay Asians in a bar. Usually, a non-Asian friend would introduce them to the gay scene. Because Asians were not, as one narrator put it, a "commodity" at that time, many felt ignored or unwelcome in these establishments. Here lies the first contradiction: These bars were the few spaces that they could claim as gay men, yet they could not completely own them because of their racial difference. Their experiences in these spaces were sometimes discouraging, and in cases where Asians were refused entrance, even humiliating. The environment coerced many into dissociating their racial identity from their sexual identity.

The development of "rice bars," such as the River Club in the mid-'70s and Mugi's in the early '80s, was to some gay Asians a godsend. These supposedly gay Asian spaces, however, often functioned as sites of ethnic tourism for "rice queens," or white men who had a particular and often exclusionary sexual interest in Asian men. I even argue in this chapter that the set-up of these gay Asian bars served these white men's interests. Furthermore, as many narrators suggest, there were "barriers" among the various ethnicities. Gay Asians were polite but guarded, and often they competed for the same white men who frequented these bars. This contradiction is much more complex than the first. All the narrators considered these places fun to visit every weekend. They knew they would not be turned away at the door, and these spaces were virtually the only places in Los Angeles where they could find a significant number of gay people who looked like them. Despite the ethnic cliques, informal networks did develop out of these spaces.

Yet many gay Asians were cautious about saying that there was an organized community. What bars like the River Club did was to highlight the problematic dynamics among Asians in more visible ways than ever before. Until the River Club, it was rare to find a handful of Asians frequenting the same bar at one time. With the congregation of more than a hundred Asians in these rice bars every weekend, it became impossible for them to escape the observation that what could be their racial commonality had been a wedge keeping them apart. It was for this reason that most founders of the A/PLG decided to organize to bring these various ethnicities and factions together. The lack of a network among gay Asians and the dependence on non-Asians, especially whites, to gain entrance into the gay world had informed how some gay Asians related to one another. The rice bars perpetuated this legacy. However, while gay Asians were not able to define in these spaces a coherent sense of identity and community that integrated both their race and their sexuality, many in the A/PLG leadership credited them for speeding the process of community formation.

Asians in Mainstream Gay Bars

Until the mid-1970s, there were few places in Los Angeles where one could find a significant congregation of gay Asian men. RB*, a Caucasian narrator who in the 1980s became active with the A/PLG and was employed as a bartender at Mugi's, a gay Asian bar in Los Angeles, ran a bar in Hollywood called the Stopover from 1973 to 1977.[1] He did not recall having seen any Asian patrons in his bar during that period. In fact, even RB, no stranger to the bar scene in Los Angeles and a onetime bar owner himself, did not become "aware of Asian gays until I started going to Mugi's in the early 1980s [as a patron before he joined the staff]." Of course, gay Asians had been frequenting gay bars for decades, but before the mid-'70s, their presence was scattered, and they seldom traveled in pairs, let alone groups. The narrators often commented on how rare it was to find another gay Asian man in a gay establishment. As RK said, "When I first started going to different bars [in the mid-'60s], I didn't see that many Asians yet. Most of them were white. There were Asian people who were gay, but they were so spread out. Like Roy T. Maybe I'd see him in this bar one night, and then I wouldn't see him for the longest time. Suddenly, he would pop up again. Same things with other guys, because they had their own [non-Asian] friends or social scene."

It is interesting to note that, because there was no sense of a gay Asian community for most of the narrators, the people who introduced them to the gay LA scene were non-Asian. These guides could be friends they had known from work, the military, or even personal ads. So startling was an encounter between two Asians that they often did not know how they should react. Should they nod or wink in acknowledgment of their commonality? Dare they approach each other to make conversation? Perhaps not certain what this racial commonality could mean in a gay context, many simply looked away.

Furthermore, the gay scene was not a positive reinforcement for most gay Asian men at that time. EW* said:

I feel that the whites set the standards of everything in this life. Whether we realize it or not, we tend to follow those standards and emulate them, which was no different in gay circles at that time. The selective process in the bar scene was just deadly, because the whites were going for other whites at the time, and Asian types were not a commodity. The whites at that time, I feel, viewed us as more of the subservient type. And then as soon as we opened our mouths and started talking, they discovered that we were just as Americanized as them. Then they felt intimidated. Or they came off condescending or patronizing. Of course, you could see through that, and you took it. On the one chance that somebody might be attracted to you, you went along with it and thought, "Well, okay. Let's see where this'll go." But after a while, it just became too ridiculous, and it became apparent that they were either stupid or ignorant. Then you let them have it. They didn't know what was going on because, "Well, he's an Asian; how come he's behaving this way? He's just like the white queens: vicious, just as vicious." Well, we learned.

The prevailing environment made it difficult for Asian men to become assertive. This in turn reinforced the stereotypes of passive, "subservient" Asian men. As EW continued:

I mean, you didn't have a chance [in the bars] if you were an Asian. We were just a novelty they might try or something. That's the type of prevailing feeling we [Asians] had when we were in the bar environment or gay scene. I wasn't a troll or a reject. I was reasonably attractive in my younger days. I could have suitors and so forth, but I never got that satisfaction [from the bars]. You'd have to be really exceptionally beautiful or something for them to give you the time of day. And rejection is the keyword here. The fear of rejection was really my biggest fear. Going to the bar scene, I would never approach anybody because I couldn't take the rejection.

Other patrons' indifferent reactions to Asians could often be internalized. CC* said:

I was very reserved in that kind of atmosphere. I don't know if that's because of the Asian in me or I'm not a very extroverted person. I would be just standing there and waiting for somebody else to take charge and make the first move. Very rarely would I get asked or picked up. That made me feel like, Well, people don't like Asians. I don't know if you can call that discrimination. It could be just people's taste.

I never saw myself as a sexual being. Being Asian in the gay community, I didn't see that I could be attractive to anyone. And if they were sexually attracted to me, then it was like, "Wow, there's something wrong with them. *[He laughs]*. What's with this guy, you know?"

Indifference was not the worst. Sometimes white patrons and staff had blatant ways to let people of color know they did not belong there. As HP* recalled, "I've seen people give dirty looks to someone when they walked in because of their race. I've heard snide remarks, just bitchy remarks: 'What's that nigger doing here? How come that chink is here?' Dirty looks. Facial expressions. Turning their backs. You name it. It was there."

Discrimination became more blatant in in the late 1970s and early '80s as West Hollywood became the gay Mecca and the large dance clubs moved in to replace the local bars as major sites of assembly for gay men. Even now, for example, DG* says he does not visit West Hollywood often, "because I had a very bad taste of going into West Hollywood, where Asians were carded and asked for three pieces of picture ID and all that good stuff." LJ* remembered one bathhouse that was particularly difficult for him to get into. "I think it was discrimination," he said. "The rumor was that, if you weren't white and really attractive, you couldn't get in. I did get turned away the first time I tried to get in. So I had to get a friend of mine to refer me. Even then, they asked for three pieces of ID, which I had, which I gave to them. I did get a membership, but I think they were discriminating at the time." LJ went prepared because stories about discrimination circulated in the community. Even those who usually had no trouble gaining entrance regard these urban legends as credible. Many, such as SR, suffered the indignities firsthand. An immigrant who was not naturalized until 1980, he had had trouble gaining entrance to West Hollywood bars with his green card. He recalled, "You could show them [the bouncers] a fake California ID and they would accept that. But a green card—they would not know shit about green cards. Either they were ignorant or stupid, or they were just discriminating." Even in the early 1980s, during the first years of the A/PLG, some of its members led delegations and protests against bars that allegedly had discriminated against Asians.

According to PC*, because Asians were not held up as objects (let alone subjects) of desire, some of his acquaintances denied their ethnicity and tried to "pass." He said:

There was [my partner's] chiropractor. He didn't want to be Japanese. So he thought if he permed his hair and wore dark glasses, he could look Hispanic. He just looked like a Japanese guy with a perm and dark glasses on. And the artist we met at the Garden Show—he was a West Hollywood clone: short crewcut, big muscles, worked out [at a] gym. He only socialized with other West Hollywood clones. They would not go to rice bars or join the A/PLG.

To avoid disappointment or negative reinforcement, others resigned themselves to frequenting mainstream gay spaces with lowered expectations. As DC* said, "People were not as friendly [at the West Hollywood bars]. You had white men there that were not into Asians, and that's okay. I went there just to have fun with my friends, not to seek attention or anything of that sort." DH*, too, resolved that outings to these places would not be romantic or sexual in nature. He said:

Going to Studio One [a large dance club in West Hollywood] was more like partying around, dancing with your friends and things like that. It was not an outlet for me to find and to have sexual encounters. I would not go to Studio One on my own because I didn't find it to be entertaining going alone. I didn't want to stand there like a model.

For immediate sexual gratification, some turned to and found more success in the anonymous sex scenes—bathhouses, gloryholes in public restrooms, and "cruisy" parks—where one's ethnicity was not such a factor in choosing a partner. EW said, "I used to go [to the parks] a lot. All of this stuff just to have sex for expedience. That way I didn't have to go through this tiresome thing of drinking drinks that I didn't want and talking and talking. Everybody knew what they were there for under those circumstances in the parks. I mean, they were not there to get a drink. They were not there to engage in conversations. They wanted sex. I was relatively successful on that turf."

Blatant discrimination, subtle rebuke, plain indifference, and a scattered density made organizing among gay Asian men virtually impossible during this period. In the mid-1970s and early 1980s came the River Club and Mugi's, respectively, bars that many gay Asians and their "admirers" would frequent. The development of these rice bars is a mixed blessing in the history of the gay Asian community in Los Angeles.

Rice Bars (Part 1)

No one remembers exactly when the River Club became a "gay Asian bar." Before the mid-'70s, it had catered to a mostly Latino clientele, with some black, Asian, and white customers. Because the River Club had a strong presence of people of color, Asians knew that they would not be hassled at the door or feel unwelcome inside. By the mid-'70s, word began to spread that the River Club was where many Asians would go, thereby attracting even more gay Asians and their "admirers." "There was no discrimination," recalls RK*. "People who went there knew there was a mixture of different groups. So there was no problem about that."

Many narrators expressed their wonderment as they discovered, for the first time, a space occupied regularly by people who looked like them. Yet this familiarity did not translate into a shared identification. Instead, they acted like strangers to one another. "You would have the Asians all in different groups," RK said. "You had the Japanese in one, the Chinese in one, the Filipinos in one, and the foreign-born in another. All staring at each other. [*He laughs.*] Give each other dirty looks, like competitors. We never came together." And as SL* said:

> During that period, there was this real feeling amongst Asians—and I would share this feeling, too—that it was harder to approach another Asian. At the same time, you kind of viewed them as competition, competition for primarily white men, although I was actually interested in dating other men of color.
>
> I knew this one Asian guy there who was about two years ahead of me in high school. He would always come to the bar also. And we consciously avoided each other because of that connection. I've talked to him more recently, and I don't think we ever talked about that period. I do remember sometimes I felt like saying hi to him, but it seemed so taboo and scary to connect with somebody who you knew from suburban Asian America. Certainly there was some fear that he might tell other people back home. I'm sure that's why he avoided me. Secondly, I think there was a lot more things that would reinforce low self-esteem and internalized homophobia during that period. Not having any sense that there were groups for gay Asian men, positive types of organizations, I felt more fear in confronting my own feelings about being Asian and gay, and the fact that you were dealing with a gay man that was also Asian [would force me to confront those feelings.]

This, however, does not mean that gay Asian men like SL were ashamed of their race. Quite the contrary. SL, for example, was active in the Asian American movement in the late 1970s and early '80s, and many of his comrades knew about his sexuality. Race and sexuality simply did not relate to each other at that time. As SL explained:

> I separated things so much at the time. On the one hand, I was very political and very much into Asian American identity and how I looked at race critically. But I couldn't put the two [gay and Asian] together. During that time, I did date some Asian men, but we

really never talked that much about our backgrounds. I would think I was even avoiding the topic. That wasn't our connection.

The competition for white men could also take place within one's own ethnic group. SR was reticent in his association with his "fellow Filipinos" in the River Club, where he used to go every weekend. He recalled, "There were two occasions I had a good-looking guy I was going out with. Before I knew it, they were almost snatched or stolen by Filipinos. So I said, I'm not going to associate with them anymore. It was much better for me to be with a different kind. I felt more safe. I'm not putting them down, but that's a bad experience I had. Even if you're with your own kind, there's always some problem that might occur."

Neither was this dynamic specific to Los Angeles. TG*, a narrator who had emigrated from Hong Kong and who spent some time in San Francisco before relocating to Los Angeles, encountered a similar dynamic in both cities. He said:

I remember meeting this Caucasian guy at Rendezvous in the early '70s in San Francisco. Rendezvous was the equivalent of Faces [in LA], which was a place where there were quite a number of Asians and mostly Caucasians who were interested in Asians. I dated this guy several times, and he introduced me to a friend of his, a Chinese guy, in Rendezvous. The two of us hit it off very well, and he got really upset. He actually left the two of us. The next day, he gave me a line that I would always remember. He said, "Asians never like other Asians." That wasn't my experience. It made me feel something was wrong with me, although I didn't buy it. It sounded quite ludicrous to me. In fact, we never dated after that.

At the same time, it seemed like at that place, the Asians all saw each other more as competitors for the attention of these white guys than as friends. I found that in the River Club, as well. Like most bars, there was a lot of posturing and positioning and trying to attract. It was competitive along racial, ethnic lines, too, in those days. So I think he was quite accurate in terms of assessing how things were, true to a certain extent. That was his experience. But it doesn't have to be.

This is a reflection of the primacy of whiteness in the gay community, the "white standards" that EW meantioned earlier. "Now that I look back on it, I think it was very racist in a sense," DG reflected. "Asians were not attractive to me. My models were primarily Caucasian models. Everything up to that time that I read or saw within gay publications and things was all white. Therefore, to me, white became the object of my sexual fantasies, you might say."

Invisibility has often been used to explain why Asian–Asian relationships were discouraged. One familiar refrain was, "We couldn't find each other." Furthermore, they did not find representations of themselves in either the mainstream (read, white) gay community or the mainstream (read, straight) Asian American community. Not only were they led to believe that other gay Asian men were not desirable, but, feeling unworthy themselves, they could find validation only from white gay men, not from one another.

But numbers cannot explain everything. It may be true that before the 1970s gay Asians were few and scattered, but certain dynamics persisted even at the River Club and Mugi's, sites where 100 to 200 hundred gay Asians congregated every weekend.

Even in these environments, in which Asians were clearly the majority, the feeling of alienation persisted. When one gay Asian man met another, there were already sets of expectations that informed how they would relate to each other. As long as those expectations were left unchallenged—no matter what kind of space gay Asians occupied or how many of them occupied it—those expectations would inevitably be inscribed in the spaces around them.

Although I do not deny the importance of this theme of invisibility in the narrators' lives, a closer examination of gay bars in Los Angeles reveals a much more complex and strategic geography. Michel Foucault argues that "discipline proceeds from the distribution of individuals in space" (1977: 41). One of the techniques of this distribution is what he calls "enclosure":

> Its aim was to establish presences and absences, to know where and how to locate individuals, to set up useful communications, to interrupt others, to be able at each moment to supervise the conduct of each individual, to assess it, to judge it, to calculate its qualities or merits. It was a procedure, therefore, aimed at knowing, mastering and using. (Foucault 1977: 43)

The gay bars constituted these sites of "enclosure," with their own rules and manners, which in turn enforced an identity for those populating them. Gay Asian men were simultaneously invisible *and* conspicuous in their marginalizaton. This spatialization of desire is another layer of the power dynamics between white and Asian gay men. By looking at where gay Asians men were invisible and where they were conspicuous, we gain deeper insight into this power relationship.

Rice Bars (Part 2)

The spaces of mainstream gay bars and gay Asian bars were clearly delineated for many gay Asians. Although West Hollywood was a gay Mecca in one of the largest cities in the United States, it was not, as the narrators described in the previous section, particularly inviting to people of color in the 1970s and early '80s. When an Asian man wanted to find a sexual partner, he had better chances at the gay Asian bars, where he could be sure the white men there would be interested in Asians sexually or romantically. As RK said, "I enjoy the gay Asian bars, like Mugi's. The Caucasians that went there, you know they were interested in Asians, so you didn't have to guess or play mind games."

Mugi's (in East Hollywood) and the River Club (in Los Feliz) were situated relatively far away from the increasingly centralized gay scene in West Hollywood. In the pursuit of love or something less permanent, gay Asian men found themselves exiled in these ghettos. This separation put the Asians in their place and retarded racial integration in West Hollywood. In addition, this spatial arrangement delineated a border that made crossing more of an authentic "slumming" experience for the white men. I find the concept of "ethnic tourism" to be useful in analyzing these spaces. Using this concept to characterize the behavior pattern in such a relationship is not new. Lillian Faderman describes Harlem in its heyday during the 1920s as a tourist site for white gay men and lesbians. She writes, "White fascination with Harlem seems to have smacked of a 'sexual colonialism,' in which many whites *used* Harlem as a commodity, a stimulant to sexuality. And as in many colonized countries, Harlem itself, needing to encourage tourism for economic reasons, seemed to welcome the party atmosphere" (1991: 68). This kind of relationship is rife with both possibilities of exploitation and opportunities for all parties involved. However, this in no way implies that power and access were equal in these bars.

One example of the power dynamics of sexual ghettos is particularly telling. *Pacific Bridge*, a magazine based in San Francisco, is devoted almost entirely to personal ads between Asians and non-Asians. In the introductory letter to its first issue, published in May 1982, the editor asks, "How can gay Asians and non-Asians get together? Sure, there are 'specialty bars' in New York, San Francisco, and Los Angeles. And some of us are able to travel overseas. But for most of us, meeting new friends is a difficult, time-consuming process."[2] Here the "specialty bars" are portrayed as a sort of ersatz tourism for white men; the ads are even cheaper and less time-consuming, almost like being a tourist without leaving the comfort of your own home. Using the word "specialty" to characterize gay Asian bars also reinforces the primacy of whiteness in gay men's desire. Who is the "specialty"? And for whom? Browsing through *Pacific Bridge*, it becomes obvious who the "us" is in the introductory letter with whom the editor identifies. It is always the non-Asian (overwhelmingly white) men who are the "tourists."

This is also evident in a 1984 article in the gay magazine *Stallion*. In it, the author, an "Occidental" named Blade, writes,

> Gay travelers, whether they're civilians on business or vacation, or members of our own armed forces, have been hooked on Asians ever since Butterfly met Pinkerton, but those of us who aren't free to travel must try to satisfy our cravings here at home. It isn't all that difficult. Practically every large American city has its "in" place (a meeting ground for East and West), usually a bar or restaurant where yellow-or-tan-skinned fellows, young, willing, and exotic may contact Occidental men who (perhaps recognizing their self-imposed stereotype) have dubbed themselves "rice queens," men who seem to prefer submissive, effeminate little "geisha guys" or "sing-song boys." The stereotype of "old and white" plus "young and yellow" remains so strong that at first glance an outsider might easily be led to think he'd stumbled into a pedophile's club.[3]

Similar to the personal ads in *Pacific Bridge*, this article shows rice bars or "in" places as privileging white men as the primary audience.

In the rice bars, the narrators might have escaped discrimination and harassment at the door or blatant racism from other patrons or staff. However, they also found the same sexual hierarchy reinscribed in these supposedly gay Asian spaces. All the narrators commented on the ethnic segregation, as well as their competition for the same object of desire. Certainly, language and cultural barriers played a role in the exclusivity of cliques. But the hostility and suspicion may be explained better by the perceived notion of Asian–Asian sexual incompatibility, which reinforced white gay men as the prize for which they would compete against one other. As noted earlier, RB, who is white, was a regular patron of Mugi's and later became one of the club's bartenders. He provided a unique vantage point in the sociology of these bars as he describes the following mating ritual:

> The out and up purpose of Mugi's was a gay meeting place for Caucasians to meet Asians, and 99 percent of them were ex-service people that were over in Asia. I was in Japan for several years. The word got around, of course, from white people who liked Asians that if you wanted to meet an Asian, Mugi's would be the bar to go to. So Mugi's became really popular in the '80s.
>
> At that time, Mugi's, to be blunt, became a very good pick-up bar for Asians. Now, if you were going to go into Hollywood, you'd find a smidgen of Asians. Maybe out of 300 in a bar, you'd be lucky to count five Asians. If you were single in Mugi's, you'd make friends very fast with [the owner. He] had gotten me a couple of dates.
>
> For instance, there were a couple of Japanese kids here on vacation, and they were talking to [the owner]. Now, they were looking to meet a Caucasian. So Yoshi picked up on this, and he got an inkling what they were looking for. Or, let's say, somebody saw me and liked me. Yoshi would talk to me and say, "Hey, I want you to meet this person." And you would pick up on it and go home together. As you got to be a regular customer, you mingled with other regulars, too. It's called cruising.

This environment manifested the various aspects of ethnic tourism: the "tourist" who consumes exoticism; the native, or "touree," who puts himself on display for sexual-economic reasons; and the "tour guide," who brings the two together and facilitates the transaction. Further, this arrangement was naturalized so that clients knew what to expect. RB continued:

> I felt pretty free in that environment because, first of all, everybody in there was gay. You knew the Asians were looking for Caucasians, and the Caucasians were looking for Asians. So that's the atmosphere that you'd already built up. It wouldn't be like going into a disco bar cold turkey, where you didn't know anybody. You might be in there all night and still go home alone. When you went to Mugi's, you were pretty sure that you would meet some people.

In addition to matchmaking, the staff, as the middlemen, tried to minimize the potential for exploitation in these fleeting encounters by steering patrons away from regulars who had bad reputations. RB explained further:

> I ended up bartending at Mugi's on and off between '83 and '88. Since I had been a steady every weekend, I knew pretty much everybody. Most of the people I knew were already paired up or they were dating. Once in a while, I would introduce somebody. Or if I knew there was a bad dude there, I'd do the same thing as Yoshi. When you bring a trick home, you stand a good chance of getting ripped off if you don't know who the person is. But if Yoshi knew somebody had ripped somebody off, he would tell you. That's the advantage of going to Mugi's or what I call a neighborhood bar. But Yoshi had his own Japanese crowd, which a lot of other customers resented in a way. He had his clique and would get them preferences. I told him a few times. I said, "You ought to speak English more."

To maximize profits and maintain the clientele, the "tour guides" had to fulfill a certain expectation that the club would be "a very good pick-up bar for Asians," inadvertently reinforcing the sexual hierarchy in which whiteness was prized. This arrangement certainly gave the white men tremendous advantages. They were free to "tour" the different cliques. Often they would meet other Asians through Caucasian friends or their partners or dates. Under one another's watchful eyes, however, the Asians were relatively immobile.

The "tourees" were not always the stereotypical victim in this kind of relationship. Although some resented being on display, others "modif[ied] their behavior and their cultural artifacts in response to tourist demand, and [sought] to derive economic benefits from literally making a spectacle of themselves" (Van Den Berghe 1994: 15). On learning about rice queens, PB* felt the kind of validation that had eluded him in mainstream gay bars and turned their gazes into spotlights. He said:

> When I found out about this group of guys called "rice queens" who were attracted to Asians, I thought it was a joke. How could you be just attracted to Asians? I'm attracted to guys who are cute. Having grown up in the Philippines, there were a lot of cute Asians there, so I was attracted to them, as well. In high school here, it was all white kids, so I was attracted to cute white kids. This idea that all they were attracted to were Asians was really bizarre. I had a sudden surge of self-worth that I had never felt before. The idea that there was this special attraction was great. When I walked into the River Club, it was the first time where every eye in the place all of a sudden turned to me. It was like someone had turned on a spotlight.

Similarly, PC recognized that Asians were not a commodity in mainstream bars. So the fact that their ethnicity was prized in the gay Asian bars conferred on them certain power when negotiating with white men. However, PC was also conscious of the fact that this in no way suggests that the power dynamic between whites and Asians was equal. He said:

> Of course, I understood, either unconsciously or consciously (probably unconsciously for the longest time), that when a man is only attracted to me because I'm Asian and he's not attracted to other people, that gives me some sort of power. And I could use that power. Going outside of rice bars and finding that I did not match those people's sexual fantasies, more or less,... caused me to think I did have power in those situations with the rice queens. But that limited me to this one group of men. I think the limits were what bothered some of us.

This power to manipulate is a dangerous one. As bell hooks suggests, "Marginalized groups, deemed Other who have been ignored, rendered invisible, can be seduced by the emphasis on Otherness, by its commodification, because it offers the promise of recognition and reconciliation" (1992: 3). Submitting to this seduction leaves a problematic racialized sexual ideology unchallenged and reinforces our Otherness.

Denied other sexual outlets, discouraged from seeing their Asian brothers as potential partners, and limited in numbers and supportive institutions and other resources, many gay Asian men, not suprisingly, did not regard rice bars categorically as something negative or debased, as later generations of gay Asian men, having inherited both a history and a geography, might have. Foucault (1977) suggests that the power of discipline does not reside solely in laws and regulations. Its genius often lies in the way the ideology of the ruling power is embedded in the spaces around us, so we must see one another through the eye of power, yet at the same time we know we are constantly being watched in the same way. In other words, through specific spatial arrangement, we discipline ourselves. It is no different with the gay Asian bars.

For example, many of the narrators describe Asians as passive and ascribe this trait to Asian culture in general, even though many of them are not the type to be pushed around. They cite this as one reason that they would not approach one another—or anyone, for that matter. I believe that it is not Asian culture per se but the specific culture within the gay Asian bars that enforced "shyness" among gay Asian men. I agree with PB, who said:

> [The bars] promoted this thinking that we couldn't possibly be assertive. I mean, if you don't think you're marketable, why would you even dare to go out and try to pick up someone? How could you? You'd probably think he's probably attracted to white guys, like the rest of them are. You'd think you're the only one who didn't get the formula.

RK expressed a similar sentiment: "I think I just never pursued Asians because of the feedback. It's like, there was no sense trying, because you were not going to get anywhere with an Asian. He probably wouldn't be interested." Even though a conventional cultural explanation is often used to account for "Asian passivity," it is more probable that a strict sexual code was already embedded in these spaces. Lack of access to one another prevented gay Asians from conceiving a panethnic sexual identity, let alone a community with any sense of racial solidarity. Under this kind of arrangement, it was easy to see why Asians viewed one another suspiciously.

The gay Asian bars of the 1970s and early '80s were indeed contradictory spaces. They presented sexual opportunities to gay Asian men and offered them a refuge from the sometimes hostile and racist gay community. However, they did not foster an openness and intimacy among gay Asian men. As HP pointed out:

> You have to take into the consideration the time period and the fear of raids and the fear of giving out too much information about yourself. Because if there is a raid, subconsciously you don't know if the other person is going to fink on you. There is always that threat, that fear. So it was better to be anonymous. It was just like an unwritten law. Unless I give you permission, unless I want to tell you my last name, where I live and whatever, you never ask. And you never give out that kind of information freely.

Even among the circle of friends who eventually became the leadership of the A/PLG barriers existed in the beginning. Tak Yamamoto, the group's first president, recalls his pre-A/PLG days:

> We never got deep because I think there was a certain reluctance to reveal yourself. You knew nothing of confidentiality. You didn't know any of this was going to go anywhere. You didn't know if it was worth even delving into. You didn't know if there was an interest in any heavy dialogue at all. . . . Not until the formation of A/PLG did we actually develop heart-to-heart.

These bars were not places where these men could begin to share a collective history. Yet these spaces presented a powerful visualization of their fragmented identities. The bars highlighted the contradictions they had felt all along. Why did they not find other Asians attractive anymore? Why did they have to look beyond themselves for validation? Why could they not talk to one another? For the first time, gay Asians found themselves congregating in the same space. and they could not avoid these questions any longer. RK said, "We got more exposure to more cultures at these venues. We noticed more groups than we otherwise would've been able to see." In effect, these gay Asian bars hastened the process of community formation.

Given this context, the A/PLG is significant not only because it was the first gay Asian organization in Los Angeles; it also represents a disrupture in how gay Asians in Los Angeles related to one another. The A/PLG was formed in reaction to the ethnic segregation of the rice bars. In the A/PLG's first few years, the leadership was very clear about the organization's mission. They organized educational presentations and activities focusing on various Asian cultures in an attempt to foster a sense of panethnic solidarity. By involving the membership, the A/PLG also sought to develop gay Asian leadership in the community, so gay Asians would not have to look elsewhere for validation. It was truly the first collective effort among gay Asians to merge their racial and sexual identities.

There were limits to this disrupture, however. Because white men were so integrated in whatever informal networks gay Asian men had formed, the A/PLG necessarily had an open membership policy. This meant that the existing sexual hierarchy was imported into the organization, and early A/PLG leaders found themselves contesting it constantly. Different members brought different agendas to the organization. Although the leadership saw the A/PLG as an opportunity to develop leadership and foster a sense of gay Asian pride, many members, both Asian and white, regarded the organization as a "dating service," a more benign alternative to gay bars.

The most glaring casualty of this clash was the participation of Asian lesbians. Framing the formation of the A/PLG as a response to this gender-specific racial dynamic, as this chapter does, can have an unfortunate and false implication that Asian lesbians were absent or passive in the organization. This was not the case at all. Although the women were outnumbered from the beginning, a minority of women did count among the early A/PLG leadership. However, the major controversies that preoccupied the organization in its first years derived from the very sexual hierarchy that is discussed in this chapter, and the controversies alienated so many women that their participation remained small, despite the organization's staggering growth in its first few years. Later, the women found it necessary to organize on their own, and in the 1990s the A/PLG changed its name to Asian/Pacific Gays and Friends (A/PGF) to reflect its membership profile more accurately. Although the history of organizing among Asian lesbians could be traced to the A/PLG, the historically limited participation by women in the A/PLG further illustrates the persistence of the racial dynamics that preceded the organization. What was different from before, though, was that this sexual hierarchy could no longer claim a monopoly. With the A/PLG, a new paradigm for how gay Asians in Los Angeles would relate to one another was clearly emerging.

Notes

1. I have used initials to protect the identities of all narrators in this study; in addition, some of the initials stand for pseudonyms. They are marked with an asterisk on first reference.

2. *Pacific Bridge* (San Francisco), May 1982.

3. Blade, "Hard-Boiled Rice: Are the Days of 'Rice Queens' and 'Geisha Boys' Giving Way to a Tough New Breed of Oriental Men?" *Stallion* (May 1984), 48.

References

D'Emilio, John. 1992. "By Way of Introduction: Notes from One Gay Life." Pp. xiii–iv in John D'Emilio, *Making Trouble: Essays on Gay History, Politics and the University*. New York: Routledge.

Faderman, Lillian. 1991. *Odd Girls and Twilight Lovers: A History of Lesbian Life in Twentieth Century America*. New York: Penguin Books.

Foucault, Michel. 1977. *Discipline and Punish: The Birth of the Prison*. New York: Pantheon Books.

hooks, bell. 1992. *Black Looks: Race and Representations*. New York: Routledge.

Van Den Berghe, Pierre L. 1994. *The Quest for Other: Ethnic Tourism in San Cristobal, Mexico*. Seattle: University of Washington Press.

CHAPTER 5

Emily Noelle Ignacio

Pilipino ka ba? Internet Discussions in the Filipino Community

Internet communities are particularly exciting sites to study because they are formed in transnational places and potentially consist of thousands of people located around the world. Many scholars have shown that the organizing principles of cyberspace communities differ from communities based on physical proximity (see, for example, Bromberg 1996). In particular, an "empathetic proximity" exists in virtual and non-virtual communities that are based on common interests, tastes, and ideas (Lemos 1996). This empathetic proximity, in turn, creates an imaginary boundary, or "symbolic territoriality," around the community. Thus, although there are many parallels between real-life and virtual communities, studying communities in cyberspace will help us broaden our ideas about what constitutes community as well as what purpose communities serve. This chapter focuses on the various criteria members of a diaspora use to build a Filipino community on the Internet, not on the reasons for community formation itself. In doing this, I show how technology broadens definitions of community.

Soc.culture newsgroups on the Internet (for example, <soc.culture.china>, <soc.culture.canada>) are communities whereby participants can be in empathetic proximity with others who want to discuss the delineated culture. Members of Asian American and Pacific Islander American communities in particular log onto these newsgroups because they want to communicate with people "back home" and to deepen their knowledge of issues pertaining to their homeland. In addition, many want to discover their "authentic" culture. The Internet also gives immigrants an especially efficient means for communicating with family members in the homeland. Thus, solidarity between diasporic members and people in the homeland can be initiated or maintained.

Why is solidarity so important? One of the dilemmas affecting Asian Americans and Pacific Islander Americans is the inability of most non-Asian Americans to distinguish between Asian and Pacific Islander ethnic groups and between Asians and Asian Americans (Espiritu 1986). Because of this, the approach to combat racism is twofold. First, many Asian Americans have learned that they must derive strength in numbers. As a result, political activists and scholars advocate forming racial coalitions (see San Juan 1992). In addition to forming strong racial coalitions, Asian Americans must try to show the diversity within Asian America. By doing both, Asian Americans assist in highlighting the social construction of "race."

Many scholars focus on a colonial group's construction of the "Other" (see Stoler 1997; Young 1995) and how this construction justifies imperialism. In this article, I focus on how the "Other"—that is, Filipino participants in <soc.culture.filipino>—defined Filipino identity against the backdrop of the U.S.–Philippine colonial relationship. Specifically, I analyze debates about language against the backdrop of U.S. colonialism and show that there is a powerful relationship between images or memories of homelands and political issues (especially U.S. colonialism) in the articulation and negotiation of a Filipino diasporic identity.

Despite the participants' keen awareness of transnational networks and the permeability of national and regional borders, they actively chose to define themselves using notions of fixed cultures rooted within particular national borders. This is true largely because naming is always done against the perceived rigidity of ethnic, racial, and cultural classification systems and in reference to local political issues (Clifford 1994; Haraway 1991; Lippard 1990). Although members of the diaspora wanted to clarify their common group identity and form a cohesive community, they still often defined themselves in relation to the current local and global classification systems in order to create a strong, political subject position in opposition to the United States.

Some members also found it possible to form a new hybrid, yet resistive, Filipino community by transcending old boundaries. Dissonance occurred when the participants discussed the authenticity of Tagalog and whether it is possible to disentangle "American" words from Tagalog. Interestingly, in the heat of the debates, some participants emphasized the "Filipinized" way to pronounce English words and letters. These participants wanted to show that the incorporation of English words or letters does not necessarily point to a colonial mentality; rather, it can be a form of resistance. In stressing this, they emphasized hybridity and fluidity, which transcends the American–Filipino dichotomy.

Methods

From 1995 to 1997, I logged on to the newsgroup at least once a week to see how the participants were talking about, debating, and defining Filipino identity.[1] I saved all posts that contained any reference to identity. Although I mostly "lurked" (i.e., read but did not post), I did enter the discussion when a group member wrote something that I felt needed clarification. Because I was a participant observer, my own stories and posts are included in the empirical material. If something within the discussions made me rethink my own identity, I either wrote it down in my notes or posted it on the newsgroup. In a year and a half, I printed out and analyzed more than 2,000 posts using the method of instances.[2]

When I began my research, newsgroups were considered public spaces. Thus, I could claim ownership of anything that was posted on the newsgroup. Still, I wanted to preserve the confidentiality and anonymity of the participants on <soc.culture.filipino>. Thus, all names, except "mom" and "dad," are pseudonyms. Furthermore, although I did not observe many anonymous posters, any who are quoted here have had their pen names changed, because finding anonymous posters' "real-life" names is relatively easy. In addition, because the archives for Usenet groups (for example, DejaNews at www.dejanews.com) can easily be searched, I have not included exact dates, real names, or real subject headings for any of the discussion threads in order to protect the participants' anonymity. To give readers some sense of context, I do provide the participants' location and the general time period of the posts.

Creating a Diasporic Community on the Internet

In late 1994, when I started participating in <soc.culture.filipino>, members of the newsgroup were optimistic about the speed and efficiency of e-mail and newsgroups. They hoped to use the Internet to meet Filipinos worldwide, learn about Filipino history and culture, and find long-lost relatives. All also desired to understand the issues that affect Filipinos worldwide. It appeared that <soc.culture.filipino> was a virtual homeland to which diasporic Filipinos could return. Although newsgroup communication is not synchronous, it still allows one potentially to interact with thousands of people around the world through the simple act of typing words on a keyboard. Efficiency and speed equals "nearness" on the Web; thus, in this newsgroup, the Filipino diaspora appeared to collapse. As one participant exclaimed, "It's a small world and the Net totally shrinks it!" We had, as Kling and Iacono (1995) warned, believed the hype of the "computer revolution."

People constantly rearticulate their identity in non-virtual locations; I had witnessed this throughout my life. Although these events were sporadic, I saw my aunts rearticulate their identity as each relative from the Philippines or as third-generation Filipino Americans visited our home. In addition, M. Bello and V. Reyes (1986–87) have shown that transnational Filipino political communities have been formed in the past, outside the Internet. In the 1970s, when President Ferdinand Marcos declared martial law, many Filipino Americans formed anti-Marcos political organizations and kept up with political developments by reading newspapers, watching the news, visiting the Philippines, and pressing relatives from the Philippines who came to the United States for a visit. As a result, "those in the Philippines acknowledged that their counterparts here knew more than they did about what was happening back home" (Bello and Reyes 1986–87: 76). Eventually, transnational anti-Marcos ties were formed that, Bello and Reyes argue, helped overthrow the Marcos government. The widespread dissemination of information about the Marcos dictatorship aggravated thousands of Filipinos worldwide and brought this political issue to the forefront. As a result, strong world powers (such as the United States) could no longer stand by Marcos in good faith; thus this relatively peaceful revolution succeeded. Although the newsgroup participants knew that many Filipinos' had no access the Internet, we still felt we could begin a political revolution there, then let others in our respective real-life locations join in.

Before Filipinos could mobilize, however, we needed to establish what it means to be Filipino and what issues affect us most. The primary purpose of <soc.culture.filipino> was to

> discuss relevant Filipino issues in a newsgroup that would single out Filipino culture. Currently, there are several other nations that have started their newsgroups. . . I believe that there will be a consistent flow of news, especially with the state our country is in presently. This newsgroup may help others to understand what our culture is really like and not what it is rumored to be.

By separating Filipinos from "others" in the last sentence, the newsgroup's founder moved Filipinos from the periphery to the center, from the background to the forefront. This newsgroup simultaneously was to offer "authentic" Filipino history and information and serve as a virtual space where people could return home and form a community. However, as we will see, community building was a challenge precisely because the participants' main goal was to find "what our culture is really like and not what it is rumored to be."

Dealing with Historical Erasure

Because I take my writing seriously and I try to give my readers something honest, something that comes from the heart, I experimented by submitting manuscripts based on personal experiences. I figured this was the real thing, that my writing would be as Filipino as I am. Wrong. My American companions' comments included:

- *There is nothing Filipino here;*
- *This could have been a New Yorker attending Sacred Heart College;*
- *Gives no flavor of the Philippines*

I wondered if my American companions wanted a stereotype of the Philippines—swaying coconut trees, little brown girls traipsing on the seashore; or, better yet, Igorota running around barefoot and bare breasted on the rice terraces.

—© Cecilia Manguerra Brainard (Brainard 1991: 1)

Renato Rosaldo (1989) has described Philippine history as "350 years in a monastery and 50 years in Hollywood," which refers to Spanish and American occupation and to the corresponding "erasure" of Filipino culture as a real culture. That is, many social scientists believe that, because of the many years of colonial rule, Filipinos no longer have a unique culture and authentic Filipino identity. Therefore, they claim, there is no use in studying Filipino culture.

This relative lack of scholarship has had harmful effects on many Filipinos world-wide. Many of the newsgroup's participants said that characterizing the Philippines as "Americanized" and "Westernized" delegitimizes Philippine culture. Thus, they hoped that discussions on <soc.culture.filipino> would help uncover their hidden history. This emphasis on discovering an authentic Filipino culture has, however, led to some fiery debates. Like the passage by Cecilia Brainard quoted earlier, descriptions of the Philippines or Filipino culture that contain Western images were discounted or, often, presented as evidence of a participant's colonial mentality.

Because the media and other institutions often portray cultures as rigid, separate entities, any crossing of the boundaries draws suspicion, particularly when it involves the crossing of a former colonial power to a formerly colonized country. As stated, Westernized images of the Philippines incite accusations of "colonial mentality," dependency, and neo-colonialism. Although some may argue that these are in fact present, drawing such inflexible boundaries between cultures essentializes cultures and, as shown in this chapter, makes it difficult for diasporic Filipinos to establish a Filipino community. This essentialization, however, is strategic for many reasons. In the next section, I discuss how racial and multicultural issues influence the identity- and community-formation process.

Racism, Multiculturalism, and the Importance of Defining Identity, Culture, and Community

AMERICAN BEATS OUT KWAN FOR FIGURE SKATING TITLE

> — *Scrolling marquee, MSNBC Website*
> *(<http://www.msnbc.com>), 20 February 1998*

Several scholars have argued that we must take into account hybridity (such as race, gender, class, and culture) within social groups and stop reifying notions of natural, essential identities because social groups are socially constructed (Bowker and Star 1999; Butler 1995; Cole 1986; Haraway 1991; Lorde 1984; Scott 1995; West 1995). The classification schemes and standards that are created and reified are used to marginalize and control people, animals, and things. Thus, the attempt to fight domination by using the same classification schemes is futile because it only maintains the status quo.

However, as William and Dorothy Thomas stated, "If men define situations as real, then they are real in their consequences" (1928: 572). For example, in the United States racism and laws that are contingent on race are constant reminders that, although racial categories are constructed, race indeed matters. In addition, the media often portray "Americans" only as "white." The MSNBC headline quoted earlier is just one example of how Asian Americans in particular are marginalized in the United States. For months before the 1998 Winter Olympics, many Asian Americans were ecstatic because an Asian American athlete was receiving media attention. Michelle Kwan, a Chinese American figure skater and the favorite to win the gold medal, had appeared on numerous magazine covers and had been interviewed on many television shows during 1997. Yet MSNBC still treated her as an outsider.

Although the marquee was quickly corrected, and despite an apology from MSNBC's sports editor (Edmundo Macedo), Asian American groups around the country were deeply outraged. Brandon Sugiyama of the Asian American Journalists Association sarcastically suggested alternative headlines, including WHITEY BEATS OUT SLANT and U.S. BEATS OUT RED CHINA. This mistake was not taken lightly among these Asian American organizations, or by Asian Americans in general. (Mom and Dad, avid skating fans, bitterly complained that "the yellow peril hasn't gone away.") Thus, despite the increasing visibility of Asian Americans in the media, this incident (among others) highlights the marginality of Asian Americans.

As a result, many political activists and scholars have advocated forming viable racial coalitions instead of merely deconstructing race (San Juan 1992). Yet to combat marginality, many Asian American groups simultaneously want to show the diversity *within* Asian America. As a result, many members of ethnic subgroups within the Asian American race want to articulate their separate ethnic identities, as well.

The participants in <soc.culture.filipino> often expressed the desire to meet both of these goals. Their immediate concern was to learn about Filipino culture, because "knowing [the] culture is what makes one rich." But because the Philippines was a U.S. colony, some participants wanted to rid Filipinos of their "colonial mentality" and articulate their pre-colonial culture. The following section describes some of the debates that occurred on <soc.culture.filipino>.

Using Language to Reify Boundaries

"Wall Street English" and Colonial Mentality

The resistance to colonialism was frequently expressed in the arguments about the use of English and the English alphabet in the Philippines. Associating the control of one's language with resisting the dominant group is not unique to Filipinos on this newsgroup. Many scholars argue that retaining one's language is fundamental to retaining one's identity (Anzald'a 1987; Radhakrishnan 1996). On this newsgroup, some participants believed that instruction in English would only foster colonial mentality. Others argued that Filipinos should be pragmatic and put their nationalism aside because knowing English can only help the Philippines (as Jeff stated):

> Many Filipinos equate instruction in English as a throwback to colonial days. Were English not the international language of business and industry, I might agree. The great advantage Filipinos enjoy over many is their ability in English. This has unfortunately been eroded in the past two decades by those who oppose English language education for

nationalistic purposes. Nationalism and pride in one's country and culture is GOOD, but being fluent in the "International" language (which happens to be English but could be anything) is also a great advantage in an ever shrinking world.

In this part of the post, Jeff's argument parallels the arguments of the classical modernization school—that is, that for nations to become more advanced, they should emulate the more advanced nations in the world, such as the Western European countries and the United States (So 1990). Jeff then alludes to American colonization, but in contrast to some participants, he says that it has helped Filipinos (at least in their ability to speak English). He went on to say:

> The fact that Filipinos are fluent in Pilipino/Tagalog, their native dialect, and English is something to be proud of. Nationalism aside, I believe President [Fidel] Ramos's policy of English comprehension in education and government is a positive step towards allowing the [Republic of the Philippines] to take their rightful place among the ranks of the Economic Tigers of Asia.

Chris, a Filipino in the Philippines, completely disagreed, saying that knowing English is not necessary for progress:

> What we need for sustained progress is a language that will unite our people. And it doesn't have to be english. Again, look at Japan, Korea, France, Italy, and more. In China our company signed a 4150M communication contract. In Korea another $80M for network and computer outsourcing deals. On both cases we needed local interpreters to win the projects.

Chris's post is interesting for a number of reasons, the first being that he downplays the importance of doing business in English. Even in France, a country that Chris uses as an example, signs appear in many public spaces advertising agencies that can teach businesspeople how to speak "Wall Street English." I argue that the reason it was important to downplay Western—particularly American—influences is that the participants believed that one of the major weaknesses of Filipinos is "colonial mentality." It was believed that Filipinos could not for a strong, national community without first stripping the culture of American influences and then articulating a united national culture.

Ironically, the majority of debates on this newsgroup were written in English, because the participants were aware that not all of the members of <soc.culture.filipino> were proficient in the official national language, Pilipino.[3] Yet Chris maintained that Filipinos need their own national language and, consequently, need to conduct business using that language. This led to a discussion about the authenticity of Tagalog. The most interesting debate about English and the authenticity of Tagalog occurred when participants discussed the (relatively) new Filipino alphabet and the authenticity of Tagalog.

Mind Your *P*s and *F*s

In 1987, the Department of Education, Culture, and Sports of the Philippines issued a memorandum stating that the Philippine alphabet had been changed from the

Pilipino–Tagalog Abakada version (which has twenty letters and excludes C, F, J, Q, V, and Z) to a new alphabet (with twenty-eight letters).[4] For many Filipinos (inside and outside the newsgroup), the point of contention has been the letter F.

The arguments that the participants had on this thread echoed the arguments in which Filipino scholars have been enmeshed for the past two decades. Some argue that, because the original Tagalog alphabet does not contain the letter F, Filipinos technically should be called "Pilipinos." Proponents of the old alphabet state that Filipinos should not have an F in their language because it is not authentic. More specifically, the letters C, F, J, Q, and V should not be in the alphabet because they signify both American and Spanish colonialism. They argue that one of the ways to show independence from the colonial powers is to control one's culture and language; thus, keeping the traditional "Abakada" is one way to assert Filipino control over the culture and identity. Others argue that because F is not in the traditional language, it is difficult for many Filipinos to pronounce the letter's sound. Thus, rather than forcing Filipinos to use the F, it should be eliminated.

Others argue, however, that not having the F in the alphabet is a form of "dumbing down" Filipinos. Claiming that many Filipinos cannot pronounce the letter F, they argue, makes it appear as if Filipinos cannot speak "good" English and are less educated than other groups, which reinforces negative stereotypes. Another argument is that many Filipinos could not spell their own names using the traditional alphabet. Thus, the new alphabet was adopted for practical reasons. A debate between participants named Allan and Brian contains almost all of the arguments that I have presented (Brian's original posting is demarcated by carat marks):

```
Dear Allan. . . .
>An impressive post, especially the sections written in "old
>tagalog spelling".

Thank you. I always make sure that certain relevant facts that
haven't surfaced are made known so that all of us could arrive at
appropriate opinions which aren't based on ignorance or plain gut-
feel.

>I'd like to point out, however, that the adoption of the
>Spanish alphabet was during the time when Pilipinos still had no
>concept of themselves as a nation.

I also wanted to point out that the proper term now is "Fil-
ipinos," and not "Pilipinos". About the concept of nation. . . .
Even until now, culturally speaking, the Philippines still isn't a
single nation. We aren't homogeneous like the Japanese and the
Germans whose countries are prime examples of Nation-States.
```

In this first part of the debate, Brian (aware that his post could reach thousands of participants) attacks the authenticity of the use of the Filipino "Abakada" (and the idea of a static culture in general) by relying on words that symbolize legitimacy, such as "facts" and "proper." Although Allan's original post contained a great deal of information, Brian uses this omission to his advantage, as any good debater would. In addition, he invokes the *F* versus *P* debate immediately by correcting Brian's spelling of Filipinos. This sets up his stance as one who rejects the idea of an authentic, unchangeable language and culture. Interestingly, his assertion that the Japanese and Germans are homogenous was never debated by any of the participants, although this, too, is a contested point.

```
> The "ridiculous Abakada" was part of an attempt of to
> foster the nascent national identity of a newly supposedly
> independent state. An independent nation is hoped to be
> independent in thought and identity as well.

But I thought you said (in your earlier posts) that you didn't
like the government departments who took matters into their own
hands like what [Department of Education, Culture, and Sports] did
when it chose to use the complete Roman-Latin alphabet. . . . The
adoption of the Abakada was itself an arbitrary decision by the
Institute of National Language and didn't hold a plebiscite or a
Congressional hearing in order to arrive at that decision. I'm
sure you didn't mean to contradict yourself, but really, that's
what you've already done. . . . As it turns out, the Abakada was
a mistake because Filipinos can't spell their names using it . . .
so the government has the right to rectify it by adopting the
more practical complete Roman-Latin alphabet.
```

This section of the debate mirrors a debate between those who purport that the incorporation of colonial culture signifies "colonial mentality" (for example, the belief that colonized peoples who have embraced elements of the colonizer's have "sold out" and lost their heritage) and those who believe that cultures are fluid and constantly evolving and changing. Allan's insistence on retaining the original alphabet, the "Abakada," reflects his anticolonial stance. By giving a historical account of the simultaneous development of the nation and language, Brian attempts to reify the authenticity of Tagalog. However, Brian used the idea that Tagalog was created (especially by a governmental body) to delegitimate the authenticity of Tagalog. In his view, whether it is imposed by a colonial body or by an anticolonialist body does not matter. The fact that it is created and imposed only shows that culture and language are constantly in flux. Interestingly, Allan could not spell his last name without the new letters. Brian eventually pointed that out to the newsgroup to support his position that the new alphabet should stand.

To summarize: This exchange debated two intertwined issues—the authenticity of the "Abakada" and whether the new alphabet and the use of English words constitutes "colonial mentality" and the loss of culture. Here, the agency of Filipinos is at stake. Allan feared that the use of English takes away the Filipinos' agency—that is, if Filipinos do not use the authentic language, then they are merely neo-colonial subjects and victims of globalization. Brian believed that the inclusion of English words (and letters) signifies not a colonial mentality but progress. For him, using English words is a matter of practicality, not a denial of one's culture. To stop the argument between *F*s and *P*s, one person posted the following: "As long as we frounounce our f's froferly, I think there's no froblem with that."

The conversation about *F*s and *P*s then shifted and revolved around this post. Specifically, participants ended the debate by intentionally misusing the letters to lighten the mood. Here is an example of the replies to this post:

```
> Iksyusmi,
> Did yu jas sey "ep"?? [Excuse me, Did you just say
> "F"?]

Ang "P" ay ipo-pronawns mo as "PEE"; ang "F" naman "EFF"—Did you
get my foint? [You should pronounce "P" as "PEE" and "F" as
"EFF"—Did you get my foint?]
```

Throughout this interchange, it is obvious that the posters know the difference between *P* and *F* and and exactly where each letter is used. The posters were careful to pick words that began with *P* or *F* to make the point. The transposition of *P*s and *F*s is not a completely "innocent" gesture. Instead, I argue that it points to something more significant: the imposition of the Tagalog structure over English. This is, I argue that, in addition taking pride in the "Filipino way" of pronouncing English words, to some participants used it as a subtle form of resistance. Of course, what is intended to be humorous is not always perceived as humor, especially if it resembles negative stereotypes that are commonly attributed to the marginalized group.

Nine months after the *P*s and *F*s debate, and following the recent "Ebonics" (so-called black English vernacular) controversy, some Filipinos started a "FLIPbonics" thread that highlighted what they considered to be the "Filipino" way to speak English. The thread was intended to be humorous, so most of the participants framed their responses as jokes. For example:

```
> I think they ought to teach "FLIPbonics in schools. I'll
> give you an example . . .
> "Today I went to the store driving my behicle and
> bought some fancake mix and then saw a fregnant lady there"
> LOL [laugh out loud]

Well actually it would be like this:

"Today I went to da estore dribing my bicycle and bought some
fancake mix and I saw a fregnant lady dere."

If you're gonna go FOB [fresh off the boat], then do it right....
=)
```

Despite the smiley face at the end of the message, the thread deeply offended one participant, Paul, who argued that the messages made fun of recent immigrants to the United States and that those who posted them should be ashamed of themselves. He ended by stating:

```
> It's already too much that whites and blacks
> make fun of filipino immigrants and assuming all the time that we
> are "foreigners" in this damn country... do you really have to
> add insult to the problem?
```

He cites those he perceives as common adversaries—whites and blacks, specifically—to show people that Filipinos cannot afford to be divisive. In addition, he reminds the participants that Filipinos in the United States, even those who have been here for generations, are perceived as "foreigners" and are targets of discrimination. In addition to discrimination because of skin color, Filipinos face the problem of "Orientalism" (that is, the separation of "Asian" culture and "Western" culture). Thus, they are perceived as less American than some Filipinos in the Philippines imagine. By invoking these common adversaries, Paul reminded the participants of their goal of unity.

Instead of apologizing, Robert implied that the ability to laugh at oneself is "Filipino":

> I have always believed that if there's one thing about Filipinos (or Pinoys or Flips), [it] is that they have an incredible sense of humor. That, plus their love of music, which makes them quite unique.
>
> Filipinos seem to be renowned as a very jolly people, finding things to laugh about even in the worst situations. Call it a racial coping mechanism, but I believe it helps us to be strong in the face of adversity. And one of the things that Pinoys love is a joke based on word-play, specifically, word-play based on how we pronounce words, how english words sound if taken in a filipino context, etc.

In an interesting twist, Robert states that the Flipbonics thread is not an indication of internalized racism, as Paul suggested, but very Filipino. Instead, the ability to laugh at the word play in the Flipbonics threads was not only a racial coping mechanism but a redirected resistance to continued colonialism. After associating humor with "Filipinoness" and suggesting that "Filipinizing English" is a subversive act, Robert critiqued Paul:

> With that said, I believe you should lighten up and take the thread for what it is—a thread of jokes. And do not take our ability to laugh at our own account (which, I have been told, can sound quite bizarre to some native English speakers) as an inability to appreciate our own culture. Far from it, our ability to laugh at it indicates how much we appreciate it. I mean, let's face it: our unique accent when talking in English is part of our culture, as well as our sense of humor!

Interestingly, shortly after Robert posted this letter, <soc.culture.filipino> members began a "You might be Filipino if. . . " thread whose jokes often incorporated Filipinized English (Ignacio 1998).

In this article, I have demonstrated how the participants in <soc.culture.filipino> defined Filipino identity against the U.S.–Philippine relationship. I argue that, because U.S. cultural and economic influences are still prevalent, the construction of Filipino identity often involves dichotomizing "American" and "Filipino." Thus, in Stuart

Hall's (1990) terms, the participants articulated Filipino identity against a relation of difference.

Marginalized cultural groups often attempt to authenticate their culture by controlling their language (Anzald'a 1987). The participants on <soc.culture.filipino> are no different; noting the use of American English in the Philippines, the prevalence of "Taglish," and the change in the traditional alphabet, some alarmed participants wanted to strip the lingua franca of U.S. colonial influence. But the various knowledge bases in this newsgroup and the experiences of each participant collided and, in the end, led members of <soc.culture.filipino> to question the authenticity of Tagalog and, by extension, the strength of Filipino culture. Because many members were so inclined to demarcate "Filipino" and "American" clearly, this knowledge appeared to be a setback to forming a cohesive Filipino community.

However, the hope of establishing a community was rekindled when the participants stressed that "Filipinized" American English showed that Filipino cultural traits continue despite the Westernization of Philippines. With this move, they attempted to *transcend* the "Filipino"–"American" dichotomy and emphasize cultural syncretism and resistance. There, participants wanted to demonstrate that colonial mentality could be transcended by showing that what was once thought of as colonial mentality (that is, the incorporation of English words into Tagalog) could take the form of resistance by creating English words that were almost but not quite, American. Although the debates also caused much confusion, discussions such as these give rise to the possibility of a new, fluid Filipino identity and the formation of a new, inclusive Filipino community.

Notes

1. Before I began my research, I posted a letter to the newsgroup informing the participants of my study and encouraging them to e-mail me if they had any questions. Because of the large turnover in newsgroups, I re-posted the letter every few weeks.

2. I address the laborious system of analyzing newsgroup data elsewhere: see Ignacio 1998.

3. Pilipino is mostly based on Tagalog, a language spoken most heavily in the northern regions of the Philippines.

4. The Pilipino/Tagalog Abakada alphabet contains the following letters: *a b k d e g h i l m n ng o p r s t u w y*. The new alphabet contains: *a b c d e f g h i j k l m n ñ ng p q r s t u v w x y z*.

References

Anzaldúa, Gloria. 1987. *Borderlands/LaFrontera: The New Mestiza*. San Francisco: Aunt Lute Books.

Bello, M., and V. Reyes. 1986–87. "Filipino Americans and the Marcos Overthrow: The Transformation of Political Consciousness." *Amerasia* 13: 73–84.

Bowker, Geof, and Susan Leigh Star. 1999. *Sorting Things Out: Classification and its Consequences*. Cambridge, Mass.: MIT Press.

Brainard, Cecilia Manguera. 1991. *Philippine Woman in America*. Quezon City: New Day Publishers.

Bromberg, Heather. 1996. "Are MUDs Communities? Identity, Belonging and Consciousness in Virtual Worlds." Pp. 143–52 in *Cultures of Internet: Virtual Spaces, Real Histories, Living Bodies,* ed. Rob Shields. Thousand Oaks, Calif.: Sage Publications.

Butler, Judith. 1995. "Subjection, Resistance, Resignification: Between Freud and Foucault." Pp. 229–49 in *The Identity in Question,* ed. John Rajchman. New York: Routledge.

Clifford, James. 1994. "Diasporas." *Cultural Anthropology* 9, no. 3: 302–38.

Cole, Johnetta. 1986. "Commonalities and Differences." Pp. 1–30 in *All American Women: Lines That Divide, Ties That Bind.* New York: Free Press.

Denzin, Norman K. 1998. "In Search of the Inner Child: Co-dependency and Gender in a Cyberspace Community." Pp. 97–119 in *Emotions in Social Life,* ed. Gillian Bendelow and Simon J. Williams. London: Routledge.

Espiritu, Yen Le. 1986. *Asian American Panethnicity.* Philadelphia: Temple University Press.

Hall, Stuart. 1990. "Cultural Identity and Diaspora." Pp. 222–37 in J. Rutherford, *Identity: Community, Culture, Difference.* London: Lawrence & Wishart.

Haraway, Donna J. 1991. "A Cyborg Manifesto: Science, Technology, and Socialist-Feminism in the Late Twentieth Century." Pp. 222–37 in *Simians, Cyborgs, and Women: A Reinvention of Nature.* New York: Routledge.

Ignacio, Emily Noelle. 1998. "The Quest for a Filipino Identity: Constructing Ethnic Identity Within a Transnational Location." Ph.D. dissertation, Department of Sociology, University of Illinois, Urbana-Champaign.

Kling, Rob, and Suzi Iacono. 1995. "Computerization Movements and the Mobilization of Support for Computerization." Pp. 119–53 in *Ecologies of Knowledge,* ed. Susan Leigh Star. New York: State University of New York Press.

Lemos, André. 1996. "The Labyrinth of Minitel." Pp. 3–48 in *Cultures of Internet: Virtual Spaces, Real Histories, Living Bodies,* ed. Rob Shields. Thousand Oaks, Calif.: Sage Publications.

Lippard, Lucy R. 1990. *Mixed Blessings: Art in Multicultural America.* New York: Pantheon Books.

Lorde, Audre. 1984. "Age, Race, Class, and Sex: Women Redefining Difference." Pp. 114–23 in *Sister/Outsider.* Santa Cruz, Calif.: Crossing Press.

Psthas, George. 1995. *Conversation Analysis.* Thousand Oaks, Calif.: Sage Publications.

Radhakrishnan, Rajagopalan. 1996. *Diasporic Mediations: Between Home and Location.* Minneapolis: University of Minnesota Press.

Rosaldo, Renato. 1989. *Culture and Truth: The Remaking of Social Analysis.* Boston: Beacon Press.

San Juan, E., Jr. 1992. *Racial Formations/Critical Transformations: Articulations of Power in Ethnic and Racial Studies in the United States.* Atlantic Highlands, N.J.: Humanities Press.

Scott, Joan W. 1995. "Multiculturalism and the Politics of Identity." Pp. 3–12 in *The Identity in Question,* ed. John Rajchman. New York, NY: Routledge.

So, Alvin Y. 1990. *Social Change and Development: Modernization, Dependency, and World-System Theories.* Newbury Park, Calif.: Sage Publications.

Stoler, A. 1997. "Educating Desire in Colonial Southeast Asia: Foucault, Freud, and Imperialist Sexualities." Pp. 27–47 in *Sites of Desire, Economics of Pleasure: Sexualities in Asia and the Pacific,* ed. Lenore Manderson and Margaret Jolly. Chicago: University of Chicago Press.

Thomas, William I., and Dorothy Swaine Thomas. 1928. *The Child in America.* New York: Alfred A. Knopf.

West, Cornel. 1995. "A Matter of Life and Death." Pp.15–19 in *The Identity in Question,* ed. John Rajchman. New York: Routledge.

Young, Robert J. C. 1995. *Colonial Desire: Hybridity in Theory, Culture and Race.* London: Routledge.

Part II

Communities in
Transformation:
Identities and
Generations

CHAPTER 6

*Debbie Hippolite Wright
and Paul Spickard*

Pacific Islander Americans
and Asian American Identity

Item: One widely used textbook on Asian Americans includes chapters on several ethnic groups—Pacific Islanders along with Chinese, Japanese, Filipinos, Asian Indians, Koreans, and Southeast Asians (Kitano and Daniels 1988). Another textbook does not address Pacific Islanders at all. (Chan 1991)

Item: A posting on the main Asian American studies Internet listserve describes a Seattle Samoan boy who was the celebrated lover of his sixth-grade teacher as "a lovestruck, messed-up young yellow brother." (Kim 1998)

Item: More than fifty universities teach Asian American studies courses. Only five teach a course on Pacific Islander Americans, and none of those is in an Asian American studies program or department.[1]

Item: As the 2000 Census drew near, some community activists called for the separation of Pacific Islander figures from the Asian and Pacific Islander aggregate; others called for Hawaiians to be grouped with Native Americans. (U.S. Office of Management and Budget 1997)[2]

These items all point toward ambivalence in Asian American communities and in Asian American studies circles about the relationship between Asian Americans and Pacific Islander Americans. One often sees the term "Asian Pacific Islander" or an analogue in print (Rimonte 1989). In what senses and for what purposes may one consider Pacific

Islanders to be Asian Americans? For more than two decades, Asians and Pacific Islanders have been linked in the eyes of some government agencies, some community activists, and some ethnic-studies scholars. Yet Pacific Islanders have never been central participants in the construction and performance of Asian American identity and institutions. They have been marginal at best—guests at the Asian American table, if you will.

In the 1970s and early 1980s, some scholars pointed toward what they believed would be an emerging panethnicity that would include such peoples as Chamorros, Hawaiians, and Samoans along with Chinese, Koreans, Vietnamese, and other Asians. At the end of the century, Pacific Islanders seem to be moving in rather a separate direction. This chapter addresses the historical assertion that Pacific Islanders belonged in the same social category as Asian Americans; the forces that tended to support that gathering of disparate peoples; and the forces that currently are loosening that assertion of panethnic connection.

Lumping the Unlumpable: Ascription by Outsiders

According to a lot of people who are neither Asians nor Pacific Islanders, these groups belong together. That most official expression of white American racial thinking, the U.S. Census, says so. In 1980 and 1990, the census listed, essentially, five racial categories or panethnicities: white, black, American Indian or Alaskan Native, Hispanic, and Asian or Pacific Islander (Espiritu 1992; Lott 1998: 31).[3] Few people at the Census Bureau really thought that Fijians, for example, were some variety of Asians, but there were not very many Fijians or other islanders, and the Census Bureau had to put them *somewhere*.

This feeling—that there must be a larger box in which Pacific Islanders belong, and the Asian box will do—is a legacy of the Enlightenment yearning after universal laws and a place to put everything. The result for racial thinking in America and Europe is the pseudoscientific idea of race. This is perhaps the ultimate modernist project, built out of the perceptions of other peoples formed by northern Europeans as they colonized the world. The idea of the Swedish taxonomist Linnaeus was that all living things can be classified into a descending pyramid of kingdom, phylum, class, order, family, genus, and species, with the several items at each level entirely separate from one another and neatly nested in a larger box above. Blumenbach and Gobineau took that idea one step further and came up with a definitive list of four or five discrete races into which all varieties of humankind must be made to fit. The idea, of course, was hash, but it caught on. And so the racists had to find a place for people who did not fit the system neatly: Arabs, for example, were stuck into the white race, and Pacific Islanders, eastern Turks, and others got to be Asians (Marks 1995; Spickard 1992; Tucker 1994).

The artificial planting of Pacific Islanders in the Asian category is related to the fact that people who are neither Asians nor Pacific Islanders often cannot tell them apart. They seem to many European-derived Americans to come from more or less the same place: somewhere west, over the ocean, far away and exotic. It is no accident. The

bringing together of Asian and Pacific Island peoples as workers in plantation agriculture was U.S. colonial policy and planter economic practice in Hawai'i, just as it
was British policy and practice in Fiji. In each case, the creation of ethnically divided
Asian and islander working classes reinforced the hegemony of the colonizing power
and the planter class, at least initially (Takaki 1983; see also Beechert 1985; Bennett
1994; Lal 1983, 1992; Walker 1989).[4] So colonialism put Asians and Pacific Islanders
together in the minds of many Americans. Many non-Asian or Pacific Americans
associate both Asians and islanders with Hawai'i—and, to be sure, there are a lot of
Asians and islanders in Hawai'i. Waikiki attractions and tourist advertisements frequently place Asian dancers (especially women) in island costumes (Buck 1993). The
fact that island racial identities are more fluid and inclusive than those on the U.S.
mainland may further confuse outsiders (Spickard and Fong 1995; Tyau 1996).

By ascription, then, outsiders lump Asians and Pacific Islanders into a single Orientalist melange. Everyone from Honolulu to Suez sort of blends together in the eyes
of most white Americans (Said 1978).

Asian Americans: The Inclusion of Pacific Islanders, and Not

Asian Americans have not been quite so quick to gather Pacific Islanders into their
racial group. The project that made the idea "Asian American" began in the 1940s and
1950s. Before World War II, there was no Asian America; there were instead several
separate ethnic communities whose ancestry derived from various parts of Asia.
There was a Chinese American community, a Japanese American community, and a
Filipino American community, each with its own separate history, culture, and institutions. There were smaller communities of South Asians and Koreans, with less-
well-developed institutions, but likewise with no significant links to any other Asian
group. In fact, there was considerable animosity among some of the Asian American
groups—notably, between immigrant-generation Japanese Americans and Chinese
and Filipino Americans—on account of politics in Asia during the 1930s and '40s
(Burrows 1939; Hertzler 1949).

The idea of a pan-Asian American identity began to grow during World War II in
Hawai'i and in the years after the war on the U.S. mainland. In neighborhoods such
as Kalihi-Palama in Honolulu and Seattle's Central District, American-born children
of Chinese and Japanese immigrants, and to a lesser extent Filipinos, grew up together without the intra-Asian ethnic prejudices that had kept their parents apart. They
went to high schools such as Garfield in Seattle, Galileo in San Francisco, and Far-
rington and McKinley in Honolulu. Orientalized together by the non-Asian people
around them, they bonded with one another in ways that previous generations of
Asians had not. The Chinese and Japanese Americans had similar experiences of Confucian family dynamics, and all three groups dealt with similar experiences growing
up in migrant communities. In those same schools and streets they witnessed other
neighbors, African Americans, achieving a measure of empowerment through the
Civil Rights and Black Power movements.

In the late 1960s, as the first generation of Asians to enter college in large numbers, these young people who had begun to think of themselves as Asian Americans witnessed the student movements for black and Chicano studies and took part in the movement against the Vietnam War. They, too, began to agitate for study programs that addressed their own histories and cultures. And like those other racial groups, they connected their work on campus with work in their communities of origin. Increasingly in the late 1960s and 1970s, young Asian activists crossed ethnic lines: Chinese students agitated to save San Francisco's International Hotel, a residence mainly for Filipino elders; Japanese youths worked at clinics in Chinatown. In school and community, Asians began to come together, regardless of their ancestral nationalities, to learn and struggle, and a pan-Asian identity was born (Espiritu 1992: 31–49). William Wei describes the development of this identity: "As an ethnic-consciousness movement, the Black Power movement made Asian Americans realize that they too had been defined by European American attitudes and dominated by an Eurocentric culture. They had to rethink who they were and re-create their own cultural identity, forging distinct Asian ethnic group identities into a pan-Asian one. The foundation for this unique identity was their experience as Asians in America—a common history of oppression and resistance that would serve as the basis for a 'bold culture, unashamed and true to itself'" (Wei 1993: 42).

Pacific Islander Americans had no part in this creation of an Asian American panethnic identity. There were no appreciable numbers of Hawaiians, Chamorros, Tongans, Samoans, or other islanders in those West Coast public high schools and colleges in the 1960s and 1970s. And the first stirrings of the Asian American movement did not include Pacific Islanders. The first major books of an Asian American sort, *Roots* (Tachiki et al. 1971) and *Counterpoint* (Gee 1976), published by the UCLA Asian American Studies Center in, had almost no material on Pacific Island peoples. Early Asian American studies programs and pan-Asian community-action movements had few if any Pacific Islander participants.[5] In Hawai'i, the Pacific Island peoples lived alongside Filipinos, Chinese, and Japanese, but island social dynamics were different, and no common identity was formed.[6] Pacific Islanders suffered discrimination from whites, but it was not common discrimination suffered together with Asians.[7] It was on the mainland that Pacific Islanders were added to the "Asian and Pacific Islander" category, and the addition was made in their absence.

For more than twenty years, starting in the mid-1970s, some Asian American institution builders and writers have sought to include Pacific Islanders in their group, at least in name. It has happened more in Southern California than in the northern part of that state; and more in California than elsewhere. As a founding moment, some people point to an early government directive lumping Asians and Pacific Islanders. Others point to this or that meeting where a group adopted an API name. But no one seems to have a definitive starting point for the lumping of Pacific Islanders into the Asian American category. The governmental-origin theory is supported by the fact that the inclusive label has been most commonly used by education analysts and social-service agencies that deal with the government. Thus, the *Asian Pacific Community Directory* (1991: 7–16) lists several dozen "Asian Pacific" counseling, health-care, legal, and social-service agencies—few of which have any significant component of Pacific Islander staff or clients.[8] This is not a criticism of the intentions or work of those agencies. They do important things, and most mean to be inclusive. It is just that, in the vast majority of cases, the term "Asian Pacific" is really just a longer way to say "Asian."

In 1982, four scholars tried to sort out the Asian Pacific American tangle: Alexander Mamak and Pat Luce of the National Office of Samoan Affairs; Sucheng Chan of the University of California, Berkeley; and Douglas Lee of the University of Washington. Chan (1982: 3, 41–2, 44) wrote:

> Some years later [after the beginning of the Asian American movement], the adjective "Pacific" got grafted onto the term "Asian Americans" to form the compound label "Asian Pacific Americans." This, too, was a political act. . . . It was thought that lumping the two groups together would increase our political strength. Government officials and funding agencies seemed to have welcomed such a compound label, for it. . . was convenient. . . . Most Asian Americans are quite ignorant about Pacific Islanders. . . . This sad state of ignorance is true not only of the public but of scholars as well. Unfortunately, this includes scholars who teach in Asian American Studies programs. . . . The differences between Asian Americans and Pacific Islanders are much greater than the similarities between them. . . . The people with the greatest vested interest in keeping the two groups aggregated are government officials and bureaucrats in funding agencies, for treating the two umbrella groups as one simplifies the work which such people have to do.

What Chan wrote in 1982 is no less true today. Mamak and Luce (1982: 31) agreed that Asians and Pacific Islanders did not have much in common despite the government's insistence on lumping them together, and noted "Pacific Americans' dissatisfaction with the term 'Asian Pacific American'. . . [because] continued use of the present term will produce a total loss of Pacific American identity."

Luce and Mamak were too pessimistic about the fate of Pacific Islander identity. Hawaiian culture and identity have enjoyed a renaissance and are far stronger in the 1990s than they were in the 1970s. Samoan, Tongan, and Chamorro identities in overseas communities remain strong as numbers grow and community institutions proliferate. There are many Samoan churches in Southern California, Tongan community associations in Utah, and so on. As we shall see, there is also, as the century turns, the beginning of a pan-Pacific Islander identity, as well, a parallel to the pan-Asian ethnic identity that grew after World War II. What there is not is any significant melding of Pacific Islanders into a larger Asian Pacific Islander group.

There have been some parts of Asian America where Pacific Island people and subjects have been welcomed. The scholarly society in the field was once called the Association for Asian/Pacific American Studies. From time to time, the association's annual conference has included papers by scholars working on Pacific Islander issues—especially on the question of Hawaiian sovereignty in recent years. In 1999, the association elected an ethnic Hawaiian to its board for the first time. The editors of the book in which this essay appears made an unusual effort to recruit writers with Pacific Islander perspectives to include in the volume. That attention to Pacific Islander issues has been followed by a minority of scholars working in Asian American studies. Yen Le Espiritu's pathbreaking *Asian American Panethnicity* (1992) attempts to disaggregate Hawaiians, Samoans, and Guamanians, and to address some issues that islanders face. Lee Lee and Nolan Zane's *Handbook of Asian American Psychology* (1998) integrates data on Pacific Islanders throughout.[9]

Yet these are only pockets of inclusion. In the early 1980s, the association dropped the "Pacific" from its name and became simply the Association for Asian American Studies (AAAS). Although it has Pacific Islander members and presenters, they have not always been welcomed. At the 1995 national meeting in Oakland, Pacific Islander participants reported being asked by Asian conference staff members, "What are *you* doing here?" At an earlier meeting in Ithaca, New York, several Asian American scholars burst in shushing when a Hawaiian presenter chanted his genealogy at the start of his paper. He was not being loud but, rather, was performing a necessary element of Pacific Islander etiquette that would enable his audience to know the people from whom he came—hence, to know him and to place the meaning of his words. To interrupt his presentation was culturally insensitive in the extreme, although he was gracious in forgiving those who interrupted.[10]

Unlike Espiritu, Lee, and Zane, most writers in Asian American studies have little or nothing to say about Pacific Island peoples. Nearly all the major textbooks and interpretive treatments in the field ignore Pacific Islander Americans, except a few references to Hawaiians, whom they treat not as part of Asian America, but as background factors in the experiences of real Asian Americans in Hawai'i (Chan 1991; Fong 1998; Okihiro 1994; Takaki 1989).[11] Excellent books on "the state of Asian America," on racial categorizing of Asian Americans, on Asian Pacific American workplace issues, and on the history of immigration policy toward Asian Americans have all virtually ignored Pacific Islanders (Aguilar-San Juan 1994; Hing 1993; Lott 1998; Wu 1997).[12] Even a fine book on the teaching of Asian American studies carefully avoids dealing with any Pacific Islander American issues (Hirabayashi 1998).

Pacific Islander Americans are not the only people to be placed on the margins of Asian America. It is no secret in Asian American studies circles that Chinese, Japanese, and Korean Americans have long been regarded as more central to the making of Asian America than have, for example, Filipino or South Asian Americans (Spickard 2001). The marginalization of Filipinos was highlighted in 1998 when the AAAS awarded a prize to Lois-Ann Yamanaka for her novel *Blu's Hanging*, whereupon a furious protest was lodged against what many alleged was the book's anti-Filipino racism. A group of South Asian American scholars succinctly characterized their position vis-à-vis Asian America as "a part, yet apart" (Shankar and Srikanth 1998). Pacific Islander Americans' hold on a place in Asian America is, if anything, even more tenuous.

Ethnic-Identity Formation for Pacific Islander Americans

Identity issues have sorted themselves out somewhat differently for Pacific Islander Americans than they have for Asian Americans. The major mainland Asian peoples have tended to emphasize boundaries, separation, and distinction when expressing or describing ethnicity. The emphasis in scholarly writings about Asian ethnicity has been on attributes, mainly on ancestry and cultural knowledge. The lines are clear, not just between Chinese and Japanese, but between Shanghainese and Cantonese (Dik^tter 1992, 1998; Hayashida 1974; Spickard 1996). In the islands, perhaps because of the large amount of mixing that has gone on for a very long time, the emphases are on centers, not boundaries, and on multiplicity and flexibility of ethnic definitions. The focus in scholarly writings about Pacific Islander ethnicity is on relatedness, on cultural practice, on connection to place, and on maintenance and expression of the group's historical narrative (Spickard and Fong 1995; Linnekin and Poyer 1990).

Such narrative is a crucial element out of which Hawaiian or Samoan or Tongan ethnicity is made. When Pacific Islanders meet one another in a formal situation, they each tell their ancestry to help the other locate and begin to know them. As Haunani-Kay Trask (1993: 1) writes: "In Polynesian cultures, genealogy is paramount. Who we are is determined by our connection to our lands and to our families. Therefore, our bloodlines and birthplace tell our identity. When I meet another Hawaiian, I say I am descended of two genealogical lines: the Pi'ilani line through my mother who is from Hana, Maui, and the Kahakumakaliua line through my father's family from Kaua'i. I came of age on the Ko'olau side of the island of O'ahu. This is who I am and who my people are and where we come from."

So one's individual location of identity is dependent on the narrative of one's ancestors. So, too, group identity in the Pacific and in the Pacific diaspora is built on a sense of common narrative. Stephen Cornell (2000: 42) emphasizes the power of shared narrative as ethnic glue: "When people take on, create, or assign an ethnic identity, part of what they do—intentionally or not—is to take on, create, or assign a story, a narrative of some sort that captures central understandings about what it means to be a member of the group. . . . 'We are the people who. . . .' Now you know who we are. Now we can talk."

The Hawaiian collective ethnic narrative is built out of a history many hundreds of years old and recounted in ancient chants and modern documents. Great voyaging canoes brought people to the islands in premodern times. They built what many Hawaiians regard as a golden age of social harmony in close relationship with nature. In what Europeans reckon as the eighteenth century, Europeans first found their way to the islands, and King Kamehameha brought political unity to the peoples of the several islands, with some help from Western intervention and weaponry. In the nineteenth century, the descendants of Kamehameha built a nation that came ever more intimately into contact with the colonial designs of Europeans and Americans. The Hawaiian population was decimated by foreign diseases. Hawaiian leaders gave up the *kapu* system that regulated behavior in favor of Christianity. Hawaiians' control over their native lands was undercut by the *mahele* of 1848, which gave common lands into individual hands, then into the hands of foreigners. Many thousands of foreign workers were brought in to serve plantation agriculture. Great fortunes went into foreign pockets while the Hawaiian population was improverished. In 1893, foreign residents overthrew the Hawaiian monarchy, and five years later the United States annexed the islands. For generations, things Hawaiian were devalued and hidden. As the centennial of that annexation came and passed, native Hawaiians brought back to life new versions of old Hawaiian language, cultural practices, and institutions. They began to demand the return of native sovereignty, as well. This is an outline of a common version of the Hawaiian ethnic narrative, emphasizing the political impact of colonialism and the need for native self-assertion (Trask 1993; Kame'eleihiwa 1992; Dudley and Agard 1990).

There is a similar, anticolonial Maori ethnic narrative, beginning with the peopling of the islands, continuing through wars of conquest by outsiders, and currently celebrating an even stronger cultural and political renaissance than that among Hawaiians. This narrative is spoken most emphatically in Aotearoa (which European-derived peoples call New Zealand), but also among Maori who live in the United States (Awatere 1984). The Tongan ethnic narrative is less elaborately articulated outside the islands, if only because there are fewer Tongans to do the articulating. It stresses not colonial domination but the fact that Tongans, alone among island peoples, have maintained formal political if not cultural independence. The ethnic narrative of the Samoan diaspora highlights not colonialism but a longing for the islands of home among a scattered people (Wendt 1973, 1980).

Making a Pan-Pacific American Identity

Each of these expressions of identity is specific to the people who come, or whose ancestors came, from a particular set of Pacific islands—from Guam or Tahiti, from Tonga or Samoa, from Palau or Fiji, from Hawai'i or Kiribati. In the current generation there is a new development: Some Pacific Islanders are making a common panethnicity in America. Interviews with Pacific Islander immigrants and their American-born offspring reveal several themes that are relevant to the formation of a pan-Pacific Islander American identity.

Theme One: Pacific Islanders are frequently mistaken for someone else. Not so long ago on a plane from the West Coast to Illinois, a curious passenger leaned across the aisle and asked me, "What tribe are you from?" He assumed I was Native American. When I told him I was not, he replied, "Oh, you must be Mexican." When I told him I was flattered, but I was not that, either, he said, "Well, what are you?" He had never heard of Maori, but ultimately he was comfortable with the label "Polynesian." Hawaiians are Polynesians, and he thought he knew about Hawaiians (Spickard et al. 1995: v). One young man interviewed for this study said, "Depending on where I am I'm usually thought of as being from the minority group of that area. When I was in California someone began speaking Spanish to me, and someone else asked me if I was part Filipino."

Theme Two: Pacific Islanders perceive themselves as different and distinct from Asian Americans. A young woman of Tongan descent said, "I have seen the term 'Asian Pacific Islanders' written in books and articles but never thought that it related to me." Another said, "I think people view Asians very differently than Pacific Islanders in the United States, and frankly I do, too. Our cultures are very distinct and different from Asian cultures."

Theme Three: Pacific Islanders define themselves in multiple ways depending on context, stressing connection and relationship. This is a means of forming affiliation and affinity with others. Recently, I met a Tongan man at a professional conference. He introduced himself to me, because we were the only Pacific Islanders in attendance. I immediately mentioned that my grand-uncle had married a Tongan woman and told him her family name. I continued by saying that their daughter had also married a Tongan man and told my new friend his family name. We both chuckled after he recounted that he had gone to school with my cousin's husband's brother—we were practically related.

Theme Four: Pacific Islanders are a mixed multitude. Not only are Pacific Islanders from different island groups, they are quite different from one another culturally, physically, and in terms of social structure. But most have a consciousness of being mixed people. How such people construct their ethnicity is worth contemplating. One woman said, "I consider myself half-American and half-Palauan. My father is white, and my mother is from Palau. I feel Palauan because I can speak the language and communicate with my relatives there. But I feel very American, too, because I was born and raised over here. . . . I think the term Pacific Islander American fits me perfectly."

A young man who was born in Hawai'i but raised on the East Coast of the United States, whose father is Maori and whose mother is Hawaiian, said: "I thought I was just like my African American, Filipino, and Caucasian friends when I was growing up, but my parents insisted we learn about our cultures by learning Hawaiian and Maori songs and dances. Occasionally my father would have luaus for our family and friends to remind us of our Polynesian culture."

A woman of Hawaiian, Chinese, German, Irish, and Tahitian descent who was born and raised in the western United States recounted: "When I'm in Hawai'i I feel more American because I don't speak Pidgin. . . . But when I was in high school, I hung out with other Polynesians or people from the Pacific Islands. I always considered myself a Pacific Islander even though I can't speak Hawaiian. In fact, none of my friends spoke the languages spoken by their parents or grandparents."

Another woman described herself as being "a mixture of Chamorro, Chinese, Spanish, and maybe Filipino." She said, "I tell people I'm Chamorro because of the deep roots that I have in Guam. My ancestors have been there for a long time. . . . [But] sometimes I refer to myself as a Guamanian. . . . And then again, whenever I fill out government forms, I check the Pacific Islander box, but when I'm given the opportunity I check Chamorro."[13]

Theme Five: There is a localization of identity for Pacific Islanders in Hawai'i. Pacific Islanders raised in Hawai'i see themselves as more closely connected to other island peoples than to mainland Americans. An immigrant who has been in the United States for more than forty years and raised her children and grandchildren in Hawai'i said: "Although I'm a U.S. citizen and have been for a long time, I don't feel American, but I feel very local. The local culture incorporates many of my own cultural values and practices, which is not true on the mainland." There is a sense of related cultures, family systems, and colonial and postcolonial social dynamics among the peoples of the various island nations that accords well with such dynamics in Hawai'i but does not have much in common with the continental United States.[14]

Theme Six: Those Pacific Islanders who have interacted the longest and most thoroughly with outsiders feel more connected with other groups, such as Asian Americans, African Americans, and white Americans. A Samoan woman from San Francisco said: "My parents are Samoan, my name is Samoan, but I grew up having much the same type of experiences as other people in my neighborhood who were mostly black or Asian. I'm still Samoan, but I'm also like the people I grew up with."

A panethnic Pacific Islander American identity is a new phenomenon that some Pacific Islanders have incorporated as one of many ways by which they describe themselves. Some accept the term because of its utility in distinguishing Pacific Islander Americans from Asian Americans, with whom they feel they have little in common. For others, a panethnic identity of any sort—Pacific Islander or Asian Pacific Islander—does not resonate at all; for them, the salient ethnic identity is Tongan or Maori or Hawaiian or whatever their island derivation.

There are several indicators of a growing pan-Pacific Islander identity, especially among the children and grandchildren of immigrants from various island nations. In 1999, Davianna McGregor of the University of Hawai'i at Manoa became the first Pacific Islander to be elected to the national board of the AAAS. Many Pacific Islander students and scholars hope that her appointment will foster substantive discussion regarding how Pacific Islander Americans fit into the AAAS and how the association may act to accommodate islanders' future involvement. One recent development is an informal Pacific Islander caucus within the association.

Pacific Islander American academics, professionals, and students have begun to create formal associations and networks. This is evident in the development of Pacific Islander American student associations at various universities. For example, in 1991 a Polynesian Club was organized at the University of Utah. The club ran under the auspices of the Center for Ethnic Students. However, because the university lumped the Asian American and Pacific Islander students together, the Polynesian Club was advised by the counselor appointed for Asian students. It was not until 1994 that Fahina Pasi, a Tongan, became the Pacific Island student and club adviser. In 1995, the Polynesian Club changed its name to the Pacific Islander Student Association in order to be more inclusive of islanders who are not Polynesian and to expand the role of the association from being a social support to students, to fostering broader academic and professional development of Pacific Islander students at the University of Utah and beyond.

The first Pacific Islander Symposium was held in 1995 at the University of Utah. Pacific Islander students, academics, professionals, and community leaders from Utah (plus a few from Hawai'i) were invited to present on topics relevant to Pacific

Islanders in the United States. In succeeding years, the symposium grew in size and regional spread so that now participants come from social agencies and universities from northern and southern California, Utah, Idaho, and Hawai'i.

In May 2000, Brigham Young University–Hawai'i hosted the first National Pacific Islanders in America Conference, drawing on scholars, students, professionals, and community activists from all the western states, Hawai'i, and the islands of the Pacific. The conference theme was, "Who Is a Pacific Islander American?" The conference showcased research by students as well as scholars and professionals, and organized academics and professionals to mentor the younger generation of Pacific Islander Americans.

What does all this say about the relationship between Asian American identity and Pacific Islander American identity? It suggests, on the one hand, that the Internet commentator cited at the beginning of this paper was not quite accurate in his expression of Pacific Islander American ethnicity. The young man in question may have been "lovestruck" and "messed-up," but he was not quite a "yellow brother."

Pacific Islander Americans have a long history of being lumped together with Asian Americans by outsiders and by Asians, but seldom by Pacific Islanders. In general, we are grateful for the hospitality of Asian Americans, in particular the AAAS, as it has provided a place in the ethnic-studies world for us to work on our issues. Some of the issues on which we work—family, community, generational change, racial oppression, cultural morphing, and so on—are issues with which we share much with our Asian brothers and sisters. But other issues—ongoing colonialism; continuing working-class status in America; linkages to communities in Australia, New Zealand, and throughout the Pacific, and so on—are different for Pacific Islanders than Asians.

Pacific Islander Americans are beginning to form their own panethnic group, including some fledgling institutions that draw people from across the various island identities. We once were Tongans and Maoris and Hawaiians. Now many of us are beginning to see ourselves and to act together as Pacific Islander Americans. We are not any kind of Asians. But we are part of a linked struggle, and we are happy to share that struggle with Asian American friends.

Pacific Islander Americans have recently begun to emerge from the shadow of our Asian American brothers and sisters and to build our own pan-Pacific Islander community institutions and identity. Now we and Asian Americans need to begin talking about the relationships between our two communities. We need a frank, open, mutually respectful, and mutually supportive dialogue. Kehaulani Kauanui (1998) and Joanne Rondilla (2000) have recently taken steps toward beginning such a dialogue with papers on off-island Hawaiians and their relations with Asian Americans from Hawai'i and on the place of Filipinos between Asian and Pacific America, respectively. Asian and Pacific Islander Americans can and should continue to evolve a working coalition to support each other's issues, from antiracism to immigration reform to Hawaiian sovereignty. We can and should note and celebrate our differences at the same time that we affirm that the differences do not divide.

Notes

Acknowledgments: We are grateful to Rick Bonus, Edwin Napia, Eileen Tamura, and Linda Võ for comments on earlier versions of this paper.

1. At this writing, Pacific Islander American studies courses were being taught at Brigham Young University–Hawai'i; the University of California at Santa Barbara; the University of Hawai'i at Hilo; the University of Hawai'i at Manoa; and the University of Utah.

2. At this writing, the figures had not yet been aggregated. It appears there will be a separate Pacific Islander category and that Hawaiians will not be grouped with Native Americans.

3. The vestigial distinction by which the Bureau of the Census lists Latinos not as a race but as an ethnic group need not detain us here.

4. In Hawai'i, the Pacific Islanders were mainly Hawaiians and the Asians were mainly Chinese, Japanese, and Filipinos. In Fiji, the Asians were Indians and the islanders were various sorts of Fijians. It can be argued that over the long term, the introduction of Asian workers destabilized European and American colonial power.

5. William Wei makes this point by omission. In 350 pages stuffed with names and stories, there are less than a handful of references to Pacific Islanders, and all of them point to the *disconnection* between Pacific Islanders and pan-Asian movements. To wit: "Pacific Islanders. . . have found the National Network [of Asian and Pacific Women's] activities largely irrelevant to their needs" (Wei 1993: 98).

6. In fact, in Hawai'i no pan-Asian ethnic identity as such formed, despite greater numbers and more actual mixing of the Asian groups. To this day, although many people in Hawai'i possess mixed ancestry and there is a lot of mixing in such cultural areas as food and music, each of the separate ethnicities retains a strong identity; the common term used is not "Asian" but "Oriental," with all its problematic implications, and the term used for the mixed grouping is not "Asian" but "Local" (Okamura 1995; Yamamoto 1995).

7. The most conspicuous exception to this was the complex interplay between Hawaiians and various Asians in the formation of a plantation working class in Hawai'i (Takaki 1983).

8. Note that the directory also includes several agencies that do serve Samoan, Tongan, and other islander communities, although they seldom bear the label "Asian Pacific."

9. See also Barkan 1992; Ignacio 1976; Nakanishi and Hirano-Nakanishi 1983; and Yoshioka 1981.

10. Private communications with the authors. It is worth noting that in Oakland, the same impoliteness was extended to some racially mixed conference participants, although not to any white participants with whom we have talked.

11. The exception is Kitano and Daniels 1988.

12. See also Lee 1998, in which Pacific Islanders disappear into the "Other Asian" category.

13. See Spickard and Fong 1995 for an analysis of similar dynamics.

14. See Hereniko 1994.

References

Aguilar-San Juan, Karin, ed. 1994. *The State of Asian America.* Boston: South End Press.

Asian Pacific Community Directory. 1991. 5th ed. Los Angeles: UCLA Asian American Studies Center.

Awatere, Donna. 1984. *Maori Sovereignty.* Auckland: Broadsheet.

Barkan, Elliott R. 1992. *Asian and Pacific Islander Migration to the United States: A Model of New Global Patterns*. Westport, Conn.: Greenwood Press.

Beechert, E. D. 1985. *Working in Hawai'i*. Honolulu: University of Hawai'i Press.

Bennett, Judith A. 1994. "Holland, Britain, and Germany in Melanesia." Pp. 42–45 in *Tides of History: The Pacific Islands in the 20th Century*, ed. K. R. Howe, Robert C. Kiste, and Brij V. Lal. Honolulu: University of Hawai'i Press.

Buck, Elizabeth. 1993. *Paradise Remade*. Philadelphia: Temple University Press.

Burrows, Edwin C. 1939. *Chinese and Japanese in Hawaii during the Sino-Japanese Conflict*. Honolulu: Institute of Pacific Relations.

Chan, Sucheng. 1982. "Asian American–Pacific American Relations: The Asian American Perspective." Part 1 of *Asian American and Pacific American Relations: Three Studies*. Seattle: Association for Asian/Pacific American Studies.

———. 1991. *Asian Americans: An Interpretive History*. Boston: Twayne.

Cornell, Stephen. 2000. "That's the Story of Our Life: Ethnicity and Narrative, Rupture and Power." Pp. 41–53 in *We Are a People: Narrative and Multiplicity in Constructing Ethnic Identity*, ed. Paul Spickard and W. Jeffrey Burroughs. Philadelphia: Temple University Press.

Dikötter, Frank. 1992. *The Discourse of Race in Modern China*. Stanford, Calif.: Stanford University Press.

Dikötter, Frank, ed. 1998. *The Construction of Racial Identities in China and Japan*. Honolulu: University of Hawai'i Press.

Dudley, Michael Kioni, and Keoni Kealoha Agard. 1990. *A Call for Hawaiian Sovereignty*. Honolulu: Na Kane O Ka Malo Press.

Espiritu, Yen Le. 1992. *Asian American Panethnicity*. Philadelphia: Temple University Press.

Fong, Timothy P. 1998. *The Contemporary Asian American Experience*. Upper Saddle River, N.J.: Prentice-Hall.

Gee, Emma, ed. 1976. *Counterpoint: Perspectives on Asian America*. Los Angeles: UCLA Asian American Studies Center.

Hayashida, Cullen Tadao. 1974. "Identity, Race, and the Blood Ideology of Japan." Ph.D. dissertation, University of Washington, Seattle.

Hereniko, Vilsoni. 1994. "Representations of Cultural Identities." Pp. 406–34 in *Tides of History: The Pacific Islands in the 20th Century*, ed. K. R. Howe, Robert C. Kiste, and Brij V. Lal. Honolulu: University of Hawai'i Press

Hertzler, Virginia B. 1949. "A Sociometric Study of Japanese Students in a Polyethnic High School." M.A. thesis, Department of Sociology, University of Washington, Seattle.

Hing, Bill Ong. 1993. *Making and Remaking Asian America Through Immigration Policy, 1850–1990*. Stanford, Calif.: Stanford University Press.

Hirabayashi, Lane Ryo, ed. 1998. *Teaching Asian America*. Lanham, Md.: Rowman and Littlefield.

Ignacio, Lemuel F. 1976. *Asian Americans and Pacific Islanders*. San Jose: Pilipino Development Associates.

Kame'eleihiwa, Lilikala. 1992. *Native Land and Foreign Desires*. Honolulu: Bishop Museum.

Kauanui, J. Kehaulani. 1998. "Off-Island Hawaiians 'Making' Ourselves at 'Home': A [Gendered] Contradiction in Terms?" *Women's Studies International Forum* 21, no. 6: 681–93.

Kim, Ben <benkim@fortune4.com>. 1998. <AAASPosts@uclink4.berkeley.edu> (15 May).

Kitano, Harry H. L., and Roger Daniels. 1988. *Asian Americans: Emerging Minorities*. Englewood Cliffs, N.J.: Prentice-Hall.

Lal, Brij. 1983. *Girmitiyas: The Origins of Fijian Indians*. Canberra: Journal of Pacific History.

————. 1992. *Broken Waves: A History of the Fiji Islands in the Twentieth Century.* Honolulu: University of Hawai'i Press.

Lee, Lee C., and Nolan W. S. Zane, eds. 1998. *Handbook of Asian American Psychology.* Thousand Oaks, Calif.: Sage.

Lee, Sharon M. 1998. "Asian Americans: Diverse and Growing." *Population Bulletin* 53, no. 2 (June).

Linnekin, Jocelyn, and Lin Poyer, eds. 1990. *Cultural Identity and Ethnicity in the Pacific.* Honolulu: University of Hawai'i Press.

Lott, Juanita Tamayo. 1998. *Asian Americans: From Racial Category to Multiple Identities.* Walnut Creek, Calif.: AltaMira Press.

Mamak, Alexander, and Pat Luce. 1982. "Asian American–Pacific American Relations: The Pacific American Perspective." Part 2 of *Asian American and Pacific American Relations: Three Studies.* Seattle: Association for Asian/Pacific American Studies.

Marks, Jonathan. 1995. *Human Biodiversity.* New York: Aldyne DeGruyter.

Nakanishi, Don T., and Marsha Hirano-Nakanishi, eds. 1983. *The Education of Asian and Pacific Americans.* Phoenix: Oryx Press.

Okamura, Jonathan. 1995. "Why There Are No Asian Americans in Hawai'i: The Continuing Significance of Local." P. 243 in *Social Process in Hawai'i: A Reader,* 2nd ed., ed. Pater Manicas. New York: McGraw-Hill.

Okihiro, Gary Y. 1994. *Margins and Mainstreams: Asians in American History and Culture.* Seattle: University of Washington Press.

Rimonte, Nilda. 1989. "Domestic Violence among Pacific Asians." Pp. 327–37 in *Making Waves: An Anthology of Writings by and about Asian American Women,* ed. Asian Women United of California. Boston: Beacon.

Rondilla, Joanne. 2000. "The Filipino Question in Asian and Pacific Islander America." Paper presented to the Pacific Islanders in America National Conference, Brigham Young University–Hawai'i.

Said, Edward. 1978. *Orientalism.* New York: Random House.

Shankar, Lavina Dhingra, and Rajini Srikanth, eds. 1998. *A Part, Yet Apart: South Asians in Asian America.* Philadelphia: Temple University Press.

Spickard, Paul. 1992. "The Illogic of American Racial Categories." Pp. 12–23 in *Racially Mixed People in America,* ed. Maria P. P. Root. Newbury Park, Calif.: Sage.

————. 1996. *Japanese Americans: The Formation and Transformations of an Ethnic Group.* New York: Twayne.

————. 2001. "Who Is an Asian? Who Is a Pacific Islander? Monoracialism, Multiracial People, and Asian American Communities." Pp. 13–24 in *The Sum of Our Parts,* ed. Teresa Williams-León and Cynthia L. Nakashima. Philadelphia: Temple University Press.

Spickard, Paul, and Rowena Fong. 1995. "Pacific Islander Americans and Multiethnicity: A Vision of America's Future?" *Social Forces* 73, no. 4: 1365–83.

Paul R. Spickard, Debbie Hippolite Wright, Blossom Fonoimoana, Karina Kahananui Green, David Hall, Dorri Nautu, Tupou Hopoate Pau'u, and John Westerlund, eds. 1995. *Pacific Islander Americans: An Annotated Bibliography in the Social Sciences.* La'ie, Hawai'i: Institute for Polynesian Studies.

Tachiki, Amy, et al., eds. 1971. *Roots: An Asian American Reader.* Los Angeles: UCLA Asian American Studies Center.

Takaki, Ronald. 1983. *Pau Hana: Plantation Life and Labor in Hawai'i.* Honolulu: University of Hawai'i Press.

———. 1989. *Strangers from a Different Shore: A History of Asian Americans*. Boston: Little, Brown.

Trask, Haunani-Kay. 1993. *From a Native Daughter: Colonialism and Sovereignty in Hawai'i*. Monroe, Maine: Common Courage Press.

Tucker, William H. 1994. *The Science and Politics of Racial Research*. Urbana: University of Illinois Press.

Tyau, Kathleen. 1996. *A Little Too Much Is Enough*. New York: W. W. Norton.

U.S. Office of Management and Budget. 1997. "Recommendations from the Interagency Committee for the Review of the Racial and Ethnic Standards to the Office of Management and Budget Concerning Changes to the Standards for the Classification of Federal Data on Race and Ethnicity," *Federal Register*, vol. 62, no. 131 (July 9), 36919–26.

Walker, Ranginui J. 1989. "Colonisation and Development of the Maori People." Pp. 152–68 in *Ethnicity and Nation-Building in the Pacific*, ed. Michael C. Howard. Tokyo: United Nations University.

Wei, William. 1993. *The Asian American Movement*. Philadelphia: Temple University Press.

Wendt, Albert. 1973. *Sons for the Return Home*. Honolulu: University of Hawai'i Press.

———. 1980. *Pouliuli*. Honolulu: University of Hawai'i Press.

Wu, Diana T. L. 1997. *Asian Pacific Americans in the Workplace*. Walnut Creek, Calif.: AltaMira.

Yamamoto, Eric. 1995. "The Significance of Local." Pp. 138-50 in *Social Process in Hawai'i: A Reader*, 2nd ed., ed. Pater Manicas. New York: McGraw-Hill.

Yoshioka, Robert B., et al. 1981. *Mental Health Services for Pacific/Asian Americans* San Francisco: Pacific Asian Mental Health Research Project.

CHAPTER 7

Rebecca Chiyoko King

"Eligible" to Be Japanese American: Multiraciality in Basketball Leagues and Beauty Pageants

In the year 2000, when the Office of Management and Budget changed the way that race was enumerated in the U.S. Census to allow people to self-report more than one race, many Asian American communities came face to face with the fact that their demographics are shifting to include an increasing number of multiracial members. In general, Asian American community groups did not support changing the census to allow multiraciality to be expressed because they worried that the inclusion of a "multiracial" category would decrease the proportion of people who reported themselves as Asian American (U.S. Department of Commerce 1997: 2). Because financial and other resources available to Asian Americans are often determined by the size of the community, and because this size is determined by the census numbers, many worried that the change would summarily deplete Asian American communities of needed resources.

In addition, Asian Americans traditionally have been undercounted in the census. This was of increasing concern, because overall the Asian American community is small relative to other groups.[1] The debate over the changes in the 2000 U.S. Census put the attention squarely on one of the fastest-changing demographics in Asian American communities—mixed-race Asian Americans. This chapter examines the issues surrounding recognition of multiraciality through two case studies in the Japanese American community—beauty pageants and basketball leagues. In particular, it focuses on the racial eligibility rules that guide participation and access to these two community institutions.

The evolution of a larger multiracial population within Asian American communities illuminates a new demographic trend that will continue to have an effect on how those communities are defined. In addition, the increasing number of multiracial Asian American people provides a case to examine possible strategies for racial and ethnic community change.[2] Mixed-race Asian Americans could point to this blurring of racial and ethnic lines when they transgress racial and ethnic boundaries to identify with both their Asian American group and their other racial or ethnic group. Although Asian America historically has had its multiracial people—for example, Sui Sin Far, often touted as one of Asian American literature's first voices, was multiracial—the issue of multiraciality is relatively new in the community (Root 1996: xiv). Multiracial Asian Americans have not always found being "mixed" easy in a community that, until the 1960s, was relatively monoracial. Unlike in the African American community, whose history of "mixing" is long recognized, mixed-race Asian Americans have found themselves a new and often rejected part of the Asian American community (King and DaCosta 1996). In addition, many Amerasians or Eurasians were "faces" that reminded people of war (for the Vietnamese and South Koreans) and therefore were often seen as "the dust of life" (Valverde 1992: 148).

Are multiracial Asian Americans the future of Asian American communities as they remain in the United States and come to intermingle with other racial and ethnic groups? Or are mixed-race Asian Americans symbols of Asian American communities' being swallowed up by assimilation? Traditional scholars of racial and ethnic relations have argued that the longer a racial community remains in the United States, the more culturally and structurally assimilated it becomes (Gordon 1964). Because of rising socioeconomic status, educational levels, and intermarriage rates, Asian Americans have often been targeted as one of the most assimilated racial and ethnic groups. Others, however, point out that assimilation is not the only possibility—that there is in fact evidence of the development of "panethnic" Asian American institutions and communities (see Espiritu 1992). These panethnic organizations tend to bring previously disparate Asian ethnic groups together around a common political or social goal.

In this chapter, however, I argue that there is a third option for racial and ethnic community development, one that is neither panethnic nor assimilationist. This process, which I call a "transracial ethnic strategy," is being used among Japanese Americans community to incorporate people of mixed Japanese American people into the community while excluding members of other Asian ethnic groups and other racial groups. As I will show, in the basketball leagues, multiracial Japanese Americans are seen as "authentic" and rightful participants in Japanese American organizations and are given priority over members of other non-Japanese American (Caucasian, black, Chinese, Korean, Filipino, etc.) groups. This represents not a joining together of Asian ethnic groups in a panethnic formation but a distillation of Japanese Americaness.

The Japanese American Example

In this chapter, I examine one Asian American community, Japanese Americans, that has undergone a significant demographic shift in the past thirty years. With an aging

TABLE 7-1.   Population

	Japanese	Filipino	Chinese	Korean	Vietnamese
1900	85,716	0	118,746	—	—
1910	152,745	2,767	94,414	5,008	—
1920	220,596	26,634	85,202	6,181	—
1930	278,743	108,424	102,159	8,332	—
1940	285,115	98,535	106,334	8,568	—
1950	326,379	122,707	150,005	7,030	—
1960	464,332	176,310	237,292	n.a.	—
1970	591,290	343,060	436,062	69,150	—
1980	716,331	781,894	812,178	357,393	245,025
1990	847,562	1,406,770	1,645,472	798,849	614,547

Source: Based on material from Barringer et al. 1993: 39.

community, low levels of immigration, and high out-marriage rates, Japanese Americans have found their community "shrinking" within Asian America (see Table 7-1). In addition, Japanese Americans tend to be less likely to be recent immigrants (see Table 7-2).

Because Japanese American immigration has been slow in the past twenty years, and because Japanese Americans have been in the United States for almost five generations, they are often considered among the more acculturated and established groups within the Asian American community. This has also been posited as one of the reasons that Japanese Americans out-marry more than any other Asian American group. According to estimates by Larry Shinagawa (1994: 155), 47.7 percent of all Japanese Americans marrying out of the community, versus 26.1 percent of Chinese and 43.3 percent of Filipinos. If other Asian American communities continue to

TABLE 7-2.   Immigrants Admitted by Country of Birth

	Japanese	Filipino	Chinese	Korean	Vietnamese
1866–1870	185	—	40,019	—	—
1901–1905	64,102	—	12,792	—	—
1906–1910	65,695	—	7,813	—	—
1921–1925	29,927	—	22,330	—	—
1936–1940	520	528	2,464	—	—
1956–1960	31,022	11,592	22,501	6,182	213
1961–1965	21,342	15,929	20,954	10,179	773
1966–1970	21,911	85,636	75,748	25,618	3,788
1971–1975	25,989	153,254	86,645	112,493	15,250
1976–1980	21,925	206,962	116,877	159,463	163,431
1981–1985	20,020	221,166	126,830	166,021	234,875
1986–1990	23,228	273,805	143,751	172,851	166,544

Source: Based on material from Barringer et al. 1993: 24–6.

increase their out-marriage rates, they will be on the path that the Japanese American community is now following. In this sense, the Japanese American community may be the face of the future for Asian Americans, and that face may be decidedly multiracial. Many people see this as a threat to community survival, and discussion about ways to replenish Japanese American culture through new immigrants or marriage within the community has increased among many Japanese Americans.[3]

Finally, whereas Japanese Americans used to be of the largest and most established Asian American groups, they are now facing a numerical decline within the Asian American community as ongoing immigration has swelled the numbers for groups, such as South Asians, Chinese, and Filipinos. Further, Japanese Americans are among the smaller racial and ethnic groups within the United States; thus, the growth of mixed-race people as a percentage of the community is faster than it would be for other, larger communities. Finally, the number of aging Japanese Americans has not been offset by new immigrants in the same way that has occurred within the Chinese American and Filipino American communities.

With immigration currently under serious attack in the United States—particularly in California, where many Asian Americans reside—and immigration from Asia declining because of the economic crisis there, the Japanese American community may provide an example of the dilemmas that face other Asian ethnic communities in dealing with shifting demographics and the consequent shifting notions of group membership.

Negotiating Membership in the Japanese American Community

Within the Japanese American community, these demographic changes have increased the attention paid to multiracial and multiethnic members. For example, "community" events such as film screenings and panel discussions about interracial families have increased. The *Hokubei Mainichi* and *Nichi Bei Times* (Japanese–English newspapers in San Francisco) published New Year's issues in 1998-99 focusing on mixed-race people within the Japanese American community, and an increasing number of books (e.g., *American Knees* [Wong 1995]) and films (e.g., *Doubles* [Life 1995]) have appeared dealing with the issue of mixed-race Japanese Americans. All of this shows that mixed-race Japanese Americans increasingly are being discussed and debated within the Japanese American community. When the community accepts mixed-race members over and above other Asian ethnics, this is an example of a transracial ethnic pattern of group definition, not of a panethnic formation.

To examine this issue, I draw on fifteen months of ethnographic fieldwork and seventy in-depth interviews completed in 1995–96 in two Japanese American community institutions: beauty pageants and basketball leagues. I interviewed participants and organizers of both the pageants and basketball leagues in four cities: Honolulu, Los Angeles, San Francisco, and Seattle. I chose the pageants and leagues as sites for study because both have a long history within the Japanese American community (predating World War II) and both featured (racial) "eligibility" rules governing participation.

The practice of these rules allowed me to see the process by which mixed-race people were construed as members of the community—that is, as eligible to play in the leagues or participate in the beauty pageants.

I found that, with increased multiracial and multiethnic participation, there has been a shift in the definition of who is considered to be Japanese American. By examining the racial eligibility rules (i.e., some percentage of your ancestry must be Japanese to play or participate), I show that some beauty pageants and basketball leagues within the Japanese American community have shifted their understanding of who is Japanese American from a race-oriented to an ethnicity-oriented basis. This expansion of racial definitions of who is Japanese American to include mixed-race Japanese Americans and not monoracial Asians of other ethnic groups is an interesting example of how pan-Asian ethnic identity can be directly challenged.

My research shows that the traditional racial strategy assuming that all Japanese Americans are 100 percent racially Japanese can no longer be maintained, and that many Japanese American community members and organizations have had to change their criteria for participation or membership because of the decline in the number of monoracial ("full") members. As noted earlier, the pageants and basketball leagues I examined used what I call a transracial ethnic strategy, allowing mixed-race Japanese Americans but not monoracial Chinese Americans (or other Asian ethnic groups) to participate. This also might be termed a "cultural-pluralism" approach, because the organizations incorporate people of different racial backgrounds and mixes as long as they have some Japanese racial background at the same time that they of exclude other (full-blooded) Asian ethnic groups.

For the most part, the Japanese American organizations under study did not use a transethnic racial strategy. That strategy would involve opening up access to the pageants and basketball leagues to all "Asians" but maintaining a racial basis for participation. An element of cultural nationalism is embedded in the transethnic racial strategy in it shows that the organizers would rather allow other Asian ethnic groups than mixed-descent Asian Americans to participate. An example of this strategy can be found in Russell Jeung's (1998) research on the formation and growth of panethnic Asian American churches, which gather different Asian ethnic groups together not around a political or cultural issue but in order to use a pre-existing social network of Asian Americans to make the churches viable. Although I recognize that a trend toward panethnic organizing exists within the Asian American community, I argue that straight assimilation and panethnic formations are not the only options. There is a simultaneous trend toward transracial ethnic identity formation that has implications for Asian American identity formation, and it may at times conflict with the pan-Asian ethnic strategy.

Case Studies

Japanese American Beauty Pageants

Beauty pageants are not a traditional site for studying community identity, but they are important, because the beauty queen comes to represent not just herself but an entire racial or ethnic community. In addition, the Japanese American community has a long tradition of electing beauty queens attached to such events as the Cherry Blossom Festival in San Francisco, which ushers in the spring, and the Nisei Week Queen and Festival in Los Angeles, which originally celebrated the accomplishments of second generation Japanese Americans (Nisei). The association of these queens with important festivals and holidays in Japanese American communities makes them an important cultural institution in which we can see a multiracial transition happening.

Although the Japanese American communities in Honolulu, Los Angeles, San Francisco, and Seattle are different in many ways, they all hold queen pageants, and each pageant has racialized rules about how much Japanese ancestry one must have in order to participate—in other words, that participants have some percentage of "Japanese ancestry" (ranging from 25 percent to 50 percent) in order to participate. Basing participation on ancestry requirements assumes that "blood quantum" determines Japanese American identity. With this idea come related assumptions about culture and language. In other words, the ancestry rules also rely on the idea that the candidates will have some corresponding Japanese culture and that the queen will "look" Japanese. This is important, because, as a symbol of the community, the queen needs to be seen by others as Japanese American.

Therefore, it is not enough for a mixed-race contestant to see herself as Japanese American. She must also be "legitimated" and seen so by other Japanese Americans in order to be an authentic and successful queen. The fact that the rules exist at all and are based on the same criteria in each city signifies agreement across various communities that, to be a representative of the Japanese American community, one must be racially (that is, believed to be of a bloodline) Japanese. Although the cultural, or ethnic, component is important, it is clearly not the only criterion in selecting the queen. If success were dependent only on culture, a white or black person who had lived in Japan and was sufficiently familiar with Japanese or Japanese American culture would be acceptable. In this case of these beauty pageants, it is not.

The racial component and rules thus are important indicators of what the various local Japanese American communities consider important. But the rules are not the same in every city, and these variations signify important differences in negotiating race and ethnicity in these diverse Japanese American communities. I argue that the variability of the racial rules in these communities is directly related to the demographic size and political and economic power of each. This can be seen by the fact that the 42nd Annual Cherry Blossom Queen pageant held in 1995–96 in Honolulu, which has the largest Japanese American community of the four cities under study (and the largest ethnic and racial group in Hawaii; see Table 7-3), required that contestants be of 100 percent Japanese ancestry. By contrast, the rules for the Cherry Blossom Queen of Northern California pageant in San Francisco in that year stated that "at least one parent must be of 100% Japanese ancestry."

In the Honolulu pageant, candidates were asked to prove that they were of 100 percent Japanese ancestry, thus confirming their racial "authenticity." Most showed U.S. birth certificates on which the "race" of each parent was recorded.[4] Japanese nationals, whose birth certificates do not record parents' race, and U.S. citizens whose cer-

TABLE 7-3. Racial Rules in 1995–96

City	Racial Rule	First Pageant	Japanese American Population	% of the Total Local Population	Number of Applicants	Criteria
Honolulu	100%	1953	247,286	22%	50 or more	beauty
Los Angeles	50%	1935	159,440	2.5%	about 35	beauty, community
San Francisco Bay Area	50%	1968	45,133	1%	6–10	essay, community, talent
Seattle	25%	1960	22,289	1%	3–5	scholarship, talent

Source: The figures for Japanese American Population and % of Total Local Population are derived from 1990 U.S. Census data.

tificates had no "race" category were asked to bring their families in to be interviewed (in Honolulu) or to draw their family trees (in Seattle). Again, compliance with this rule has been regulated in different ways in different cities. Contestants in Los Angeles's Nisei Week Queen pageant, for example, were sponsored by local Japanese American community organizations and had to participate in local competitions before arriving at the finals. According to the pageant's coordinator, it was up to the local organizations to ensure that each candidate was eligible and met the racial rules. Therefore, the Nisei Week Queen committee trusted the word of the local organizations. In Hawai'i, each potential candidate was interviewed at home along with her parents, allowing the pageant organizers to ensure that the racial rule was being maintained. These racial rules clearly divide those who are "sufficiently" Japanese American to represent the community from those who are not—those who are "in" and a part of the community from those who are "out" and not eligible to be a part of and represent the community.

Where mixed-race women were allowed to participate in 1995–96—that is, in Los Angeles, San Francisco, and Seattle—debates over the racial rule and the ability of mixed-race queens to represent the community brought to the fore changing understandings of race, ethnicity, and community membership. In the 1980s, members of Los Angeles's Japanese American community argued over whether a mixed-race woman could be a Japanese American pageant queen if she did not "look" Japanese: How can she be queen, they asked, if she does not represent the "average" Japanese American? Even in Honolulu, where mixed-race women were barred from participation, there was still debate and discussion about the possibility of allowing them to run in the future and the impact this would have on the pageant. The conclusion was that mixed-race women should not be allowed into the Honolulu pageants because their participation would dilute the pageants' "ethnic integrity."[5] In other words, allowing mixed-race women to run is seen as representing a descent along the slippery slope of the end of the community. Thus, the presence of mixed-race women and their participation (or debated participation) in these pageants highlights the very question of who is Japanese American. And because the mixed-race women are usually half-white, it also gives rise to questions about the relationship Japanese American communities have to the larger (usually white) society.

The other noticeable difference among the pageants involved the variation in the blood-quantum rules imposed in each city. In 1996, these rules varied in direct relation to the size of the monoracial (assumed to be 100 percent Japanese) population in each location. Honolulu, for example, was able to maintain its "100 percent Japanese ancestry" rule because its Japanese American community was so large that the pageants never wanted for candidates. Seattle, by contrast, canceled its pageant in 1996 because the organizers could not find enough candidates who were "of Japanese ancestry." The point here is that the pageants seemed to lower the percentage of Japanese ancestry required in order to widen the pool of potential candidates. However, some pageant organizers seemed to feel that, if enough candidates who were at least 25 percent Japanese (and thus physically identifiable as Japanese) could not be found, they should just "close up shop" and not hold a pageant anymore.

Where the rules have been altered to expand the definition of who is "legitimately" Japanese American, pageant organizers have prioritized the attempt to maintain "Japanese Americaness" over expanding the criteria to include members of other Asian ethnic groups. In other words, although the organizers could simply turn the contests into panethnic Asian American pageants, they have not. Instead, they have held fast to their ethnic ideas of Japanese American identity, even when it has involved shifting the corresponding racial concept to include mixed-race women. Apparently, they would rather have a half-white or, in some cases, a half-black woman with some Japanese ancestry than a full-blooded Chinese American woman as Cherry Blossom Queen. Thus, they are able to maintain their ethnic ideas of authenticity and legitimacy by expanding the racial definition of who is Japanese American—or by making racially mixed women legitimately "Japanese American."

Finally, a hierarchy existed among the mixed-race women in the pageants. Those who were "mixed" with "other Asian" were considered by judges and other pageant participants to have a "better chance" of winning the pageant—that is, they were considered more acceptable in the Japanese American community—than those who were half-white. And both Japanese–other Asian and Japanese–white mixed-race women had advantages over those who were half-black. In summary, the pageants show how Japanese American beauty pageants use transracial ethnic rules to guide participation, thus giving priority to women of mixed Japanese descent women over women of other, monoracial Asian ethnic groups.

Japanese American Basketball Leagues

I found a similar transracial ethnic strategy in use in the Japanese American Basketball Leagues (or J-Leagues). Japanese American sports leagues began as a result of racial discrimination. Excluded from playing on varsity and community teams before and after World War II, Japanese Americans formed their own leagues to encourage participation in sports and in the local racial and ethnic community. Japanese American volunteers were key to the foundation, maintenance, and evolution of these leagues before, during, and after the internment of Japanese Americans in World War II. These leagues allowed people of all the generations (Issei, Nisei, and Sansei) to come together, create community cohesion, and learn sportsmanship, which many thought would help Japanese Americans to be accepted as "true Americans." Today, Japanese American sports leagues, particularly basketball leagues, have increased in popularity, and members of other Asian ethnic groups want to participate in them.

This has caused problems, both legal and social, because most leagues' eligibility rules require players to be "of Japanese ancestry." For example, in 1986, the bylaws of the Bay Area Nikkei League (BANL)[6] stated that new players must "be a participating member of the sponsoring organization (usually a church or other Japanese American organization) and that the organization must be predominantly Japanese American and that no more than two non-Japanese players can be in the game for one team at any given time."

In 1993, the BANL altered its eligibility rules because fewer and fewer Japanese American youth were participating in the league and the number of those of other ethnicities—primarily other Asians, especially Chinese Americans—wanting to get into the league had increased. The league's bylaws were changed to read: "An unregistered player of Japanese ancestry must be a participating member of the sponsoring organization at the time of roster approval" (the time was left unspecified) and "an unregistered player of no Japanese ancestry must meet the following conditions: a) the player or parent must be an active participant in a predominantly Japanese American sponsoring organization; b) the player must not be over six feet tall; c) the player must not be an impact player recruited for the purpose of dominating play in the league." Finally, the rules stated that "each season all team rosters must have more than 50 percent of the players of Japanese ancestry, but no more than three non-Japanese players."

In other words, players of Japanese ancestry only had to be participating members of the sponsoring organization; there were no restrictions on their height or skills. At the same time, non-Japanese players were subjected to more stringent rules. This proved true in practice as well as on paper: Some Japanese players were able to sign up to play on a team at the last minute while non-Japanese players who had not signed up at least a year in advance were disallowed. Although the change from permitting only two non-Japanese players on the court at a time to allowing no more than three on a team shows that the leagues wanted to accommodate more non-Japanese players, they still kept a large number of other Asian-ethnic players, particularly Chinese Americans, from participating.

According to the definition set forth by the league, one either is of Japanese ancestry or one is not. Unlike the beauty pageants, the basketball league in question did not use blood-quantum rules per se to determine eligibility. As one of the league's organizers explained to me, referring to the quote of three non-Japanese players per team, "If they have some Japanese ancestry, they are a non-quota player." In other words, multiracial Japanese Americans who can prove that they are part Japanese are considered "Japanese" and therefore are not subject to the "three non-Japanese players" rule.

In reality, mixed-race Japanese Americans who play in the league are questioned at times about their "authenticity." At one BANL board meeting, there was considerable debate about the "legitimacy" of one of the mixed-race players. Eventually, the board decided to ask the player, who did not have a Japanese surname, about his ancestry. When he responded that his mother was Japanese but absent, he was taken at his word.

Other leagues, such as the Nikkei Adult League (NAL) (age 18 and older), have used strident methods to ensure "ethnic integrity." According to the eligibility requirements in the NAL's 1994 bylaws:

A. Japanese Players
    1. One or both natural parents must be Japanese.
    2. In case of adoption, both parents must be Japanese.
B. Chinese players
    1. Both natural parents must be Chinese.
    2. Each team may have a maximum of three (3) Chinese players.

These bylaws also state that "All new players must submit birth certificates before they are deemed eligible to play in the NAL."[7]

The second rule under "Japanese Players" is interesting. Although it requires that players who are adopted be raised as culturally Japanese and that both of the adoptive parents be Japanese, it does not specify the *player's* ancestry in terms of race. Therefore, the player technically could be white or black. Thus, the rules show a separation between race (e.g., in rule number one for Japanese players) and culture (e.g., in rule number two for Japanese players); however, both race and culture are viewed as legitimate criteria for "eligibility" to be Japanese and play in the league. There is not the same understanding for adopted Chinese players, who are excluded completely. Clearly, the hierarchy of preference in this league follows these line: full Japanese Americans, mixed-race Japanese Americans, adopted but culturally defined Japanese Americans, then, finally, full Chinese Americans.

In addition, the NAL's rules set out strict penalties for teams that used illegal or ineligible players—that is, those that used too many non-Japanese players. These penalties ranged from forfeiting all the games in which the illegal player had participated to players' being banished (and having their kids banished) from the league for life. This is a clear example of the "gate-keeping" that is done to ensure "ethnic integrity": Teams that have too many Chinese players or that allow someone who is "falsely eligible" (who has no Japanese ancestry) to play could be thrown out of the league.

I asked one of the league's board members whether this had ever happened. He said that "fraud" had become so routine that the league had started asking players for their birth certificates. Even then, he said, some players falsified their "race" on their birth certificates, changing it from "Chinese" to "Japanese," to meet the league's eligibility requirements. The NAL was starting to get involved in verifying players' birth certificates in order maintain the "ethnic integrity" of the league.

Because of these rules, many Chinese American players have become upset with the leagues and threatened to sue on the grounds of "racism" and "discrimination."

One such case was brought against the BANL in the late 1980s. The league explained to the player who had brought the suit that, if he continued, the league would fold because the league was made up of volunteers and was not financially able to withstand a lawsuit. The player's family dropped the suit because they did not want to be responsible for destroying the league and taking basketball away from other Asian kids. Their panethnic loyalty may not have paid off, however, because after the suit was droppped, the BANL's board bought insurance that will protect both its individual members and the league as an organization against liability when (not if) a case like this comes up again.

Thus, these two leagues are not broadening their definition of Japanese American to include other Asian ethnic groups, and they are not moving toward a pan-Asian ethnic identity. Neither are they continuing to depend on traditional notions of Japanese Americaness (that is, 100 percent Japanese ancestry). Instead, they are expanding the definition of who is Japanese to include mixed-race Japanese Americans and, in so doing, are shifting the criteria for membership and participation.

In other words, the BANL and the beauty pageants are using a transracial ethnic strategy (that is, one can be mixed or from many different races as long as one is racially part-Japanese) rather than a transethnic racial strategy (that is, one can be from any Asian-race-based ethnic group). The NAL, however, seems to be mixing these two strategies in that it allows both monoracial Chinese American players (although in a limited way) and mixed-race Japanese Americans access to the league. Interestingly, the NAL technically does not allow people of mixed Chinese descent to play at all.

Interestingly, the rosters of the teams, which are drawn form the Japanese American sponsoring organizations, appear to be increasingly diverse. One roster given to me in 1996 listed eight players:

Challat, Carl (Ishii) *Japanese*
Chang, Elvin
Englehardt, Tom
Fung, Kevin (Yoshio) *Japanese*
Peralta, David (Hara) *Japanese*
Shaw, Mike (Takeo) *Japanese*
Takahashi, Corey *Japanese*
Yoshihara, Kazuo *Japanese*[8]

Of these eight players, only two were "full Japanese" (Takahashi and Yoshihara). Four more "Japanese" players were counted toward the total (Challat, Fung, Peralta, and Shaw) because they were of mixed Japanese descent, which the coach noted by adding their Japanese middle name or mother's Japanese surname in parentheses. Even Kevin Fung, who one can assume is part-Chinese and part-Japanese, is counted as Japanese in order to make room for the two non-quota players: Elvin Chang (full Chinese) and Tom Englehardt (white).

These two case studies, basketball leagues and beauty pageants within the Japanese American community, illustrate how the Japanese American community is working to incorporate multiracial people. By looking at eligibility rules in both of these contexts, one can see shifting notions of who is eligible to be Japanese American. These rules also demonstrate a shift over time from completely "race"-based definitions of to a more "ethnicity"-based technique of designating who is considered an "in-group" or community member. These people of multiracial Japanese descent are crossing into the Japanese American community, and with their acceptance comes a redefinition of the criteria by which one is determined to be Japanese American.

This chapter has also shown that basketball leagues and beauty pageants in local Japanese American communities are not using only panethnic or assimilationist strategies; instead, they may be intermixing these strategies with a transracial ethnic strategy. This newer strategy of prioritizing mixed-descent Japanese Americans (and considering them "authentic" Japanese American participants) over other, monoracial Asian ethnics shows that there may be a distillation of the ethnic definition of Japanese Americanness, but also that the concept of race in this instance may be more fluid than it once was. When people of mixed Japanese descent are considered more legitimate participants than, say, monoracial Chinese Americans, this means that the the definition of "community member" has been expanded to include those who are half-white or half-black as long as they are also half-Japanese but not to include those who are "full" Chinese. This seems to be a strategy that is different from, and sometimes competes with, strategies that aim toward pan-Asian ethnic formations.

Finally, this theoretical point may shed light on other racial and ethnic identity-formation processes at work in the re-formation of the Asian American community as it grapples with demographic changes. This may mean that the boundaries of ethnic and racial groups for Asian and Pacific Islander Americans are shifting as these groups become more acculturated to allow members to have multiple and overlapping memberships and loyalties not only with other Asian ethnic groups, but also with whites and blacks. This does not mean, though, that the assimilationist model is the only way in which Asian and Pacific Americans relate to whites. Instead, it means that they may be using other strategies to negotiate "mixing" with other racial (white or African American) communities. Theoretically, this is a new way of thinking about community membership that is not just assimilation or just panethnic formation. Instead, it is a way of thinking that recognizes ethnic differences while transcending racial lines—in other words, transracial ethnic formation.

Notes

1. In California, where almost 50 percent of Asian Americans resided in 1990, Asian Americans made up only 10 percent of the total population (Oliver et al. 1995: 1-1).

2. There is tremendous theoretical slippage between the terms "ethnic" and "racial." When I refer to ethnicity as a basis for community membership, I am using the operative definition that respondents provided—that is, they used the term "ethnicity" to refer to culture, language, and food, and "race" to refer to ancestry and phenotype.

3. This can be seen in such events such as the April 1998 "Ties That Bind" conference in Los Angeles and the Nikkei 2000 conference, "Empowering Our Community in the 21st Century,"

in San Francisco. These conferences represent efforts to bring together various Japanese American community groups to work together to "save" a declining community and ask, as does a Nikkei 2000 Conference poster, "What binds us together as Japanese Americans? How can we redefine and broaden the definition of community?"

4. Most of these participants were born in the 1960s and 1970s, and their U.S. birth certificates collected data on "mother's race" and "father's race." It is interesting that these certificates were accepted as "proof," because there was no way to "confirm" that the mother and father were 100 percent Japanese.

5. The eligibility rules in Honolulu changed in 1999 to allow multiracial women (50 percent or more Japanese ancestry) to participate in the pageant. This change, which caused a great deal of disagreement in the Hawaiian Japanese American community, is an interesting case of having to include mixed-race women because they have become a demographic fact of the community.

6. The names of the leagues have been changed to protect the identities of the participants. The BANL is a youth league in the San Francisco Bay area serving children age 8–18; the NAL is an adult league (age 18 and older) in California.

7. Note that the racial rules are more stringent for adopted adults and that Asian American groups other than Chinese Americans are not mentioned at all. The league organizer with whom I spoke said that Chinese Americans made up by far the largest group of non-Japanese players in the league. However, she also mentioned that increasing numbers of Filipino Americans and Korean Americans "wanted into" the league.

8. The names on the roster have been changed, but I have preserved their ethnic format. That is, I substituted a Japanese surname for a Japanese surname and so on. The italics are added for emphasis.

References

Barringer, Herbert, Robert W. Gardner, and Michael J. Levin. 1993. *Asians and Pacific Islanders in the United States*. New York: Russell Sage Foundation.

Espiritu, Yen Le. 1992. *Asian American Panethnicity: Bridging Institutions and Identities*. Philadelphia: Temple University Press.

Gordon, Milton M. 1964. *Assimilation in American Life*. New York: Oxford University Press.

Jeung, Russell. 1998. "The Formation and Growth of Evangelical, Panethnic Asian American Churches." Paper presented at the Pacific Sociological Association Conference, San Francisco, April.

King, Rebecca Chiyoko, and Kimberly DaCosta. 1996. "Changing Face, Changing Race: The Making a Remaking of Race in the Japanese American and African American Communities." Pp. 227–44 in *The Multiracial Experience: Racial Borders as the New Frontier*, ed. Maria P. P. Root. Newbury Park, Calif.: Sage Publications.

Life, Reggie. 1995. *Doubles*. Video recording.

Oliver, J. Eric, Frederic C. Gey, Jon Stiles, and Henry Brady. 1995. *Pacific Rim States Asian Demographic Data Book*. Berkeley: University of California, Office of the President.

Root, Maria P. P., ed. 1996. *The Multiracial Experience: Racial Borders as the New Frontier*. Newbury Park, Calif.: Sage Publications.

Shinagawa, Larry Hajime. 1994. "Intermarriage and Inequality: A Theoretical and Empirical Analysis of the Marriage Patterns of Asian Americans." Ph.D. dissertation, Department of Sociology, University of California, Berkeley.

U.S. Department of Commerce. 1997. "Findings on Questions on Race and Hispanic Origin Tested in the 1996 National Content Survey." U.S. Bureau of the Census, Population Division, Working Paper no. 16. Washington, D.C.

Valverde, Kieu-Linh Caroline. "From Dust to Gold: The Vietnamese Amerasian Experience." Pp. 144–61 in *Racially Mixed People in America*, ed. Maria P. P. Root. Newbury Park, Calif.: Sage Publications.

Wong, Shawn. 1995. *American Knees*. New York. Simon and Schuster.

CHAPTER 8

Pensri Ho

Young Asian American Professionals in Los Angeles: A Community in Transition

In the urban sprawl of Los Angeles, young Asian American professionals use social networks to mobilize their individual and collective efforts strategically to secure and perpetuate middle-class ascendancy. Yet this community of young professionals is in transition, professionally and spatially. In their mid-twenties to mid-thirties, these men and women are in the process of discovering their professional niche and negotiating the complexities of establishing a dominant presence in their respective careers. This endeavor sometimes forces these professionals to become increasingly mobile; in their pursuit of lucrative employment or in compliance with employers' demands, they must travel or relocate throughout the region, the country, and the world. Given their mobility, these men and women created a deterritorialized community that relies on overlapping local, regional, national, and international social networks dominated by Asian American professional peers.

One formalized manifestation of this community is the voluntary Asian American Professional Network (AAPN).[1] This chapter discusses how the AAPN enables professionals strategically to secure and perpetuate middle-class ascendancy without resorting to the dismissal or rejection of racial self-identification. Instead, the organization encourages members to develop an Asian American consciousness. Although alienated at times by a larger Asian American community that is troubled by its class-privileged insularity and its embodiment of the model-minority myth, these professionals continue their efforts to forge ties with other Asian American constituencies through community-service activities.

Research for this chapter is based on ethnographic fieldwork and intensive interviews conducted among young Asian American professionals in Los Angeles from 1995 to 1998.[2] Although primary research was conducted among the AAPN membership, interviews and fieldwork were also conducted among non-AAPN professionals. To ensure respondents' anonymity, pseudonyms have been assigned to reflect both their ethnicity and given names. Some of the professions and regions (states and cities) of origin were also altered slightly to ensure their anonymity. However, the pseudonymous details reflect the general integrity of each person's background. For example, a museum curator would be recast as an art historian.

Asian American Professional Network

Since its founding in 1994, the AAPN's membership has grown to 500 active members and nearly ten volunteer directors, who implement and coordinate all the operations and programming logistics of the organization. Equally divided between men and women, most of the members are of East Asian descent and are college-educated professionals in the corporate, legal, medical, entertainment, technology, and engineering fields. A little more than half were born or raised in Southern California. Although several were born or raised in Midwestern and Southern cities or suburbs, a majority of the remaining members were born or raised in the Midatlantic states (the northern East Coast). All but a few members were raised outside their respective ethnic-enclave communities. Raised by immigrant parents who secured middle-class to upper-middle-class standards of living for their families in the United States, these 1.5-generation[3] to third-generation Americans average twenty-six years of age.

The voluntary AAPN was founded by a small group of friends and acquaintances who wanted to create an organization of young professionals who were interested socializing with their age peers and developing their professional potential. Although several well-established professional organizations existed at the time, the AAPN's founding members felt that these organizations did not cater to the age-specific needs and interests of younger members. In response, the AAPN was created to schedule recreational sporting, cultural, community-service, and social-networking events. These activities were balanced by more career-enhancing programs, such as professional-development workshops and leadership seminars.

Because of its effective programming and marketing strategies over the years, the AAPN receives recognition and praise from numerous established and well-respected corporate and Asian American organizations, as well as from leaders in Southern California and, to a small degree, across the nation. Several Southern Californian Asian American corporate and political leaders lent their efforts to promote the visibility of the AAPN in the larger Asian American, corporate, and more "mainstream" communities in the region.

These leaders usually inform their professional peers about the AAPN and help the organization secure corporate and community sponsorship of its professional-development and community-service events. The AAPN is a nonprofit organization and relies on these leaders' assistance to raise annually tens of thousands of dollars in cash and in-kind donations to support its programs. Impressed by the youth, professionalism, and energy of the membership and the association's directors, these corporate and professional leaders sometimes encourage young professionals they encounter outside of the AAPN to join the organization. When asked why she chose to join the AAPN, Sheila recalls:

> My father's fraternity brother works for Xerox and was invited to one of the events. His wife was so incredibly impressed [by] the caliber of young people at [the AAPN] that she said, "[Sheila], you've got to get involved." She's actually been trying to get her son involved, too. Every young Asian person she met, she tried to get them involved 'cause she was so impressed with the group of people.

Although Sheila did not remember whether the woman's husband had been invited for his corporate or community leadership, the impact of this couple's interaction with the AAPN directors and members nevertheless inspired the wife to recruit members for the organization.

The ability of the organization's directors to garner such support is impressive. However, their endorsement can be counterproductive when these political and corporate leaders pressure the AAPN's directors to support their agendas. For example, several Asian American politicians have attempted to secure the AAPN's endorsement of their election and re-election campaigns over the years. As a federally recognized nonprofit organization, AAPN must remain nonpartisan under federally mandated guidelines. Hence, requests for political endorsements cannot be fulfilled. Further, when invited by the AAPN to attend events as VIP guests or to give brief speeches praising or endorsing their support for the AAPN and its programs, several of these politicians have stated their political platform to the association's membership, circumventing the AAPN's directives. Yet despite these challenges, the AAPN continues to win community support and recognition from these leaders.

Class Privilege

AAPN members seek increased wealth and social-status acclamation, both of which theoretically would give them access to and active participation in the conspicuous-consumption and leadership of American culture as defined by American middle-class standards. Very much a reflection of the times (1990s) and the regional climate of Southern California, AAPN members' apathy and early access to class privilege generally lessen their social awareness and concern for social issues that affect the Asian American community.

In many cases, these members' lifestyles and lack of social-conscious-raising activities as undergraduates explain their lack of interest in community activism, especially when such activities involve the working class. Their lifestyles reflect their life-course priorities at an age at which work and friendships are primary concerns, and interaction is usually limited to those who share similar lifestyles and apathy toward social issues. The apathy arises from two primary sources. First, these members' leisure activities usually revolve around socializing with friends, pursuing hobbies, and engaging in sports activities (spectator and participatory); they rarely involve reading news periodicals and discussing current events in ways that go beyond sensationalized mainstream-media news bites and work-related topics. Second, before they were consumed by their work, a slight majority of the AAPN members pursued undergraduate majors that would lead to careers in engineering, medicine, or business. The disciplines' concern with practical application rather than with Aristotelian, Confucian, or Emersonian pursuits of knowledge may reflect the social climate of the 1980s—the decade in which members were coming of age. The 1980s were shaped by escalated downward mobility, streamlined middle management, and decreased job security (Newman 1988). The fear and anguish experienced by the middle class during this decade, compounded by pressures from immigrant parents intent on having their children perpetuate the middle-class standard of living they maintained in the United States, shaped the educational and career choices of this generation of young professionals.

The AAPN reinforces these professionals' middle- to upper-middle-class values by giving its members opportunities to network with people from diverse professions.[4] Non-members consistently mention their alienation from AAPN members. One non-member, Kazu Yoshimura, a second-generation Japanese American raised in the Midwest, commented:

> Now, I'm not saying for all [AAPN] members, but some [AAPN] members I felt a slight social class difference. What people talk about and their interests tend to be a little materialistic. But a positive thing is there's people that [are] aware of their minority backgrounds and certain difficulties they might face in the professional environment as a result of being Asian American or Asian Pacific American. So it's good to have some kind of organization be a support group, be able to help with that aspect.

Later in the interview, Kazu conjectured that the materialism of some AAPN members might be attributable to the regional influences of Southern California, and Los Angeles in particular. Other non-members stated similar disapproval of AAPN members' materialism and seeming disregard for individual and collective responsibility to less fortunate members of the Asian American community. Yet their criticisms were tempered by comments acknowledging these professionals' awareness of social and community issues. Another non-AAPN member, Celeste Change, a second-generation Chinese American, offered a slightly more amusing description of AAPN members. A graduate student in planetary sciences, she discussed her and her husband's perception of the AAPN:

> Definitely not our usual crowd. It's, for us, a little too much into the money and business aspect. But I joke with people, "Somebody's got to fund us. Right?" Someone's got to make the money and give us, donate some money to us. And I think that is what AAPN is for us.
>   We are thankful that there is a group that does community work. And even if that is really a small percentage, but they have the big parties, make a lot of money and give it to community groups. We really respect that.

We have very mixed feelings about AAPN. They're not very political. I mean, at least people at AAPN know about the internment. At least there's general political awareness, I think. I mean, there are people who would understand Asian American issues, at least.

Hence, AAPN members' materialism is partially excusable given their awareness and nominal commitment ("really a small percentage") to the Asian American community. Whereas Kazu attributed members' awareness of discrimination to their coalescing into a support group, Celeste attributed their awareness to their fundraising efforts and their general familiarity with Asian American issues ("know about the internment"), despite the organization's non-partisan stance. Their rationale for the evidence of members' social conscience prevents them from completely dismissing an organization with a seemingly dubious record of community service and social responsibility.

Deterritorialized Community

Because the AAPN's members reside and work throughout Los Angeles County and portions of Orange County, California, they rely on a complex social network to foster a sense of community. As a major hub in the social network, the AAPN provides members with opportunities for greater social interaction through sponsored programs, organizational meetings, and unofficial organizational gatherings where members meet for lunch or dinner and a recreational activity. Given the rise of transnational political and economic forces, changes in mobility and communication technology also allow these social networks to persist, despite the growing absence and weakening significance of geographically fixed locations.[5] Hence, the lack of a territorialized community for these professionals does not negate the existence and vitality of a spatialized community sustained through a complex social network.[6]

This deterritorialized community of young Asian American professionals is collectivized through shared markers of identity that are not limited to racial self-categorization. Rather, their Asian American identity rests on a complex overlapping of local, national, and international social networks that primarily comprise other Asian American professionals. The AAPN's directors and members implement adaptive strategies shaped by these social networks in an attempt to counteract potential occupational, racial, and age-based barriers in the professional and managerial positions of their respective occupational sectors. Professionals tap into this network to secure mentors, advice on the best methods to maneuver for promotions in their respective fields, possible job opportunities, moral support, and professional references.

The AAPN is the Southern California chapter of a nationally based young Asian American professional organization, the Asian American Coalition of Professionals (AACP), with more than ten affiliates across the country. Although their regional (local) and national affiliates are based on official associations, their international social networks stem from relationships cultivated either while in the United States or when they attended study tour programs in East Asia, as was the case for nearly half of the professionals interviewed for this study.

The professional and personal lives of two AAPN members, Terence Ho and Maria Wong, best illustrate how regional, national, and international social networks reinforce the salience of a deterritorialized community and can become a reliable resource for professional development. A 1.5-generation Chinese American from Ohio, Terence enrolled in the Taiwanese Study Tour Program the summer after he graduated from high school. Among the people he befriended were a Southern California woman named Maria and a Northern Californian man named Wei-Liang Chu. When he completed the program, Terence moved to Michigan to begin employment at a *Fortune-500* company. While in Michigan, he maintained contact with Maria and Wei-Liang and joined the local chapter of the AACP. After a year of working seventy hours a week, he decided to leave his high-paying job to become an entrepreneur by using his family contacts in Asia and his friendship networks from the study tour and the AACP. His company would help American service corporations gain access to the Asian and Asian American market.

To gain this access to the Asian American market, Terence moved to Los Angeles, because the city had emerged as a hub for Asian and Asian American commerce in the United States. Several theorists and economists discuss how global restructuring has changed the character of certain cities, such as Los Angeles. Saskia Sassen (1991), an urban planner, insists that certain cities, such as Los Angeles, have become global cities. Instead of serving to integrate regional and national entities, these cities have emerged as centers of the new global world order. These global cities vary in their specific functions, but they generally are the hubs of world trade; house the headquarters of transnational companies; and serve as financial centers. Their main role centers on coordinating the international flow of capital, production, and trade. While Sassen described New York, London, and Tokyo as leading examples of global cities in the 1980s, one can see that Los Angeles had made the transition to a global city by the 1990s.[7]

Through the Michigan chapter of the AACP, Terence contacted the AAPN, the Los Angeles chapter, to ease his transition into the city. Within a few months of his arrival, he had co-founded a company with Wei-Liang and other study tour alumni. Because his business venture required him to travel frequently to East Asia, he maintained contact with study tour alumni employed in the region. Maria was one of those friends. Unlike Terence, Maria pursued various job opportunities first in Taiwan, then in Hong Kong. Although she did not intend initially to go to Hong Kong when she decided to work temporarily in Asia, the city became a viable alternative to Taiwan when she discovered that a childhood friend was employed there. Eager to pursue additional work experience, she moved to Hong Kong after her friend offered encouragement and temporary accommodations until she could secure full-time employment. While in Hong Kong for business, Terence told Maria that when she returned to Southern California, he would introduce her to the AAPN, an organization that had been formed during her absence. In the fall of 1995, Maria returned to Southern California and became involved with the AAPN through Terence's insistence and in an attempt to familiarize herself with a city that had changed during her four-year absence.

The collective experiences of these people resonates in the experiences of many of the AAPN members. Their travel and work-related relocations in the United States and the Pacific Rim appear to affirm and confirm their self-identity as Asian Americans, despite the differences in the circumstances surrounding each relocation. These networks enable members to construct a spatially salient community without jeopardizing individual members' desire to affirm their membership in the amorphous and theoretically fractured Asian American community.

Cultivating Professional Success

Socializing with Asian American professionals in other industries extends one's professional networks. John Chow, a second-generation Chinese American and a founding member of the AAPN, explained the potential benefits of an extensive social network:

> If I just keep in contact with the same number of people that I do right now, at least half have a head on their shoulders, they're gonna be goin' somewhere. . . . I think, somewhere along the line, [the network] would bode well for anybody involved in the current network. I will benefit from that as well, being in the middle of it for so long.

Later in the interview, he discussed how a social network of successful professionals can serve as an effective resource for personal and professional gain. The network can be a source of job and investment referrals, legal and medical advice, and potential investors in his anticipated entrepreneurial endeavors. Although John's expectations are a specific example of how social networks can provide professional empowerment, he nevertheless illustrates the opportunistic perspective shared by many other AAPN members.

Although possibly attributable to self-centered egotism, this opportunistic perspective also reflects the corporate mentality shared by a significant portion of the membership. Although different professions have different organizational cultures and dynamics, success in nearly all fields is partially dependent on one's professional networks and the mentors one secures. Sometimes who one knows is just as important as—if not more important than—what one knows. The sociologist Robert Jackall (1988) has examined how professional networks in a large American corporation are crucial to managerial success. These alliances, which "are rooted in fealty and patronage relationships" (Jackall 1988: 38), are encouraged. Conforming to informally understood guidelines, professionals are expected to "choose one's social colleagues" selectively to leverage their own advancement or to garner protection in times of need (Jackall 1988: 39). Although limited to alliance-building within one's work environment, the opportunistic agenda of Jackall's managers is comparable to that of John and other AAPN members who rely on regionally and nationally based social networks.[8] While Jackall addresses the importance of maintaining professional networks, a study commissioned by the executive-search firm Korn/Ferry International discusses the importance of securing mentors and role models. In 1988, Korn/Ferry International, in conjunction with the Columbia University Business School, conducted a study of the highest-paid, most successful minority executives in corporate America. Among the study's findings was that securing role models and mentors played a pivotal role in the eventual professional success of these executives.[9]

Some professionals attribute their ability to overcome their reluctance to approach more established professionals for guidance partly to their involvement as active leaders in the AAPN. Although many of the association's directors and event organizers had prior experience as undergraduate student leaders, involvement in the AAPN allowed them to develop effective leadership strategies and managerial skills to program successful events or strategize operationally viable methods to sustain the growth of the nonprofit organization. These skills were crucial for AAPN leaders to cultivate, because the organization's primary source of income is corporate sponsorships. Brad Chan, a member and former director, best articulated how some directors view the AAPN as a vehicle for personal and professional growth:

> Professionally, it definitely helped me, because I always had a problem. I hate talking to people who are older than me. I meet a fifty-year-old professional and I just have nothing in common. In respect, that I get introduced to these people, now or I actually approach them for money. That's really forced me to understand how to relate with my "superiors," per se. So on a professional level, AAPN has certainly helped me learn how to deal with successful people out there.

Working on behalf of the AAPN, directors and event organizers are given a rare opportunity to interact with successful professionals in a capacity that usually is unavailable to them in the workplace, where they may be placed in lower-middle-management positions, or in more established professional organizations. The latter have directors who are generally older and better established in their careers. Hence, they might not allow younger, less-experienced professionals to be put in positions that could jeopardize their procurement of funds. Overcoming one's self-imposed intimidation of established upper-management professionals better enables one to approach and secure mentorships and professional advice from these people, a strategy that Jackall and the Korn/Ferry study determined was one of the best for achieving professional success.

Asian American Awareness

These professional networks also engender greater Asian American awareness and solace, a point that was best articulated by Miranda Tam, who is pursuing a career in entertainment, and Winnie Fong, an advertising executive. Miranda, a second-generation Chinese American, confided:

> AAPN is a great place to meet people who are doing a lot of different things... [to] show people what Asian Americans really are *doing* right now. They're U.S. assistant attorneys. They're [television] network execs. They're entrepreneurs. They're going to business school. These are things that are achievable. And, I think that we can be those role models. I mean, however big or small.

Whereas Miranda was inspired by the variety of professions pursued by her age peers, Winnie found solace in the company of those who were employed in careers that are not conventionally pursued by Asian Americans:

It was nice to see Asians who weren't necessarily engineers and scientists *(laughs)*. Well, it's just such a *relief* to know that I'm not the only one. I wanted to hear what their experiences were in the work world as Asians. I thought it would be interesting to hear their experiences and see if they were similar to mine because *(sighs)* a lot of those people were not necessarily doctors, lawyers, and engineers. I think those specialties have different things that they have to overcome versus someone who is just in the "business world." And, you know what? I had always hoped that someone would help me [when I graduated from college]. Maybe I would've not been as lost for a while. So I always felt like it would be nice to give back.

The successes and diversity of conventional and unconventional professions pursued by age peers inspired these women and other professionals to strive within their own professions. Whether intentionally or unintentionally, the AAPN provides a forum that replicates the competition that these professionals have encountered since childhood. In an effort to conform to upper-middle-class standards of success, they succumbed to various pressures imposed by peers, teachers, and mentors who were influenced by the model-minority myth. These pressures were compounded by the high expectations of their well-educated immigrant-generation parents, who were eager to see their children replicate or exceed the middle- to upper-middle-class standards of living that they had provided for their families in the United States.

Many Asian American professionals echoed Winnie's and Miranda's stated interest in serving as mentors not only for one another, but also for younger Asian Americans. Several professionals and community leaders have stressed that AAPN members are at an age at which they can make the most direct and compelling impact on communities in need. Unlike the more established professionals, AAPN members may have both the time and age proximity to contribute their energy to helping youth. In response to this interest from the AAPN membership and leadership, a mentorship program was established in 1998 that pairs AAPN professionals with Asian American college students in Los Angeles and Orange counties. Hence, not only does the organization provide opportunities for professionals to secure mentors among age peers and more established professionals; it also gives them the option of becoming mentors to other Asian Americans. Among all of the variables offered by the these professionals to justify or explain their involvement in the AAPN, community service is the most directly motivated by a sense of Asian American identity.

However, the pan-Asian dimension of many of these professionals' identity formation did not occur until college or their socialization with other Asian American professionals at work, in graduate school, or through professional organizations such as the AAPN. For the few who developed panethnic affinities in college, their experiences were characterized primarily by friendships with other Asian Americans in non-activist contexts. For the few who developed panethnic affinities in graduate school, their experiences resulted primarily from friendships arising from involvement in pan-Asian student activist organizations. Unfortunately, the disparity in activism lacks any consistently definitive variable. Meanwhile, the primary source of panethnic identity formation for nearly 75 percent of the professionals interviewed for this study was interaction with Asian American professionals at work or in professional organizations such as the AAPN. <u>Many of them adopted the term "Asian American" uncritically because it is commonly used among their Asian American professional peers.</u>

At times, professionals used the terms "Asian American" and "Asian American community" to describe themselves, their peers, and their community, despite skepticism about the existence and cohesiveness of such social categories. Winnie Fong is one such skeptic. Having been raised in the Midwest in a predominantly European American community, she did not interact with other non-Chinese Asian age peers until she moved to Southern California after graduating from college. At one of her jobs she was befriended by a Vietnamese American co-worker, who encouraged her to socialize with the other Asian Americans in the company. After a few months, this co-worker encouraged Winnie to join the AAPN. Curious about Asian Americans in general, and open to new experiences, she chose to socialize with her Asian American co-workers and to participate in some AAPN events while maintaining her friendship networks with non-Asian co-workers. Although she identifies more as Chinese than as Asian American, she said:

> You know what? I think "Asian community" for me is something that was defined by other people 'cause I probably just thought of it as helping young Asian professionals like me. I don't necessarily, I guess, define them as a community, but other people do. Other people in [the AAPN] call it the Asian community. Always talking about giving back to the Asian community. So, I probably used that term because I hear it so much.

Hence, Winnie's growing involvement in the <u>AAPN led her to adopt a panethnic sensibility "because</u> I hear it so <u>much." Willingness to assert the existence of an Asian American collectivity despite uncertainty or ambiguity about its existence is endemic among a majority of the professionals.</u> This contradiction is not problematic for these professionals because their lives are characterized by an ambiguously constructed racial self-identity and conflation of their internalized American and Asian ethnic identities.

Meanwhile, in the sentence "Always talking about giving back to the *Asian* community," Winnie specifically refers to the directors of the AAPN, who consistently emphasize the importance of community service among the membership. Because Winnie's circle of friends in the AAPN at the time of the interview was primarily limited to directors and associate directors of the organization, she was most likely influenced by the organization's leaders. Given this influence, one would assume that the directors—the advocates of the membership's involvement in the Asian American community—have a clear definition or understanding of the Asian American community. Ironically, many of the leaders are equally baffled. Yet despite this uncertainty, the leaders and numerous other professionals who experience similar uncertainty focus their efforts and energy on helping other Asian American professionals primarily because this is the group with which they can best identify and empathize. Because their interaction with other Asian Americans is primarily limited to socialization with other Asian American professionals, they are more prone to develop a biased and privileged Asian American identity. Given this bias, can they possibly generalize their commitment to the larger Asian American community—

a large percentage of whom serve, advocate on behalf of, or belong to the under-privileged immigrant population?

Because many of the professionals are unfamiliar with current policy changes affecting Asian Americans and have limited interaction with Asian Americans who are not professionals or kin, they rarely question their ability to succeed unhindered by discrimination. Fortunately, their involvement in race-specific professional organizations such as the AAPN does occasionally expose them to perspectives that either challenge or cause them to reflect on their idealistic preconceptions. The AAPN schedules occasional seminars at which Asian American leaders in various industries are invited to offer speeches and engage in discussion with members about their professional pursuits and achievements. One such seminar focused on advocacy and politics in the Asian American community. Registration was limited to fifty members to allow maximum interaction with the five invited Asian American politicians and community leaders, including Matt Fong, California's State Treasurer, and Angela Oh, then a member of the U.S. Commission on Race. Each leader was placed with ten AAPN members, and all participants discussed topics ranging from Asian American representation in politics to Asian American politicization.

The members noted that this seminar gave them their first opportunity to familiarize themselves with Asian American issues and politics. This opportunity is one of several offered by the AAPN to educate members about issues that could affect them. While other AAPN seminars focus on specific industries and how one should maneuver to maximize one's success in the face of possible adversity, this political-advocacy seminar educated members about pressing issues in the larger Asian American community, such as the variable reception of Asian American presence in American society. Hence, occasional exposure to Asian American community, professional, and political leaders at AAPN events can minimize these professionals' idealism of race in American society. At the same time, however, these leaders' mere presence and personal successes can also fuel members' optimism. The precedent set by these accomplished men and women is a source of inspiration for members who are optimistic of their chances for professional success.

In their speeches and discussions with the membership, these leaders stressed social responsibility and encouraged the young professionals to serve the Southern California Asian American community. Aware of the importance of service to the community, the AAPN develops programs for members to volunteer their time at a community-service activity or contribute money at a fundraiser for a designated Asian American service agency. Sometimes non-AAPN members are drawn into these altruistic endeavors through members' social networks. Thus, young professionals' efforts to increase aid to community agencies is not limited to AAPN members. Even though their individual commitments vary in terms of sincerity and impact, their collective attempt to be socially responsible to a larger Asian American community is welcomed and appreciated by receiving agencies. Hence, although class polarization and segregation can undermine panethnic solidarity (Espiritu and Ong 1994), acts of social responsibility spurred by leaders and peers can partially alleviate the damage wrought by class privilege.

Asian Americans can collectively achieve personal and professional success outside the ethnic-enclave community without suppressing or denying their racial identities. AAPN members have shown that their efforts to achieve success depend on their membership in a supportive and dynamic, deterritorialized community of Asian American professional peers. The lack of a clearly delineated, physically tangible area in which to congregate and interact, such as an ethnic enclave, does not weaken this community's vitality. Instead, advances in communication and transportation technology allow these professionals to rely on an expansive social network rooted in friendship, kinship, and work- and school-related relationships that traverse local, national, and international boundaries to support and strengthen their deterritorialized community. The versatility and breadth of these Asian American social networks illustrate the perceived benefits of being a member of a community of young Asian American professionals, as well. Membership offers benefits and opportunities that are unavailable or inaccessible through non-Asian American social and professional networks. Thus, to maximize their success, many of these professionals rely on both Asian American and non-Asian American networks.[10]

The AAPN members use their professional identities and the skills, knowledge, and personal networks they have established and fostered through their involvement with the association to empower themselves personally and professionally. Despite their opportunistic objectives, they all eventually develop an Asian American identity that is specifically rooted in professionalism and classism. Although a majority of the members surveyed had a fair understanding of their Asian American identity, they, too, eventually developed a similarly biased version of a racialized identity. However, despite this distinction, members and directors do attempt to aid less privileged Asian Americans in a show of their commitment to being social responsible to the Asian American community in Southern California. Thus, although this community of young professionals embodies the model-minority myth, it also contradicts some of the stereotypes associated with this appellation. Despite their general lack of awareness and understanding of American racial dynamics, these professionals' decision to socialize with other Asian American professionals, join an Asian American organization, and occasionally serve the larger Asian American community through volunteerism or donations suggests they are not ignorant of the limits of their individual efforts to achieve professional success in American society and that they not unwilling to aid the Asian American community as a whole. Although they may embody the model-minority myth, the myth does not define them.[11]

Notes

1. The name of the organization has been changed.

2. During the research period, I became a director and board member of the AAPN. For a discussion on the pedagogical ramifications of this experience, see Ho 2000.

3. The 1.5 generation is defined as those who were born overseas but raised primarily in the host country.

4. Such organizations are typical of such exclusionary upper-class social clubs as certain country clubs and the Junior League (Aldrich 1988; Ostrander 1984). Although the AAPN is not as exclusive as these upper-class social clubs, the organization provides similar services, enforcing class exclusivity for its members.

5. The salience of geographical territories is weakening in relation to the growing significance of spatial configurations. But the significance of geographical territories to people's sense of self and community will never disappear, because people continue to ground their experiences conceptually partly on social interactions and experiences rooted in a physical location.

6. Gupta and Ferguson argue that "in the pulverized space of postmodernity, space has not become irrelevant; it has been reterritorialized in a way that does not conform to the experience of space that characterized the era of high modernity. It is this reterritorialization of space that forces us to reconceptualize fundamentally the politics of community, solidarity, identity and cultural difference" (1997: 37).

7. See the chapter on Los Angeles in Soja 1989 for further support of this assertion.

8. Similar use of social networks is evident in other communities. For example, the welfare mothers studied in Stack 1974 illustrate how social networks can be used for personal benefit in securing both basic goods and potentially expensive services, such as child care.

9. Many in the study were African Americans whose role models and mentors were primarily European American men.

10. This is not to imply that these networks are exclusively Asian American or non-Asian American, for individuals of all races can be included in both networks.

11. For a more critical discussion of the model-minority myth and the complicity in these professionals' actions, behavior, and experiences, see Ho 2000.

References

Aldrich, Nelson W. 1988. *Old Money: The Mythology of America's Upper Class.* New York: Vintage Books.

Espiritu, Yen Le, and Paul Ong. 1994. "Class Constraints on Racial Solidarity among Asian Americans." Pp. 295–321 in *The New Asian Immigration in Los Angeles and Global Restructuring,* ed. Paul Ong, Edna Bonacich, and Lucie Cheng. Philadelphia: Temple University Press.

Gupta, Akhil, and James Ferguson. 1997.*Culture, Power, Place.* Durham, N.C.: Duke University Press.

Ho, Pensri. 2000. "(E)rasing the Model Minority? Racial Ideology Among Young Urbanized Asian American Professional." Ph.D. thesis, University of Southern California, Los Angeles.

Jackall, Robert. 1988. *Moral Mazes: The World of Corporate Managers.* New York: Oxford University Press.

Newman, Katherine S. 1988. *Falling from Grace: The Experience of Downward Mobility in the American Middle Class.* New York: Vintage Books.

Ostrander, Susan A. 1984. *Women of the Upper Class.* Philadelphia: Temple University Press.

Sassen, Saskia. 1991. *The Global City: New York, London, Tokyo.* Princeton, N.J.: Princeton University Press.

Soja, Edward W. 1989. *Postmodern Geographies: The Reassertion of Space in Critical Social Theory.* London: Verso.

Stack, Carol. 1974. *All Our Kin: Strategies for Survival in a Black Community.* New York: Harper & Row.

CHAPTER 9

Mary Yu Danico

Internalized Stereotypes and Shame: The Struggles of 1.5-Generation Korean Americans in Hawai'i

I didn't like being Korean at one time, but instead of ignoring it, I decided that I wanted to change that perception so I wouldn't feel bad about being Korean.

—Sean Chung, research field notes, May 1997

In the early 1970s, Charles Kim, a reporter for *Koreatown*, the English edition of the *Korean Times/Hankook Ilbo*, wrote an article describing people like himself who were neither first- nor second-generation Korean Americans as the "1.5" generation, or *ilchom ose* (Koh 1994). In the past decade, interest has been growing in the identities and affiliations of Korean immigrants and of 1.5- and second-generation Korean Americans. Although the majority of Korean Americans immigrated to California and New York after the 1965 Immigration Act, according to the 1980 and 1990 U.S. Censuses, the history of Korean immigration to the United States began in Hawai'i (Lee 1993; Patterson 1988, 2000). Thus, the ethnic identities of Korean Americans vary by geography, culture, and generation.

When Koreans moved to Hawai'i after the 1965 Immigration Act, many immigrated with their children, who are sometimes called the 1.5 generation (or 1.5ers). As child immigrants, they are demographically first-generation Korean Americans, much like their parents. Through the process of relocating from traditional Korean culture, and negotiating with the host culture, the 1.5 generation creates a "separate" group identity that is different from the identities of the first and second generations (Danico

1999a, 1999b). Since the inception of this "1.5 generation" label, discussions have surfaced about the ideal definition of the 1.5 generation and the factors that characterize it. The 1.5ers have been described as those who immigrated during their formative years (Hurh 1980; Koh 1994; Ryu 1990) and even those who are "native-born" (Park 1999). Hence, the term "1.5ers" has been used to describe all Korean Americans who are not considered immigrants. Such generalizations minimize the complexity of the generation by merely categorizing them as the *other* Koreans. The 1.5 generation Korean Americans have their own position on how they should act in a given situation (Danico 1999a). Consequently, their ethnic identities are negotiated, created, and questioned depending on the situation (Cerulo 1997; Espiritu 1994; Lal 1983, 1993; Nagel 1994; Okamura 1981; Tuan 1998).

Korean American 1.5ers have different experiences from their parents and from American-born (second generation) Korean Americans. The 1.5ers are Korean-born but were raised in Hawai'i and therefore are bicultural, bilingual, and are able to negotiate between their ethnic boundaries. What makes these 1.5ers distinct, however, is their lack of identification and their consciousness of not being first or second generation but "somewhere in-between." The feeling of being "neither"—and, to some extent, invisible—has demarcated 1.5ers from other Korean Americans in Hawai'i (Danico 1999a).

A variety of factors shape ethnic identities and communities in Hawai'i. Depictions and perceptions of Korean Americans are based largely on the stereotypes and impressions that the larger local community has of first-generation Korean Americans and how first-generation Korean American present themselves to the local and Korean community. Consequently, such impressions affect how 1.5-generation Korean Americans identify and define being both Korean American and local in Hawai'i.[1] Stereotypes of Korean Americans in Hawai'i are widespread in the schools and among peers, local media, and non-Korean Americans. They influence 1.5ers to disassociate themselves from other Korean Americans in Hawai'i and create their own Korean American identity and community.

The stereotypes of Korean Americans are largely driven by a perception of Keeaumoku Street and Waikiki as representative of the Korean American community. The larger society holds stereotypes of Korean Americans as aggressive, rude, and hot tempered, and as holding jobs as bar hostesses and taxi drivers. Such stereotypes have branded Korean Americans in general and have had negative consequences for the 1.5ers. The shame and embarrassment they feel because of the stereotypes pushes them away from identifying with "Korean Koreans" to associating with locals and non-Koreans.

Korean American 1.5ers also learn what it means to be Korean American, or "local," from their non-Korean peers at junior high school and high school. In order to disassociate themselves from the stereotypes held by the larger society, they look for alternative ethnic options with which to identify. Drawing on my fieldwork, twenty case studies, and fifty informal interviews with 1.5ers in Hawai'i,[2] I will examine in this chapter how stereotypical perceptions affect 1.5ers' identification with being Korean American. Specifically, I will look at how such impressions foster a desire for 1.5ers to define their own identity and community.

Perceptions of the Korean American Community

Ask any Korean American or local person in Hawai'i where one can find Korean businesses, restaurants, or, more generally, the Korean American community and most, if not all, will point to Keeaumoku Street and Waikiki. Keeaumoku is in the heart of Honolulu, near the Ala Moana Shopping Center and Waikiki, and stretches its way into a residential section of Makiki. The commercial area is a busy part of town where one can find a combination of local and tourist foot and car traffic. More than in other areas of Honolulu, there is a Korean presence along Keeaumoku that is visible even to the non-local eye.

As one walks or drives along Keeaumoku, one sees restaurants, shops, and other businesses with Korean-language signs. Small plazas on Keeaumoku house mostly Korean businesses. Sam Sung Plaza, for example, has become visibly Korean in the past few years. Once, the plaza included the Sam Sung store, a Japanese restaurant, a Japanese book store, a karaoke bar, a cosmetics store, and a Korean restaurant that had no visible sign. Nothing about the plaza distinguished it except the Sam Sung store's reputation for carrying reasonably priced electronics. As the Korean economy developed and tourists started visiting the islands, however, the plaza began to reshape itself. The electronics store was renovated as a department store; a bakery and juice bar, alteration and tailor store, herbal store, and dry cleaner emerged with Korean signs.

What was once an undistinguished shopping plaza has, in the past three years, became more visibly Korean. Keeaumoku itself has become a smaller version of Koreatown in Los Angeles—an area that some locals are starting to call "Koreamoku," although Korean Americans have not adopted this term. The idea of Keeaumoku representing the Korean American community has generated mixed reactions among Korean Americans.

Do Keeaumoku and Waikiki Represent the Korean American Community?

From the early 1970s to the present, Keeaumoku has been known for its restaurants and drinking establishments—or, as locals call them, "Korean bars." These bars employ Korean American and other ethnic hostesses circulate the bar, hook up with male customers, and ask the customers to buy them drinks. The patrons buy drinks for the hostesses and tip the hostesses to sit and drink with them; in some cases, the hostesses receive a percentage of the drink sales.[3] The hostess bars have become such an integral part of the local community that people often equate them with Koreans (thus, the name "Korean bars"). The bars also carry certain connotations. First, they portray Korean Americans—especially women—as sexually loose, as bar-girl types who want to be bought a "drinkie-drinkie." Second, they give the impression that Koreans are primarily involved in a business that is marginally close to prostitution. As a result, a group of first-generation Korean Americans has pressured the press and television media to stop using the term "Korean bars" in news stories. During an interview, a historian at the University of Hawai'i said that the social pressure from the first-generation Koreans resulted in a change in the term "Korean bar" to "hostess bar."[4]

Although the press does not commonly use the term "Korean bar" any more, locals do. Regardless of whether a bar is Korean-owned, the idea of the "Korean bar" is now a part of the larger community's vocabulary.

In the 19 May 1998 issue of the *Honolulu Star-Bulletin*, Bill Kwon, a sports reporter, wrote about the victory of a Korean American golfer. His article sparked anger from the Korean Jaycees. It read:

> They're dancing in the streets of Seoul. And, I imagine, on Keeaumoku [Street] too; especially during happy hour; and Who knows? Maybe there even might be a Club Se Ri on Keeaumoku [Street] some day.[5]

In response to the article, a Jaycee member named John e-mailed the paper's editor, saying:

> We are not exactly sure what Mr. Kwon was trying to express in these sentences, but one can't help but think that all Koreans live on Keeaumoku, or that all Koreans attend "happy hours," or that all Koreans engage in liquor businesses (i.e., "Club Se Ri"). What is most certain however is that Mr. Kwon's comments stereotype Korean Americans as being at least associated with these activities. In effect and in a subtle way, Korean Americans are attributed with socially undesirable characteristics. We sincerely question Mr. Kwon's judgment in making these statements. It is possible that Mr. Kwon was trying to add humor to his article, however, this type of humor is not only offensive to Korean Americans but can lead to racist treatment toward Korean Americans.[6]

Another Jaycee member named Don e-mailed a message saying, "As you can imagine, this is not very culturally sensitive, and is offensive to many Koreans who are disturbed by the association that people make with Koreans and the 'hostess bars' in Hawai'i." The *Honolulu Star-Bulletin*'s editor replied:

> I agree with you. The remarks were offensive and never should have been published. The fact that Bill is of Korean ancestry does not make it acceptable. I apologize and will see to it that those responsible are aware of your displeasure and mine.[7]

Stereotypical comments about Korean Americans such as these are common in Hawai'i. An interviewee named Hilary, a twenty-seven-year-old law student who had immigrated to Hawai'i with her parents when she was two years old, said that she was embarrassed by the stereotype of the Korean bar hostess:

> In Hawai'i, the ongoing thing is that Koreans own hostess bars and that Korean women work in these establishments. The thing is, why do they have to focus on the hostess bars? I mean, there is so much more to the community than the hostess bars, but that is what we are linked to. They never talk about Korean doctors, lawyers, or other professionals. It's always the Korean hostess bars.[8]

Hilary noted that although some of the bar hostesses are Korean, others are Thai, Vietnamese, Filipino, and Caucasian; yet whenever people talk about the bar workers, they single out the Koreans. Such stereotypes give a wrong impression, she pointed out, and perpetuate the image of Koreans as sex workers, which has more negative implications for Korean American women than men. Hilary also said that if there were more positive stereotypes of Korean Americans—like those of Japanese and Caucasians as being rich—the hostess stereotype would not be as bad. The stereotype of Koreans as bar hostesses is only one example of the factors that influence the ethnic identity of 1.5- and second-generation Korean Americans. Newspaper articles and the assumed stereotypes are mere reminders of a label that causes them embarrassment and shame.

Waikiki, a major tourist destination, has also gone through some changes in the past decade. For tourists, Waikiki represents Hawai'i: hotels, shops, restaurants, clubs, and other retail businesses catering to tourists. The International Market Place in the heart of Waikiki has been in business for decades. It consists of small vendors spread throughout an outdoor mall who sell a variety of goods, such as jewelry, Hawaiian artifacts, "aloha wear" (Hawaiian shirts, dresses, surfwear, and sarongs), candles, and other tourist souvenirs. Since the 1970s, this area has housed predominately Korean American vendors who cater to tourists, often selling goods at prices that far exceed the products' worth and haggling with customers so that they feel they've gotten a bargain.

In the 1980s, a proposed new convention center threatened to replace the mall. The merchants, many of them first-generation Korean Americans, demonstrated in front of the International Market Place to discourage construction. Their methods, however, became a point of criticism in the local community. Several things worked against the merchants in their demonstration. First, there was a language barrier: Most of the merchants did not speak English or spoke with heavy accents; thus, they were not able to express their views to the larger community when the news media interviewed them. Second, they used demonstration tactics that were common in Korea but that, to non-Korean eyes, were unsettling. For example, they cut their own fingers to write their protest signs in blood, and cried and screamed in Korean. To non-Koreans, the merchants presented an image of uncivilized, irrational, and barbaric Koreans. Of course, the blood the merchants used to make their signs symbolized the blood and sweat that they had put into building and running their businesses and earning their livings. In the end, the convention center was not built, though it is not clear whether the demonstration played a role in stopping the project.[9]

The image of the Korean American merchants in the International Market Place has influenced tourists' and people's impression that Koreans in Hawai'i are mostly small, money-hungry, first-generation vendors who aggressively "wheel and deal." Although Koreans do dominate the International Market Place, vending is not the only source of income for Korean Americans. For 1.5- and second-generation Korean Americans, such impressions constitute another layer of stereotype that contributes to others' sense of their ethnic identity and another image from which they distance themselves and try to change.

The International Market Place is still in business, but the ethnic composition of the vendors has changed—most notably, through growth in the number of Vietnamese merchants. Although one can still find many Korean American merchants in the mall, Koreans increasingly have been selling their space in the past ten years and taking larger retail space in hotels, shopping complexes, and department stores, and along Waikiki's main strip, Kalakaua Avenue. This is a sign of upward mobility, as the merchants go from small outdoor carts to enclosed retail space. Ten years ago, the primary foreign language spoken and written on the doors of businesses in Waikiki was Japanese. Today, Koreans and Korean signs on businesses have increased because of the increase in Korean tourist shoppers. Recently, however, the influx of Korean tourists has slowed, and it is unclear how this will alter the presentation of shops in Waikiki.

Implications of the Current Korean American Community Image

Although Keeaumoku Street and Waikiki offer the most visible signs of Korean American presence, they are not representative of the heterogeneous community. Korean-owned businesses, retail stores, and restaurants are also scattered throughout Oahu. There are growing communities in Mililani, a suburban area fifteen miles from Honolulu; on Makiki, an area that is about two miles from Keeaumoku Street; and in Kalihi, a working-class area of Honolulu, five miles from Keeaumoku. These areas are often left out of the discussion of Hawai'i's Korean American community. Even less visible in the local and Korean American community discourse is the presentation of non-Korean-focused businesses. An impression exists that only those businesses bearing Hangul (Korean) signs are Korean-owned. Sean Chung, a twenty-nine-year-old administrator who immigrated to Hawai'i with his single mother and brother when he was five years old, noted that the community comprises doctors, chiropractors, lawyers, and other professionals who do not work under Korean marquees. Yet they do not represent how Korean Americans are viewed in Hawai'i.[10]

Aside from the visible signs of a Korean American community, the people who lead the community are a clear reflection of why and how Koreans are presented in Hawai'i. Having Korean signs on businesses can have divergent effects. On the positive side, the signs can attract and call out to first-generation Koreans to patronize businesses. They also send out a message to the predominantly Korean-speaking first generation that one does not need to speak English and can thus communicate effortlessly and purchase what one wants from these businesses. And the signs reflect the message of pride in being Korean and owning a business. They are a marker for the Korean American community that the establishments are owned by Korean merchants and business people who have established themselves in Hawai'i.

On the other side, the Korean marquees may cause some to question whether Koreans tend intentionally to exclude non-Koreans. The local Japanese, Chinese, and Filipino communities, for instance, do not market their ethnicity to the community to the same extent. Businesses that bear Korean-language signs may also have Korean-speaking employees whom locals and 1.5- and second generation Korean Americans perceive to be more cordial to Koreans than to members of other ethnic groups. Pat, a twenty-nine-year-old retail manager who immigrated to Hawai'i with his single mother, brother, and sister when he was seven years old, echoed such impressions when he said:

Koreans have a bad habit of exclusively associating with other Koreans. They don't have a diverse group of friends. There's a distinction between those with a diverse group of friends [1.5 and second-generation] and those without [first generation].[11]

When Pat referred to "Koreans," he meant first-generation Korean Americans. Because the larger community interacts with, and sees more of, the first-generation business community, they may assume that all Koreans are exclusive. The 1.5ers say that the Korean signs and businesses that employ Korean-speaking employees give off an impression that one is not welcome as a customer if one does not speak Korean. Although this is not necessarily the signs' intent—for all businesses want customers, regardless of ethnicity—the Korean business community until now has marketed itself to the first generation without clear consideration of non-Koreans in the local community.

Because it has limited exposure to other Korean businesses and professionals, the larger society has little understanding of the Korean American community. For Korean Americans of the 1.5 and second generations, it is difficult to express positive images of Korean Americans. As Pat said: "It's easier to think about the bad things. We only see the negative image of the Korean culture."[12] The dominant image of the first-generation Korean American community contributes to the division between generations and to the 1.5 and second generations' feeling of alienation.

If we believed the stereotypes and the visible representation of Korean Americans in Hawai'i, we would assume that first-generation Koreans were characteristic of all Korean Americans. The 1.5ers themselves have bought into such stereotypical images. When asked to describe Korean Americans in Hawai'i, 1.5ers called them "materialistic," "hot tempered," "forward," "outspoken," "too much into saving face," "too gossipy," "judgmental," "conservative," "backward," "chauvinistic," and "narrow-minded." When one points out to the 1.5ers that their impressions of Koreans in Hawai'i are not positive, they tend to call on model-minority stereotypes of Korean Americans as being hardworking and dedicated to their families, but the recital of negative characteristics flows more freely (Kim and Hurh 1983).

The significance of these negative images of first-generation Korean Americans lies in the fact that they show that the 1.5ers do not see themselves as "Korean Koreans." When 1.5ers describe the characteristics of Korean Americans, they are describing first-generation Korean Americans or Korean nationals. In this process, the 1.5ers embrace the stereotypical images and come to feel shame and embarrassment about being Korean.

The face of the Korean American community has changed and will continue to transform with each generation. The image of the community, however, is still dominated by how local and mainstream society view Korean Americans in Hawai'i. Unfortunately, the impressions of Koreans are based on stereotypes and images provoked by Keeaumoku Street and Waikiki. As they internalize these stereotypes, the 1.5ers conclude that Korean Americans are a group to be ashamed of. Thus, their understanding of what it means to be Korean American is connected to the larger society's views of Korean American.

Education and Peers

Korean American 1.5ers learn what it means to be Korean American and "local" not only from the larger society's stereotypes but also from their interactions with peers at school. The types of schools 1.5ers attend, and the ethnic compositions of their classes, are closely related to the area in which they live. The limited educational experience of working-class parents makes it difficult for them to see qualitative differences between public and private schools. Still, working-class parents encourage their 1.5-generation children to attend school, graduate, and attend a professional or vocational school or college. Mr. Lee, a fisherman and the father of an interviewee named Jenny (who was a twenty-three-year-old college student who immigrated to Hawai'i at age six with her parents, sister, and brother), said that he always regretted not getting his high-school diploma and pursuing an education. Although he made enough money to send his children to private school, he felt that the most important thing was that his children receive a college education.[13]

Being an "FOB"

Generally, 1.5ers remember vividly what it was like to be "FOBs" ("fresh off the boat") at school, and many 1.5ers reported observing in the early part of their education a significant difference in the way immigrants were treated by locals. They remembered being picked on for their "Fobby" clothes and feeling alienated from other students, which reinforced their desire to become "local" or "American." The pressure to break away from the foreigner image is compounded by the idea that Asian Americans in general are "forever foreigners" (Tuan 1998). Language was a distinguishing factor for many Korean American 1.5ers at school. Their inability to communicate with non-Koreans and their Korean accents triggered teasing by their peers, which affected their self-esteem. Travis, a twenty-eight-year-old banker who had immigrated to Hawai'i at age nine with his parents, two brothers, and a sister, recalled: " When I was younger, I was insecure about my surroundings, and I became embarrassed [of my English]. It was around fifth or sixth grade that I became comfortable with others." [14]

Although Korean 1.5ers eventually learn to speak English with little to no accent, they carry memories of feeling ashamed of and embarrassed about their ethnicity. Even when other Korean-speaking students were around, the 1.5ers remained embarrassed about their foreignness. Thus, the memory of being picked on and picked out as "different" has remained. Consequently, many 1.5ers sought friends among non-Koreans and locals, who in turn influenced their understanding of what it meant to be local and Korean American, not "Korean Korean."

From elementary school to high school, Korean American students were always around, but, like other 1.5ers, Jenny K., a twenty-five-year-old college student who had immigrated to Hawai'i with her parents when she was seven years old, did not pay much attention to other Korean Americans until high school. She explained:

They were too "cliquey"; they only spoke Korean, hung out with Koreans, and isolated themselves from others. We did not want to hang out with "just" Koreans, particularly those at our schools. We wanted to blend in with the rest of the school and wanted to associate with the local students.

Korean Americans who immigrate during their high-school years face another problem: Although most are bilingual (with accents), they are not bicultural, and they are not able to relate to the local culture or to what it is like to grow up in Hawai'i. Thus, Korean 1.5ers treated them as they did other first-generation Korean Americans. The stereotypes of the first generations are then given to all Korean Americans by the 1.5ers, and they distance themselves from other Koreans in attempt to fit in with the dominant group. Such beliefs hindered 1.5ers from fostering relationships with other Korean Americans and perpetuated the internalized shame of their own ethnic group.

Befriending Local Peers

To get away from the stereotypes of Korean Americans in Hawai'i, 1.5ers tended to develop close relationships with local students, often believing that they had to make a choice between hanging out with Koreans or with non-Koreans. Because the 1.5ers saw all Koreans as the same, they could not view other 1.5-generation Korean Americans as similar to them or as different from the first generation, so they looked to non-Korean groups at school to befriend. As Chris, a twenty-five-year-old banker who had immigrated to Hawai'i at age five with his parents and three brothers, recalled: "I opted to hang out with the 'nons.'" Among the 1.5ers who chose non-Koreans as friends were those who tried to pass as members of the dominant group, whom many 1.5ers in Hawai'i at the time saw as Japanese Americans. Pat recalls wishing that he was Japanese: "In intermediate and high school, I wanted to be [local] Japanese 'cause it's the respected race in Hawai'i. Because everyone's name was Japanese, and Japanese were more Westernized. Chinese and Koreans were refugee, like."

The experiences of these 1.5ers reflect the division between immigrants and locals and the ethnic stratification that exists in Hawai'i. Pat's experience reflects not only the dichotomy between locals and immigrants, but also the ethnic stratification that existed in his school. To be a part of the dominant "local" group, one had to be Japanese or have Japanese students as close friends.

The pool of potential friends is, of course, largely determined by the ethnic composition of each school. The 1.5ers who attended private schools had mostly non-Korean friends, largely because few Korean Americans were fellow students. But the internalized stereotypes of Korean Americans also affected the 1.5ers choice of friends. Hilary, for example, said that most of her school friends were Chinese, Japanese, or haole[15] but admitted that her own stereotypes of Korean Americans hindered her interest in fostering relationships with other Koreans. She never spoke Korean at school, she said, and in fact was often taken for Chinese. "I get mistaken for Chinese all the time," she said. When 1.5ers are mistaken for members of other ethnic groups, they rarely correct the error, because they see the error as a backhanded compliment—that is, it implied that they were local, a part of the dominant group, and no longer seen as the outsider.

Private schools shielded some 1.5ers from pidgin-speaking friends (i.e., those who spoke Hawaiian Creole); the 1.5ers who attended public schools had more contact with pidgin-speaking locals and thus were able to construct a positive sense of being local. Some 1.5ers reported learning to speak pidgin, to appreciate and understand the different peoples and cultures of Hawai'i, and to take pride in belonging to Hawai'i's multicultural population. Belonging to and identifying with local culture allowed them to dismiss their Korean ethnicity. For those who attended public schools, it was easier to identify with being local than "American." Under their environmental conditions, it was more beneficial for them to appear local than *haole*. Chris said that he could never think of himself as "American," because to him "American meant being white:

> Being white means that assuming everyone is like you. Your impressions are everyone's impression. Even when there are five blacks present, you assume your perception of the world is shared by all. Whites see differences as quaint, as if the "culture I'm used to is the standard we measure things against."

Chris's explanation of race relations in Hawai'i is influenced by his belief that race relations are an issue between white people and people of color. His observations of the socioeconomic hierarchy put the whites at the top; thus, he explained that the issues go beyond race. Because his peers at school were non-Koreans, Chris says, "I think of myself as local first, Asian American second, and Korean last. I think it was when I went to Korea that I realized I wasn't like them. When I went to the mainland, I wasn't like [the other Asian Americans] either." Dan, a twenty-seven-year-old travel agent who had immigrated to Hawai'i with his father when he was seven years old, also identified with locals when he was in school. At McKinley High School, all of his friends were local, he says, and he was closer to them than to his own family. His local friends took him in, fed him, let him sleep at their homes, and introduced him to their families. Consequently, he adopted pidgin as his second language and switched from pidgin to English to Korean.

For some Korean 1.5ers, having pidgin-speaking local friends brought about a greater appreciation for local culture. Others, however, interpreted speaking pidgin as a sign of lower social class and level of education. Such attitudes among Korean American 1.5ers cross class lines. It appears to matter less which social class a 1.5er comes from than whether he or she had close relationships with pidgin-speaking locals in school. Hilary said that she had never spoken pidgin and that when she was in high school, she believed that pidgin-speaking locals were ignorant, poor, and uneducated.

Other 1.5ers say that the way schools segregate native English speakers from non-English speakers establishes the foundation for negative stereotypes. According to Mark, a twenty-five-year-old entrepreneur who immigrated to Hawai'i at age five with his parents and sister:

> I think intermediate school is more of a factor. There is the age factor, like the English as a Second Language [ESL] students stay with Korean and have less to do with Western

culture. With ESL, you isolate the Koreans and make them feel like they're less worthy in class. Like they are stupid, and the negative stuff weighs more on them. If you can go to the regular classes, you're likely to learn more and improve self-pride because you're forced to learn. ESL is backwards; they speak Korean or their own languages [in class].

Korean American 1.5ers at this point in the process have not consciously embraced their 1.5 ethnic identity. Thus, their understanding of what it means to be Korean American and local stems from their experiences from the larger local community and peers at school. Some Korean Americans stay at this part of the process, remaining ashamed of their Koreanness and disassociating with their Korean ethnicity while taking on a local or non-Korean Korean identity.

Other 1.5 Asian Americans

As the Korean American 1.5ers learned to negotiate the new ethnic options at school, they also sought out non-Korean friends who could relate to their experience. Because second-generation ethnics and locals have a difficult time identifying with their immigrant experience, the Korean American 1.5ers find that they better identify with other 1.5 Asian Americans. Like them, other 1.5-generation Asian Americans have had the experience of being immigrants; 1.5-generation Asian Americans also can identify with living and coping with first-generation parents, negotiating between two cultures, and feeling marginalized in the larger society.

As a result, Korean American 1.5ers who developed close friendships with other 1.5 Asian Americans express feelings of belonging to this generational identity early on. As Travis said:

At McKinley [high school] I had other 1.5 Cambodian, Vietnamese, and Laotian friends. There was racial tension [between the 1.5ers and locals]. I got along with local Chinese and local Japanese; they were the more integrated group. There were no defined cliques, but I didn't get along with other local Samoan and Hawaiians. They were the dominant group who stuck together.

Because his Asian American friends also came from the 1.5 generation, Travis felt that they could relate to his immigrant experiences of growing up in Hawai'i. He felt tension with other local students because he did not establish close relationships with any of them at that time. He also did not seek out other 1.5-generation Korean Americans as friends, perhaps because of the stereotypes noted earlier—that the Korean Americans in his schools were "cliquey" and exclusive of other ethnic groups, speaking primarily Korean outside class and hanging out only with Koreans. So although there were other Korean American 1.5ers at school, the 1.5ers assumed that they were like all Korean Americans. At this point of their process of becoming 1.5-generation Korean Americans, the 1.5ers have developed a sense of what it means to be Korean American and local, but they do not have a clear understanding of what it means to be a Korean American 1.5 generation. Only when they interact with other Korean American 1.5ers do they discover the uniqueness of their generational identity.

Ethnic stratification in Hawai'i creates a situation in which ethnic minorities experience alienation and shame about their ethnicity. Although members of the second and subsequent generations express feelings of shame about their ethnic group (Espiritu 1994; Kibria 1998; Tuan 1998), they at least have the comfort of knowing that they are "American citizens" and that English is their native tongue. The language barrier and initial feelings of being outsiders are vivid memories for all 1.5ers. In addition to suffering the inner frustration of learning a new language, the 1.5ers are reminded of their language abilities by both Koreans and native English speakers. Hilary said that when she tells people she was born in Korea, "they assume that my English is not as good as theirs and act differently toward me." Hilary's case marks how non-Koreans assume the power to critique those who are not American-born. In other situations, Hilary said, "Americans" act surprised when she speaks English well: "Wow! You don't sound [Korean]; you don't have an accent." Although such comments are meant as "compliments," they demarcate the 1.5ers from the native speakers and first-generation immigrants. Although such criticisms and "compliments" ease as the 1.5ers mature, the stereotypical images and anti-immigrant comments become imbedded in their sense of identity as being non-native, a foreigner, someone different from those born in the United States.

The need to conform to the dominant society and, even more important, to "pass" as an intelligent second-generation or "American-born" Korean often results from shame—specifically, frustration at not understanding English, being treated as "second-class citizens," and feeling alienated from the larger Hawai'i community. Although the 1.5ers I interviewed said that they do not experience these things today, they still observe the difficulties of their parents and other immigrants.

The 1.5ers are also ashamed because, in Hawai'i, Korean Americans are stereotypically depicted as materialistic, hot tempered, pushy, and money hungry. The images of Korean bars and hostesses are the stereotypes that embarrass the 1.5ers the most. Although they know that the "Korean hostess" is a stereotype, the jokes and comments of local friends and the island community reinforce their embarrassment and shame. Although some may argue that stereotypes should not be taken seriously, they have damaging effects on 1.5ers' sense of identity and self-worth. The 1.5ers also are aware that they should not take the stereotypes seriously, but at the same time they cannot help but be disturbed by the depictions of Korean Americans.

Finally, the 1.5ers' experience at school contributes to their shame in being Korean American. From elementary school to high school, 1.5ers experience firsthand how it feels to be outsiders, and they observe how locals treat other FOBs. Having to attend special ESL classes marks them as different from native speakers. Teachers remind them in classes and on their papers that their grammar and overall writing style need improvement, but they discount the problems by saying, "After all, English is not your first language." To avoid the stigma of being immigrants, many 1.5ers avoided contact with other Koreans who were overtly Korean or "Fobby" and presented themselves as Korean American or local. Thus, by disassociating from those who reminded them and others of the existing stereotypes of Korean Americans, they could avoid being perceived by the larger society as "typical" Koreans.

Embarrassment and shame at being Korean American is largely affected by a combination of external forces and the interpretation of these images by 1.5ers themselves. The shame is due in part to 1.5ers' not fully understanding their experiences and how they shaped their sense of ethnic identity. At this part of the process, 1.5ers disassociate from their Korean identity and affirm their Korean American or non-"Korean Korean" and local identity. The conditions at this time create a social environment in which being Korean or an immigrant is not something with which they want to identify. This process is a part of their discovery in becoming a 1.5er.

Notes

1. See Okamura 1994.

2. To meet 1.5-generation Korean Americans, I hung out at Korean businesses (hotels, restaurants, bars, etc.), churches, and organizations. From there, I found respondents through snowball sampling. Interviews were conducted at coffee shops, restaurants, places of business, beaches, and homes. The informal interviews lasted from two to four hours each. The twenty case studies were followed over a period of one and a half years. Using an ethnographic approach, I not only interviewed the subjects but also observed them with family, friends, and co-workers. I was also able to conduct informal interviews with their family and friends. All of the interviews and observations were made between January 1996 and August 1997.

3. From my research field notes (hereafter, field notes) dated February 1996–July 1997.

4. Ibid., May 1996.

5. Bill Kwon, "Pak's Victory Celebration Touches Seoul," *Honolulu Star-Bulletin,* vol. 3, no. 99 (19 May 1998), D1.

6. E-mail, 19 May 1998. The names have been changed to protect confidentiality.

7. E-mail, 20 May 1998. The names have been changed to protect confidentiality.

8. Field notes, August 1997.

9. For a documentary report on the International Market Place demonstrations, see *Fighting for Our Lives,* prod. Alice Yun Chai, video recording (30 min.), c. 1990.

10. Field notes, May 1997.

11. Ibid., October 1997.

12. Ibid., January 1997.

13. Ibid., June 1997.

14. Ibid., May 1997.

15. *Haole* is used in Hawai'i to refer to whites or caucasians. See Hormann 1996.

References

Cerulo, Karen A. 1997. "Identity Construction: New Issues, New Directions." *Annual Review of Sociology* 23: 385–409.

Danico, Mary Yu. 1999a. "The Changing Korean-American Family." Pp. 45–63 in *Till Death Do Us Part: A Multicultural Anthology on Marriage,* ed. S. Browning and R. Miller. Stamford, Conn.: JAI Press.

———. 1999b. "1.5 Generation: A Case Study of the Korean American Jaycee in Hawaii." *Korean and Korean American Studies* Bulletin, vol. 10, nos. 1, 2.

Espiritu, Yen Le. 1994. "The Intersection of Race, Ethnicity, and Class: The Multiple Identities of Second-Generation Filipinos." *Identities: Global Studies in Culture and Power* 1, no. 2–3: 294–73.

Hormann, Bernhard L. 1996. "The Haoles." *Ethnic Sources in Hawai'i: Social Process in Hawai'i* 29: 22–32.

Hurh, Won Moo. 1980. "Towards a Korean-American Ethnicity: Some Theoretical Models." *Ethnic and Racial Studies* 3: 4

Kibria, Nazli. 1999. "What 'Asian American' Means to Me": College and the Identity Pathways of Second-Generation Chinese and Korean Americans." *Amerasia Journal* 25, no. 1: 29–51.

Kim, Kwang Chung, and Won Moo Hurh. 1983. "Korean Americans and the 'Success' Image: A Critique." *Amerasia* 10, no. 2: 3–21.

Koh, Tong-He. 1994. "Ethnic Identity in First-, 1.5-, and Second-Generation Korean-Americans." Pp. 43–53 in *Korean Americans: Conflict and Harmony,* ed. Ho-Youn Kwon. Chicago: North Park College and Theological Seminary.

Lal, B. B. 1983. "Perspectives on Ethnicity: Old Wine in New Bottles. *Ethnic and Racial Studies* 6, no. 2: 185–98.

———. 1993. "The Celebration of Ethnicity as a Critique of American Life: Opposition to Robert E. Park's View of Cultural Pluralism and Democracy." In *Robert E. Park and the "Melting Pot,"* ed. R. Gubert and L. Tomasi. Trento, Italy: Reverdito Edizioni.

Lee, Yoon Mo. 1993. "Interorganizational Context of the Korean Community for the Participation of the Emerging Generation." Pp. 189–202 in *The Emerging Generation of Korean-Americans,* ed. Ho-Youn Kwon and Shin Kim. Korea: Kyung Hee University Press.

Nagel, Joane. 1994. "Constructing Ethnicity: Creating and Recreating Ethnic Identity and Culture." *Social Problems* 41: 152–76.

Okamura, Jonathan. 1981. "Situational Ethnicity." *Ethnic and Racial Studies* 4: 4.

———. 1994. "Why There Are No Asian Americans in Hawai'i: The Continuing Significance of Local Identity." *Social Process in Hawai'i* 35: 161–78.

Park, Kye Young. 1999. "'But I Really Feel Like I Am 1.5!': The Construction of Self and Community by Young Korean Americans." *Amerasia* 25, no. 1: 139–65.

Patterson, Wayne. 1988. *The Korean Frontier in America: Immigration to Hawai'i 1896–1910.* Honolulu: University of Hawai'i Press.

———. 2000. *The Ilse: First-Generation Korean Immigrants in Hawaii, 1903–1973.* Honolulu: University of Hawai'i Press and Center for Korean Studies, University of Hawai'i.

Ryu, Charles. 1990. "1.5 Generation." In *Asian American.* Boston: Twayne.

Tuan, Mia. 1998. *Forever Foreigners or Honorary Whites? The Asian Ethnic Experience Today.* New Brunswick, N.J.: Rutgers University Press.

CHAPTER 10

Lisa Sun-Hee Park

Asian Immigrant
Entrepreneurial Children

Jack, a Chinese American college junior, recalls his early days at his family's restaurant:

> When we were little, we were known as the Fu Shou kids. The restaurant is called Fu Shou. We would create hell. I remember that. We were basically let loose. My brothers and I were known for being really close. Then, in sixth grade—that's when I started working. I started peeling shrimp at the restaurant. Doing all the grunt work and whatever dirty jobs that needed to be done. Little jobs here and there. Like laundry. Me and my brother washed laundry at the restaurant. We washed dishes. Cleaning up and stuff like that. As I got older, I got more responsibilities and less of the grunt work. It was like a second home. During high school, my friends came over all the time to hang out. It was like our own little "Cheers."[1]

This chapter examines the community experiences of Korean and Chinese American adolescents and young adults who grew up in small family businesses.[2] Departing from other immigrant entrepreneurial stories, this study focuses on the children who play an integral yet largely invisible role in these businesses. This chapter seeks to analyze the ways in which children negotiate the connections among work, family, and community. It demonstrates that, by solidifying immigrant children's connection to their parents and ethnic community, the family business helps foster a sense of ethnic identity. In this way, the small family business serves as an extension or embodiment of the ethnic community in the lives of the second generation.

The ethnic community has an important function in the process of immigrant adaptation and mobility. The term "community" may embody geographic, cultural, religious, or political boundaries (Hunter 1974; Suttles 1972;). The community helps to establish the norms that guide the behavior of those who interact within its boundaries. In this regard, the small family business, as a community institution, reinforces the norms of acceptable behavior of Korean and Chinese American community members.

Nancy Abelmann and John Lie (1995: 178) explain that the "home" provides the nurturing environment, while the larger "community" protects the "home." As members of both the family and the larger community, children are integral community participants with significant roles to play. What these roles are and how such responsibility affects adolescents and young adults is a central concern in this study. Elucidating such experiences helps clarify both the ways in which children of immigrants interact with their ethnic community and some of the resulting tensions.

The Small Family Business and Asian American Communities

The immigrant family business plays an integral part within the Asian American community. It is both an economic reality and a symbolic representation of many Asian American communities. This is the case for both Korean and Chinese American communities. Korean Americans have the highest rate of self-employment (24.3 percent) in the United States (Yoon 1997). The Chinese American community hovers just above the national average at 10.8 percent and has a long history of entrepreneurship dating back to the end of the California Gold Rush in the late 1880s (Siu 1987).[3]

Although the majority of Chinese and Korean Americans do not own small businesses, the symbolic representation of Asian Americans as merchants is pervasive. During the Los Angeles rebellion in April 1989, many journalistic accounts of the event identified Korean Americans as a whole as prosperous ghetto shopkeepers (Abelmann and Lie 1995: ix). Because of their image as small family entrepreneurs, Asian Americans were stereotyped as a "model minority" by politicians and others who viewed the unrest in strictly superficial, individualistic terms. Abelmann and Lie (1995: 177) critiqued this view, saying: "Inequalities and divides of class, gender, and race are ultimately meaningless; rugged individualism reigns supreme in this social view. Put simply, people with talent and who work hard succeed, while others do not. Those who fail, then, have no one to blame but themselves."

The reality of most small businesses reveals a different story. The romantic notions to which Abelmann and Lie refer ignore the social structures that limit one's self-employment options, including the ability to mobilize resources such as capital and labor. In addition, quality of education, racial and gender discrimination, intense competition within a small market, and difficult working conditions pose significant barriers to successful self-employment. The strong presence of immigrant entrepreneurs in the United States is partly a result of the productive use of human and physical capital, particularly the use of unpaid family labor (Borjas 1990; Portes 1994). However, the measurable benefits of self-employment are debatable (Light and Bonacich 1988, Portes and Zhou 1993). Asian American entrepreneurs' lives may in fact resemble the life of the real Horatio Alger: He was a frustrated writer who never achieved his own ambitions, not an embodiment of the rags-to-riches novels he wrote (Abelmann and Lie 1995).

However, the rags-to-riches narrative continues to form the foundation of the American dream, and for this reason the Asian American community plays an important part in espousing this ideal. In the United States, the immigrant family business is deeply imbued with sentimentality. Romantic notions of family values, upward mobility, and the model-minority myth cloud the uncertainty, vulnerability, and everyday stresses of growing up in an immigrant entrepreneurial family.

In today's political environment, immigrant family businesses have come to symbolize the "good" immigrant—those individuals with "family values," a solid work ethic, successful children, and no need for government assistance. The good immigrant stands in marked contrast to the "bad" immigrant, who places a burden on the state by using government services, who is vocal about exploitative working conditions, and whose has children who face real problems. As Judith Goode and Jo Anne Schneider (1994: 15–6) explain, "The ideology of the 'good immigrant' affirms the American belief in equal opportunity, which is central to a generalized understanding of democracy in the United States." Through this ideological lens, immigrant businesses symbolize an open society without a rigid class structure in which poor, uneducated immigrants with nothing but their determination can make it in the United States.[4] This image of immigrant businesses reinforces the myth of Asian Americans as model minorities.

Immigrant Entrepreneurial Children and Ethnic Communities

Although it has been largely silent on the role of children, the sociological literature on the importance of family in immigrant entrepreneurial life is well established.[5] Jimmy Sanders and Victor Nee (1996: 235) write, "The family can be viewed as a network of obligations that embodies the social, economic, and cultural investments made prior to immigration, and that immigrants draw on and continue to invest in during the process of adaptation." Family cohesion in an entrepreneurial household is absolutely essential not only for the sake of the family members but also for their livelihood. Family members must get along not only to keep a family unit intact but also successfully to run a family business in which unpaid family labor is a necessity. For many families, impending downward mobility acts as a strong cohesive mechanism. Miri Song (1997: 16) writes, "Experiences of racism, discrimination, and social marginalization could intensify feelings of family solidarity." This effect is exaggerated within immigrant families wherein the "family is often the main social organization supporting the establishment and operation of a small business" (Sanders and Nee 1996: 235).

Asian American communities are largely defined by issues related to work and family. Children of immigrant entrepreneurial families are in key positions to elucidate the complexity of children's relationship to their larger ethnic community. Research by Philippe Aries (1962), Lloyd DeMause (1974), Valerie Suransky (1982), and Viviana Zelizer (1985) indicates that childhood is socially constructed by a variety of seemingly "adult" issues, such as the economy and politics. This is particularly true for minority, poor, and immigrant children, who have fewer buffers from "adult-like" concerns of the larger community (Furstenburg 1990). Financial security, discrimination, and familial stability are worries shared by both the parents and children of entrepreneurial households. Song (1997: 15) corroborates this observation in her study of young Chinese adults who grew up in small family restaurants in Britain: "All the young people in the sample seemed to have a heightened awareness of the precariousness of survival. Most young people were highly aware of being integral to the viability of their take-away business." For these children, the business solidifies their connection to their parents and community and consequently fosters a sense of ethnic identity.

This study demonstrates that businesses play a pivotal role in immigrant families' everyday life. Children who grew up in immigrant entrepreneurial households described a family life built around the business. Their daily activities, career plans, sense of identity, and relationships with family members revolved around the needs of the family business. This is not to say that immigrant entrepreneurial families are simply work-centered. Nor are the relationships found in entrepreneurial families simply family-centered. The stories of the children of immigrants reveal a much more complex, circular tale in which the needs of the business stem from the needs of the family.

To understand better how the business helps define the child's place within the family and community, this chapter documents and examines immigrant children's work in the family businesses. The children's duties as problem solvers and translators will be addressed. Particular attention will be paid to their role as translator, because it is especially revealing of children's place within both the business and the family.

For this project, I focused on two Asian American groups in two different life stages. I conducted forty-three in-depth interviews with Chinese and Korean American adolescents and young adults whose families owned small family businesses while they were growing up.[6] These enterprises rarely had more than two non-family employees, and their main source of labor was family members. Twenty-eight interviewees were female and 15 were male. Their ages ranged from 15 to 24 years old. The initial interviews lasted one to three hours long. I then conducted follow-up interviews that varied from 30 minutes to two hours. In addition to the in-depth interviews, I also facilitated focus groups and conducted participant observation at some of the family businesses.

During this process, I had the opportunity to get to know a number of the children's parents, siblings, and extended relatives. I visited their homes, schools, and businesses. I deliberately incorporated multiple research methods—in-depth interviews, focus groups, and participant observation—to avoid making unwarranted assumptions about groups based solely on the observation of a few individuals. Also, my theoretical considerations are derived from careful inductive, or "grounded," theory (Glaser and Strauss 1967), which starts with observed data and, in stages, develops substantiated generalizations.

Those who responded to my interview requests were almost exclusively Chinese or Korean American. Twenty-one respondents were Chinese (this includes three of mixed Chinese and Vietnamese heritage and two Taiwanese Chinese), and twenty-two were Korean. Despite the limited ethnic diversity of respondents, however, the variation in businesses was great. The largest category was restaurants (nine), followed by dry cleaners (six), but the range included an auto-mechanic shop, a fortune-cookie factory, and a shoe store. Early in the research process, I decided not to narrow the type of business. I found the similarities across the diverse individuals striking. It appears that regardless of the type of work involved, the children shared experiences.

Problem Solver

Although there is some variation in their degree of involvement, most of the children in my study played an integral role at the family's business at one time or another. These children occupied a variety of roles within the family and business, including problem solver and translator (and often both roles at once). Only two of the families I interviewed had the luxury of shielding their children from the everyday duties of the business.

For many, unpaid family labor is essential to business survival (Abelmann and Lie 1995; Light and Bonacich 1988). Such is the case for Trinh's family. Trinh described her duties at her family's restaurant:

> [I do] everything! Just kidding. I am the one who does the organizing. I supervise others when I'm there and wait on tables, ring up checks, and take orders when it gets busier.

Trinh generally works about eight hours on Saturdays, five hours on Sundays, and on occasional Friday evenings when there is an emergency or someone calls in sick. During the summer, she works full time. In addition to these duties, Trinh performs latent tasks. For example, she is the family mediator, a job that is just as important to the daily operation of the business as any other. She said:

> I think I'm the family's therapist, really. I set things straight for my parents and give them my honest opinions of how things can improve at the restaurant, in their lives, with family, etc. After so many years of hell with my rebellion and what not, I try to be a refreshing, peaceful entity to them *(laughs)*, and I try to mediate and give them different perspectives.

Trinh described her adolescent years as "hellish" and filled with constant arguments with her parents, particularly her mother. She recounted those years as a time in which both she and her parents "grew up" and learned from each other. Trinh explained:

> Around that time, we ran into many family problems. I was sixteen or seventeen going through changes on my view of society and this world. I was increasingly rebellious and outspoken. I disagreed with the way she ran things sometimes and offered suggestions. She thought I was "talking back" to her. On top of that, my brother was on the edge of

joining one gang after the other—he was stealing and vandalizing and eventually getting arrested for doing soft-core criminal activities. My father and my mom also went through a realized period of power struggle. My mom was the "queen" of the household, and my dad viewed himself as her servant, somebody she could order around. They got into fights almost every night—sometimes I thought he would kill her. Another time it got so bad that my mom threatened divorce—the second time in eight years—and proposed an ultimatum for me and my siblings to either live here or move with her to the West Coast. In the end, she decided to salvage the family, and my siblings and I got closer and decided to work as a team.

Trinh's feeling of responsibility for the business is intense, largely because the business is seen as a way of bringing and holding the family together. In this way, she feels a deep commitment to ensuring the success of the business. In addition, she feels guilt for her past role in causing stress among the family members. The family business is presented as the solution to their family problems. As the oldest of three other siblings, Trinh expressed a strong sense of responsibility in modeling certain behavior and acting as a mediator in an effort to compensate for her difficult behavior during her teenage years.

The role of mediator or problem solver is common among immigrant children. In addition to their everyday duties, many children are brought into the business particularly during times of trouble. This was evident in Judy's response to my inquiry about her involvement in the family business. She said:

I don't really make any decisions that have to do with running the business—machines or supplies—but a few times, we've had legal problems or just daily customer problems, and they asked me, "Do you think this is the American way?"... Those kinds of decisions started coming when I was younger, but now, as I'm older, they pretty much consult me with a lot of the decisions that come to the store.

I asked how she handled these situations. She explained:

I think I was pretty confident. I had ideas of what I thought was right and wrong. Sometimes, they would just say, "Oh, she's just a kid." But most of the time, they took me seriously. And at times that I thought it was serious enough, I told them that they needed to talk to a lawyer. So we have this unofficial lawyer that we consult with once in a while.

In her capacity as a problem solver, Judy functions as a cultural interpreter. She not only helps solve the problem; she also defines what is and is not a concern. That is, she is often charged with constructing the "definition of the situation" (Thomas 1923). Given the seriousness of many of these issues, Judy displayed a sense of confidence beyond her years.

Robert, a college senior, exhibited similar attributes in his job description:

Generally, day-to-day operations my dad can take care of now. He's got someone working with him now—Carol—who's very good being helpful to him. I tend to take care of things that arise that are problematic that Carol wouldn't know about and my dad wouldn't know about. For instance, what's going on these days is our shopping center wants to move us from where we are in the front of the shopping center because they want to put in a Cubs Food Store or something. So they want to use that whole area. But along with that relocation, we have to make sure that all the legal documents are straight, that they are going to provide all the same things that we had in our store in the new area and that we don't have to pay for any of it. I mean, that's like a two-, three-month-long thing. That's the kind of thing that I would take care of on Sundays, things that would arise during the week that my dad or Carol couldn't take care of.

Robert confided that he feels forced to participate in the daily business operation at a level at which he feels uncomfortable. He described his parents as "dependent" on him and explained that the burden this places on his shoulders is enormous.

I asked him whether he found any sense of enjoyment from working at the store. He replied:

I think now it's more stressful than ever because I know that if I am [going] to have a career and my own life *(laughs)* I can't be this concerned with the store. Right now, I'm really concerned with this move; basically, I'm making sure we're not getting screwed over by the management company. My parents are always calling on me—and rightfully so, because they need help, and they don't have anyone to call when they need help. This should be fine with me, but sometimes it's not. You know, when you're really busy with other stuff, you get this call. It's more stressful now because I know that I have to start my own thing sooner or later. It's just hard because of that weird self-inflicted guilt. And the thing is, I know that they can handle it because they're adaptable people. But there's something in me that says, "What if they can't? What are they going to do?" It's that general guilt. That's what I'm grappling with the most these days. I want to wean myself, and I'm trying, but every time I try to wean myself, something big comes up, like this whole moving thing. My sisters have children, families, jobs, and everything, so they can't put in the time that I can as a college student.

Robert vacillates from one position to another. He feels torn between his obligations to his parents and his own personal goals. His responsibilities are overwhelming, but he is at a loss to find another person willing to accept the duties. In some ways, the buck stops with him—as he is the youngest sibling of the family. The burden is on him to carry his parents and the family business. When asked when he would finally feel at ease, he replied: "Unless they just stop doing the business altogether, which we have begged them to do, I'm never going to stop worrying. It's so annoying."

Later in the interview, Robert lamented his decision to stay in town for college. He had hoped to go away to college and lead a "normal" student life, "where you don't have to worry so much about stuff." Unfortunately, things are never so easy. Judy, whose family owned a dry cleaner, described her involvement with her small family business:

I end up usually doing the counter work. Interacting with the customers. I usually make phone calls if there is any kind of problem or things that have to do with English-speaking people. Even when I'm at school, they usually call me if they have problems.

Judy purposely moved out of state for college. Like Robert, she reported a high level of dependence by her parents. The distance between her hometown and her college minimizes her parents' dependence but does not eliminate it. These days, Judy's parents call only when there is a problem and a mediator is required. In addition, Judy generally finds a list of chores—business- and home-related—waiting for her during visits home.

Those adolescents and young adults who regularly work at the family business generally occupy a "frontstage" role (Goffman 1959). The children are the counter workers, customer managers, or hosts and hostesses. This is generally more so for the women than the men. They take orders, answer the phone, ring up the cash register, and make small talk with customers.

Maria described what she does at her family's restaurant:

> I guess I do the carry-outs, talk with customers, handle the up-front kind of things—like behind the counter, up front, and I take care of the daily accounting. Sometimes I watch the restaurant for my dad. One time he had to go in for hernia surgery, and another time he had to go to my sister's graduation, and somebody had to look after the business.

As the "front person," Maria functions in a variety of roles. She is the family representative at the business, particularly during times of crisis or during special events. Closing the family business is rarely an option, even during serious illnesses. A successful immigrant family business, like businesses in general, requires a back-up or safety net in case of emergencies, and children often fulfill this role. Given the central role of the business in family life, the parents are extremely protective of their business. Consequently, children—not non-family employees—are asked to look after the store in the parents' absence. Such is the case for Kyung Ah's family. She explained:

> Just my parents and sometimes the kids helped out. I think it was always an issue of not trusting other people, or even if it was a relative, not feeling like they could run the business. There was always the sense of proprietary interest. My mom always had to know what was going on.

Just as one carefully screens babysitters, small family-business owners put much care and thought into finding a suitable individual to look after the store, even for very short periods of time. In many ways, the small family business resembles a family member in these situations.

Translator

The role of "front person" brings with it peculiar familial circumstances. Such is the case when children become translators in their role as problem solvers. Status inconsistencies may occur between parents and children in these situations.

Trinh recalled her first experience as her parents' translator.

> I was my parents' translator since the age of eight or nine, when my dad told me to talk to the plumber guy. That was a scary experience 'cause I realized that I knew something more than my dad did. It was a weird, superficial sense of superiority. From then on, I translated most of their legal papers. I remember my mom dragging me to her lawyer a couple of years ago and [telling] me to literally decipher a mass of forty documents for her within the hour. I also talk to my dad's credit-card companies, deal with phone bills, gas bills, etc., etc., etc.

Trinh's "weird, superficial sense of superiority" alludes to the reversal of roles she experienced: For the first time, she understood something that her father did not. She simultaneously feels proud of her newfound authority and unsure of her new responsibility as interpreter. Her senses tell her that something significant has changed in her relationship with her father, but she is uncertain about what this means.

This role-reversal may be particularly difficult for immigrant families because it may compound the powerlessness that many adult immigrants—particularly men—experience as a result of their new status as a minority in the United States. In light of their former position as the male head of a strict hierarchical household in a nation where they were the ethnic majority, adult immigrant Asian American men may feel a greater loss of control.[7]

Robert, whose decision-making duties are considerable, talked about the role-reversal that occurred in this family.

> [My dad] feels like he can't make the decisions because all of a sudden after I got into college, he thinks that he's not going to be good at anything anymore. That's horrible, but I can see him thinking that way.

Once Robert surpassed his father's educational level, he found himself in a role of authority. At the age of eighteen, he found himself in an adult role for which he was unprepared. Furthermore, he had no desire to play this part in this family business. Robert described his relationship with his parents as "stressful." While he understood his role as a child, he never anticipated how the burden of the business would complicate his familial relationships. He was a child with adult-like worries: He was expected to deal with adult concerns at the business but behave as a child with his parents. This balance was particularly difficult to achieve during times of disagreement. Robert explained that he had to present his opinions in a respectful way and comply with his parents' final decision, despite what he might truly think. The boundary between adult and child is at times as complicated as the boundary between work and family.

This was also the case for Kyung Ah. She recalled several instances in which she had intervened as translator:

> The only times I can think of is when there is a misunderstanding between a customer and my parents. Something about just the way my mom was saying something would come off the wrong way, and I would step in if I was there and just kind of explain. . . . I think my mom's English just got worse if she got excited and angry. So I would just step in and be calm and try to settle the situation.

Like her peers, Kyung Ah must mediate in times of stress. She functions as a cultural bridge between her parents and customers. To do this, she must show deference to her parents while exercising her newfound authority as an English speaker.

Jack recalled similar circumstances:

> I handled advertisements, I dealt with lawyers, customers, stuff like that. I think that, as kids of our parents, that was one of our main jobs. I think all of us, not just those of us in the restaurant business. All immigrants.

Jack is matter-of-fact about his translator role. In fact, he viewed this role as a *child's* responsibility. Jack's experience is a telling example of the differences between immigrant and non-immigrant childhoods. Today, growing numbers of adolescents are working in the service economy, where there is a proliferation of part-time jobs requiring little skill and the ability to work at "off" hours (Greenberger and Steinberg 1986). Most of the teenagers in this economy are white, middle class, and suburban, and their employment is no longer motivated primarily by their families' financial need; rather, their income goes toward discretionary purchases (Greenberger and Steinberg 1986). This experience is very different from that of immigrant children, who often are unpaid and work in a family business, where child labor laws do not apply. More important, their labor is not discretionary but required for family survival.

In her study of Chinese immigrant children, Betty Lee Sung (1987: 183) writes that a "reversal in parent–child roles is a frequent occurrence in Chinese American homes, especially those where the parents are not well educated and do not speak English." This role-reversal may be exaggerated within an entrepreneurial setting in which the parent is dependent on the child to provide translation or mediation, often on a daily basis.

The role of the translator requires more than language proficiency. One must also be an astute observer to act as a cultural bridge, particularly in times of stress. Scholars of color have discussed minorities' ability (and necessity) to juggle several spheres of knowledge in order to navigate successfully among different, and sometimes contradictory, worlds (Collins 1990; King 1990). This is also true for immigrant children. At an early age, immigrant children become savvy cultural negotiators. However, costs are incurred in achieving this ability, including the danger that the pressures of an adult role may hinder a child's development (Bronfenbrenner 1986; Burton et al. 1996). There is also concern for the parents' ability to demonstrate authority and adult modeling. A *New York Times* article illustrated this issue: "As more children take on the role of interpreter for those who do not speak English, some social science experts express concern that the practice could interfere with the children's psychological development.... Social workers here say that because children play an adult role in doing the translating, they may grow up too quickly and resent or lose respect for their parents."[8]

This role-reversal is understandably a demeaning and uncomfortable phenomenon for both parties, who must now manage a different relationship.

Negotiating Work, Family, and Community Boundaries

A number of studies of immigrant youths have found that the ethnic community can be used as a resource to improve adaptation (Portes and Rumbaut 1996; Suarez-Orozco 1989; Sung 1987; Zhou and Bankston 1994). The community's function as a "mediator" has positive effects on immigrant families, including adolescents and young adults. Min Zhou (1997: 85) writes:

> Ethnic social structure can sometimes play an important role in mediating between individual families and the large social setting. Immigrant children and parents often interact with one another in immigrant communities. If patterns of interaction are contained

within a tightly-knit ethnic community, these children and parents are likely to share their similar experiences with other children and parents. In this way, the community creates a buffer zone to ease the tension between individual self-fulfillment and family commitment. The community also serves to moderate original cultural patterns, to legitimize reestablished values and norms, and to enforce consistent standards.

Family businesses often serve as a conduit to the larger society for immigrant children growing up in entrepreneurial households. For this reason, the family business parallels the ethnic community in its role as mediator between the family and the larger mainstream society. The small family business helps establish the norms and boundaries of acceptable behavior for immigrant children, who ride the fence between two generations and two cultures but are belong fully to neither. However, these norms may feel overly burdensome for these immigrant entrepreneurial children as they try to negotiate the differing boundaries of work, family, and community. These interviews raise the question as to how much community involvement is too much.

At times, adolescents and young adults viewed their experience with the family business as crossing the line from a "buffer zone" to a battle zone. Their intense shared experience with their parents and other members of the ethnic community at the family business left the children with little room to ease the tension between individual self-fulfillment and family commitment. However, some children in these situations found creative modes of adaptation: They formed tightly knit communities of their own. Using ethnic churches and ethnic organizations such as the Korean Dry Cleaners Association, children of immigrants formed a network and created a routine in which members telephoned one another from their respective businesses to complain about being bored. When asked what she gained from working at her family's family dry cleaners, a college junior said:

> I guess I've always accepted [the family business] as part of what I see as part of my culture. Most of my friends are dry-cleaner kids, and we all had the same experience. We call each other from cleaner to cleaner, "Are you there yet? When are you getting out there?" I ended up spending a lot more time with my Korean friends than my American friends. The schedule was different. All my white American friends would hang out during the day and all the Korean kids had to work until 5 P.M. or 6 P.M. We had to go out afterward.

In this scenario, the respondent is part of a community with shared norms and defined boundaries that helps to "normalize" her experiences. In this way, the burden of the children's responsibilities is shared by the collective.

The respondents' roles as problem solvers and translators are integral to the routine functioning of both the business and the family. For some, the problem-solver role begins early. The accompanying responsibility grows into a sense of burden as the child grows older and his or her role within the business shifts from "helping out" to "working" (Song 1997). As the problem solver, the child becomes a representative of their family, the business, and, at times, the ethnic community. As the cultural bridge between parents, business, and ethnic community and the larger mainstream American society, children feel the burden of their central role. The circumstances require the child to adhere to the ethnic community's norms while interpreting the norms of the larger American society. Within this central role, they must incorporate the expectations of both.

As translators, the adolescents and young adults experience similar constraints. Establishing boundaries between adult and child responsibilities becomes difficult as their roles become reversed. In times of status inconsistency, the children find themselves cautiously exhibiting competence in dealing with a potentially stressful situation, while also showing deference to their parents. For the young people, it is important to remain their parents' children while performing adult-like duties. More than simply fulfilling a familial or business role, the adolescents and young adults understand their position as contributors to their parents' (sometimes fragile) sense of positive self-identity.

Like Evelyn Nakano Glenn's study of Japanese American domestic workers, immigrant entrepreneurs have trouble finding "satisfaction in work that most people consider unchallenging at best and repugnant at worst" and in maintaining "self-esteem and an independent identity in a situation where one is personally subordinated and accorded little respect" (Glenn 1986: 168). The children, then, feel an obligation and a burden to "clean" the "dirty work" (Glenn 1986; Hughes 1971) by ensuring the success of both the business and family. Cleaning other people's underwear, washing dishes, and pumping gas are transformed into a source of pride when these activities are viewed as acts of great sacrifice for the sake of the children. In turn, the children must appear appreciative even as they stagger under the burden of adult-like worries. As cultural mediators, the children appear all too conscious of their delicate role.

For these children, the business solidifies their connection to their parents and community and consequently fosters a sense of ethnic identity. The adolescents and young adults in this study experienced intense involvement with work, family, and community. This study illustrates some of the consequences of community involvement. Although the ethnic community, as embodied in this case by the small family business, can be used as an ethnic resource, it can also produce strains in the lives of children who have few barriers from the adult world.

How immigrant children in entrepreneurial families manage their numerous roles provides important clues to understanding how ethnic communities can contribute to or hinder the children's relationship with their parents—and, consequently, the outcome of their adaptation. This study also emphasizes the immigrant children's role as significant community participants. Children of immigrant entrepreneurial families are not simple bystanders. Rather, they help shape the daily experience of the ethnic community. In fact, they play a pivotal role in connecting the ethnic community and its first-generation members to the larger American society.

Notes

1. "Cheers" refers to a popular television show of the early 1990s about friends who congregate in a local bar.

2. I refer to both adolescents and young adults as "children" of immigrants even though some of the young adults were in their twenties. I do this to highlight their relationship to their parents.

3. According to Yoon 1997, the national average of self-employment is 10.2 percent.

4. In reality, for many immigrants owning a small business is an act of downward mobility. Rather than a source of pride, many small family businesses are a source of shame (Abelmann and Lie 1995; Yoon 1997).

5. See Coleman 1988; Fernandez Kelly and Schauffler 1994; Light and Bonacich 1988; Sanders and Nee 1996.

6. Almost all of the respondents lived in the Midwest.

7. See Nee and Nee 1972: 168.

8. "For Immigrants' Children, an Adult Role," *New York Times* (15 August 1991), C7.

References

Abelmann, Nancy, and John Lie. 1995. *Blue Dreams: Korean Americans and the Los Angeles Riots.* Cambridge, Mass.: Harvard University Press.

Aries, Philippe. 1962. *Centuries of Childhood: A Social History of Family Life.* New York: Alfred A. Knopf.

Borjas, George J. 1990. *Friends or Strangers: The Impact of Immigrants on the U.S. Economy.* New York: Basic Books.

Bronfenbrenner, Urie. 1986. "Ecology of the Family as a Context of Human Development: Research Perspectives." *Developmental Psychology* 22, no. 6: 726–42.

Burton, Linda M., Dawn Obeidallah, and Kevin Allison. 1996. "Ethnographic Insights on Social Context and Adolescent Development Among Inner-City African-American Teens." Pp. 397–418 in *Essays on Ethnography and Human Development*, ed. Richard Jessor, A. Colby, and Richard A. Shweder. Chicago: University of Chicago Press.

Coleman, James. 1988. "Social Capital in the Creation of Human Capital." *American Journal of Sociology* 94: S95–120.

Collins, Patricia H. 1990. *Black Feminist Thought.* New York: Routledge.

DeMause, Lloyd. 1974. *The History of Childhood.* New York: Psychohistory Press.

Fernandez Kelly, M. Patricia, and Richard Schauffler. 1994. "Divided Fates: Immigrant Children in a Restructured U.S. Economy." *International Migration Review* 28: 662–89.

Furstenberg, Frank. 1990. "Coming of Age in a Changing Family System." pp. 147–96 in *At the Threshold: The Developing Adolescent*, ed. S. Shirley Feldman and Glen R. Elliott. Cambridge, Mass.: Harvard University Press.

Glaser, B., and A. Strauss. 1967. *The Discovery of Grounded Theory.* Chicago: Aldine Publishing.

Glenn, Evelyn Nakano. 1986. *Issei, Nisei, War Bride.* Philadelphia: Temple University Press.

Goffman, Erving. 1959. *The Presentation of Self in Everyday Life.* New York: Anchor/Doubleday.

Goode, Judith, and Jo Anne Schneider. 1994. *Reshaping Ethnic and Racial Relations in Philadelphia: Immigrants in a Divided City.* Philadelphia: Temple University Press.

Greenberger, Ellen, and Laurence Steinberg. 1986. *When Teenagers Work: The Psychological and Social Costs of Adolescent Employment.* New York: Basic Books.

Hughes, Everett. 1971. *The Sociological Eye.* Chicago: Aldine-Atherton.

Hunter, Albert. 1974. *Symbolic Communities: The Persistence and Change of Chicago's Local Communities.* Chicago: University of Chicago Press.

King, Deborah. 1990. "Multiple Jeopardy, Multiple Consciousness: The Context of a Black Feminist Ideology." Pp. 265–95 in *Black Women in America*, ed. Micheline R. Malson et al. Chicago: University of Chicago Press.

Light, Ivan H., and Edna Bonacich. 1988. *Immigrant Entrepreneurs: Koreans in Los Angeles, 1965–1982*. Berkeley: University of California Press.

Nee, Victor G., and Brett De Bary Nee. 1972. *Longtime Californ'*. New York: Pantheon Books.

Portes, Alejandro. 1994. "Introduction: Immigration and Its Aftermath." *International Migration Review* 28: 632–9.

Portes, Alejandro, and Ruben Rumbaut. 1996. *Immigrant America: A Portrait*, 2nd ed. Berkeley: University of California Press.

Portes, Alejandro, and Min Zhou. 1993. "The New Second Generation: Segmented Assimilation and Its Variants Among Post-1965 Immigrant Youth." *Annals of the American Academy of Political and Social Sciences* 530: 74–96.

Sanders, Jimmy M., and Victor Nee. 1996. "Immigrant Self-Employment: The Family as Social Capital and the Value of Human Capital." *American Sociological Review* 61: 231–49.

Siu, Paul C. P. 1987. *The Chinese Laundryman: A Study of Social Isolation*. New York: New York University Press.

Song, Miri. 1997. "Children's Labour in Ethnic Family Businesses: The Case of Chinese Takeaway Business in Britain." *Ethnic and Racial Studies* 20: 690–717.

Suarez-Orozco, M. 1989. *Central American Refugees and U.S. High Schools: A Psychological Study of Motivation and Achievement*. Stanford, Calif.: Stanford University Press.

Sung, Betty Lee. 1987. *The Adjustment Experience of Chinese Immigrant Children in New York City*. Staten Island, N.Y.: Center for Migration Studies.

Suransky, Valerie Polakow. 1982. *The Erosion of Childhood*. Chicago: University of Chicago Press.

Suttles, Gerald D. 1972. *The Social Construction of Communities*. Chicago: University of Chicago Press.

Thomas, William I. 1923. *The Unadjusted Girl*. Boston: Little, Brown.

Yoon, In-Jin. 1997. *On My Own: Korean Businesses and Race Relations in America*. Chicago: University of Chicago Press.

Zelizer, Viviana A. 1985. *Pricing the Priceless Child: The Changing Social Value of Children*. Princeton, N.J.: Princeton University Press.

Zhou, Min. 1997. "Growing Up American: The Challenge Confronting Immigrant Children and Children of Immigrants." *Annual Review of Sociology* 23: 63–95.

Zhou, Min, and Carl L. Bankston III. 1994. "Social Capital and the Adaptation of the Second Generation: The Case of Vietnamese Youth in New Orleans." *International Migration Review* 28: 821–43.

Part III

Communities of
Alternatives:
Representations
and Politics

CHAPTER 11

Karen Har-Yen Chow

Imagining Panethnic Community and Performing Identity in Maxine Hong Kingston's *Tripmaster Monkey: His Fake Book*

In Maxine Hong Kingston's 1989 novel *Tripmaster Monkey: His Fake Book*, the stream-of-consciousness narrative of the protagonist Wittman Ah Sing's random thoughts and actions is not a meandering journey to self-identity but a journey that is driven by a purpose outside and beyond Wittman himself. What appears as undirected blending, hybridization, and intertextualization of actions, language, and ritual is a series of negotiations that acknowledges panethnicity as the nature of Asian American community. Wittman's desire to create art in drama ends up enacting community in a play—and further, it enacts community and ethnic identity (as far as such identity is communally formed) *as* performance and play. That is, the novel negotiates the fusion and fission processes operating at multiple levels in the "everyday life" of the budding Chinese American playwright Wittman Ah Sing.

The movement of time in the novel is erratic: Some scenes and dialogues are slowed down and drawn out with much detail, and other sections of the narration, especially the episodes of mythical stories, are chronologically suspended. This invites the narrator and reader to step outside the novel's setting and consider Kingston's epigraph: "This fiction is set in the 1960s, a time when some events appeared to occur months or even years anachronistically" (Kingston 1989: n.p.). Kingston, perhaps intentionally, never explains which events are anachronistic. The erratic timing of the narrative, however, reflects the historically interrupted processes of Asian immigration to America, which has a significant role in Asian American community formation.

Further emphasizing the novel's making of community through individual identity, the first-person discourse represents not only Wittman's thoughts but also the voice of an unidentified, anonymous narrator who performs many functions. These include freely commenting on events and characters, introducing new chapters, foreshadowing later moments in the novel, critiquing the characters, and correcting their views. The first-person narration oscillates with no breaks between Wittman's voice and the omniscient voice. Kingston directed our interpretation of this split narration when, in a 1989 interview in the *New York Times Magazine*, she identified the omniscient narrator as "a woman.... She's always kicking Wittman around and telling him to do this and that and making fun of him.... She's Kuan Yin, goddess of mercy" (Loke 1989: 28).

Isabella Furth has read *Tripmaster Monkey* as an allusive and elusive text that enacts the slipperiness of such a hyphenated identity. Furth sees that when Wittman adopts the famous Chinese mythological Monkey King as his alter ego, he also adopts the Monkey King's secret weapon—his magic pole stored like a toothpick behind his ear. Furth notes, "The magic pole is a staff that can change from toothpick to giant's staff, an axis of transformations, negotiations, and subversions" (Furth 1994: 36). Like the pole, then, "perspectives [within the narrative] shift, narratives multiply, significations oscillate through multilingual puns, and the straightforward, stable equation balanced on a hyphen is revealed as a reductive appropriation" (Furth 1994: 36).

As a Chinese American, Wittman Ah Sing is large and asserts multitudes of identities. He imagines himself as a poet, a playwright, an antiwar pacifist, a warrior god, a lone artist, and, conversely, a community builder. Like many young artists who were part of Berkeley in the 1960s, he is smitten with the countercultural ideologies of that period and imagines himself to be a cultural radical. Underlying all his identities are his concerns with being Chinese and Asian American. He expresses that identity literally on his body: He is long-haired and bearded and chooses to wear green because "some dorm guy said 'we look yellow in that color.' It had to do with racial skin. And from that time on, he knew what color he had to wear—green" (Kingston 1989: 44).

Even as Wittman retells episodes of the Chinese epic "Journey to the West," about the Monkey King and other travelers' pilgrimage to India, he himself is on a journey to negotiate what his Asian American identity means and how he, as an artist, ascribes meaning to it. In negotiating its meaning and his understanding of it, he wrestles with a dilemma facing the multivalenced cultural matrix that is America. The novel phrases this dilemma in the form of the question that has been particularly contentious and critical for Americans who identify with being part of ethnic minority groups: How does one reconcile unity and identity? And it seems to answer: through play and performance.

Drama and performance use language to convey an aesthetic of everyday living. The growing popularity of Asian American theater and film in the 1980s and 1990s has raised the stakes of representations and revived the questions about the role of art and literature in defining ethnic identity and community. Kingston's text adds to these discussions by complicating the deceptively binary oppositional nature of the debate between "constructed" and "authentic" Asian American culture by problematizing the valuation of "real" over "fake," as well as the notion that a "real" is always distinguishable from the "fake" in Wittman's perspective.

From Wittman's perspective, what is "real" and of value to most people is selfish, limiting, silly, and unimaginative. When he listens to a Wall Street stock-market report, for instance, he hears, "Friday's Tao up 2.53 points" and feels "pleased with himself, that he hadn't lost his Chinese ears. He had kept a religious Chinese way of hearing while living within the military-industrial-educational complex" (Kingston 1989: 85). Wittman is acutely concerned with making passion, art, and interpersonal connection part of the everyday lives of most people. For Wittman, those things are tied to social concerns, such as criticizing and correcting racism, but like many people he does not confront every incident and does not understand why he sometimes acts on his anger and sometimes does not. He is sullenly silent when watching racist depictions in films, but while on his honeymoon he publicly confronts the teller of a racist joke in an expensive restaurant and storms out in indignation.

To further unpack what drives this narrative, we must consider Wittman's name, which is a pun on Walt Whitman, the literary model for this young, twenty-something, philosophizing, playwright–poet, sixth-generation Chinese American. Walt Whitman is read as a poet who embraces the marginalized and traditionally voiceless people in American history and published texts. Likewise, Wittman's desire to write and his artistic development are activated by locating a minoritized, ethnic subject—Chinese Americans—and using it as a starting point for his epic, panethnic play. By titling the first two chapters of the book "Trippers and Askers" and "Linguists and Contenders," after lines in Whitman's epic poem "Song of Myself," Kingston further announces Walt Whitman's shaping of her vision.

Although both "Song of Myself" and Kingston's novel can be read as epics of America, their strategies are quite different. Both texts embrace a large scope of democratic American society, with many characters appearing, but their protagonists' voices still dominate. Both could be called "dramas of identity" because the first-person narrative lists a multitude of images that the narrator embraces and makes her own. However, whereas Whitman's multitudes are anonymous, Wittman Ah Sing makes innumerable intertextual references to Western literature, poetry, film, and popular culture and to Chinese mythology. The speaker's language alternates between English and the Toishan dialect of Cantonese Chinese, with an occasional sprinkling of Spanish and French. These make for some of the most humorous moments in the text. For example, one scene plays with the Cantonese phrase *hoi mun*, which means "open the door": "Knock knock. Hoimun. Hoimun who? Hoimun, I want to come in, ah. Haha, get it? Herman, open the door" (Kingston 1989: 254).

The hyphenated space between Asian and American, like Monkey's toothpick, is where Wittman plays with performing identities. Although he seeks entry into a national identity, a unitary "I" that is unmarked by the hyphen, he finds himself constantly challenged. His identity is reactive, proactive, and performative rather than formed around a singular essential identity. What I refer to as "performance" is not limited to theatrical or staged performance but includes the performances we all carry out in living everyday life. I turn to Michel de Certeau (1988) here in defining everyday life not simply as a passive environmental matrix that encompasses us, but as systems of operational combinations composing a "culture" that we selectively act in and on. Performance is the moment of emergence, or the process of becoming, involving an actor and delivery, and as such it invites consideration of multiple gaps and conditions of identity. It can be broken down into the setting and narrated conditions of the enactment of performance, the words or descriptive action performed, the means of delivery, and the reception by intended and non-intended receivers, who may be the reader, other characters, or the speaker himself or herself. Ethnic community solidifies around individuals' enactment of these performances, thus reinforcing recognition of commonality in language and cultural practices. Wittman literally enacts a connection to an old-time, first-generation Chinese immigrant, an "old fut," and persuades the old-timer to allow him use of the Chinese Benevolent Association by invoking and performing his ethnic associations and connections. In their exchange, Wittman uses Cantonese words, opening with invocations of relatives and familial connections (Kingston 1989: 255–5), enacting the Chinese mythical story of the Twenty-Three Outlaws of the Water Margin and ending with the customary Cantonese farewell, "Meet again."

Kingston's use of words and language to enact performance and identity in performance also focuses on the gap between what Ferdinand de Saussure (1986 [1959]: 648) calls the signifier and signified. In other words, it invites scrutiny of how identity is being represented, how language can create and limit what is "real" for us. Wittman clarifies this further in his musings on hair:

> People look at blondes with discernment. When you think about it, aren't blondes sort of washed out? Pale? But there's an interest in them. Everybody looks at them a lot. And sees distinctions, and names the shades. Those four heads were each a different black. Kettle black. Cannonball black. Bowling-ball black. Licorice. Licorice curls. Patent-leather black. Leotard black. Black sapphire. Black opal. And since when have ashes been blonde? Ashes are black and white. Ash black. And his own hair. What color was his own hair? He pulled a mess of it forward. It's brown. But he always put "black" on his i.d.s. I've got brown hair. And never knew it though combing it at the mirror daily because when you think of Chinese, Chinese have black hair. (Kingston 1989: 59)

These musings both defy mono-ethnic typing and embrace panethnic consciousness. Wittman ties his hair back, for example, not simply into a "ponytail" but into a "samurai–Paul Revere–piratical braid" (Kingston 1989: 44), asserting, in that phrase, the hairstyle's multiple historical and cultural "roots."

Theater of the "Other"

The novel's slippage and never-ending referentiality seem to reinforce that there are no real objectives or stakes, only play, in its representations. But Wittman has a purpose that drives this disjunctive narrative: He wants to produce a play, but not a play that will simply entertain. He wants to revive a lost tradition of American theater—the traveling theater, theater for the masses, which he traces not only to traveling shows and the vaudeville popular in nineteenth- and early-twentieth-century America, but also to Chinese traveling theater. That tradition includes traveling operas and paper-puppet shows that performed well-known epics and myths.[1] In her novel, Kingston imagines this form of Chinese performance coming with Chinese American immigrants to the United States. American vaudeville traveling shows and Chinese theater both have a history of being roving forms of entertainment for the masses that showcase the unusual and fantastic. But American shows displayed Asians as oddities—take, for example, Barnum and Bailey's "Siamese Twins," Chang and Eng; "Flying Lings"; and "First Chinese Woman in America." The Chinese opera/theater cast fantastical characters such as the Monkey King as heroes and warriors in allegorical tales. For example, one of the one hundred and eight outlaws, the heroes of the famous epic "Journey to the West," is Li Kwai— Black Li, a "Black Chinese." By combining figures of American vaudeville and Chinese epics in his story of the American West, Wittman creates a distinct, all-inclusive, American community. He imagines a scene that borrows elements of the famous myth and refashions them for his goal:

> There the stranger, the weird and the alienated make their own country. And have one hundred and seven brothers and sisters. The one hundred and eight banditors, banished from everywhere else, build a community. Their thousands of stories, multiples of a hundred and eight, branch and weave, intersecting at the Water Verge. (Kingston 1989: 261)

Like Walt Whitman, Wittman Ah Sing identifies with the marginalized, the so-called riffraff of society. Wittman is a frustrated and mostly unemployed recent college graduate struggling to find recognition as a writer, but he finds renewed purpose for his work as a playwright who will use theater to build panethnic community. His vision is that performing Asian American identity and enacting community participates in developing a panethnic consciousness that is transmuted throughout other means of American experience and culture. As he explains:

> I'm going to start a theater company. I'm naming it The Pear Garden Players of America. The Pear Garden was the cradle of civilization, where theater began on Earth. Out among the trees, ordinary people made fools of themselves like kings and queens. As playwright and producer and director, I'm casting blind. That means the actors can be any race. Each member of the Tyrone family or the Lomans can be a different color. I'm including everything that is being left out, and everybody who has no place. My idea for the Civil Rights Movement is that we integrate jobs, schools, buses, housing, lunch counters, yes, and we also integrate theater and parties. (Kingston 1989: 52)

Wittman feels his marginalization in the Chinatown community as well as in the mainstream culture. Although he lives in Chinatown, he is called a "*jook tsing*," or "bamboo node," a term used by first-generation immigrants to alienate culturally the young American-born Chinese. While searching for a Chinese word for Chinese American, he can think only of "*jook tsing*," for which he creates a linguistic community by placing it alongside "*ho chi gwai*" ("ghost likeness," where "ghost" refers to whites) as well as *mestizo* and *pachuco*, Mexican American terms whose implications are similar to that of "*jook tsing*." Just as the mythical Monkey finds himself free to move between communities, these people who are not completely accepted either in mainstream American community or in ethnic communities have less individual cultural investment at stake and are in more fluid positions to do the work of panethnic cross-ings. Yet like Monkey, who is a king and representative to the celestial gods, these peo-ple also remain marked by and responsible to these communities. When cajoling the doubtful president of the Chinese Benevolent Association to open his hall for the stag-ing of a play, Wittman argues:

> Listen, we must play in here. Else, what Association for, huh? collecting dues? What you do, huh? You bury old men. You be nothing but one burial society. Better you let United Farm Workers use the bathroom and kitchen. Let them crash overnight. Be headquarters— Hello, Strike Central—for unions of waiters and garment workers. . . . We make our place— this one community house for benevolent living. We make theater, we make community. (Kingston 1989: 255, 261)

Homi Bhabha (1990) defines the "performative" as one part of nation narration. He sees the performative as a temporal space of slippage that both gives response and adds to a nationalist pedagogy—or, in other words, what is accepted as the central history of the nation.

Shades of Yellow

If we define the epic as Mikhail Bakhtin (1981) does—as a national tradition that re-cre-ates and affirms a national past—then Wittman's unusual epic theater, like Walt Whit-man's *Leaves of Grass,* is forged as a new epic of America, one that embraces every indi-vidual's song of himself as well as the traditionally celebrated heroic vanguards and forefathers. This strategy of using performance to articulate and enlarge America has a long tradition, running from Whitman in the nineteenth century to Alan Ginsberg and the Beat poets in the 1950s. By Wittman Ah Sing's time, it has also been adopted by the countercultural social-left theater of the 1960s, as well as by the Black Arts movement of the 1960s and 1970s. It should be recognized, then, that Wittman's artistic vision for panethnic community is significantly shaped by the social conditions of the 1960s.

In the late 1960s and early 1970s, the Yellow Power movement created and shaped that panethnic consciousness and community. According to the sociologist Yen Le Espiritu (1992), the university-student-led Yellow Power movement, as an offshoot of the larger Civil Rights Movement, was also influenced by the Black Power move-ment's political and organizational tactics. Yellow Power's unique locus of unity was the internal colonial model, which stressed commonalities among "colonized groups." Declaring solidarity with other Third World minorities, as well as with fellow Asian Americans, students rejected the term "Oriental" and proclaimed themselves to be "Asian Americans." They acknowledged that Asians in America experienced and shared histories of struggles that included racial violence against Asians, Japanese American internment, Asian-exclusion acts, anti-miscegenation laws, and other leg-islative and social restrictions on their participation in American culture. According to the historian Amy Uyematsu, they sought "freedom from racial oppression through the power of a consolidated yellow people" (1971: 12) In the summer of 1968, a conference titled "Are You Yellow?" at the University of California, Los Angeles, convened one hundred students of diverse Asian ethnicity to discuss issues of Yellow Power, identity, and the war in Vietnam. In 1970, a new pan-Asian organization in Northern California called itself the "Yellow Seed" because "Yellow [is] the common bond between Asian-Americans and Seed symboliz[es] growth as an individual and as an alliance" (Espiritu 1992: 32).

However, the term "yellow" itself soon became a site of contestation over the construction of Asian American identity and community. The first objection to the term "yellow" came from Filipino American activists who did not reject being called "yellow" because they objected to the pan-Asian framework. On the contrary, they rejected it because it excluded them from that grouping. That moment illustrates the fission and fusion process that characterizes not only specifically Asian American but also a general American panethnic identity. Other groups such as South Asian Americans, Southeast Asian Americans, and bi- and multiracial Asian Americans have made similar protests of marginalization in order to be more fully participatory and included as Asian Americans. Through the many changes in Asian American diversity in the late twentieth century, it is remarkable that Asian American panethnic identity has not been rejected but, rather, expanded and redefined since the 1960s.

Although these intersections are in flux and indeterminate, the formation of Asian American identity in the 1960s and 1970s continues to provide reference for Asian American identities today. It is the focus of struggle between Asian American cultural nationalists, who want to keep Asian American history at the center of Asian American identity, and transnationalists, who increasingly see Asian American identity as multi- or even post-national, with hybrid, modern cultures of the Pacific Rim as the heart of Asian American identity. The distinction is apparent in widely distributed periodicals produced by and for Asian Americans. The San Francisco current events weekly *AsianWeek* focuses on political and community issues and events of Asian American groups around the nation. The monthly *aMagazine* focuses more on pop culture, fashion, and trends that appeal mostly to students and young professionals. *Giant Robot*, now a nationally distributed and professionally produced magazine, began as an alternative 'zine; it was penned by a handful of contributors and featured articles on imported Asian music, candy, toys, and cinema. All these publications seem to define Asian Americans with different interests. But at the same time, they maintain different influences of the Asian American movements of the 1960s and '70s. *AsianWeek* articles are steeped in rights-centered orientation of political struggles for equal rights—reporting, for instance, on community organizations' efforts to preserve Medicaid benefit for elderly Asian immigrants. Alternatively, *Giant Robot* has featured a cover story on the seminal figures of the Yellow Power movement and its intersections with the Black Power movement. And *aMagazine*, acknowledging that its readership draws significantly from students who are exposed to Asian American studies courses (a field of study that owes its origins to the Yellow Power movement) ranks "the best colleges and universities" for Asian Americans, noting such factors as Asian student populations on campus and the presence of Asian American studies programs and cultural centers.

Community Theater

The finale of the novel, the staging of Wittman's community play, itself demonstrates not the resolution of these issues but, rather, their articulation. The play lasts three nights and concludes with a long soliloquy by Wittman in which he raises an amalgam of issues around Asian American identity. In shaping Asian American panethnic community, the play and the soliloquy do not simply replicate unproblematic celebrations of multiculturalism such as those criticized by Lisa Lowe (1996). Lowe has objected to the way in which a multicultural festival in Los Angeles represented the city as

> a postmodern multicultural cornucopia, an international patchwork quilt ... although the "signifiers" were the very uneven, irreducible differences between these diverse acts, the important "signified" was a notion of Los Angeles as multicultural spectacle. In the process, each performance tradition was equated with every other, and its meaning was reduced and generalized to a common denominator whose significance was the exotic, colorful advertisement of Los Angeles. Despite tensions between the narratives of authenticity, lineage, and variety, all these narratives effect, in different ways, the erasure and occlusion of the "material" geographies of Los Angeles. (Lowe 1996: 89)

What distinguishes the play's seamless connection of Chinese myth to Chinese American, Asian American, and other ethnic American culture and experiences from what Lowe calls a "multicultural spectacle" that dangerously masks and therefore erases differences that are felt by minorities in the cultural hegemonic structures of their lives?

For one, the play showcases the talent and accomplishments of many uncelebrated Asian Americans in America's history and exhibits multifaceted Asian American cultures while it presents a story of origin, telling a Chinese American hybrid tale of Chinese immigration to America using elements of the Chinese myth The Romance of the Three Kingdoms. Unlike the sort of multicultural festival Lowe describes, the community play does not simply showcase Asian American "success" stories of "making it" in America. For instance, Chinese American gang members show up to tell the story of the martial artist Bruce Lee as a critique of the racist Hollywood studios that told Lee that "Chinese man has no Star Quality"; the story turns Lee's failure to become a Hollywood star into a heroic triumph: "The hell with them. Good for me. I did not let Haw-lee-woot change me into the dung dung dung dung dung with the little pigtail in back" (Kingston 1989: 281).

The play's opening is a discomforting critique of how Asian Americans occupy a problematic space in the American cultural imagination. The portrayal of the original Siamese Twins dramatizes the problematic meaning of "Asian American" itself, looking at the term as seemingly signifying something freakish, monstrous. A linked pair of acrobatic twins somersault across the stage—Chang and Eng, the conjoined Siamese twins, both wearing one green velveteen suit. They are played by a Japanese American and a European American, and they can neither find consensus about their identities nor survive without each other. They are both pulled involuntarily into American society as war draftees, where they re-enact moments of domestic conflict in America—the Civil War anxiety of brothers fighting brothers, as well as the Vietnam War-era resistance to the draft. They are also forcibly marginalized as freaks and put on display. Inciting a riot when they refuse to let the curious crowd see the ligament that joins them, they are arrested. Between the bars, Chang yells: "We know damned well what you came for to see—the angle we're joined at, how we can have two sisters for wives and twenty-one Chinese–Carolinian children between us. . . . You want to know if we feel jointly. You want to look at the hyphen. You want to look at it bare" (Kingston 1989: 293).

The play/revue continues the following night in carnivalesque fashion. Helen Gilbert and Joanne Tompkins have described the carnival as a form of postcolonial drama that is "characteristically exuberant, non-naturalistic, and self-consciously theatrical. . . drawing attention to public space, communal activity, and vernacular languages" (Gilbert and Tompkins 1996: 78). Thus, the carnival proclaims Asian Americans' historical and continued presence in America, but it does so in a way that is farcical, both parodying the American carnival that exhibited Asians as freaks and appropriating the forum for depicting alternative, Asian American self-made images and revisionist histories. Following the appearance of Chang and Eng are Sui Sin Far and Jade Snow Wong, who are female Chinese American writers and Kingston's predecessors. These women, the omniscient first-person narrator asserts, are not "bucktoof myopic pagans. . . . These excellent dark women should have overcome dumb blondes forevermore" (Kingston 1989: 296).

The play goes on to represent history as myth, blurring the boundaries between fact and fiction. A re-enactment of the violent history of the lynchings of Chinese Americans in the frontier period of the mid-nineteenth century merges with performances of The Romance of the Three Kingdoms. The stage is alive with scenes of multiple stories, and the narrator notes, "As in real life, things were happening all over the place. The audience looked left, right, up, down, in and about the round, everywhere, the flies, the wings, all the while hearing reports from off stage. Too much goings-on, they miss some, okay, like life" (Kingston 1989: 298). Amid all this activity, the narrator acts as interpreter, setting straight some cultural misperceptions: "The police break up the riot started by a lynch mob in a store and arrest the grocers for assaulting officers. So Chinese Americans founded the Joang Wah for the purpose of filing legal complaints with the City of New York against lynchings, illegal arrests, opium, slavery, and grocery-store licensing. A tong is not a crime syndicate and not a burial society. It is organization of community, for which Chinese Americans have genius" (Kingston 1989: 298).

As the participants experience the "theater as community" that Wittman has envisioned, a disruption occurs. The play is interrupted by police sent to investigate the cacophonous goings-on. Yet when the policemen come to the Benevolent Organization to investigate, they do not make any arrests or write citations because, ironically, as the narrator explains, "the Chinese are allowed more fireworks than most people" (Kingston 1989: 299). Thus, the exoticism of Chinatown acts to marginalize it but also to create spaces that have certain kinds of subversive agency—that is how Chinatown remained exempt from some restrictions, such as setting off fireworks without permits.[2]

The fireworks are the climactic conclusion of the epic portion of the play, which has taken place over two evenings. This conclusion ends up drawing the audience into the action, with a fighting free-for-all that spills outside the theater into the streets. This is not an apocalyptic moment, however. It is, rather, a collective performance of fighting, of people physically engaging with one another, that is ultimately brought to climactic closure with the fireworks show.

Playing with Himself

The end of the play is subdued as Wittman has the last word—there has been no mention of him in the description of the play up to this point. Wittman all but disappears for the first two nights of the play, then finally reappears for his long soliloquy at the play's conclusion. Although Wittman is the director and writer of this play, he has no interest in becoming a curator or ethnographer who simply "imports" culture to the stage without dealing with the accountability of making a spectacle of performed identity.

Wittman's soliloquy provides a solitary spoken voice at the end of the Kingston's novel. Deborah Geis describes the soliloquy as a

> kind of monologue that generally suggests introspection. . . . A soliloquy usually involves the verbalization of the speaker's interior feelings or thoughts and often entails a revelation or decision that may not be ordinarily rendered in speech outside of a theatrical framework but which is enacted aloud for the benefit of the audience (e.g., Hamlet's soliloquies). (Geis 1993: 8)

In his soliloquy, Wittman clearly constructs a community around him, one that is positioned against Sinophiles, Orientalists, consumers of an Asian culture that is a product of their own imagination. For Wittman, this means ferreting out racism disguised even in the form of praise of his work. By critiquing seemingly positive newspaper reviews of the play, he reveals how they reinforce stereotypes of Asian exoticism. He asserts that, contrary to reviewers' characterization, the play is distinctly American, the "West": "There is no East here. West is meeting West. This was all West. All you saw was West. . . . I am so fucking offended. Why aren't you offended? Let me help you get offended" (Kingston 1989: 308). Wittman's rejection of "the East" is not an internalized racism or self-hatred of his Chinese ethnicity; rather, it is a rejection of "Sinophiles" who see the East as exotica, as a culture to be consumed and found amusing. To further dramatize his rejection of exoticism, he begins cutting off his own hair while on stage, because long Asian hair is often depicted as a marker of this exoticism.

When criticizing the reviewers' Sinophilic use of food metaphors to describe the play, Wittman seeks to engage the audience in the community of the theater. This moment is also a rupture in that community—the Sinophiles formerly and currently in the audience are now the other, "them": "They think they know us—the wide range of us from sweet to sour—because they eat in Chinese restaurants. They're the ones who order the sweet-and-sour shrimp" (Kingston 1989: 308). In that moment, community is fissured between the "we-authentic-Chinese" and the "they-not-Chinese." However, as the larger communal "we" is still "America," those of non-Chinese descent who would not commit the error of mistaking the falsely exoticized as "authentic" could still feel included in Wittman's "we."

But by directly addressing the audience, Wittman also fuses the gap between them and himself: They become part of the play, even when they are passive spectators. The "audience" he addresses at one point appears to be Asian Americans who would identify with the collective "we," as in: "We're about as exotic as shit. Nobody soopecial here. No sweet-and-sour shit" (Kingston 1989: 308). The addressed "you" also includes non-Asian Americans, especially in the remarks enclosed in parentheses within Wittman's speech, which are moments of slippage, doubled voice, ambiguity in the speaker—is Wittman or an unnamed "omniscient" narrator speaking? "Okay, let's say in this soap opera, they hear bad news about their only son—killed in war. (Don't you whites get confused, he's killed fighting for *our* side. Nobody here but us Americans)" (Kingston 1989: 309).

The nature of soliloquy does makes it a problematic vehicle with which to build community, because the notion of having a solitary speaker creates community by silent consensus. As Geis argues:

> When a monologue seems to address the audience directly, the paradoxical position of the audience in respect to the speaker intensifies. It is possible to argue that this type of monologic utterance simultaneously includes the spectators in a more direct way than otherwise and reasserts their very powerlessness. The audience seems to be addressed, yet its members are not (except in certain forms of experimental theater) in a position to respond, for doing so would, as Goffman explains, involve breaking the "dramatic frame." (Geis 1993: 14)

Yet even as Wittman directs and performs his monologue (driven by his indignance with America's treatment of Asians and Asian Americans and by his performed rejection of Asian stereotypes), his "authority" as the soliloquist is diffused by two types of disruption. One type involves outbursts from the audience, which Wittman welcomes and encourages; the other type involves the omniscient narrator's comments on Wittman's words and the audience's reactions in the theater.

One part of Wittman's soliloquy, which he considers to be "his craziest riff, the weirdest take of his life at the movies" (Kingston 1989: 314), is naming famous male American movie stars who have appeared on screens as "cowboys with Chinese eyes." To Whitman's delighted surprise, his admission does not lose his audience. They stay with him and verbally volunteer *more* names of actors with "Chinese" eyes who have played cowboys. The long list that eventually develops can be imagined as a powerful affirmation of "Chinese eyes" as "American-heroic," especially if movie clips of the following actors were strung together: Roy Rogers, Buck Jones, John Wayne, John Payne, Randolph Scott, Hopalong Cassidy, Rex Allen, John Huston, John Carradine, Gabby Hayes, Donald O'Connor, Lee Marvin, Steve McQueen, Gary Cooper, Alan Ladd, Jack Palance, Gregory Peck, Robert Mitchum, Richard Boone, and Clint Eastwood.

The second disruptions occur when Wittman delves into a lengthy condemnation of racialized beauty perpetuated by Hollywood, as well as by Asian women themselves when they agree to have their eyes surgically remade into "Westernized" eyes (slicing the eyelid to create an epicanthic fold). Here he again splits his audience. As Tana, his wife, and the omniscient narrator both note, "bad Wittman did not let up" (Kingston 1989: 312). He is committing the rude act of insulting his audience and misogynistically criticizing the women themselves rather than the self-esteem-damaging societal messages that they have internalized. Although Tana and the feminist-omniscient narrator may be listening silently, they are also in disagreement. Their disapproval suggests that performing the desire for and acquisition of Western eyes and performing the outrage against this means of "beautifying" oneself are oppositional discourses of being "Asian American."

The effect of Wittman's critique and rejection of stereotypes, coupled with the audience's and narrator's dialogic response to him, explodes the uniformity of the term "Asian American." Kent A. Ono suggests that we may be in a cultural moment that demands a "re/signing" of the term "Asian American" as an ideograph for "multiple struggles over language and power relevant to contemporary political practices." Ono explains:

> The ambivalent use of the term, "re/signing," in my title is purposeful. There are two meanings I hope to evoke by using it. First, I suggest that use of the term "Asian American" should be questioned; it may have to be resigned, scrapped, or disused. Second, I suggest that another possibility is available: rather than resigning the term, we may be able to re-sign it. . . . By shuttling between the two meanings: resigning (retiring) and re-signing (refiguring), I hope to enact a critical, rhetorical practice that creates slippage between using and disusing the term, Asian American. (1995: 68)

Wittman expresses frustration at the lack of a satisfactory name for Americans of Asian descent and addresses this issue of nomenclature that is an issue of negotiation for Asian American identity. It is easier for him to articulate what he is *not* than what he is:

> Where's our name that shows that we aren't from anywhere but America?. . . Look at the Blacks beautifully defining themselves. "Black" is perfect. But we can't be "Yellows.". . . Nah, too evocative of tight-fisted Chang. Red's our color. But the red-hot communists have appropriated red. . . . We are not named, and we're disappearing already. We want a name we can take out in the street and on any occasion. We can't go to the passport office and say, "I'm a Han Ngun.". . . Once and for all: I am not oriental. . . . There's no such *person* as a Sino-American. (Kingston 1989: 326–7)

The end of the play, then—as might be expected—is not so much an "ending" as it is an "opening" of panethnic Asian American community and the tensions within it. The community of the play is in a bonding moment, but one that is chronologically situated in a time at which Americans' sense of wartime unity had shattered and had never been recovered. Wittman's pacifism is affirmed as he vows that he will not serve in Vietnam, but this decision threatens his status as a loyal member of the American community: As a disloyal American, he will defect to the U.S.-Canadian border at Niagara Falls with Tana, his white, European American wife, as his paper-wife escort. Yet renegade spaces continue to "open up" America for Wittman: "He had memories of dug-out dressing rooms that were part of an underground city where Chinese Americans lived and did business after the L.A. Massacre, nineteen killed. He and other draft dodgers could hide in such places until the war was over" (Kingston 1989: 340).

Thus, this ending/opening signals the discomforting tension inherent in forming community: The aim to form connections and commonalities elides difference and can lead to misunderstanding. Wittman chronicles the degeneration of his marriage into a neglected domesticity of shrimp shells, dirty dishes, cat feces, and mold, and he tells Tana he loves her "Unromantically but" (Kingston 1989: 339). The restrictive "but," as in Bharati Mukherjee's short story "A Wife's Story" (1988), signals an ambivalence that threatens to unravel unity and complicity. However, the audience chooses to focus on hearing "I love you," willfully misreading Wittman's frank deconstruction of marriage into a celebration of idealized romance. Like it or not, the community blesses Wittman. And he has to admit, "he was having a good time." Although not everyone has heard everything, he fulfills a pacifist goal: "our monkey, master of change, staged a fake war, which might very well be displacing some real war" (Kingston 1989: 306). In the end, Wittman re-assigns value to the terms "real" and "fake" whereby the "fake war," in "displacing some real war," questions the value of "authentic" essentialist identities that form the basis of nationalist posturing that can engender war. Finally, Wittman reconstructs not only Chinese America and Asian America but even America insofar as it stands for a utopic heterotopia.

Notes

1. According to the Chinese folklore scholar Robert Moss, the tradition of drama and storytelling first became very popular in the Yuan dynasty, beginning around 1260. Moss further traces the Yuan storytelling tradition to the Northern Song, when public recitations of the myth of Three Kingdoms were performed in the dynasty's commercial centers. Moss also mentions that notices of Three Kingdoms shadow plays (in which backlighting was used to illuminate hand-manipulated puppets against a screen) also have been found in the Northern Song. See Moss 1991: 957–8.

2. Such subversive potential, however, is increasingly limited. In 1997, for example, the New York City Police Department decided, for public-safety reasons, to prohibit fireworks in the city's Chinatown for Chinese New Year festivities. The new prohibitions raised many protests, to no avail.

References

Bakhtin, Mikhail Mikhailovich. 1981. *The Dialogic Imagination*. Austin: University of Texas Press.
Bhabha, Homi K. 1990. "DisSemination: Time, Narrative, and the Margins of the Modern Nation," Pp. 291–322 in *Nation and Narration*, ed. Homi K. Bhabha. London: Routledge.

de Certeau, Michel. 1988. *The Practice of Everyday Life.* London: University of California Press.

De Saussure, Ferdinand. 1986 (1959). "Nature of the Linguistic Sign." Pp. 646–56 in *Critical Theory Since 1965*, ed. Hazard Adams and Leroy Searle. Tallahassee: University Presses of Florida.

Espiritu, Yen Le. 1992. *Asian American Panethnicity: Bridging Institutions and Identities.* Philadelphia: Temple University Press.

Furth, Isabella. 1994. "Bee-e-een! Nation, Transformation, and the Hyphen of Ethnicity in Kingston's *Tripmaster Monkey*." *Modern Fiction Studies* 40, no. 1: 33–49.

Geis, Deborah. 1993. *Postmodern Theatric(k)s: Monologue in Contemporary American Drama.* Ann Arbor: University of Michigan Press.

Gilbert, Helen, and Joanne Tompkins. 1996. *Postcolonial Drama: Theory, Practice, Politics.* London and New York: Routledge.

Kingston, Maxine Hong. 1989. *Tripmaster Monkey: His Fake Book.* New York: Alfred A. Knopf.

Loke, Margaret. 1989. "The Tao Is Up." *New York Times Magazine* (30 April).

Lowe, Lisa. 1996. *Immigrant Acts: On Asian American Cultural Politics.* Durham, N.C.: Duke University Press.

Moss, Robert, comp. and trans. 1991. *Three Kingdoms: A Historical Novel* (attributed to Luo Guanzhong). Berkeley and Los Angeles: University of California Press.

Mukherjee, Bharati. 1988. *The Middleman and Other Stories.* New York: Random House.

Ono, Kent A. 1995. "Re/signing 'Asian American': Rhetorical Problematics of Nation." *Amerasia Journal* 21, no. 1–2: 67–78.

Uyematsu, Amy. 1971. "The Emergence of Yellow Power in America." Pp. 9–13 in *Roots: An Asian American Reader*, ed. Amy Tachiki, Eddie Wong, and Franklin Odo. Los Angeles: UCLA Asian American Studies Center.

MAIN POINTS

- SOUTH ASIAN WOMEN'S ORGANIZATIONS (SAWO) & MOVEMENT TO HELP SOUTH ASIAN WOMEN IN ABUSIVE SITUATIONS
- CONCEPT OF "MODEL MINORITY" AND IT BEING A MYTH

DEFINE "COMMUNITY"

- GRP OF PPL WILLING TO HELP OTHERS EITHER TO RECOVER FROM A BAD SITUATIONS / HELP SUPPORT THEM THROUGH A CERTAIN TIME

TIME / DO NOT TIME

- TIME: EXPLAINED REASONS WHY PPLE (ASIAN PPL) IGNORE & TRY TO HIDE THE ABUSE SITUATIONS B/C THEY DON'T WANT IT AFFECTING THEIR IMAGE OF BEING SO FAMILY ORIENTED

CHAPTER 12

Margaret Abraham

Addressing Domestic Violence and the South Asian Community in the United States

I have been working in the area of domestic violence in the South Asian American community for more than a decade. My entree was as a researcher, but, like many other South Asian women, I became a part of a small but growing movement in the 1990s that addresses a spectrum of issues confronting South Asians in the United States.[1] Although my identity as a researcher and the goal to write about domestic violence was always central, I frequently found myself reflecting on the notions of South Asian community identity and the complexities of organizing against domestic violence.

Notions of South Asian American community identity have been undergoing considerable change in the past two decades. Much of the early impetus for this change came from the mobilizing activities of South Asian women's organizations (SAWOs) that addressed domestic violence in the South Asian community. These organizations, together with many other progressive South Asian groups, have played an important role in redefining the community identity in ways that recognize the diversity of its population in terms of ethnicity, class, gender, and legal status. Mobilizing the South Asian American community to address domestic violence and other social problems has forced many SAWOs to struggle with a range of issues and approaches in organizing for progressive change.

In this chapter, I examine the changing dynamics of South Asian community identity in the United States in the 1980s and 1990s and the complexity of organizing against domestic violence in a community that has been labeled a "model minority." Specifically, I focus on the social construction of the model-minority image for South Asians, the emergence of South Asian women's organizations that challenged this image, and my own reflections on the strategic tactics with which these organizations have to contend in their politics of transformation.

South Asian Americans and the Model-Minority Image

Approximately 2 million South Asians live in the United States. Until the 1990s, this community was viewed almost uniformly as a model minority—one whose members adhered to the valued principles of economic success in the public sphere while retaining strong cultural values in the private sphere. Not only did the dominant group in the United States refer to South Asians as a model minority, but segments within the South Asian community identified and represented themselves as such. The tendency to highlight South Asians' economic success, especially among Indians who came to the United States before the 1980s, can be seen in the works of various writers, including Nathan Glazer, Harry Kitano, and Parmatama Saran (Kitano and Daniels 1995). Glazer characterized the Indian population in the United States as "marked off by a high level of education, by concentration in the professions, by a strong commitment to maintaining family connection, both here in the United States and between the United States and India" (1976: vi).

For many members of the South Asian community, who had immigrated to the United States as professionals in the 1960s, the model-minority image was to be promoted and sustained. It was perceived as good for business and as a way for South Asians to distance themselves from other, lower-status minorities with whom they did not want to identify, lest such identification decrease the status of their own ethnic group in the U.S. social hierarchy. Mainstream and community leaders portrayed the South Asian community as a monolithic whole—as a model minority that believed in strong family ties, that was well educated and economically successful, and that had achieved a fine balance between upholding the cherished values of South Asian culture while simultaneously adopting the principles of modern American capitalism.

In the 1980s and 1990s, "chain migration"—the immigration of sponsored relatives of South Asian U.S. residents—changed the demographic composition of the South Asian community. It brought considerable variation along such dimensions as education, occupation, class, and gender experiences and on such axes as language, religion, region of origin, and class. Despite these new subgroups, the South Asian community continued to be represented within the United States by a small number of business people and wealthy professionals, who defined the image, activities, and interests of the community. Often, their politics and articulation of community interests, especially in New York and New Jersey, lay in those areas that protected the interests of businesses.

The 1980s also gave rise to a more visible phenomenon: the predominance of South Asians—again, especially in New York and New Jersey—in the newsstand business, as taxi drivers, and as motel owners. Many ethnic investors purchased stores in strategic locations as investments and in order to take advantage of the cheap ethnic labor provided by chain immigration. Thus, a complex stratification system arose within the larger American economic system involving the leasing and subleasing of property. In that system, extremely wealthy, oppressive immigrant owners hired cheap immigrant labor. Yet it was the small-business owners and employees who worked fourteen-hour days at kiosks, gas stations, and motels who became the visible "image" of the South Asian community (Khandelwal 1997). These employees, many of them South Asian women, confronted language barriers and limited economic opportunities; thus, they often were compelled to work exploitative hours to support themselves and their families in these low-paying jobs.

In the 1990s, the image of ethnic homogeneity in the South Asian American community was—internally, at least—replaced by a class- and region-based heterogeneity. A class system comprising at least three tiers now exists. The upper class is made up of wealthy businessmen and certain professionals, including doctors, lawyers, and computer technologists; the middle class is composed of college students and mid-range professionals; and the lower-class embraces blue-collar workers, low-wage earners, and, in some cases, undocumented workers. Yet, despite this heterogeneity in class and income, the South Asian American population continues to be represented generally as an economically successful community.

Until the mid-1990s, acknowledging the problem of domestic violence within the South Asian American family was extremely problematic, because it challenged the very concept of "good family values and strong family ties"—or what Linda Gordon (1989) calls the "myths of harmony of the normative family." The public image of the South Asian community in the United States has been defined primarily by men, and women have served as the cultural transmitters. Although South Asian immigrant women deal with the multiple forces of international migration, the economic demands of the American economy, and various familial and cultural obligations, their gender identity is culturally defined primarily in terms of the home. As the main symbol of cultural continuity, women face external and internal pressures to uphold the culture in specific ways, including adhering to culturally prescribed gender roles. Thus, South Asian women in the United States became responsible for upholding not only the family's honor but also the honor of segments of the model-minority community.

Domestic patriarchy, considered a given within the mainstream immigrant community, was not a subject for public discussion. In this social environment, issues such as domestic violence lay unaddressed. After all, they did not fit into the concept of the model minority or the happy, harmonious South Asian home. To talk about domestic violence within the community was to shatter the social construction of the community's image, challenge domestic patriarchy, and threaten the moral solidarity of community—a moral solidarity that was frequently reflected in the rhetoric of the various collective and religious practices of the community (Rayaprol 1993). It would then appear that, in the immigrant context, although South Asian women were supposed to be economic contributors, they were also to be increasingly constructed in cultural terms, with the immigrant home as the site for defining gender relations and ensuring traditional patriarchy. At the same time, immigrant women and men were struggling against the ethnic and gender images that made them targets for ethnic, class, and race discrimination in American society.

Many South Asians worried about their community image. In reaction to the dominant American society's racism and cultural imperialism, they often avoided looking at their own community critically. They became so invested in portraying South Asians in positive ways that they oppressed some segments of the community, including women—for example, by denying the violence perpetrated against them. Because the family lay within the private realm, and social control of domestic violence entailed an intrusion of the community into normative domestic patriarchy, problems such as domestic violence were not addressed, and instances that came to light were ignored, denied, or explained away. It was with this backdrop that South Asian women's organizations emerged to challenge the model-minority image by publicly addressing the problem of domestic violence in United States.

SAWOs' Role in Redefining Community Identity

The 1980s saw the rise of South Asian women's organizations in the United States. These organizations, which, together with other progressive organizations, address domestic violence have contested the model-minority image, arguing that it is a myth that has played a pivotal and problematic role in shaping community-identity politics in the United States (Abraham 2000). By their very existence and through their work, the SAWOs have demonstrated that the model-minority image denies the diversity of individuals of groups within the South Asian immigrant community. That is, it forces the community to be treated as a monolithic entity. The SAWOs also point out that model-minority status is extremely problematic because it frequently means denying or making invisible issues that do not fit within the label, such as poverty, AIDS, homosexuality, substance abuse, and domestic violence.

Although South Asian organizations existed before 1980, they were mainly symbolic representations of immigrants' ties to their home country that focused on cultural activities. South Asian men had greater visibility than women in these organizations and tended to be the locus of control. Those organizations did not address the differing experiences of immigrant men and women (Vaid 1989). In fact, the social institutions of the family and the social and religious organizations of the South Asian community reinforced the gendered division of labor.

At the same time, the specific concerns of ethnic-minority women were frequently ignored by white U.S. feminists, thus marginalizing South Asian and other immigrant women. Some South Asian women thus increasingly felt a need to organize to address the problems within their community and challenge the model-minority myth (Abraham 1995). This is illustrated in the following lines by Shamita Das Dasgupta, a cofounder of Manavi, the first SAWO to address domestic violence:

Discarding the security of the mainstream movement was not easy. Neither was my conscious decision to wed my feminist agenda with my ethnic identity. Until then my relationship with my Indian community had been based on my birth; now my relationship became an act of choice. As a symbol, I gave up wearing all Western clothing. However, this was not enough. I had to develop a feminist agenda in the context of the South Asian community.

I realized I was not alone in my efforts. Serendipitously, I came together with five other Indian women, all runaways from mainstream feminism. Reclaiming our community was an intricate task. We had to dig through its surface crust of conservatism, absolutism and androcentrism. In turn, the community had to receive us in our many faceted roles: mothers, activists, professionals, students, wives, feminists, single women. (Dasgupta and DasGupta 1994)

Similarly, Mallika Dutt, one of the five founders of the SAWO Sakhi for South Asian Women in New York, says:

I've worked for many years with the women's movement in the United States, predominantly around issues of women of color and sexuality. I have also done some work around violence in general. . . . We [another founding member] started getting to a point where we really felt we wanted to work with other South Asian women because all of our work had been done in the larger context of sort of mainstream America.[2]

Kanta Khipple, one of the founding members of the Chicago SAWO Apna Ghar, told me that she and a couple of other women who were working with service organizations saw a dire need to provide services within the South Asian community. According to Khipple, no South Asian organization was doing such work in Chicago at the time. Further, ethnic organizations were not providing services for abused women, Khipple said, which made it hard for those who needed help to get any real service from the community and resulted in many women being trapped in abusive relationships. The lack of such services and the complexity of a couple of cases at the time thus became the impetus for the creation of Apna Ghar.

The beliefs, vision, and commitment of these organizations' founders and initial volunteers resulted in the emergence in the 1980s of a new set of South Asian organizations whose focus was South Asian women. In the short span of fifteen years, many SAWOs have been established as part of a growing social movement to address the problem of violence against women in their community. These include Sakhi for South Asian Women in New York; Service and Education for Women Against Abuse (SEWAA) in Philadelphia; Apna Ghar in Chicago; Sneha in Connecticut; Maitri and Narika in California; Asian Women's Self-Help Association (ASHA) in Washington, D.C.; Saheli in Austin; Chaya in Seattle; Daya in Houston; Raksha in Atlanta; and many more throughout the United States. These organizations create a space for South Asian women in the United States to discuss issues that are pertinent to them as women and as South Asians, provide tangible support and services for abused South Asian women, and, in the process, challenge the myth of the model minority.

As I was conducting my research in the early 1990s, challenging the model-minority image and redefining community identity for SAWOs involved organizing South Asian women, ending domestic violence, and educating the community (Abraham 1995). Speaking about their most intimate relationships allowed South Asian women to begin to organize around their most individualized and atomized experiences. As the larger women's movement found, defining and sharing private problems and experiences can expose the need to mobilize and organize around manifestations of oppression.

The SAWOs identified a need to challenge and reform institutions such as the family, the economy, education, law, the state, media, and politics, all of which perpetuate violence against women in general and against immigrant women in particular. Domestic violence within the community provided a concrete issue around which to organize. Central to these organizations was the belief that organizing South Asian women would lead to solidarity and empowerment. Although varied in their approach, most of the SAWOs tried to bring women together around issues pertinent in their lives, particularly issues that result in inequality and oppression. This focus on organizing was a particularly important part of what I have called "value-oriented" organizations (Abraham 1995). As Mallika Dutt says:

> We are very aware of gender issues, of power around gender. We're also both very aware of the connections between sexism, between sex and race and class and sexual orientation and a whole range of other things. We saw and felt very much the need to organize around domestic violence, to organize around South Asian women and to organize within our community because there wasn't anybody doing the work around women at all at any level whatsoever. There was AIWA [Asian Indian Women in America]. . . . But in terms of our political voice, in terms of a voice that really challenged some of the cultural norms and some of the sexism and patriarchy that exists in our communities, we didn't see anybody doing that work in New York.
>
> So we decided that we needed a mechanism through which to do the consciousness-raising work and to do the organizing work. Domestic violence seemed to be one of those issues, which allowed women to come together across class, across race, across sexual preference.[3]

South Asian public events have also offered an avenue for organizing women by providing opportunities to draw attention to social concerns and to demonstrate publicly against abusers. This was done for Syeda Sufian, who was doused with gasoline and set on fire by her husband, Mohamed Mohsin, a middle-class South Asian. Sakhi for South Asian women organized a demonstration and publicly shamed the perpetrator and supported Sufian through her husband's trial and conviction—and important example of SAWOs challenging the model-minority myth. Through coalitions, South Asian organizations have also addressed gay and lesbian rights and workers' rights in order to represent the diversity within the South Asian American community (Abraham 2000).

For most of the SAWOs, domestic violence became a concrete organizing point. Although domestic violence occurs all over the world, the South Asian community in the United States is marked by its own set of cultural and structural factors. One of the SAWOs' key goals was to address domestic violence at the macro and micro levels. At the macro level, the SAWOs focused on advocating for issues affecting women's rights, with a focus on immigrant women's rights, in order to bring about legislative reform and cultural sensitization in the law-enforcement and medical-care systems. Some SAWOs also teamed up with other organizations to sensitize the courts, the police, medical services, and educational institutions to the needs of various immigrant communities.

At the micro level, the SAWOs provided assistance through individual advocacy and victim-support groups. A number of the South Asian women who approached these organizations had suffered physical abuse, sexual abuse, isolation, economic deprivation, and threats of deportation from their spouses and extended kin (Abraham 1998a, 1998b, 1999). The SAWOs gave abused women relevant information, suggested options available to them, listened to their problems, created support groups, provided counseling, and helped women to take the steps necessary to end the cycle of violence. In the support groups, abused women could meet other survivors, discuss their problems, support one another, and empower themselves (Abraham 1995, 2000).

SAWOs have been at the forefront of addressing the needs of abused South Asian immigrant women for the past decade. In 1990, Apna Ghar, a shelter in Chicago, opened to provide services for abused South Asian women. In 1997, Manavi established the transitional home Ashiana. These and other SAWOs, such as Narika, Sakhi, Saheli, and Sewaa, have provided handbooks to law-enforcement and health-care personnel and held discussions of the issues with mainstream services. Sakhi and Manavi have made considerable strides in organizing and empowering women in New York and New Jersey, respectively. These organizations have developed contacts with job-training centers and checked their accessibility for South Asian women; initiated language-training classes and connected victims with existing programs; and provided help in obtaining work permits, writing resumes, and finding jobs.

Because social change for South Asian women cannot be achieved without addressing the perception and structure of the South Asian community, one of the SAWOs' most important goals was community education. Religious institutions play a critical role in community identity and moral legitimacy among South Asians, so the SAWOs targeted these institutions for inclusion in efforts to bring about social change. They met with the leaders, discussed the problem of domestic violence, sensitized the laity about gender issues, held classes, and initiated programs that increased the South Asian community's social awareness in a variety of ways. Getting community and religious leaders to recognize the prevalence of domestic violence in the South Asian community and drawing attention to the need for these leaders to address the problem is a major step toward the SAWOs' goals.

Evidence for growing awareness of domestic violence in the South Asian community can be found in increasing numbers of abused South Asian women approaching the SAWOs, larger pools of volunteers to staff the organizations, and rising levels of funding from within and outside the community. Although nearly all the SAWOs initially faced negative reactions from the community, the situation has been gradually changing. Although not all of the reaction is now positive, the SAWOs are increasingly being accepted, as seen in the individual donations that they receive from the public; in their access to religious institutions and cultural functions to conduct public education; and in the coverage they have received in the mainstream South Asian press. However, the SAWOs task remains a difficult one. Thus, the last section of this chapter focuses on my reflections on the strategic tactics with which these SAWOs must contend in their politics of transformation.

Tactics Toward Our Communities

My research focused on SAWOs that address domestic violence; over the past decade, however, the U.S. South Asian community has seen increased mobilization around other important issues, such as health, poverty, religious fundamentalism, gay and lesbian rights, and domestic workers' rights (Dasgupta 1998; Khandelwal 1997). The South Asian population has doubled; new South Asian organizations have proliferated; and many more scholars, including a new generation of South Asian students, have begun to write about issues that affect our lives. The past decade has also seen the coming of age of a second generation of South Asians in the United States who are addressing the diverse concerns that have grown out of their perceptions and experiences of American and South Asian culture. The differing backgrounds of these men and women in terms of country of origin, age, class, sexuality, ethnicity, region, education, and socioeconomic status, as well as their own personal histories, have all seem to play into the way in which community identity is represented, contested and redefined.

Because the community is diverse and competing loyalties are a part of identity politics, the question remains: How do we bring about substantive progressive change within the community? We know that major segments of the South Asian community are still reluctant to acknowledge domestic violence as a social problem. For way too long, members of the South Asian community have bought into the model-minority image as good and desirable and ignored the many ways in which such images oppress us and obscure the problems we need to address within our community and in our relations with other ethnic minorities.

Many mainstream South Asians think that challenging the oppressive elements of our culture means discarding our South Asian identity. All too often, wealthy male members of and religious leaders in the community "manage" our identity: They become gatekeepers, controlling the image that is presented of the South Asian community. Although the gatekeepers' interests often do not truly represent the community's needs, they are able to take advantage of the relative power that their socioeconomic status provides within the community or in the larger American society. Further, many South Asian women collude in maintaining these identity constructions. Tension therefore inevitably exists among the diverse segments of the community as members' struggle with competing forces that shape community identity and the actualities of the lives we live.

Although there is no doubt among SAWOs that pressure must be applied to bring about social change within the community, there is contention over tactics. Some factions within the movement see confrontation as the most effective tactic for bringing about long-lasting gains. Others feel that negotiating, or persuading the community, is SAWOs' best course in addressing issues such as domestic violence, because it is more likely to gain popular appeal and enable transformation from within.

Persuasion may hold great appeal, but I believe it also poses a danger—it can lead to limited, issue-based change without essentially challenging the core of dominant and subordinate relations within the community. So although persuasion has its merits, those who focus on it alone must be careful not to compromise the larger agenda in favor of small gains within the community. Persuasion can also imply that the onus of bringing about change lies primarily with the SAWO and, as such, minimizes the responsibility of the community for its own actions. At the same time, those who choose a confrontational approach must carefully weigh whether such tactics really provide a base on which to maintain control of the important issues. After all, the act of confrontation can become a limited end in itself.

Given the social construction of South Asian identity and the arenas in which it is symbolically articulated, those addressing domestic violence cannot afford to be excluded from mainstream cultural activities. Rather, we should use these arenas as sites for challenging the status quo in multiple ways. Sometimes this may entail using persuasive tactics and participatory activities that creatively challenge the normative order while strategically claiming a space that is otherwise denied to us. At other times, confrontation may be essential so that we do not blunt the challenge or shield the very people and acts that we fight against. I believe that, in the absence of a serious commitment to progressive change, participatory activities run the risk of compromise and collusion. Similarly, continuous confrontation can push away those we want to include in our struggle.

Bringing varying degrees of pressure through all means possible, rather than assuming only one definitive way exists, must be part of the mobilization process. It is important for those involved in SAWOs to understand that immigrants do not always fit into an either–or categories as defined by the dominant culture. Therefore, the mobilization process must not limit itself to an either–or approach; it should also use an additive approach to achieve shared values and address common concerns. Immigrants frequently draw on cultural values that are based in their immigrant histories and look for possibilities to create "imagined communities" in a foreign country (Anderson 1991; Bacon 1996). This is an important part of the transnational experience and the process of renegotiating ties and bonds in a foreign country. Therefore, rather than totally dismissing the cultures of these imagined communities, organizations should use both tactics strategically to redefine our communities. We should articulate that our community is best served when *all* segments of community consciously discard those elements that oppress some of us. We also need to convey that addressing problems, both within the community and in mainstream American society, should be perceived not as detrimental to the community image but as an important part of progressive change. Although the community should not be given opportunities to deny the existence of social problems or attitudes and acts of discrimination, it also behooves organizations to think about their tactics when dealing with our communities. In the political climate of anti-immigrant and racist sentiment that our communities confront, SAWOs must always be conscious of the meaningfulness and relevance of our tactics. There will always be some tension between the issues we seek to address and the tactics we choose. The movement is best served, however, when our tactics carefully link vision with pragmatism as we work within, at the margin of, and from outside the communities we seek to transform.

The movement is still quite young, and its future direction and long-term outcomes are still to be seen. We will have to evaluate the SAWOs' ideology, goals, structure, and activities from time to time to remind members of maintain organizational integrity and modify the organizations' structures when necessary as we find the most effective directions in which to point future efforts. To address domestic violence, we need to mobilize the different segments that make up the South Asian community and transcend ethnic, national, religious, class and gender divisions. We must simultaneously shift the community's away from its dependence on the model-minority image and stop scapegoating the lower socioeconomic classes for the community's problems. As long as we are vested in such an image, we will not be able respond effectively to any problem, be it domestic violence, substance abuse, AIDS, or poverty, for fear of eroding a community image that is perceived as good and desirable. And we must remember that defining and redefining our communities is an ongoing process in which all of us need to engage. We are our communities—our communities ourselves.

Notes

Acknowledgments: I thank Hofstra University, the SAWOs, and the women who participated in my research and made this study possible.

1. The term "South Asian" is a social construct that refers to people who trace their roots to countries known today as Bangladesh, Bhutan, India, Nepal, Pakistan, and Sri Lanka, and who have immigrated to North America in the twentieth and twenty-first centuries. Its evolution and use, especially by South Asian activists in the United States in the 1980s, came indirectly out of the interaction between these immigrant groups and the dominant American culture. The "South Asian" label has been used in a variety of ways, including as a cultural identification, as a regional identification, and as the basis for collective action. Although the term is still used popularly, large segments of the South Asian population today identify themselves primarily in terms of specific nation-states in South Asia.

2. Mallika Dutt, interview with the author, 24 April 1991.

3. Ibid.

References

Abraham, Margaret. 1995. "Ethnicity, Gender, and Marital Violence: South Asian Women's Organizations in the United States." *Gender and Society* 9, no. 4: 450–68.

———. 1998a. "Alienation and Marital Violence Among South Asian Immigrant Women in the United States." Pp. 175–196 in *Designs for Alienation*, ed. Devorah Kalekin-Fishman. Jyväskylä, Finland: SoPhi.

———. 1998b. "Speaking the Unspeakable: Marital Violence Against South Asian Immigrant Women in the United States." *Indian Journal of Gender Studies* 5, no. 2: 215–41.

————. 1999. "Sexual Abuse in South Asian Immigrant Marriages." *Violence Against Women* 5, no. 6: 591–618.

————. 2000. *Speaking the Unspeakable: Marital Violence Among South Asian Immigrants in the United States.* New Brunswick, N.J.: Rutgers University Press.

Anderson, Benedict. 1991. *Imagined Communities: Reflections on the Origin and Spread of Nationalism.* London: Verso.

Bacon, Jean. 1996. *Life Lines: Community, Family, and Assimilation Among Asian Indian Immigrants.* New York: Oxford University Press.

Dasgupta, Shamita Das, ed. 1998. *A Patchwork Shawl: Chronicles of South Asian Women in America.* New Brunswick, N.J.: Rutgers University Press.

Dasgupta, Shamita Das, and Sayantani DasGupta. 1994. "Journeys: Reclaiming South Asian Feminism." Pp. 123–30 in *Our Feet Walk the Sky: Women of the South Asian Diaspora,* ed. Women of South Asian Descent Collective. San Francisco: Aunt Lute.

Glazer, Nathan. 1976. "Foreword." Pp. vi–viii in *The New Ethnics: Asian Indians in the United States.* New York: Praeger.

Gordon, Lisa. 1989. *Heroes of Their Own Lives: The Politics and History of Family Violence.* London: Virago Press.

Khandelwal, Madhulika. 1997. "Community Organizing in an Asian Group: Asian Indians in New York City." *Another Side* 5, no. 1: 23–32.

Kitano, Harry, and Roger Daniels. 1995. *Asian Americans: Emerging Minorities.* Englewood Cliffs, N.J.: Prentice-Hall.

Rayaprol, A. 1993. "Gender Dynamics in Cultural Practices Among South Indian Immigrants." Paper presented at the Annual Meeting of the Association of Asian American Studies, Ithaca, N.Y., June.

Vaid, Jyotsna. 1989. "Seeking a Voice: South Asian Women's Groups in North America." Pp. 395–405 in *Making Waves: An Anthology of Writing By and About Asian American Women,* ed. Asian Women United of California. Boston: Beacon Press.

CHAPTER 13

Edward J. W. Park

Asian Pacific Americans
and Urban Politics

As we reflect on the transformative impact of Asian Pacific Americans (APAs) on American society, urban politics emerges as one of the most prominent sites of change and struggle. Since the passage of the Immigration Act of 1965, the rapid growth of the APA population and communities has become an important source of new urban tension. The growth of the APA middle class has resulted in "white flight" and backlash politics in once quiescent suburban communities (Saito 1998). In an interview with a *Los Angeles Times* reporter, a white resident articulated a common reaction to APA-led neighborhood transition. Protesting the influx of Chinese Americans into Monterey Park, California, she said: "I feel like I'm in another country. I don't feel at home anymore" (as quoted in Fong 1994: 64). Since the 1980s, this sentiment has expressed itself powerfully, as city after city has debated and passed English-only laws that seek to curtail the visible signs of Asianness.

Even as middle-class APAs displace whites in suburban and affluent neighborhoods, American cities have seen rising tension and conflict between APAs and other racial minority groups. From New York to Los Angeles, conflict between Korean American liquor-store owners and African American community activists has resulted in highly publicized protests and boycotts (Min 1996; Rosenfeld 1997). In San Francisco and Houston, the influx of Southeast Asians into traditional African American neighborhoods has been met with growing tension and violence as these communities compete for affordable housing, social services, and economic opportunities (Rodriguez 1995).

Along with demonstrating the continuing significance of race and the growing multiracial complexity of American cities, APAs are throwing off their image as the silent and apolitical minority and are actively mobilizing to win their share of political power. Although their small numbers often frustrate efforts to win national and state-level offices, APAs have achieved a measure of success at the urban level, where they can more effectively leverage their demographic concentration in certain metropolitan areas (Fong 1998). From their traditional base in San Francisco to newly settled Houston, APAs have become the fastest-growing segment of urban political leadership in the nation (Nakanishi and Lai 2000). In their mobilization, APAs reveal a great deal about their political ideology and agenda, internal diversity and divisions, and, ultimately, the future of urban politics in America.

In this context of profound change and rapid mobilization, this chapter seeks to take a critical look at APAs in urban politics. A number of groundbreaking works have appeared recently on the issue of suburban community transition; this chapter, however, will focus explicitly on the issue of inter-minority politics in the urban setting (see Fong 1994; Li 1999; and Saito 1998). The first part of the chapter examines the academic literature on race and urban politics—in particular, the "liberal-coalition model," which remains the dominant way of thinking about racial minorities and urban politics. Using the experience of Los Angeles, a city closely identified with the model, this part of the chapter questions the relevance and the utility of a model that is steeped in the political realities of the Civil Rights Movement and the mobilization of African Americans in the context of a biracial society.

In the second part of chapter, I will examine the experience of Korean Americans in Los Angeles as a case study that brings into focus some of the key issues as APAs mobilize politically in a multiracial, multiethnic setting. In particular, the discussion highlights the complex relationship between Korean Americans and African Americans—clearly the most important and senior partner of the liberal coalition. Finally, I will conclude by highlighting some of the lessons for building a more compelling framework for understanding urban politics and for building a more inclusive and just American city.

The Liberal-Coalition Model

One of the most enduring assumptions in the urban politics literature has been that the political incorporation of racial minorities is inextricably linked with their participation in liberal coalitions (Browning et al. 1984; Sonenshein 1993). This liberal-coalition model has been fundamental to, and pervasive in, studies of race and power in contemporary American cities for compelling reasons. For much of American's urban history, conservative coalitions have actively and uniformly sought to exclude all racial minorities from the political process, with devastating consequences not only for their political rights but also for their economic development and social lives.[1] Faced with hostility and recalcitrance from conservative coalitions, racial minorities found a measure of political unity among themselves and worked with allies among white liberals whose political commitment included individual rights and representative justice (see Boussard 1993; Taylor 1994). Working in coalition with white liberals, racial minorities—with the leadership of African Americans—ushered in the most dramatic urban political change in U.S. history during the 1960s and the 1970s (Browning et al. 1984).[2] Although many have questioned the varying terms and parameters of cooperation and cohesion between racial minorities and white liberals, most have viewed the political incorporation of racial minorities through their successful integration into liberal coalitions (Browning et al. 1984; Carmichael and Hamilton 1967; Sonenshein 1996).

Perhaps more than in any other city, urban politics in Los Angeles has been shaped by the liberal-coalition model. From the beginnings of its expansion in the 1880s to its emergence as one of the largest cities in the nation by the 1960s, Los Angeles politics was dominated by white Protestant migrants from the Midwest who wanted to avoid the "fate" of large Eastern and Midwestern cities—cities that they perceived to be dominated by the corrupting influences of Catholic immigrants, labor unions, and racial minorities (Fogelson 1967; Sonenshein 1990: 34). Despite the increase in racial and ethnic diversity ushered in by the massive migration of blacks, Mexicans, Jews, and APAs since the 1920s, Los Angeles's urban political leadership was almost exclusively white until the 1960s. Moreover, the city's leadership was committed to a conservative vision of urban government in which the scope of its activities were limited to maintaining law and order, fostering a pro-business environment, and upholding racial boundaries in residential and social spheres (Romo 1983; Sonenshein 1990). Even as the city's social-service needs exploded with the growth of the poor and the working class, political leaders in Los Angeles remained steadfast in their policies of fiscal austerity and refused to fund social programs. Under this political regime, racial minorities who faced unequal access to the labor market, severe housing segregation, and inferior social services suffered the brunt of conservative leadership. The last conservative mayor representing this brand of politics in Los Angeles was Sam Yorty, whose legendary conservatism included staunch support of the controversial police chief William Parker in the aftermath of the Watts riot of 1965 and the refusal of millions of dollars of federal funds for urban programs because he feared that these new resources would politically empower the African American community (Horne 1995).

Los Angeles was one of the first major American cities to have a successful liberal coalition. In 1973, the African American councilman Tom Bradley defeated Yorty and was elected mayor in a city whose population was less than 20 percent African American. As Raphael Sonenshein (1993) has convincingly shown, Bradley was able to win the closely contested election in 1973 by building a biracial coalition of African American and Jewish voters, running on a platform that promised a more inclusive city leadership and bureaucracy, more expansive social-services and community programs, and, to appease the powerful business community, a pro-business policy that would transform Los Angeles into a "world city." Since then, other major cities have seen the emergence of liberal coalitions, punctuated by the election of William Goode in Philadelphia, Harold Washington in Chicago, and David Dinkins in New York.

In Los Angeles, Bradley handily won re-election in 1977, 1981, 1985, and 1989, each time broadening his formidable "Bradley Coalition" to include the growing Latino and APA population by aggressively diversifying the city bureaucracy and championing Latino and APA candidates for elective office. Michael Woo, the only APA to be elected to the Los Angeles City Council, was identified closely with the Bradley Coalition—a key asset when he was elected to the council in 1985 (Regalado 1998). As an insurgent movement that opened up white-dominated city hall and actively addressed the needs of neglected minority communities, liberal coalitions enjoyed enthusiastic and uniform support among the majority of racial minority groups (see Browning et al. 1990).

By the 1970s, the Civil Rights Movement had transformed urban politics; since then, major social and political changes have unfolded in American cities. More than 7 million immigrants from Mexico, Central America, and Asia entered the United States in the 1980s alone (Portes and Rumbaut 1996). These newest Americans bring new multiracial complexities and challenges to the urban political process and pose daunting challenges for liberals in maintaining their traditional claim on racial-minority incorporation. At the same time, racial politics has gradually moved from the simplicity of unequivocal white supremacy to the more nuanced and complex dynamics of "post-Civil Rights" politics (Marable 1995). As Michael Omi and Howard Winant (1994) persuasively argue, conservatives have successfully reframed the discourse of American race relations in the post-Civil Rights era so that charges of "reverse discrimination" and "black racism" are not only part of the mainstream political vocabulary but have engendered powerful political movements, including the national attack on affirmative action.

As liberals find themselves struggling with new challenges, some conservatives have attempted to reconfigure their relationship with racial minorities and have reached out for their votes and support. Whether these attempts reflect their anxiety in the face of demographic change or genuine commitment to racial inclusion, conservatives are increasingly reluctant to write off racial minorities politically, especially in large cities and diverse states where racial-minority voters can shift the electoral balance. In the 1990s, Los Angeles and New York both saw liberal candidates for mayor lose to conservative Republicans, even as the minority population in these cities boomed. In 1993, Richard Riordan defeated Michael Woo in Los Angeles, and Rudolph Giuliani defeated David Dinkins in New York. In their campaigns, both Riordan and Giuliani openly appealed to racial-minority voters and won a considerable number of votes (Sonenshein 1993; Marable 1995).

A striking example of these complexities can be found in the tense relationship between Cuban Americans and African Americans in Miami, an experience that provides an important comparative perspective on the Korean American experience in Los Angeles. In their landmark study *City on the Edge* (1993), Alejandro Portes and Alex Stepick trace the rise of Cuban American political power in Miami despite the fierce resistance of the city's Anglo elite. As Cubans entered Miami in 1950s, Miami's urban political scene was dominated by the all-white Chamber of Commerce, which catered exclusively to the needs of downtown business and the tourist industry (Warren et al. 1990). The mutual need for community development, social programs, and political representation brought a measure of cooperation among African Americans and Cuban Americans, especially among the middle class in these two communities, whose economic and political aspirations were effectively frustrated in this segregated Southern city.

As the number of Cuban refugees and immigrants became massive during the 1970s and 1980s, however, the relationship between these two communities became increasingly strained.[3] At the level of everyday interaction, Cuban Americans and African Americans increasingly saw themselves as competitors in the lower segments of the labor and the housing markets, for small-business opportunities, and for municipal services and social programs. Perhaps even more important, Cuban Americans who entered during these decades did not experience the same kind of social exclusion that African Americans and earlier waves of Cuban refugees encountered—saving them from both the most blatant forms of discrimination and an important political socialization that provided a basis for political cooperation. At the level of political leadership, Cuban American politicians—sensing correctly that the tremendous population growth would translate into a decisive voting block—decided to reject coalition politics with African Americans and go their own way (Warren et al. 1990). Any last hope that these two communities could work together was dashed in 1986, when two Cuban American candidates faced off for the mayoral race. In a divisive campaign, Raul Masvidal, who received solid support from the African American community, lost the election to Xavier Suarez, who appealed narrowly to the Cuban American community and was financially supported by the Anglo business community, which promised large investments in Little Havana. Reflecting on this crucial moment, Portes and Stepick (1993: 201) argues that it was ultimately more important for the Cuban Americans to boost the economic fortunes of Little Havana than to "build a new multiethnic community."

During Miami's Liberty City riots of 1980, an event that is strikingly similar to the Los Angeles civil unrest of 1992, a segment of the African American community vented its frustration against Cuban Americans who—despite their late arrival—had leapfrogged African Americans both economically and politically by the end of the 1970s.[4] When asked why Cuban American-owned businesses were targeted for attack, an African American community leader accused Cuban American merchants—particularly liquor-store owners in impoverished African American communities such as Liberty City and Overtown—of exploiting their community, "just as Jewish and other white merchants had done before" (Portes and Stepick 1993: 141). At the same time, some Cuban Americans recoiled at the suggestion that the community had betrayed its earlier alliance with the African American community. A first-year law student told the *Miami Herald*, "[Cuban Americans] have pulled ourselves up, why should we restrain ourselves? I don't think the Cuban community in Miami owes anything politically and economically to anyone. The Cuban community succeeded because it's been loyal to itself" (as quoted in Portes and Stepick 1993: 199).

When Nelson Mandela, the newly elected president of South Africa, made a stop in Miami in 1990, he visited a profoundly divided city. Two of the largest groups that gathered at the entrance of the Miami Beach Convention Center were Cuban Americans, who condemned Mandela's relationship with Cuba's Fidel Castro, and African Americans, who counter-protested the racism of Cuban Americans. One of the African

American protesters held a placard that read, "Mandela, Welcome to Miami, Home of Apartheid" (Portes and Stepick 1993: 176).

Korean Americans in Los Angeles

As the full effect of the immigration reforms of 1965 took hold, Koreans immigrated to the United States in astonishing numbers (Hing 1993; Min 1996). Like most post-1965 immigrants, they were attracted to urban areas that had large and dynamic economies and previous settlements of co-ethnics who could help them adjust to their new lives. Los Angeles, with its booming and diverse economy and the largest Korean American community in the country, quickly became the center for the Korean American population (Chang 1994; Min 1996). From 1970 to 1990, the Korean American population grew more than sevenfold, increasing from 9,395 to 72,970. By 1990, Los Angeles County had become home to 145,431 Korean Americans, representing close to 20 percent of this group's total U.S. population (Min 1996: 34). In their settlement, Korean Americans in Los Angeles transformed a twenty-square-mile area just west of downtown Los Angeles and, in 1978, won the official designation of "Koreatown" from city hall.

Despite its ethnic moniker, Koreatown is now largely Latino: Korean Americans have rapidly moved into traditionally white suburbs and now make up less than 15 percent of Koreatown's population (Min 1996). Nevertheless, with more than 3,000 Korean American-owned businesses and more than one hundred community organizations, Koreatown remains the social, economic, cultural, and psychological center of Korean Americans in Southern California, and the nation, and has made Los Angeles urban politics the most prominent site for their political hopes and dreams.

The timing of Korean Americans' migration coincided with the most dramatic change in Los Angeles's political history and reveals some of the complexities of post-Civil Rights urban politics. As noted earlier, after decades of white conservative rule, the city's liberal coalition finally elected Tom Bradley mayor in 1973 and ushered in two decades of liberal control of the city government (Sonenshein 1993). In the two City Council districts that divide Koreatown and its immediate areas, key members of the Bradley Coalition held the office, and today, both districts are represented by liberal minority politicians (Nate Holden, an African American, and Mike Hernandez, a Latino). Beyond urban politics, Koreatown has been represented by liberal politicians in Sacramento and in Washington, D.C., for nearly three decades.

In addition to winning elected offices, the Bradley Coalition actively diversified city agencies through political appointments and by aggressively pursuing affirmative-action hiring in public employment (Guerra 1987). At the same time, the Bradley Coalition remained predominantly a coalition of African Americans and white liberals, in part reflecting the decisive role of African American and Jewish voters in bringing Bradley to power (Sonenshein 1993). Although Latinos gained some prominence in the Bradley Coalition, reflecting their increasing demographic presence and, more important, the rise of important individual political leaders, APAs (especially new groups, such as Korean Americans) remained peripheral to the concerns of the liberal political leadership (Brackman and Erie 1998; Regalado 1994). On the eve of the Los Angeles civil unrest, not one Korean American served in any significant political or appointed office, and most of the social-service agencies within the Korean American community looked to their own ethnic resources rather than to city hall to fund programs.

From the point of view of Korean Americans, then, the face of political power in the city has always been ideologically liberal and racially diverse. At the same time, however, Korean Americans have felt far removed from the liberal political leaders who have controlled much of Los Angeles politics during their community's short history. These leaders have expressed little interest in the Korean American community and provided even less in the terms substantive political incorporation, such as active recruitment of Korean Americans for elected office or funding of community-based political organizations (see Browning et al. 1984). To many Korean Americans, the liberal political leaders—and, more specifically, African American political leaders, who had the highest visibility the community—looked not like an insurgent political force that had toppled the conservative and racist Yorty–Parker regime, but like an entrenched and imposing power that ultimately cared little about their community.

The Los Angeles civil unrest of 1992, the largest episode of civil unrest in the nation's modern history, stands as the single most important event in the history of Korean Americans.[5] Confronted with their greatest crisis, Korean Americans quickened the pace of their political development and vigorously participated in Los Angeles politics for the first time. Their participation has forced the community to confront its own tensions and divisions and to engage the mainstream political process. In contrast to the experiences of other racial and ethnic groups that underwent similar types of political formation through crisis mobilizing (see Boussard 1993; Portes and Stepick 1993; Taylor 1994), the political mobilization in the Korean American community has not brought intra-community unity and consolidation. Instead, it has brought a sharpening of political divisions and differences. Two case studies drawn from the aftermath of the civil unrest serve as examples of why Los Angeles's Korean Americans are a community divided and why the question of coalition-building remains open.

In the aftermath of the civil unrest, the hopes of some Korean American and African American progressive activists that the two communities could begin to work together to build a more just and harmonious Los Angeles came to a crashing halt in controversy over the reopening of liquor stores. The heavy concentration of liquor stores in inner-city communities has long been a sensitive political issue for liberals in Los Angeles. For many inner-city residents, the preponderance of liquor stores in their neighborhoods has represented betrayal by liberal politicians who favor the tax revenues that these stores create over the welfare of the communities. The destruction of some two hundred liquor stores during the civil unrest provided a unique opportunity for the city's liberal political leadership to do something about the situation. The possibility of reopening liquor stores quickly became a racial issue when it was discovered that 187 of the stores were owned by Korean Americans. As Sonenshein (1996) has described in great detail, local political leaders, working with Democratic leaders in Sacramento, succeeded in passing an ordinance that imposed strict conditions for reopening, including providing security and parking. The restrictions were so severe that only a handful of stores were able to reopen two years after the civil unrest (Kang 1994a, 1994b). Although some of the opponents of the liquor stores valiantly worked with sympathetic members of the Korean American community to "deracialize" the issue, their efforts were stymied by others who relied on explicit racial labels and imagery to rally the political support of African Americans, including Danny Bakewell, an African American activist who equated Korean American liquor-store owners with drug dealers (Chavez 1994; Sonenshein 1996). Five years after the controversy, the liquor-store issue has become the key metaphor within the Korean American community for their political victimization at the hands of African American and liberal political power (Park 1996).

Because the liquor-store controversy was so volatile, liberals who did not directly support the restrictions stayed on the sidelines, fearing the anger and hostility that their support of Korean Americans might bring from the African American community (Sonenshein 1996). In this time of desperation, Korean Americans found their only willing allies among the conservatives who were immune to African American political power. When the Republican-led effort to overturn the restrictions finally failed in Sacramento, Korean American community leaders, side by side with business-association members and Republican activists, charged African Americans with "black racism" and blamed liberal Democrats for scapegoating the Korean Americans for decades of failed policies in the inner city (Kang 1994a). In a terse editorial in the *Korea Times*, two Republican activists aimed their comments directly at the liberal-coalition model by imploring readers to rethink carefully "who are their friend and who are their enemies" (Steel and Park-Steel 1994). Although they lost the policy battle, the conservatives within the Korean American community won a huge victory in revealing what they perceive to be a fundamental, if not fatal, antagonism between the Korean American community and the liberal coalition.

Although the liquor-store controversy energized the conservatives within the Korean American community, broader political developments in Los Angeles since the civil unrest have emboldened the community's liberals and the progressives. In addition to organizational coalition-building (Brackman and Erie 1998; Freer 1994; Park 1996; Regalado 1994), there has been a vigorous grassroots political mobilization on the left in Los Angeles. First, the statewide and national politics that have sought to undermine the political gains of racial minorities and immigrants have mobilized Korean American liberals and progressives on issues such as immigrant rights, affirmative action, and bilingual education. California's notorious Propositions 187 and 209, and the federal government's effort to eliminate legal immigrants from some Social Security programs and the food-stamp program, have created powerful reasons and desperate conditions for racial minorities to work together.

In Los Angeles, with a still liberal City Council and a growing minority electorate, conservative and centrist political leaders, including Mayor Richard Riordan, have avoided taking firm stands in favor of these legislative onslaughts and have created a conservative political vacuum within the city. Within this context, Korean American liberals and progressives have successfully linked these initiatives to what they argue are broad-based conservative attacks on immigrant and civil rights. Korean American activists succeeded in convincing the voters in the community to reject Proposition 209, even though its proponents positioned APAs, including Korean Americans, as one of its chief beneficiaries (*Crosscurrents* 1996). In addition, the Republican-led push to eliminate legal immigrants from federal-level redistributive programs, including Supplemental Security Income and food stamps, has galvanized liberals and progressives to fight these measures, which have an inordinate impact on Koreatown's large concentration of elderly and new immigrants. These state and national developments, in conjunction with the lack of vigorous conservative advocacy within the city and the community, have brought new life to the liberals and progressives within the community. The explicit anti-immigrant sentiment in these developments has placed Korean American conservatives in an awkward position in a community that remains closely connected to its immigrant roots. One conservative activist I interviewed lamented, "How can I ask Korean Americans to support the Republican Party when they are being told that it wants to yank the food out of their grandparent's mouth?" On the opposing side, the progressive head of a Korean American social-service agency said, "I don't get it. While one segment of the Republican Party puts out the welcome mat for Korean Americans, another segment hangs out the sign 'Koreans Go Home.'"[6]

In addition, Korean Americans, like most post-1965 immigrant groups, bring with them diverse class backgrounds and political visions that shape their politics. For instance, although they have one of the highest rates of college education (33 percent), Korean Americans living in Koreatown suffer from among the highest poverty rates in the city (26 percent) (Ong and Umemoto 1994). Thus, it remains an open question whether *any* existing political coalition can absorb Korean Americans, or similarly situated new immigrant groups that are characterized by dramatic intragroup diversity and difference, in toto (Abelmann and Lie 1995; Min 1996). Although models of racial and ethnic *group* incorporation have been central in the study of urban politics (Browning et al. 1984; Erie and Brackman 1995; Glazer and Moynihan 1963), the intragroup diversity and difference among Korean Americans, as well as among other new immigrants, pose a challenge to this method of understanding political incorporation.

Although the media has focused on Korean Americans as predominantly an entrepreneurial group, it is class diversity, not homogeneity, that characterizes the community. This is especially true in Los Angeles, where decades of suburbanization has left the city with Korean Americans who are disproportionately poor, often trapped in low-paying service jobs in the ethnic economy (Ong and Umemoto 1994). In his research on Koreatown's ethnic economy, Pyong Gap Min (1996) echoes the familiar charge in the inner-city that too many of the businesses in Koreatown are owned by Korean Americans who live outside the community's and the city's boundaries, leaving Koreatown with low-paying service and retail workers; recently arrived, young families; and the elderly who live in the community's numerous subsidized housing complexes. Indeed, although much is made of the community's 30 percent self-employment rate, larger numbers of Korean Americans work in low-paying jobs, with little or no benefits and with severely limited opportunities for mobility (Abelmann and Lie 1995; Light and Bonacich 1994). The class diversity among Korean Americans has played a significant role in the politics of the community, ranging from highly publicized labor conflicts to battles over relief money in the aftermath of the civil unrest (Lee 1994).

Along with these class-based divisions, Korean American political activists have made a more direct ideological appeal. On the one hand, they argue that as racial minorities, Korean Americans share a long history of racial oppression with other minority groups. For instance, Korean Americans one of the two very last groups (along with Japanese Americans) who were given the right to naturalized citizenship in 1952 (Choy 1979). In different times and in different localities, Korean Americans were excluded from immigration, prohibited from owning real property, and discriminated in housing markets and educational opportunities (Takaki 1989). Within the community, Korean American liberal and progressive activist constantly link these historical accounts with contemporary politics, drawing lessons for coalition politics. They also link contemporary political issues ranging from immigration restriction, welfare reform, and anti-Asian violence to the broader historical narrative, arguing that Korean Americans can best guard their hard-won rights and ensure future equality by working together with other members of the liberal coalition (Cho 1993; Kang et al. 1993; Kim 1994; Oh 1993). On the other hand, Korean American conservative activists have argued that the community has class-based interests and commitment to "traditional values" that puts them squarely against liberals. First, they argue that the Korean American community remains a community of entrepreneurs, and they smooth over class differences by arguing that the working class in the community will benefit most with a strong and vibrant ethnic economy. By conflating small-business interest with community interest, they rally the community's political support for both fiscal conservatism and law and order (Steel and Park-Steel 1994). Fiscal conservatism addresses the economic interests of the community, but the issue of law and order touches it more deeply. Vivid and regular reports in the ethnic and mainstream media of horrific crimes against Korean American shop owners and residents touch the raw nerve of the community and have worked to rally the community in support of conservatives who offer them tough justice and righteous vengeance (Doherty 1992; Yi 1993).

Thus, the history of racism provides an emotional connecting point between Korean Americans and liberals, while the issue of crime serves a similar function for the conservatives. In addition, Korean American conservatives view liberalism in opposition to "traditional" Korean culture, which is based on Confucian values, including respect for elders and traditional gender roles. Liberals within the community—especially liberal and progressive women—are chastised as being "too assimilated," having abandoned Korean ways for the permissive ways of the American society.

Lessons from Los Angeles

This excursion into Korean American politics in Los Angeles reveals some important lessons for the liberal-coalition model of urban politics. First, it is important to recognize that the model's central assumption of power relations in American cities can no longer be taken for granted. New immigrant groups, even those that are racial minorities, lack the personal experience of de jure racism that served as such a powerful unifying force a generation ago. For them, the face of conservative urban politicians—among them Richard Riordan and Rudolph Giuliani—is no longer that of the recalcitrant defender of white power and privilege but is the face of the competent manager who will lower taxes, grow the economy, fight crime, and reduce the bureaucracy, all the while ensconced in the multiculturalism of their cosmopolitan cities. With these changes, liberals must rethink what they have to offer—in both policies and leadership—to new immigrants and to other constituents to win their political support. In this context, the new immigrants can either revitalize the liberal coalition on a new vision of urban America or bury it under the weight of its own, but different, recalcitrance.

In addition, within the urban political context, African Americans can appear to the new immigrants as an imposing and entrenched political power rather than as an important agent for progressive political change. Although it might be tempting to call on African American political leaders to share their political power and resources with the new immigrant groups, that is made difficult by the current political and economic crisis that African American communities face (Marable 1995) and by decades of mistrust and animosity between African Americans and new immigrants (Oliver et al. 1993; Portes and Stepick 1993; Rodriguez 1995). Perhaps the greatest challenge for the liberal coalition and for the established African American political leadership will be to identify common interests around which these groups can come together so they can rebuild the mutual trust that is essential for multiracial coalition and collaboration. As recent works that focus explicitly on building multiracial coalitions show, this task is difficult but not impossible (see Freer 1993; Saito and Park 2000).

Finally, the diversity within new immigrant groups poses another set of issues that liberal coalitions must address. Class divisions within the new immigrant communities provide opportunities for liberals who have traditionally garnered support among the working class and the poor. Indeed, in Los Angeles, APAs and Latinos who reside within the city limits have dramatically increased the liberal political base, and Latino workers and labor unions in particular have recharged the city's once declining progressive left (Brackman and Erie 1998; Regalado 1998). At the same time, because race and ethnicity no longer have the same "leveling effect" in minority political formation, liberals cannot simply pursue a "one-class" strategy to win the political support of new immigrant groups as it did a generation ago. For APAs whose class composition includes large numbers of entrepreneurs and professionals, this is particularly clear. Yet what this means for the liberal coalition remains an open question, one that will be ultimately decided by the cycle of the real-world political process. Regardless, for the liberal coalition to become more fully effective, it must confront more directly the changing political and demographic realities of urban America.

Notes

1. For an extended discussion of conservative and liberal coalitions in American urban politics, see Browning et al. 1984, 1990.

2. At the national level, the Civil Rights Movement's policy victories include the Civil Rights Act of 1964, the Voting Rights Act of 1965, and the Fair Housing Act of 1968. At the urban level, these national policies have led to greater political participation of racial minorities, resulting in a number of dramatic political victories by African American and Latino candidates (see Sonenshein 1993).

3. From 1960 to 1988, the percentage of Cuban Americans grew from less than 5 percent to more than 40 percent, while the percentage of African Americans grew from 14.7 percent to 19.6 percent.

4. Similar to the Los Angeles civil unrest of 1992, the Liberty City riot of 1980 was sparked by a not-guilty verdict for four white police officers charged in the killing of an African American motorist, Arthur McDuffie. The Liberty City section of Miami erupted in violence less than three hours after the all-white jury entered its verdict.

5. The civil rest in Los Angeles was sparked by the not-guilty verdict for four Los Angeles police officers charged with beating the African American motorist Rodney King. The civil unrest raged from 29 April to 5 May 1992, resulting in the loss of fifty-two lives, 16,291 arrests, and the destruction of nearly $1 billion in property. Underscoring the multiracial dimension of the unrest: the majority of those killed were African American, the majority of those arrested were Latino, and Korean Americans sustained nearly half of the property loss. For a general description of the Los Angeles civil unrest, see Oliver et al. 1993. For the political impact of the civil unrest, see Freer 1994; Park 1996; and Sonenshein 1994.

6. Laura Jeon, interview with the author, Los Angeles, June 1998; Youngbin Kim, interview with the author, Los Angeles, June 1998.

References

Abelmann, Nancy, and John Lie. 1995. *Blue Dreams: Korean Americans and the Los Angeles Riots*. Cambridge, Mass.: Harvard University Press.

Brackman, Harold, and Steven P. Erie. 1995. "Beyond 'Politics by Other Means'? Empowerment Strategies for Los Angeles' Asian Pacific community." Pp. 282–303 in *The Bubbling Cauldron: Race, Ethnicity, and the Urban Crisis*, ed. Michael Peter Smith and Joe R. Feagin. Minneapolis: University of Minnesota Press.

———. 1998. "At Rainbow's End: Empowerment Prospects for Latinos and Asian Pacific Americans in Los Angeles." Pp. 73–107 in *Racial and Ethnic Politics in California*, vol. 2, ed. Michael B. Preston, Bruce E. Cain, and Sandra Bass. Berkeley, Calif.: Institute of Government Studies Press.

Boussard, Albert S. 1993. *Black San Francisco: The Struggle for Racial Equality in the West, 1900–1954*. Lawrence: University Press of Kansas.

Browning, Rufus, Dale Rogers Marshall, and David Tabb. 1984. *Protest Is Not Enough: The Struggle of Blacks and Hispanics for Equality in City Politics*. Berkeley: University of California Press.

———. 1990. *Racial Politics in American Cities*. New York: Longman.

Carmichael, Stokeley, and Charles Hamilton. 1967. *Black Power: The Politics of Liberation in America*. New York: Vintage Books.

Chang, Edward T. 1994. "America's First Multiethnic 'Riots.'" Pp. 101–18 in *The State of Asian America*, ed. Karin Aguilar-San Juan. Boston: South End Press.

Chavez, Lydia. 1994. "Crossing the Culture Line." *Los Angeles Times Magazine* (28 August).

Cho, Sumi K. 1993. "Korean Americans vs. African Americans: Conflict and Construction." Pp. 196–211 in *Reading Rodney King/Reading Urban Uprising*, ed. Robert Gooding-Williams. New York: Routledge.

Choy, Bong-Youn. 1979. *Koreans in America*. Chicago: Nelson-Hall.

Crosscurrents. 1996. "Affirmative Action Controversy in California," vol. 19, no. 2.

Doherty, Jay. 1992. "Black–Korean Alliance Says Talk Not Enough, Disbands." *Los Angeles Times*, 24 December.

Fogelson, Robert. 1967. *The Fragmented Metropolis: Los Angeles, 1850–1930*. Cambridge, Mass.: Harvard University Press.

Fong, Timothy P. 1994. *The First Suburban Chinatown: The Remaking of Monterey Park, California*. Philadelphia: Temple University Press.

———. 1998. "Why Ted Dang Lost: An Analysis of the 1994 Mayoral Race in Oakland, California." *Journal of Asian American Studies* 1, no. 2: 153–71.

Freer, Regina. 1994. "Black–Korean Conflict." Pp. 175–204 in *The Los Angeles Riots: Lessons for the Urban Future*, ed. Mark Baldassare. Boulder, Colo.: Westview Press.

Glazer, Nathan, and Daniel P. Moynihan. 1963. *Beyond the Melting Pot*. Cambridge, Mass: MIT Press.

Guerra, Fernando J. 1987. "Ethnic Office Holders in Los Angeles County." *Sociology and Social Research* 71: 89–94.

Hing, Bill Ong. 1993. *Making and Remaking Asian America Through Immigration Policy, 1850–1990*. Stanford, Calif.: Stanford University Press.

Horne, Gerald. 1995. *Fire This Time: The Watts Uprising and the 1960s*. Charlottesville: University Press of Virginia.

Kang, K. Connie. 1994a. "Store Owners Fight Restrictions on Reopening." *Los Angeles Times* (21 July).

———. 1994b. "Asian American Groups Organize to Fight Measure." *Korea Times* (English edition) (2 September).

Kang, Milianna, Juliana J. Kim, Edward J. W. Park, and Hae Won Park. 1993. *Bridge Toward Unity*. Los Angeles: Korean Immigrant Workers Advocates.

Kim, Elaine H. 1994. "Between Black and White." Pp. 71–100 in *The State of Asian America*, ed. Karin Aguilar-San Juan. Boston: South End Press.

Lee, Hoon. 1994. "4.29 Displaced Workers Justice Campaign." *KIWA News*, vol. 1, 6–13.

Li, Wei. 1999. "Building Ethnoburbia: The Emergence and Manifestation of the Chinese Ethnoburb in Los Angeles' San Gabriel Valley." *Journal of Asian American Studies* 2, no. 1: 1–28.

Light, Ivan, and Edna Bonacich. 1988. *Immigrant Entrepreneurs: Koreans in Los Angeles, 1965–1982*. Berkeley: University of California Press.

Marable, Manning. 1995. *Beyond Black and White: Rethinking Race in American Politics and Society*. New York: Verso.

Min, Pyong Gap. 1996. *Caught in the Middle: Korean Communities in New York and Los Angeles*. Berkeley: University of California Press.

Nakanishi, Don T., and James S. Lai. 2000. *National Asian American Political Almanac*. Los Angeles: UCLA Asian American Studies Center.

Oh, Angela E. 1993. "Rebuilding Los Angeles: Why I Did Not Join RLA." *Amerasia Journal* 19: 157–60.

Oliver, Melvin L., James H. Johnson, and W. C Farrell. 1993. "Anatomy of a Rebellion." Pp. 117–41 in *Reading Rodney King/Reading Urban Uprising*, ed. Robert Gooding-Williams. New York: Routledge.

Omi, Michael, and Howard Winant. 1994. *Racial Formations in the United States*, 2nd ed. New York: Routledge.

Ong, Paul, and Karen Umemoto. 1994. "Life and Work in the Inner-City." Pp. 87–112 in *The State of Asian Pacific America: Economic Diversity, Issues and Policies*, ed. Paul Ong. Los Angeles: LEAP Asian American Public Policy Institute.

Park, Edward J. W. 1996. "Our L.A.? Korean Americans in Los Angeles After the Civil Unrest." Pp. 153–68 in *Rethinking Los Angeles*, ed. Michael J. Dear, H. Eric Schockman, and Greg Hise. Thousand Oaks, Calif.: Sage Publications.

Portes, Alejandro, and Ruben G. Rumbaut. 1996. *Immigrant America: A Portrait*, 2nd ed. Berkeley: University of California Press.

Portes, Alejandro, and Alex Stepick. 1993. *City on the Edge: The Transformation of Miami*. Berkeley: University of California Press.

Regalado, James A. 1994. "Community Coalition-Building." Pp. 205–36 in *The Los Angeles Riots: Lessons for the Urban Future*, ed. Mark Baldassare. Boulder, Colo.: Westview Press.

———. 1998. "Minority Political Incorporation in Los Angeles: A Broader Consideration." Pp. 381–409 in *Racial and Ethnic Politics in California: Volume Two*, ed. Michael B. Preston, Bruce E. Cain, and Sandra Bass. Berkeley, Calif.: Institute for Governmental Studies Press.

Rodriguez, Nestor P. 1995. "The Real 'New World Order': The Globalization of Race and Ethnic Relations in the Late Twentieth Century." Pp. 211–25 in *The Bubbling Cauldron: Race, Ethnicity, and the Urban Crisis*, ed. Michael Peter Smith and Joe R. Feagin. Minneapolis: University of Minnesota Press.

Romo, Ricardo. 1983. *East Los Angeles: History of a Barrio*. Austin: University of Texas Press.

Rosenfeld, Michael J. 1997. "Celebration, Politics, Selective Looting and Riots: A Micro Level Study of the Bulls Riot of 1992 in Chicago." *Social Problems* 44: 483–502.

Saito, Leland T. 1998. *Race and Politics: Asian Americans, Latinos, and Whites in a Los Angeles Suburb*. Urbana: University of Illinois Press.

Saito, Leland T., and Edward J. W. Park. 2000. "Multiracial Collaborations and Coalitions." In *The State of Asian Pacific America: Transforming Race Relations*, ed. Paul Ong. Los Angeles: LEAP Asian Pacific American Public Policy Institute and UCLA Asian American Studies Center.

Sonenshein, Raphael J. 1990. "Biracial Coalition Politics in Los Angeles." In *Racial Politics in American Cities*, ed. Rufus P. Browning, Dale Rogers Marshall, and David H. Tabb. New York: Longman.

———. 1993. *Politics in Black and White: Race and Power in Los Angeles*. Princeton, N.J.: Princeton University Press.

———. 1994. "Los Angeles Coalition Politics." Pp. 205–36 in *The Los Angeles Riots: Lessons for the Urban Future*, ed. Mark Baldassare. Boulder, Colo.: Westview Press.

———. 1996. "The Battle over Liquor Stores in South Central Los Angeles: The Management of an Interminority Conflict." *Urban Affairs Review* 31, no. 6: 710–37.

Steel, Shawn, and Michelle E. J. Park-Steel. 1994. "Outcome of AB 1974: Korean-Americans Strangled Again." *Korea Times* (English ed.), 7 September.

Takaki, Ronald. 1989. *Strangers from a Different Shore*. Boston: Little, Brown.

Taylor, Quintard. 1994. *The Forging of a Black Community: Seattle's Central District from 1870 through the Civil Rights Era*. Seattle: University of Washington Press.

Warren, Christopher L., John G. Corbett, and John F. Stack, Jr. 1990. "Hispanic Ascendancy and Tripartite Politics in Miami." In *Racial Politics in American Cities*, ed. Rufus P. Browning, Dale Rogers Marshall, and David H. Tabb. New York: Longman.

Yi, Daniel. 1993. "From NAFTA to Immigration: Rep. Kim Speaks Out Before KA Republicans." *Korea Times* (English ed.), 6 October.

CHAPTER 14

Jiannbin Lee Shiao

The Political and Philanthropic Contexts for Incorporating Asian American Communities

In all of the country, [the San Francisco Bay area] is the one place I feel at home. Nowhere else do I feel accepted by strangers as a fellow citizen and human being.

—Japanese American executive director of a Bay area pan-Asian nonprofit organization

You're comparing us to organizations in San Francisco? That's no fair! They're so far ahead of us!

—Korean American president of a pan-Asian membership organization in Cleveland

On the surface, the difference between the Asian American communities in San Francisco and Cleveland is simply demographic. We would naturally expect the larger and older populations of California to possess a more developed community infrastructure than their counterparts in Ohio. However, it is not an easy step from the complexity of self-help associations prevalent among all dense ethnic communities to the structured relationships of uniquely American nonprofit organizations that interpret, carry out, and challenge our public policies (Gallegos and O'Neill 1991; Shiao 1998). And it is yet another broad step to inclusion in the dominant coalitions in urban politics (Browning et al. 1984; Hero 1992). The picture is further complicated once we observe that Asian American communities in Cleveland have had direct and private access to the mayor's office since the 1980s, while their counterparts in San Francisco had to wait until the 1990s for comparable inclusion. Many Asian Clevelanders nevertheless report that their children often choose to move to the West and East Coasts to pursue their adult lives.

The point is that the "inclusion" of Asian American communities cannot be predicted from their internal complexity or even size in a given region. I argue that Asian American "communities" have very different meanings from region to region because they negotiate distinct local cultures of civic participation. How Asian Americans represent themselves to one another and the wider regional community already accommodates local histories of minority political inclusion. Recognition of this simple fact represents an important step away from the "one size fits all," often California-based models of Asian American ethnic empowerment and interracial civic leadership.

I base this argument on a qualitative sociological comparison of local philanthropy in the San Francisco Bay and Greater Cleveland areas. The focus on local foundations presents a unique view into how Asian American community institutions develop in the context of racialized environments that are less remote than those portrayed in federal government and national media stereotypes. I chose the California–Ohio comparison because both the Bay area and the Cleveland area were 10 percent foreign-born in 1960 (U.S. Bureau of the Census 1964a, 1964b) but divergently experienced the post-1965 rise in immigration—becoming 25 percent and 5 percent foreign-born, respectively, by 1990 (U.S. Bureau of the Census 1973a, 1973b, 1981a, 1981b, 1993). And I focused on the organizational cultures and activities of The San Francisco Foundation and The Cleveland Foundation as the major community foundations in each metropolitan region (National Committee for Responsive Philanthropy 1989). The qualitative data sources included forty-five in-depth interviews with the directors of Asian American nonprofit organizations and other minority grant-seeking organizations, foundation trustees, and program officers, and local political commentators; archival oral-history transcripts of deceased foundation personnel; and thirty years of foundation annual reports. The scope of the study was 1960 to 1990, a period encompassing the Civil Rights Movement to the advent of diversity policies (Glazer 1997) in a host of private institutions—most notably, foundations, universities, and corporations. In this chapter, I reveal the links among Asian American community organizations, local foundations, and urban politics, arguing that community formation is a deeply local matter.

First I present the histories of Asian American organizational development in the two metropolitan regions. Then I demonstrate how local philanthropy channeled their differentiation and placed the communities on distinct paths to civic participation. These philanthropic influences themselves arose in turn from local political circumstances that resemble not points on a common empowerment trajectory but, rather, particularities in local history. In the conclusion, I discuss what the Bay area Asian American communities can learn from Cleveland. At stake is the implication that racial-formation scholars might take locales and private elites more seriously.

Asian American Organizations in Two Metropolitan Regions

The shape and activities of Asian American organizations crystallize the relationships between the communities in question and the wider society. In Michael Omi and Howard Winant's classic formulation of racial formation theory (1986), ethnic and ethnoracial organizations are social-movement vehicles that translate rearticulated group identities into demands for social change and eventually state action. However, social-movement organizations are not only bundles of collective will; they also have an institutional form in an ongoing—not simply reactive—civil society. For example, popular American history often notes "great men" such as Dr. Martin Luther King, Jr., but forgets the vast network of Black churches that supported him. By civil society, I refer to the whole of private organized life, from formal to informal, extra-familial collectives, that are not reducible to nonprofit organizations but are importantly crystallized in them. Although social movements may exploit the nonprofit form (Gronbjerg 1993), the nonprofit form also disciplines social movements in ways that are more nuanced than simple co-optation. For instance, Asian American communities strategically adopted a pan-Asian organizational form in part to secure the notice of the U.S. Census Bureau (Espiritu 1992). In the urban context, Asian American organizations thus represent Asian American concerns to other groups and institutions and thereby also delimit how the community defines itself. How Asian American organizations in the San Francisco Bay area became nonprofits while those in the Greater Cleveland area remained voluntary associations, albeit with unusual political access, is a story of both social movements and local institutional contexts.

Asian American organizations crystallize significant concerns and dimensions of the Asian American communities and are important voices for them in the larger society. The social history of Asian American nonprofit organizations pivots around the Asian American movement of the late 1960s and 1970s. A new generation of Asian Americans started organizations that challenged either directly or by their very presence the leadership of older ethnic-specific organizations. Shaped by the Third World college protests in California of the late 1960s, and inspired to participate in those united-people-of-color projects, the new organizations tended to have a strong commitment to panethnicity among Asian Americans. Also, whereas the older organizations tended to relate to the wider community through preserving the "respectability" of their groups in mainstream eyes, the newer organizations were more confrontational, demanding "social justice" from the same mainstream.

The social-justice organizations, however, did not necessarily replace the old organizations. In Oakland, the new organizations developed into their own infrastructure, whereas in San Francisco, the older organizations persisted. But the more traditional leadership (for example, the Consolidated Chinese Benevolent Association) had to share power with the new leadership (for example, Chinese for Affirmative Action). The use of Chinese American examples here is not incidental. The numerical predominance of Chinese in San Francisco has meant that a united Asian front was less attractive to even the new generation. In Oakland, by contrast, organizations such as Filipinos for Affirmative Action (FAA) outlived those such as the Filipino Community of the East Bay Inc. The city difference is evident in how an FAA staff member compared Asian agencies in the two cities:

> The Oakland organizations started as pan-Asian and have stayed that way. San Francisco organizations were started by a previous generation of Asians than those in Oakland

who were inspired by the Third World protests. One Oakland exception is OCCC [Oakland Chinese Cultural Center, now the Asian Pacific Cultural Center of Oakland], which is older and used to be more like the San Francisco organizations.... In the early history of FAA, there was another Filipino organization that felt we were illegitimate. Now it's no longer around. If you look at our archives, you'll see the Filipino Community of the East Bay Inc. versus FAA battles. Those leaders are now in their seventies.

A strong factor in favor of succession by those in the more assertive 1970s generation was their effort to apply for federal dollars and attract external funding for Asian social needs, which, unlike the older cohort of leadership, they did not seek to hide. What the traditional leaders saw as the positive image of "Asian respectability"—for example, low incidence of juvenile crime—the new leaders saw as the self-perpetuation of the model-minority stereotype that delegitimated Asian issues from the attention of policies designed to ameliorate racial inequality.

Like many Black and Latino organizations, a significant segment of the Asian American nonprofit sector thus had its origins in the social movements of the 1960s and 1970s. Directors of these Asian American organizations perceive other social-justice-oriented organizations, rather than more mainstream nonprofit agencies, as their peers. Elaborating on this contrast, one agency director noted that the distinction in missions somewhat coincided with a class difference between the organizations:

> Our Black and Latino counterparts are "social-justice" oriented people: Omega Boys Club, RAP [Real Alternatives Project], West Oakland Violence Prevention Project, Narcotics Education League... versus things like Girls Inc. at the YMCA, Eden Youth Center, and East Bay Conservation Corps [EBCC], who have this "social responsibility" thing—that is, "We get kids off the streets to have fun." I feel I learned a lot from EBCC but didn't like their style or culture. They don't even hire [University of California] grads, just Ivy Leaguers only. However, they are a very sophisticated nonprofit. We [the social-justice people] see ourselves as part of a larger social movement to get youth to critically analyze issues, human values, and principles, not just get straight As and get out of trouble.

In other words, the interviewee suggested a division between youth organizations that are interested primarily in the political education of at-risk youth and youth agencies that are interested mainly in inculcating middle-class behavior, such as summer recreation and grade improvement.

However, the Asian American organizations differed from their Black counterparts in terms of their organizational age. A recurring observation was that Black organizations built themselves using War on Poverty funding,[1] which had largely disappeared by the time the Asian organizations formed in the 1970s. Furthermore, as an agency staff member observed, because the expansion of Black agencies was more closely tied to political programs, policymakers had stakes in their maintenance:

> The Asian nonprofit sector has grown, but not as much as others. Blacks and Latinos, they got on the wagon a lot earlier and had more opportunities for funding because we got on board ten years too late.... And they have policymakers who focus on their issues while we don't.

Nevertheless, the Asian organizations have become fairly successful, partly because of their collaborations as a panethnic infrastructure. As one grantee suggested, these collaborations resulted from the organizations' histories of stable administration:

> The Asian American nonprofit sector benefits from a higher level of informal and formal collaboration, which minimizes competition with each other. We were able to stabilize our own organization through collaboration in initiatives with larger organizations that did-n't have to extend themselves but did. There's a stable community of administrators in these nonprofits, as opposed to a directorship changing every two or three years. In Oak-land, the Asian nonprofit sector is now being seen as something stable. That perception is fostered by our banding together.

By the 1990s, a number of major organizations were celebrating their twentieth to twenty-fifth anniversaries, and these have long been involved in collaborations with one another and with newer Asian organizations.

In Cleveland, by contrast, most of the Asian organizations have not been incorpo-rated as nonprofits. Instead of an infrastructure of panethnic and ethnic-specific non-profits, Cleveland has an alliance of ethnic-specific voluntary associations that came together to promote panethnic celebrations after 1975. Furthermore, they secured polit-ical access through a Mayor's Asian American Advisory Committee in the 1980s, some-thing that is absent in both San Francisco and Oakland. However, the generation most predisposed to panethnicity is either nearing retirement or leaving Cleveland. The core of the local panethnic efforts has consisted of former activists from the fair-housing and other desegregation struggles of the 1960s, which benefited both African Americans and themselves. Many of these senior leaders say, however, that their children have chosen to move to San Francisco rather than remain in Cleveland. The arrival of new immi-grants in the 1970s and 1980s initiated the inverse of Bay area dynamics. Rather than a U.S.-born generation challenging the traditional leadership, an immigrant generation in Cleveland began challenging the U.S.-born generation. Although the Bay area saw a similar increase in Asian newcomers in the same decades, the immigrants were absorbed significantly into the existing mix of traditional and activist organizations.

The community foundations have played pivotal roles in the emergence and devel-opment of Asian American organizations in both regions. In many cases, The San Francisco Foundation was the funder that supported organizational "start-ups" and even the subsequent development of new programs. One director reflected on her directorship of an Asian nonprofit in an earlier decade:

> We had a great relationship with San Francisco Foundation because many of the program officers have been great supporters of [ours]. They played a key role in developing key areas and programs. And we were able to use San Francisco Foundation's money to lever-age money from other funders. It's really for program staff there to approach their col-leagues at other organizations. The initiative to make contact has gone both ways. It made a big deal to connect with people there. San Francisco Foundation really promoted [our] rise in San Francisco.

Many of the social-justice organizations began looking for funding just as Martin Paley began his directorship of The San Francisco Foundation. During that time, he expanded and diversified the foundation's staff. In one year, the foundation's sole Black program officer went from being in the numerical minority in terms of both race and gender to being the senior member of a female majority on a program staff that had a bare majority of Whites. This new staff included Asian American officers who quickly learned about this new Asian infrastructure and made a significant difference in its success.

In other words, The San Francisco Foundation stepped into a funding gap left by federal policies designed around Black–White relations.[2] In addition, as immigration began to increase the Bay area's Asian population—especially with the poor refugees and immigrants of the 1980s—the philanthropy supported existing organizations' capacity to include newcomers in the panethnic infrastructure. Ironically, the foundation's traditionally small grants no longer have comparable significance now that these community institutions have grown.

In the Greater Cleveland area, by contrast, The Cleveland Foundation supported a nonprofit infrastructure that specifically addressed Black–White inequality. The Asian American activists who might have formed Asian nonprofits instead devoted their energy to participating in fair-housing and desegregation projects through the 1970s and developed Asian organizations only in voluntary form. The emergence of Asian American panethnicity in 1970s Cleveland was thus conditioned by both the much smaller population of Asians in the region and the major attention of the region's philanthropic and nonprofit sectors to inequality than to the reflection of the new diversity. The Cleveland Foundation also has a preference for large-scale initiatives; thus, the comparatively small Asian associations in Cleveland rarely received attention that would facilitate their nonprofit incorporation. However, some Asian Americans hold seats on the citywide initiatives that the foundation has preferred to sponsor.

In sum, the study of Asian American organizations reveals the interaction of numerous phenomena identified as significant by scholars of the Asian American experience. The role of traditional associations in affirming mainstream perceptions of Asian Americans, the rise of panethnic associations and institutions, debates among Asian Americans about the model-minority stereotype, and the differentiation of Asian American concerns from the African American issues dominant in "race talk" and policy—all emerge from a look at the institutions that mediate the community and the wider society. Yet these same organizations are shaped by the nonprofit infrastructure of the wider society, even as Asian Americans exploit its legal form to pursue their goals.

Philanthropic Contexts for Asian American Community Institutions

Just as ethnic and ethnoracial nonprofits crystallize certain relationships for Asian American communities, philanthropic foundations crystallize important relationships within the wider community—particularly in the nonprofit sector. Beyond being simply a formalization of voluntary impulses, the U.S. nonprofit sector handles social responsibilities administered by public sectors in social-democratic nations (Smith and

Lipsky 1993). Within this internationally unique sector, foundations function as private governments through their disbursement of capital gains that the Internal Revenue Service partially releases from tax obligations. In urban settings, community foundations bridge the affluence of many donors with private decisions made together by professional program staff and their employers—boards of trustees appointed by the mayor, the chamber of commerce, the United Way, local universities, banks, and other notable institutions. If the nonprofit sector is a middle ground between social movements and the state, then community foundations are a middle ground within the sector itself, between its "elites" and "masses." The policies of The San Francisco Foundation and The Cleveland Foundation thus weigh heavily in how the nonprofit form disciplines Asian American conceptions of "community," its needs, and its aspirations.

In this section, I briefly describe the three major race-relations projects of each foundation. Each project figured strongly in the racial objectives of distinct and successive executive-directorships. These projects therefore suggest the evolving organizational cultures within which foundation professionals framed their initiatives.

Neither The San Francisco Foundation nor The Cleveland Foundation followed the federal racial discourse of protecting "victim" populations, as exemplified in equal employment opportunity and affirmative-action policies and programs (Matsuda 1991; Takagi 1992). Instead, both followed the longstanding mode of racial discourse in the foundation world: the search for exceptional talent (Shiao 1998). However, each organization pursued that professional project in distinct ways over the decades. Both foundations have made progress in implementing their profession's conception of diversity policy, a priority to which organized philanthropy had turned its attention by the end of the 1980s. The San Francisco Foundation had advanced the recognition of diversity far in advance of the professional field's attention to it. However, the foundation did so via a traditional, now archaic mode of grant-making—that is, through the support of an uncoordinated assortment of "good causes" and "good works" instead of through proposed plans that articulated specific missions and solutions (Shiao 1998). Well before the philanthropic media was advancing diversity policy in this strategic mode of grantmaking, The Cleveland Foundation had begun implementing such strategies.

In The San Francisco Foundation's three directorships from 1960 to 1990, the major race-related programs consisted of two awards programs and a fellowship program. Over this period, race policy generally meant awards to, as a staff member quipped, people who had "made differences that were helpful rather than hurtful." Since the organization's first directorship under John May, The San Francisco Foundation Award has annually recognized notable individuals whose lives reflected that early expression of valuing diversity. Although the Koshland Awards Program preceded the start of Paley's directorship in the mid-1970s, it exemplified his ideal of multiracial community in its identification of neighborhoods in need of community (that is, social capital). The Koshland Program has pursued its goal of, as a trustee stated, "turning residents into neighbors" by identifying unknown neighborhood leaders, convening them, and giving each individual a personal award and the discretion to direct a small grant to a community-based organization. The foundation's third director, Robert Fisher, continued its individualistic focus with the Multicultural Fellows Program, which has recruited people of color into one-year internships, where they assist the foundation's program executives to improve the pipeline for minorities into professional philanthropy. Despite the organization's innovative diversity programming, its focus on "entry-level" inclusiveness and empowerment regrettably suggests how removed The San Francisco Foundation is from the major institutions in its local political system.

In The Cleveland Foundation's three directorships from 1960 to 1990, the major race-related programs consisted of two citywide governance committees and one citywide consciousness-raising project. Over this period, race policy generally meant initiatives that, in the words of a former staff member, "strengthened the role of blacks in the community." Under the foundation's fifth executive director, James Norton, it convened the Businessmen's Interracial Committee on Civic Affairs, which became the major meeting place for Black leaders and White corporate leadership to formulate policy recommendations to manage the social movements of the 1960s. The next director, Homer Wadsworth, created the Greater Cleveland Project as an informational clearinghouse and outreach effort to prepare Cleveland for school desegregation in the 1970s and to curb outbreaks of racist violence. Wadsworth also initiated the Greater Cleveland Roundtable, which functioned as the conduit for minority affairs into Cleveland Tomorrow, the organization that (again, with much foundation involvement) adopted the task of "rebuilding Cleveland" in the 1980s. When Assistant Director Steve Minter succeeded Wadsworth in the mid-1980s, he continued the foundation's involvement with the Greater Cleveland Roundtable and Cleveland Tomorrow. Minter was the foundation's first African American executive director and the only person of color among the six men to head either of the two community foundations since the Civil Rights Movement. The foundation's success with racial projects that combined business leadership, professional knowledge, and grassroots input suggests that The Cleveland Foundation has been a cornerstone in its local political system (Tittle 1992).

In terms of the breadth of groups included, therefore, The San Francisco Foundation has promoted more programs popularly associated with "diversity policies" with the result of fostering the development of a nonprofit infrastructure for Asian American communities. However, these efforts have been relatively small when compared with the major initiatives enacted by The Cleveland Foundation. Asian American organizations repeatedly have had to struggle with the popular perception of Asians as a model minority in part because of the absence of a central regional "platform" on which to build new perceptions and traditions. Asian American nonprofits—and perhaps other nonprofit subsectors in the Bay area—"do their own thing" without much coordination with one another. By contrast, although few of Cleveland's Asian American associations have developed into nonprofits, Asian American communities there have access to a regionwide infrastructure for regularly implementing large-scale initiatives.

The Roots of Philanthropic Policy in Local Political Histories

If foundation policies channeled the development of Asian American community institutions, then why did the foundations pursue such different policies? I argue that foundation strategies in the Bay area emerged from a local political context that was not only irrelevant to Cleveland but also partly disadvantageous by comparison. Although the openness of San Francisco political culture lowered the barriers to political entry for newcomers, its anti-hierarchical character also lowered the probability of sustained social policies. Between 1960 and 1990, San Francisco's policy culture shifted from the broad national focus on desegregation to a locally specific focus on "diversity," or the goal of intercultural tolerance sought through the practice of heterogeneous representation. Meanwhile, Cleveland's policy culture shifted from the broad national focus on desegregation to a specific focus on "inequality," or the task of addressing economically rooted disparities through the practice of major initiatives. The roots of the divergence between the two regions lies in their local political histories, an important part of which was the success or failure of neighborhood movements in their respective locales.

Over this period, the success of a progressive movement in the Bay area and the failure of its counterpart in the Cleveland area generated very different urban regimes. During the 1970s, both regions elected and lost progressive mayors who represented the "neighborhoods" against corporate interests. However, San Francisco and Cleveland lost their mayors for very different reasons. In the Bay area, George Moscone lost his life to an assassin who slew both him and Harvey Milk, the city's first openly gay city supervisor. The assassin, Dan White, was a former member of the Board of Supervisors whose support came tellingly from the older, conservative, White neighborhoods (DeLeon 1992). Whereas San Francisco's movement was cheated of a progressive regime, Cleveland's movement was defeated by business leadership. Mayor Dennis Kocinich saw his city fall into bankruptcy when business elites refused to roll over the city's debt, arguably to punish him for his firm opposition to the sale of a local public utility (Swanstrom 1995). The event significantly diminished Kocinich's political clout, and the next mayor paid closer attention to the desires of local corporations.

This divergence set San Francisco and Cleveland on distinct paths in the 1980s. In his study of San Francisco politics, Richard DeLeon (1992) identifies the growth, setback, and re-growth of the city's progressive movement, a coalition of three leftist groups: traditional liberals, environmentalists, and neighborhood preservationists. Recovering from Moscone's assassination, these leftist groups returned a decade later to elect Art Agnos mayor of San Francisco. Coincidentally, in the 1980s, the rise of San Francisco Tomorrow, the "slow-growth" coalition behind Agnos's election, paralleled the rise of Cleveland Tomorrow, an association of the chief executives of the city's fifty largest firms (Tittle 1992). Unfortunately, although San Francisco's leftists formed an alliance capable of blocking corporate influence that could harm the local quality of life, they were incapable of forming a proactive agenda and taking united action. Applying "ideal types" of urban regimes, DeLeon (1992: 135) identifies San Francisco as a "hyperpluralism," in which the political leadership is weak and the business elite is dispersed. Cleveland, by contrast, approximates the exact opposite conceptual regime in DeLeon's schema: a "corporatism," in which the political leadership is strong and the business elite is cohesive.

Diversity in San Francisco is a "divisive diversity": Inclusive governance is valued in a local context, where coherent action is extremely difficult. The emphasis on inequality in Cleveland is an "exclusive equality": Coherent action is predicated on the high exclusivity of decision-making power. When we refocus on the foundations' effects on Asian American community institutions, we can see that they pursued different policies to foster minority organizations that could participate in their respective urban regimes.

Lessons from Cleveland

At the outset of my research, I did not expect to discover Cleveland to be ahead of Bay area in terms of race relations. My personal prejudices had been shaped by popular visions of San Francisco as an edge city and Cleveland as the kind of place that free-thinking people escaped in order to move to edge cities (Maupin 1978). When one separates the respective nonprofit relationships from their surrounding economic fortunes, however, one finds in Cleveland a racial context that is more than a San Francisco with fewer Asians and Latinos and more African Americans. Its infrastructure for race relations is hardly antiquated. These findings suggest a need to retheorize racial-formation perspectives to account for local differentiation and elite influence.

Shifting the Bay area to a model based more closely on Cleveland would benefit Asian Americans and other minorities by increasing the potential scope of foundation involvement, creating the possibility for policies that accumulate historically and convening leadership to engage the existing Asian American nonprofit infrastructure. The Cleveland Foundation's interventions have had a greater scope because of the organization's greater capacity to coordinate local actors who also contribute resources to the common efforts. This capacity is partly a function of the foundation's local clout, but it is also premised on the existence of a relatively united power structure in the region. The difficulty of governance in the Bay area has led to a situation in which The San Francisco Foundation has been more successful at implementing "across-the-board" diversity policies than programs coordinated with city governments and corporations to address racial inequality. By contrast, Cleveland has had a tradition of convening major forces, with the community foundation as a cornerstone of race-related efforts.

If the Bay area had a more corporatist political regime, Asian Americans there might also find attractive the creation of citywide bodies that bridged the new power structure and the racialized minority groups. The concentration of corporate and government powers would require Asian American communities to participate in a single multiracial committee of civic leadership like the Greater Cleveland Roundtable. Such citywide bodies could act as bridging institutions between corporate and mayoral regimes, on one hand, and various Asian American communities, on the other. Asian Americans would potentially be able to leverage initiatives that were larger in scale than culturally appropriate recognition in existing programs or inclusion in celebrations of uniquely local diversity.

They would, however, have to accept a higher level of corporate hegemony, by which I mean not only big business's ability to win struggles over policy design but also its effects on the culture of policy formation itself. In a study of corporate philanthropy and corporate power, Jerome Himmelstein identifies this aspect of corporate hegemony as a "discursive presence":

> It is not power in the sense of prevailing in overt conflict, or being able to set the political agenda, or possessing structural indispensability. Instead it involves a more subtle and perhaps smaller-scale kind of power than any of these—a presence at multiple levels in society and a place in multiple conversations, which allows a set of voices to be heard and a set of interests to be taken seriously almost everywhere. (Himmelstein 1997: 143)

In exchange for decades of corporate hegemony, The Cleveland Foundation has almost always received corporate support in addressing racial inequality. The foundation's leaders have been able to leverage federal, state, and local government and corporate contributions to multiply their already substantial grantmaking.

An important related cost of accepting corporate hegemony might be a more exclusive, local culture of civic participation. The Cleveland Foundation pays far less attention to issues of gender and sexuality than it does to racial diversity. An interesting index of this discrepancy lies in the historical compositions of the two foundations' trustee boards. Over time, both foundations have shifted from having all-White boards to majority-White boards—albeit with important differences. The White-majority board of The San Francisco Foundation has become evenly split between men and women, so that White men, White women, and people of color constitute numerically equal "legs" of a governing tripod. By contrast, The Cleveland Foundation's board has rarely included more than a single White woman. If the Bay area's movement toward a more cohesive policy infrastructure came through the increase of White, male corporate power, the consequence of a greater intensity of racial-inequality initiatives might be a reduced attention to gender and other concerns that are currently part of the diversity valued in the city's popular and policy cultures.

Any attempt to combine both diversity and inequality in institutional policies would thus require Asian American communities to consider carefully both their own internal diversity and the major actors outside their ethnic and panethnic associations. The internal focus of many pan-Asian initiatives fits well with local traditions of hyperpluralism, where the regional culture expects residents to live in "parallel" with respectful distance. If Asian American communities in the Bay area did develop an agenda with panethnic consensus, though, they would also have to build extra-Asian institutions of governance to implement it.

Cleveland is not a backwater that needs to follow the example of the San Francisco Bay area in order to improve the way it incorporates peripheral community members. This comparison of the development of the Asian American community infrastructures in each region has revealed their embeddedness in distinct, complex interactions between social movements and philanthropic policies. In turn, these philanthropic involvements have arisen from locally specific political histories that pivot on the fate of larger progressive movements. In a double irony, I found that the city with the defeated movement had the greater capacity to convene citywide initiatives for racial incorporation, yet the less empowered city had done more for Asian American communities. Clearly, it would be inappropriate to define Cleveland or its Asian American communities as less developed than the Bay area or its Asian American communities. Rather than being at different points on the same trajectory, Asian Americans in Cleveland and the Bay area occupy different social locations and potentially have much to learn from each other. This conclusion implies not only that the construction of racial projects involves the rearticulation of ethnic identities into panethnic agendas, but also that local institutional contexts are already channeling that process of rearticulation in complex ways.

Notes

1. See Mollenkopf 1983 for a scholarly confirmation of this observation.
2. See Nicolau and Santiestevan 1991 for the similar role the Ford Foundation has played for Mexican American organizations.

References

Browning, Rufus, Dale Rogers Marshall, and David Tabb. 1984. *Protest Is Not Enough: The Struggle of Blacks and Hispanics for Equality in Urban Politics*. Berkeley: University of California Press.

DeLeon, Richard. 1992. *Left Coast City: Progressive Politics in San Francisco, 1975–1991*. Lawrence: University Press of Kansas.

Espiritu, Yen Le. 1992. *Asian American Panethnicity: Bridging Institutions and Identities*. Philadelphia: Temple University Press.

Gallegos, Herman, and Michael O'Neill. 1991. "Hispanics and the Nonprofit Sector." Pp. 1–15 in *Hispanics in the Nonprofit Sector*, ed. Herman Gallegos and Michael O'Neill. New York: Foundation Center.

Glazer, Nathan. 1997. *We Are All Multiculturalists Now*. Cambridge, Mass.: Harvard University Press.

Gronbjerg, Kirsten. 1993. *Understanding Nonprofit Funding: Managing Revenues in Social Services and Community Development Organizations*. San Francisco: Jossey-Bass Publishers.

Hero, Rodney. 1992. *Latinos and the U.S. Political System: Two Tiered Pluralism*. Philadelphia: Temple University Press.

Himmelstein, Jerome. 1997. *Looking Good and Doing Good: Corporate Philanthropy and Corporate Power*. Bloomington: Indiana University Press.

Matsuda, Mari. 1991. "Voices of America: Accent, Antidiscrimination Law, and a Jurisprudence for the Last Reconstruction." *Yale Law Journal* 100: 1329–407.

Maupin, Armistead. 1978. *Tales of the City*. New York: Harper & Row.

Mollenkopf, John H. 1983. *The Contested City.* Princeton, N.J.: Princeton University Press.

National Committee for Responsive Philanthropy. 1989. "Community Foundations: At the Margin of Change—Unrealized Potential for the Disadvantaged," Washington, D.C., 13 September.

Nicolau, Siobhan, and Henry Santiestevan. 1991. "Looking Back: A Grantee–Grantor View of the Early Years of the Council of La Raza." Pp. 49–66 in *Hispanics in the Nonprofit Sector,* ed. Herman Gallegos and Michael O'Neill. New York: Foundation Center.

Omi, Michael, and Howard Winant. 1986. *Racial Formations in the United States: From the 1960s to the 1980s.* New York: Routledge.

Shiao, Jiannbin. 1998. "Beyond States and Movements: Philanthropic Contributions to Racial Formation in Two U.S. Cities, 1960–1990." Ph.D. dissertation, University of California, Berkeley.

Smith, Steven and Michael Lipsky. 1993. *Nonprofits for Hire: The Welfare State in the Age of Contracting.* Cambridge, Mass.: Harvard University Press.

Swanstrom, Todd. 1995. "Urban Populism, Fiscal Crisis, and the New Political Economy." Pp. 97–118 in *Cleveland: A Metropolitan Reader,* ed. Dennis Keating et al. Kent, Ohio: Kent State University Press.

Takagi, Dana Y. 1992. *The Retreat from Race: Asian-American Admissions and Racial Politics.* New Brunswick, N.J.: Rutgers University Press.

Tittle, Diana. 1992. *Rebuilding Cleveland: The Cleveland Foundation and Its Evolving Urban Strategy.* Columbus: Ohio State University Press.

U.S. Bureau of the Census. 1964a. *U.S. Census of Population: 1960. Vol. 1, Characteristics of the Population. Part 1, U.S. Summary.* "General Population Characteristics," Table 63. Washington, D.C.: U.S. Government Printing Office.

———. 1964b. *U.S. Census of Population: 1960. Vol. 1, Characteristics of the Population. Part 1, U.S. Summary.* "General Social and Economic Characteristics," Table 141. Washington, D.C.: U.S. Government Printing Office.

———. 1973a. *U.S. Census of Population: 1970. Vol. 1, Characteristics of the Population. Part 1, U.S. Summary–Section 1.* "General Population Characteristics," Table 66. Washington, D.C.: U.S. Government Printing Office.

———. 1973b. *U.S. Census of Population: 1970. Vol. 1, Characteristics of the Population. Part 1, U.S. Summary–Section 1.* "General Social and Economic Characteristics," Table 183. Washington, D.C.: U.S. Government Printing Office.

———. 1981a. *U.S. Census of Population: 1980. Vol. 1, Characteristics of the Population. Part 1, U.S. Summary.* "Chapter B, General Population Characteristics," Table 68. Washington, D.C.: U.S. Government Printing Office.

———. 1981b. *U.S. Census of Population: 1980. Vol. 1, Characteristics of the Population. Part 1, U.S. Summary.* "Chapter C, Social and Economic Characteristics," Table 246. Washington, D.C.: U.S. Government Printing Office.

———. 1993. *U.S. Census of Population: 1990.* "Social and Economic Characteristics, Metropolitan Areas," Table 1. Washington, D.C.: U.S. Government Printing Office.

CHAPTER 15

Andrew Leong

How Public-Policy Reforms Shape, and Reveal the Shape of, Asian America

This is the most significant illegal immigration control bill in a genera-tion.... [The bill] will secure America's borders, reduce the flow of illegal drugs, protect American jobs, and save American taxpayers billions of dollars.

—Representative Lamar Smith on the introduction of the
Illegal Immigration Reform and
Immigrant Responsibility Act of 1996

Koreans have always voted largely as business owners, ... and Republi-cans are more pro-business than Democrats. But the anti-immigration backlash, and its impact on Koreans, has made the community start to see politics in racial terms. There's a sense of vulnerability that's related to our race now, and some Koreans are thinking, "Wait, it's the Democrats who look out for the vulnerable."

—Gyeman Chang, president of the
Korean-American Voters Association,
New Jersey

The 1990 U.S. Census shows that the foreign-born proportion of the total Asian U.S. population was gauged at 64 percent. Projections indicate that by 2020, the foreign-born proportion will still be between 54 percent and 56 percent (Ong and Hee 1993). The Asian American community[1] comprises a predominately immigrant population. A major factor determining the community's growth rate is tied directly to whether the U.S. Congress wants to admit or reduce the number of immigrants and refugees entering each year. More than a hundred years ago, the Congress easily shut out Asian immigrants (Hing 1993; Tamayo 1992).[2] Therefore, the issue of immigration policy is an essential one for this growing community.

Linked to any newcomer group is the phenomenon of scapegoating by the "natives," or "natural-born" citizens of the country. New immigrants are blamed for everything negative, from the economy to the environment. Asian immigrants and refugees are susceptible, in particular, to being blamed for coming into the country and getting on the welfare rolls. Because immigration will continue to be an important policy issue for Asian Americans in the foreseeable future, as will existence of some kind of safety net for newcomers, these two issues can easily become entangled. The confluence of these two issues—immigration and welfare—came to a head during the 1996 general election.

During the presidential election in 1996, these two topics of public-policy debate were poised to reconfigure radically the landscape of Asian America. This chapter will focus on those areas and examine how Asian Americans reacted to both, along with the reasons for their reactions. Notwithstanding the many other public policies being debated during 1996 that could have had a drastic impact on this community, including affirmative action and making English the "official" U.S. language, the two issues that remained at the center of attention for Asian Americans were immigration and welfare reform. By examining those policy debates, one begins to see the similarities and differences emerging in Asian America. In this chapter, I will first examine the legal changes that occurred in both the welfare and immigration acts. I will then analyze and examine the differing reactions from the Asian American community and explore the reasons for those differences.

Law Reform

The Welfare Reform Act

On 22 August 1996, President Bill Clinton signed the Personal Responsibility and Work Opportunity Reconciliation Act of 1996 (hereafter, the Welfare Reform Act). The act drastically changed the relationship that had existed between the federal government and the poor, reducing or eliminating social programs that had served as a safety net for the vulnerable since the New Deal era.[3] The group facing the greatest impact is "legal" immigrants.[4] The Congressional Budget Office (CBO) determined that of the $53.4 billion to be cut from the budget over a six-year period, an estimated 44 percent, or $23.7 billion, would come from the elimination of benefits to legal immigrants.[5]

The Welfare Reform Act originated in the 103rd session of Congress as H.R. 3500, titled the "Personal Responsibility Act." By the end of 1994, one anti-immigrant measure had captured the attention of the whole country, as California voters passed the Proposition 187 ballot measure (Bau 1995).[6] In 1995, in the 104th session, the Republican-controlled Congress introduced H.R. 4, which became the welfare-reform portion of the ten pieces of legislation that made up the Republican Party's "Contract with America" (Leong 1995). Although a variety of lawsuits have kept Proposition 187 from being implemented in California (Purdum 1998), anti-immigrant sentiment had already spread across the country to Washington, D.C.

The harshest restrictions in the Welfare Reform Act absolutely bar immigrants from the food-stamp and Supplement Security Income (SSI) programs.[7] The act exempts from these prohibitions veterans and military personnel, immigrants who have at least ten years or forty quarters of recorded work history in the United States, and refugees and asylum-seekers during their first five years in this country.[8] The act also allows states to bar immigrants from other joint federal–state programs, such as the Temporary Assistance to Needy Families (formerly known as Aid to Families with Dependent Children), Medicaid, and Title XX programs.[9] It also permits states to bar immigrants from programs that are entirely state-funded.[10]

Further, the act prohibits immigrants who arrive in the future from participating in any federal "means-tested" programs during their first five years in the United States.[11] This will have a serious, long-term effect on future immigration, as will the imposition of a permanent "deeming" restriction in which an immigrant's eligibility for public benefits will be determined by adding his or her income and assets to those of his or her sponsor—regardless of whether that income is actually available.[12] This will, of course, artificially inflate the income status of many immigrants and make them ineligible for benefits.[13] The act will have the most harmful effects for Southeast Asian refugees and elderly Asians—two groups that are heavy recipients of government assistance programs.[14] Since the passage of the act, a fair amount of misinformation has been widely spread (McAllister 1997), causing considerable emotional distress in the elderly immigrant population. The suicides of eighteen elderly immigrants nationwide have been linked to fear of having their benefits terminated by the government (Harlan 1997; Hastings 1998; McAllister 1997).

The Immigration Reform Act

As with welfare reform, the Republican-controlled Congress in 1995 was poised to engage in immigration reform and to make massive changes to the fundamental bases of the immigration system that had been in effect since 1965. Leaders of the anti-immigration movement proposed enormous cutbacks in legal immigration, wholesale elimination of family-immigration categories, and even severe restrictions on employment-based immigration and the entry of temporary, non-immigrant workers. In addition, the anti-immigration movement wanted even harsher measures against the undocumented. Although it achieved its goals with respect to the undocumented and was able to make several significant changes that affect legal immigration, the anti-immigration movement failed to make the radical, systemic changes it sought. So even though it had some negative effects, the final version of the Illegal Immigration Reform and Immigrant Responsibility Act of 1996 (the Immigration Reform Act), as enacted on 30 September 1996, was far less devastating than the anti-immigration legislation leaders in Congress originally intended.

In February 1995, H.R. 2202 (the Immigration in the National Interest Act of 1995) was introduced in the House of Representatives to control "illegal" immigration and reduce legal immigration. In June of that year, the Jordan Commission on Immigration Reform issued a report concluding that the immigration system needed correction and building pressure for reform. By November, Senator Alan Simpson (R-Wyoming) had introduced the Senate version of immigration reform: Senate Bill 1394. In early 1996, the debate intensified when a coalition of pro-immigration forces successfully divided the Senate bill, splitting it into two acts that dealt separately with legal and "illegal" immigration. The most controversial measure in the House bill was the Gallegly Amendment, which, similar to a provision in Proposition 187, would have allowed states to bar the children of undocumented immigrants from public education.

After much debate, and with the White House threatening to veto any bill using this language, the Gallegly Amendment was removed. Although the House bill passed in March 1996, and the Senate version passed in May, both bills were stalled in conference committee until the passage of the Welfare Reform Act in August 1996. The conference committee then commenced a flurry of activities, negotiating an agreement that the President signed on 30 September. Throughout this process, both pro-immigration and anti-immigration forces lobbied legislators aggressively. Asian American groups along with other immigration advocates, including major business leaders, organized several "lobbying days" in the fall of 1995. The same lobbying strategy was used throughout 1996 and even up to the last minute, when new provisions were included in the Immigration Reform Act to ameliorate some of the harshness of the Welfare Reform Act. If not for the Asian American organizations and community members, along with other (Asian and non-Asian) immigration advocates, the Immigration Reform Act would have been much more severe and harmful to the immigrant community as a whole.

The Immigration Reform Act primarily addressed two areas: greater enforcement to stop illegal immigration and the revision of deportation and exclusion proceedings.[15] The act also addressed the issue of the receipt of public benefits by legal immigrants, slightly modifying several provisions of the Welfare Reform Act.[16] The Immigration Reform Act will have the most negative effects on working-class and poor legal immigrants because it requires that immigrants' sponsors have an income that is more than 125 percent of the poverty threshold.[17] The 125 percent threshold will increase income stratification within Asian America because allowing only high-income petitioners to apply to bring family members to the United States will reduce the number of immigrants with working-class backgrounds.[18]

Finally, the Immigration Reform Act contains several very disturbing provisions that will affect all Asian Americans, regardless of their citizenship status. Under the earlier law, employers could be sued if they imposed greater burdens on one group of job applicants—say, Asians or Latinos—to prove their immigration status than they did on others. Employers could not demand additional documents to verify the legal status of an applicant because she or he looked or sounded "foreign."[19] The new Immigration Reform Act shields employers from legal attacks for such unfair practices unless the applicant can show that the employer consciously intended to discriminate against his or her group. This requirement in essence puts an the end to any possibility of successful lawsuits based on discrimination in hiring.

Action and Reaction from the Asian American Community

Although Asian Americans have historically made up a small portion of the U.S. population, they have been on the receiving end of a disproportional number of legal changes. Thus, Asian Americans often must react to, rather than initiate, changes. Having examined the history and impact of the recent Welfare and Immigration Reform acts, I will now turn the focus to more interesting questions: Did the Asian American community influence this reform as an actor, and if so, to what degree? Or did the community merely bear the brunt of legislation once again? One measure of the maturity of a community is its ability to affect public policy. Thus, the Welfare and Immigration Reform Acts not only provide an illustration of the political power of Asian Americans; they also illuminate the startling diversity within the group.

The public-policy debate on immigration has always intersected with the debate on welfare, and in the recent case, the movements brought about a two-prong approach to deficit reduction: 1) eliminate additional mouths to feed by preventing them from entering the country; and 2) stop feeding mouths that are already here by making them ineligible for the programs. This strategy manifested itself in the immigration debate in the form of proposals to reduce annual immigration quotas and in the welfare debate in the form of creating provisions that exclude legal immigrants from eligibility for government benefits. In the end, only the second prong of the strategy succeeded.

Is Higher-Education Assistance Welfare?

Embedded in H.R. 4 was language that would have made legal immigrants ineligible for student loans and grants; the bill defined this sort of assistance as a "federal means-tested benefit" for which immigrants would have been ineligible. Government assistance for higher education straddled both immigration and welfare reform: The deficit-reductionists viewed the loans and grants simply as more money that immigrants were taking away from citizens—thus, as a potential area for cutbacks.[20] Immediately after this proposal was publicized, immigrant students and others organized to defeat the provision. By late November 1995, campus protests had forced congressional Republicans to back away from the provision altogether (Clymer 1995). The issue of educational assistance struck a particular chord in the Asian American community because many did not view educational opportunity as welfare. Despite the many differences within this group, Asian Americans generally place a high value on education. Census statistics show that, of all populations in the United States, the Asian American community has the highest median number of completed school years (Yip 1996a). Although some Republicans did characterize immigrants' use of higher-education assistance as welfare, the issue never took hold.[21] Prior to the issue of student aid, Asian American advocacy groups in Washington, D.C. and elsewhere had disseminated information about welfare reform and its implications for the community, yet there did not seem to be a response until the education issue came to the forefront. The people interested in welfare reform impacts were policy makers, academics, and heads of social service agencies. The voice of the community, those who would be impacted most, had not been heard on issues involving the denial of welfare benefits to immigrants. Yet, the whole welfare and immigration reform took on a momentum of its own after the education issue received widespread attention. The education issue, which started as a welfare reform measure, catapulted immigration reform to the center of attention for Asian Americans, and other immigrant communities as well.[22]

Although a variety of welfare-reform bills had been introduced before 1995, a majority of Asian Americans did not notice the issue until the latter part of 1995. It was this proposed cut to educational benefits that caught the Asian American community's attention. It also led the community to see how radical the Welfare Reform Act really was. This prompted immigrants to learn about the effects of the proposed reform on other forms of benefits, including SSI and food stamps, and prompted the community to focus on the reductions in legal immigration embedded in immigration reform. The national weekly newspaper *AsianWeek* provides evidence of this phenomenon. Before 1996, it carried a smattering of articles on the immigration- and welfare-reform movements; throughout 1996, however, every single issue of *AsianWeek* had at least one article about immigration and welfare reform. At the same time, in late 1995, big business groups and others began complaining about the impact that a reduction of legal immigration would have on the supply of skilled labor in the United States. The common interests around immigration led quickly to the development of a strange coalition.

Strange Political Bedfellows

Even though Republicans were at the forefront of the reform in welfare and immigration, there were prominent Republicans such as Dick Armey, William Bennett, and even Jack Kemp (prior to his vice-presidential nomination) who took a pro-immigration position. The isolationist or protectionist stance is countered by the need for cheap labor and an open market. It creates a strange situation in which most Republicans favor closing U.S. borders because they associate immigrants (legal and undocumented) with social cost, whereas big-business and free-trade advocates, such as the Wall Street Journal, call for open borders.

On immigration reform, both the House and Senate versions in 1995 were calling for radical reductions of legal immigration in both the family-reunification and employment-related categories. In November 1995, Bill Gates, chairman of Microsoft Corporation, came forward to criticize various measures restricting employment-related immigration (Mills 1995). Even the Roman Catholic church came forward to defend the rights of political refugees. Together with these parties was an odd mixture of unlikely allies covering a spectrum that ran from a conservative think tank (the Cato Institute) to various progressive national Asian American organizations.[23]

This strange mix of organizations was especially influential during the spring of 1996 in the battle to divide the immigration bill into two parts, each dealing separately with "illegal" and legal immigration. The usual pro-immigration advocates, such as Senator Edward Kennedy and various national immigration groups, led the fight against restrictions on legal immigration. However, without the assistance of some Republicans, such as Spencer Abraham, a freshman Republican Senator from Michigan, and the coalition mentioned earlier, the bill would never been have split.

The peculiar combinations did not stop there. The Christian Coalition became involved when the issue of family reunification caught the group's attention. It considered the language to restrict or end immigration preferences for parents and siblings to be anti-family. By March 1996, Senator Simpson had been forced into a desperate negotiation to save the remnants of his bill.[24] This strange coalition, formed on the basis of pro-family, pro-civil rights, and pro-business positions, worked to split the immigration bill and essentially defeated attempts to reduce legal immigration during the 104th session of Congress.

If not for the issue of immigration, these very diverse organizations would never have been on the same side, let alone on talking terms. The "glue" that held the parties together stemmed from the traditional vision of America as the promised land of hope and opportunity. For corporations such as Microsoft and Intel, the lure was the continued availability of foreign national talent who were already attending U.S. graduate schools and would, if permitted, naturally move into positions with these companies to become a source of cheap skilled labor. The religious right saw the possibilities of additional converts with the family-value-oriented themes inherent in "reunification." For the traditional immigrant-rights, Latino, and Asian American civil-rights organizations, this coalition represented the ammunition needed to defeat the House and Senator Simpson's plan to reduce the numbers of legal immigrants. Every one of the groups believed that it got something out of being in this coalition, which was dubbed the "Left–Right Coalition on Immigration."

Even the lone Asian American Republican representative at the time, Jay Kim of California, aligned himself with the movement to split the bill. The message was easy to market: Punish those who sneak in illegally, not those who are responsible and hardworking and have taken the legal route to the United States. The plight of the Asian American community was particularly evident, because many of its citizens had filed immigration applications and had been waiting patiently—some for more than twenty years—for their relatives to immigrate. The language in the bills would have excluded even those on this immigration backlog, which estimates put at 1.6 million Asians. Various Asian American organizations clearly and effectively presented this issue of fair play.

For pro-immigrant advocates, this was one instance providing a ray of hope in the darkness behind the restrictive movement in immigration reform. Immigrant communities had already proved capable of organizing, rallying, and defeating restrictions on immigrants' access to higher-education assistance in the welfare bill. Now, diverse Asian and Latino groups were able to forge a historic coalition with mainstream groups to defeat a major provision in the immigration bill. Could this force work to remove the denial of public-assistance provisions in the welfare reform bill, as well?

Asian American Attitudes on Welfare and Immigration

Asian Americans' success in opposing cuts to educational benefits and legal immigration is important, in light of the conservative views of some Asian groups toward welfare use, because it created an entry point to mobilize this community politically on public-benefits issues. Although there are few formal studies on attitudes of different Asian American groups on certain issues, a 1996 *AsianWeek* survey of Asian American voters sheds some light on the different attitudes exhibited by the community on the issues of immigration and welfare reform.[25] This survey provides only general information about the political opinion of Asian Americans; it would have been more insightful and enlightening if it had provided information about the nationality of origin or immigrant generation of its subjects. In any case, when questioned about their political leanings, 38 percent of the survey's respondents described themselves as "liberal," 50 percent described themselves as "conservative," and 12 percent gave the unsolicited answer of "moderate" or "middle-of-the-road." In terms of party affiliation, 28 percent of Asian Americans said they were Democrats; 27 percent, Republicans; and 41 percent, switch voters. Evidently, Asian America holds no loyalty to one particular political party. If anything, Asian America represents a "swing vote" that will be affected by the issues of greatest concern to the community.

On the topic of immigration, the survey found that Asian Americans generally favor tough policies on "illegal immigration," with more than two-thirds supporting more severe penalties on businesses that hire undocumented workers (68.6 percent support, 24.5 percent oppose). Sixty percent favored banning welfare, education, and medical services to the undocumented. One interesting statistic revealed by the survey is that 68 percent of Asian Americans living outside of California supported these bans, whereas only 57 percent of Asian American Californians showed the same support. On the issue of providing welfare to legal immigrants during their first five years in the United States, the survey found that 46 percent supported banning such benefits, while 47 percent favored providing welfare. And when asked about stopping all legal immigration into the United States for the next five years, 34 percent actually supported the measure, while a 60 percent majority opposed it.

These numbers indicate that Asian Americans are tough on "illegal immigration" and are equally divided on the issue of welfare for immigrants during their first five years, but oppose by a ratio of almost 2:1 a freeze on immigration. The survey also suggested why the Asian American community agreed with the strategy to divide provisions for legal and "illegal" immigration into two bills: The poll clearly established that most Asian Americans would oppose the proposed reductions in legal immigration.

A Gallup poll conducted in April 1996 and reported in *AsianWeek* (1996) of the general voting population provides a comparison with *AsianWeek*'s survey. In both polls, the responses were similar on the following issues for the general voting population and the Asian American population:

- Cutting off federal welfare benefits to people who had not found a job or become self-sufficient after two years:
  FOR: Gallup, 71 percent; *Asian Week*, 65 percent.
  AGAINST: Gallup, 24 percent; *Asian Week*, 27 percent.

- Reducing federal spending for social programs, such as health, education, and welfare:
  FOR: Gallup, 44 percent; *Asian Week*, 37 percent.
  AGAINST: Gallup, 53 percent; *Asian Week*, 52 percent.

The *Asian Week* poll also indicated that Asian Americans' attitudes about welfare might differ depending on whether one was talking about the undocumented, immigrants, and citizens. A third survey, a 1992 poll conducted by the Republican National Committee (Gale and Gale 1993), is informative (see Table 15-1). The GOP survey examined Asian Americans' attitudes toward welfare programs by asking subjects whether they agreed with the following statement: "The government welfare programs aimed at helping the urban poor actually do more harm than good to the minorities." The results are as follows:

According to the *Asian Week* survey and Gallup poll results, Asians American appear to hold conservative attitudes toward welfare that are similar to the mainstream response. However, the GOP survey appears to show a spectrum of attitudes within Asian America toward welfare usage. The Vietnamese community had the highest "no-response" rate for this question, possibly indicating ambivalence about answering the question. When the numbers are added up for the "strongly agree" and "agree" categories, the Vietnamese have the lowest rate of response, at around 35 percent. This is not surprising for a community that uses welfare to a large degree and includes a number of refugees who required assistance when they entered the United States. Although the survey did not include such ethnic categories as Cambodians, Laotians,

TABLE 15-1. Asian American Attitudes Toward Welfare Doing More Harm than Good

Ethnic Group	Strongly agree	Agree	Disagree	Strongly disagree	No opinion
All	17.2%	36.7%	15.7%	3.7%	26.7%
Chinese	14.9%	41.7%	11.0%	4.5%	27.9%
Filipino	22.5%	35.8%	19.2%	3.3%	19.2%
Japanese	1.9%	37.7%	27.3%	0.5%	17.5%
Korean	17.7%	31.6%	10.1%	1.3%	39.2%
Vietnamese	11.8%	23.6%	20.9%	1.8%	41.8%
Asian Indian	27.5%	42.5%	12.5%	10.0%	7.5%
Others	20.4%	24.7%	14.0%	4.3%	36.6%

Source: Unpublished data from the Republican National Committee. The survey sample consisted of 5,000 Asian American adults in California, with a response rate of 27.9 percent (the survey was completed by 1,149 Asian Americans in August 1992). The participants were selected from membership directories of major Asian ethnic organizations and from an ethnic-surname database of registered voters. The ethnic composition of the respondents was: Chinese, 42 percent; Filipinos, 9 percent; Japanese, 21.5 percent; Koreans, 17.5 percent; Vietnamese, 24.4 percent; Asian Indian, 32 percent; others, 15.5 percent.

and Hmong, one could assume that the results would be fairly similar to those for the Vietnamese, for the same reasons.

At the opposite end of the spectrum are Asian Indians, a group that not only tends to be dominated by immigrants but that also, in the 1990 U.S. Census, had the highest median household income among Asian Americans, at $60,903. Among Asian Indians, the "strongly agree" and "agree" responses totaled 70 percent.

The Vietnamese, by contrast, had a median household income of $44,040 in the 1990 Census, and the Hmong had the lowest Asian American median household income, at $20,648. Thus, one could expect many members of these groups to be using certain public-assistance programs to supplement their income. Their attitudes toward welfare, based on their experiences as former recipients, would therefore differ from the attitudes of those who have never had to rely on any sort of public assistance. Other Asian American groups had response rates between 39 percent and 58 percent in the "strongly agree" and "agree" categories. Overall, the GOP survey demonstrates that there is a basic consensus against the use of welfare within Asian America.

The ability of Asian Americans to organize and lobby is affected by these attitudes toward welfare, which in turn depend on individual experiences. On the welfare-reform issue, the Asian American community seemed to have to overcome negative internal attitudes before it could be mobilized. In addition, the strong showing in the "no opinion" category for most groups suggests that it would be difficult to get these groups to rally, speak out, and fight restrictions on immigrants' access to welfare.

However, the Asian American community was united in its response against reducing legal immigration and restricting educational benefits to immigrant students, because those benefits are seen as opportunities and have overwhelming support within Asian America. Nearly two-thirds of all Asians in the United States are foreign-born (*Asian-Week* 1995), and many still have relatives overseas whom they seek to bring to the country. Thus, this group has an inherent self-interest when it comes to the issue of immigration. The positive rallying response for both legal immigration and education benefits generally crosses over ethnic and income boundary lines within Asian America.

Such a conclusion cannot be drawn regarding the response to the welfare-reform movement. This issue was met with a wide range of responses, splintering apparently along ethnic lines and most certainly along income and class lines. For middle- and upper-income Asian Americans, welfare is simply a "refugee" or "elderly" immigrant issue that does not concern them. To them, the mere association with refugees or recognition of welfare use might draw attention to the disadvantaged status of Asian Americans overall, and might even interfere with their enjoyment of "first-class citizen" status. In the end, this disunity creates further stratification within Asian America. Although there seems to be an intersection among various groups on the issue of immigration (at least, "legal" immigration), there is certainly a divergence in the way in which different Asian American groups react to welfare.

Unintended Consequences and Reactions from Asian America

The histories of the welfare- and immigration-reform movements are full of unintended consequences—results that were not foreseen because legislators failed to examine the myriad potential effects of their proposals.[26] Responses by Asian Americans to these reforms reveal the shape of Asian America. Those hurt most will be elderly immigrants, children, and refugees, who have one thing in common: They are not eligible to vote, and thus have no political power. As history—especially the history of Asian Americans—has demonstrated, it is easy to scapegoat people who have no voice in the system. This, one hopes, is where a new history will begin for the United States and for Asian America.

The unintended consequence that will reconfigure Asian America was the spurt of applications for naturalization (Verhovek 1996). Immigrants and refugees faced with an imminent termination of benefits concluded that the best solution was naturalization. As anti-immigrant sentiment has risen, a record-breaking number of naturalization applications were filed. Within the Asian American community, seniors attended naturalization classes in droves. The real surprise and most encouraging result appears to be that those who sought naturalization to keep their benefits actually cast votes. Many pundits criticized the spurt in applications as a means to protect public-assistance benefits, but they did not expect the new citizens actually to vote. This trend is changing the course of Asian American history.

Exit-poll results in the 1996 elections[27] (Cheng 1996; Nakao 1996; Yip 1996b) reveal a remarkable statistic within the community: One-third of those Asian Americans polled indicated they were first-time voters. The motivation of these first-time voters is intriguing. Is it merely a coincidental reflection that the community is a young one, and will we always have a crop of first time voters in each general election? Was it due to something deeper, such as the need to cast a vote for the pro-immigrant candidate in reaction to the general anti-immigrant sentiment? Extending that hypothesis, were these voters newly minted citizens on welfare who wanted to ensure that their benefits would be safeguarded? These questions and many others remain to be answered in future studies. Since the national election represented a means by which new citizens could voice their opinions by choosing a pro- or anti-immigrant candidate, the results of the 1996 national election would be interesting to analyze.

Although it was Bill Clinton who signed the Welfare and Immigration Reform Acts, he signed them with the promise to file remedial legislation to "correct" the harshness against immigrants, a promise that he attempted to fulfill after the election. This is particularly revealing given that the Republican challenger, Bob Dole, had taken an anti-immigration stance on many issues. There was a clear choice for Asian Americans as to which candidate was pro-immigrant in this general election. The exit poll discussed also provided the following statistics for the 1996 presidential race: 1) out of 500 Asian Americans polled in San Francisco and Oakland, 83 percent voted for Clinton, 9 percent voted for Dole, and 9 percent declined to answer or voted for someone else; 2) out of 900 Asian Americans polled in Los Angeles, 53 percent voted for Clinton, 41 percent voted for Dole, and 4 percent voted for Ross Perot; 3) out of 3,200 Asian Americans polled in New York City, 71 percent voted for Clinton, 21 percent voted for Dole, and 2 percent voted for Perot (Yip 1996b). Clinton was clearly the favored candidate in the Asian American community. This same increase in the number of first-time voters might be occurring in other immigrant communities, as well (Ayres 1996). The overall national numbers might reflect the formation of a new voting bloc. In combination with others voting on a pro-immi-grant stance, this could be the creation of a new multi-immigrant, multigenerational, multiethnic voting compact (Rodriguez 1997).

One might conclude that this phenomenon is simply single-issue voting politics. But why should this group be examined differently from other special interest groups? Why should Asian Americans not look out for the issues that affect them most? Why is single-issue oriented politics acceptable when it comes to abortion, gun control, and even tax cuts, but not when it comes to immigration or, even further, welfare reform in favor of recipients? One hopes that the first-time voters cared enough to learn about the politicians' positions on immigration and welfare, but also that they became educated on other issues. Through this entry point, we see Asian Americans grow-ing and maturing politically. It remains to be seen whether they will become a force on other issues within the mainstream.[28]

Finally, note that the polls that this chapter uses for its analysis do not include the political opinions of non-voters. If one assumes that first-time voters in the 1996 elec-tion included people who naturalized to protect their eligibility for benefits, there might also be a correlating change in attitudes toward welfare use in the Asian Amer-ican population, such as a liberalization in attitudes as future polls reflect the opinions of welfare beneficiaries. If this assumption is valid, one can expect an increase in Asian American voters among the elderly and people who formerly held refugee status. A fascinating study could be done on various Southeast Asian populations (Cambodi-an, Hmong, and Laotian) that consist of at least 60 percent non-citizens to examine whether this reform has changed the citizenship makeup of these communities.

After the 1996 election, conservatives— especially Republicans—realized that they had made a mistake with respect to the "immigrant" vote. Exit polls and studies showed that most Asians and Latinos were voting clearly along the Democratic (read "pro-immigrant") line (Vaitayanonta 1997; Wilgoren 1997). Although Asians appear to hold different attitudes toward immigration and welfare reform, their strong voice helped to alleviate much of the harshness in the proposed immigration reform, and analyses of voting patterns in the 1996 general election have created a "spillover" effect to ameliorate the harshness of welfare reform, as well. As a result, by the sum-mer of 1997, SSI and Medicaid benefits had been restored to disabled elderly immi-grants and youth who had arrived in the United States before the Welfare Reform Act was passed (Kilborn 1997).[29] Furthermore, by June 1998, President Clinton had also succeeded in restoring food stamps to 225,000 legal immigrants (Washington Post 1998). Since the 1996 election, Newt Gingrich and other anti-immigrant politicians have taken on stances that are more pro-immigrant (Dugger 1997; Schneider 1998; Wilgoren 1997). This became especially evident in the 2000 general election, where the Republican presidential nominee, George W. Bush, courted the Latino vote.

Drawing on their common experiences with immigration and institutional racism and discrimination upon arrival (Kim 1992; McClain 1994), and out of political neces-sity, Asian America has come together as one community. Yet the political formation of Asian America is problematic in light of the immediate differences in members' languages, ethnicities, and generations. This community has barely begun to understand its own differences. Asian Americans will advance as a united community only through realizing that understanding one another's contrasting features will let them create stronger bonds among themselves.

Just as the Immigration and Welfare Reform Acts will have different effects on different groups within the Asian American community, diverse segments within the community had their own distinctive effects on legal reform and on the 1996 elections.[30] Yet at the height of the election year and the struggle against the immigration- and welfare-reform movements, getting the community involved as a whole sometimes proved difficult. More Chinese Americans appeared to react to Japan's taking of the Diaoyutai Islands (Ding 1996), which the People's Republic of China and Taiwan have claimed. This controversy, which played out during the election year, hit a raw nerve in the Chinese American community and appeared to bring vestiges of Chinese nationalism and hatred against Japan back to life (Eljera 1996).

On a different note, in the same August 1992 Republican National Committee survey mentioned earlier, Asian Americans were asked about the importance of foreign policy in gubernatorial elections (Gale and Gale 1993: 20). Every single Asian ethnic group in the survey responded overwhelming by rating this as "very important" and "somewhat important," which indicates the significance of foreign affairs in local politics for the Asian American community.

Both of these points highlight that Asian America is a diverse, complex, new, and dynamic community. One must keep in mind that the "Asian Pacific Islander" category created by the U.S. Bureau of the Census includes twenty-nine Asian groups and nineteen Pacific Islander groups (AsianWeek 1996: 15–6). Such diversity may often override a common good and create divisions, especially given the differences within these communities that stem from centuries of nationalism, tribalism, and ethnocentrism developed while in Asia. The "baggage" that people have carried from Asia as immigrants or refugees cannot be dismissed simply by taking the name "Asian Americans." An indelible scar has been left on the psyche of Asian America by the historical fact that Asians are the only racial group ever to have been systematically prohibited from entering the United States and barred from naturalization. Among this community are Japanese Americans, the only group in the history of the United States to be incarcerated as a whole solely because of their ancestry. Yet many Asians who are newcomers to the United States may be ignorant of this history.[31] To them, the act of entry becomes paramount to all else. The American dream survives as long as one is able to enter the United States.

As a community, Asian America must recognize such differences when they arise and begin to deal with them. To react any other way would be detrimental to the establishment of an Asian America that can unite and organize itself on important issues affecting its existence, and co-existence, in the United States. This is not to say that Asian Americans must divorce themselves from politics in Asia. With the globalization of the world economy and advances in communications technology, it is only natural for newcomers to maintain a stake in the events of their lands of origin. The Asian American community is still young and developing—such are the qualities of the new, transnational world. What is essential is that the community begin to act as a cohesive group in its dealings with others. All of the differences in language, culture, and history among residents of Asia also pit the groups against one another in Asian America. The factors that pull the group together are their common history of exclusion, discrimination, and exploitation. As for the differences cited within the immigration- and welfare-reform debate, the Asian American community's focus on whether Asians will be allowed to enter this country and thus whether Asian Americans will grow as a group distracts them from dealing with another critical issue of how they, like other communities of color, are treated once they are here. The community's attention has been so intensely focused on entry that it has become the preeminent issue.

With the Republicans' seeming retreat from the anti-immigrant stance, at least for now, and both parties' attempting to court the immigrant vote (Schneider 1998; White House 1999), it remains to be seen how the politics of division will be used in the future. New immigrants have always been scapegoated for the ills of this country; the focus on the "cost" of immigrants during the 1996 election is simply the latest chapter in a never-ending book. Perhaps divisional politics will be used to turn the focus away from cuts in the immigration quotas,[32] and toward benefit-related issues for newcomers—including affirmative action.[33] For the Asian American community the growing concentration of high-skilled immigrant laborers, along with the 125 percent immigrant sponsor threshold, will mean a higher level of stratification in Asian Americans' overall income levels in the foreseeable future. Because most recent immigrants will be from a higher-income, "white-collar" background, there will be fewer working-class people among Asian newcomers. This could fuel the existing difference of opinion on such issues as welfare use and affirmative action. In addition, if what most people see are Asians working for high-tech companies and "Dot.com" ventures, weight will be added to the myth that Asian Americans are model minorities.

Coming out of these recent public-policy debates is the birth of a new voice for Asian America. This is evident in the number and strength of the various national groups that represented the community on immigration, welfare, and other issues, both inside and outside Washington, D.C.[34] The current trend is toward umbrella organizations, such as the National Council of Asian Pacific Americans, that aim to create a unified voice to speak on Asian American issues (*Asian Week* 1997; Yip 1997). In fact, this relatively new council grew from the need to speak with a unified voice during the campaign contribution scandal (Ragaza and Wu 1997) and the Wen Ho Lee case (New York Times 2000), in which Asian Americans were being stereotyped and scapegoated.[35] Such a group was also needed to generate support for the nomination of Bill Lann Lee to the position of assistant attorney general in the Civil Rights Division of the Department of Justice (Wu 1997). Further, we have seen in California how Asian Americans can come together, crossing party lines, to support "one of their own,"[36] and during the 2000 presidential election a similar alliance of Asian American Democrats and Republicans, the "80/20" Initiative, supported Al Gore (Fletcher 2000).

The mere acts of taking a position on an issue that affects the community and publicizing that position are signs of growth, maturation, and unification. The question that remains has to do with the capability of organizing as one community that is able to speak with one voice on issues that affect Asian Americans and issues that Asian Americans want to affect. Asian America is diverse and an artificial construct. We may not agree on every issue, but it is important that we try to come together and speak with one voice. Only the future will tell whether Asian Americans will remain in their historical role of reacting to the policies that others impose on them or whether they will be strong enough to create policies for their community.

Notes

Epigraphs: Smith, as quoted in Associated Press 1996: A16; Chang, as quoted in Llorente 1996: A1.

1. In general, I will use the term "Asian Americans" to include "Asian Pacific Americans" and the U.S. Census terminology of "Asian Pacific Islander." I use "Asian Pacific Islander" only to relate directly to census information.

2. The historical period in which the United States excluded various groups of Asians from entry runs from the Page Law of 1875, which prohibited the entry of "prostitutes" from "Oriental countries," to the formal repeal of the national-origins system by the 1965 Amendments to the Immigration and Naturalization Act.

3. The act retreats from sixty years of social-welfare policy. It affects 12.8 million people receiving welfare and 25.6 million receiving food stamps. It changes the rate of benefits for more than one-fifth of U.S. families with children. The bill replaces more than forty federal public-benefits programs with state block grants. The act creates a five-year lifetime limit per family for welfare payments, along with a work requirement for able-bodied adults after two years of receiving benefits (Pear 1996a).

4. Although the term "immigrant" has been defined in various ways, it has a specific legal definition within immigration law. Unless otherwise noted, the term "immigrant" will be used in this chapter to denote a "legal permanent resident." In addition, although "illegal aliens" is the pejorative term used to refer to people without legal status, the author prefers the term "undocumented."

5. The majority of the overall savings from the Welfare Reform Act will be made on the backs of immigrants—even though legal immigrants represent only 5 percent of the overall welfare recipients in the United States (National Immigration Law Center 1996).

6. Proposition 187 was designed to deny the undocumented access to all state-funded programs, including public education.

7. SSI is a program that provides benefits to low-income people who are 65 years old or older, blind, or disabled.

8. The five-year period is calculated from the time that an immigrant or refugee first enters the United States. For many immigrants and refugees, five years may already have elapsed since their date of entry.

9. Title XX of the Social Security Act provides block-grant money to states, which they may use for a variety of purposes, including child care, care for disabled persons, domestic-violence prevention programs, and child-abuse prevention programs.

10. Previously, the United States Supreme Court had ruled that states could not bar legal immigrants from these programs. See Graham v. Richardson, 403 U.S. 365 (1971). With the passage of the Welfare Reform Bill, the federal government has given states the legal authority to implement these types of bans. However, states may not bar those immigrants who are exempt from the food stamps/SSI bar.

11. The act does not list the specific programs that are considered "federal means-tested," but after the U.S. attorney general defines the phrase, it will most likely include all programs that determine eligibility based on income or assets. The most important of these programs is Medicaid. Under the act, an exception exists that allows immigrants to be eligible for "community programs for protection of life and safety," a term that the attorney general has the discretion to define. Some examples of such programs include crisis counseling and intervention, short-term shelter or assistance for the homeless or abuse victims, and soup kitchens: see Federal Register (30 August 1996), 45985–6. The act does exempt from this five-year ban such items as emergency Medicaid, immunizations, student loans, Head Start; Women, Infants, and Children (WIC); and job-training programs.

12. An immigrant's sponsor is the person who signs an affidavit promising that she or he will support the immigrant in the United States. Previously, no restrictions were placed on who could be an immigrant's sponsor. Under the act, only the immigrant's petitioner—that is, the person who legally can and does apply for the immigrant's entry—may be the sponsor. If the petitioner's income does not meet the minimum requirements, she or he may bring in someone else as an additional sponsor.

13. Previously, immigrants were subject to deeming only for their first three or five years in the United States for various programs (Leong 1995: 65). Under the act, deeming is permanent for future immigrants until naturalization or ten years of U.S. work history. Furthermore, if an immigrant does somehow receive public benefits, the act allows the federal or state government to recover the money directly from the sponsor.

14. See Leong 1997.

15. The act adds several new reasons to deport immigrants and exclude aliens. Most critically, the act severely restricts the rights of immigrants and the undocumented to appeal certain Immigration and Naturalization Service (INS) rulings in federal court. This denial of the right to judicial review is unprecedented in U.S. legal history, and is very disturbing because it violates a fundamental premise of American government allows the INS basically to engage in blatant lawlessness. The act also makes it easier for the INS to deport legal immigrants convicted of crimes: see Ojito 1998.

16. Because of space limitations, I cannot discuss in this chapter all of the many substantial provisions of the Immigration Reform Act that affect undocumented immigrants. It is sufficient to remark that these changes are indicative of the ever-more-virulent attacks that have demonized this population as the new "enemies of America." As an example of the act's "get-tough" attitude toward the undocumented, it calls for 5,000 additional Border Patrol agents and fourteen miles of triple fencing at the U.S.–Mexico border near San Diego.

17. In determining whether a sponsor meets this threshold, the INS will consider the income of the sponsor's family in relationship to a household size composed of both the sponsor's family and the immigrant or immigrants. This will effectively prohibit many poor and working-class families from petitioning for their family members to become legal immigrants. Under the 125 percent threshold in 1998, a husband and wife with two children who want to petition for the wife's parents to immigrate must earn more than $27,563 per year in order to be eligible.

18. The impact here remains to be examined in future studies. For instance, the entry of more skilled Asian professionals alone will drive up the overall income of Asian Americans, there-

by contributing even more to the model-minority myth. Alternatively, fewer working-class Asian Americans may lead to less economic-development activity among small businesses.

19. Despite this legal restriction, a General Accounting Office report revealed that, after the passage of the Immigration Reform and Control Act of 1986 and its "employer sanctions" provision, widespread discrimination resulted against Asian and Latino job applicants (GAO 1990).

20. Department of Education records show that roughly 390,000 legal immigrants received about 11 percent of the overall Pell grants for 1992–93, which equals $662 million (GAO 1995).

21. These Republicans had to retreat from their own plans. For instance, Representative Clay Shaw (R- Florida), who had introduced H.R. 4, eventually conceded that education "unlike welfare, is a part of the American dream" and is a "fundamental tool for being successful, and everyone should have equal access to it" (as quoted in Clymer 1995).

22. In mid-1996, this issue reappeared when the Senate version of the Immigration Reform Act, which was even more radical than the earlier House version, included a provision that subjected to possible deportation any alien who used any federal means-tested benefit for an aggregate total of twelve months during his or her first five years in the United States. Because higher-education loans and grants fell into this definition, the outrageous result would have been the deportation of students who had made use of such loans or grants for more than a year. The deportation provision was removed as part of a September 1996 compromise between the White House and Congress. which deleted the harshest provisions of the act (Schmitt 1996a). See also "Bill Tries to Balance Concerns on Immigration," New York Times (29 September 1996), 28.

23. Other groups included the National Association of Manufacturers, the Christian Coalition, the American Jewish Congress, Americans for Tax Reform, the American Civil Liberties Union, the National Council of La Raza, and even the National Rifle Association (Holmes 1995).

24. Simpson proposed to eliminate the provisions on the reduction of labor immigration and even deleted requirements for U.S. companies to pay a $10,000 fee for every foreign worker hired (Schmitt 1996a). Eventually, the strength of this unusual and diverse coalition of lobbying groups was too powerful even for the senior senator from Wyoming. In addition, Spenser Abraham of Michigan was relentless. Senator Simpson could not elicit the help of even his colleague Senator Orrin Hatch of Utah (chair of the Senate Judiciary Committee) as the bill was separated (Schmitt 1996b).

25. This survey of the political opinions of Asian Americans was conducted was a telephone between 25 June and 2 July 1996. The sample consisted of 807 Asian American voters from the following states: California (596); Massachusetts (57); Ohio (53); Pennsylvania (45); and Washington (56) (AsianWeek 1996).

26. For example, the New York Times reported that, after the passage of the Welfare Reform Act, nursing homes across the United States began checking the immigration status of seniors, because new immigrants are ineligible for Medicaid and SSI. Some advocates are worried that seniors who appear "foreign" may be unfairly deemed ineligible even if they are covered by an exception (Pear 1996b).

27. The poll was sponsored by the National Asian Pacific American Legal Consortium and conducted interviews of approximately 4,600 Asian American voters in San Francisco, Oakland, Los Angeles, and New York City. See also Chung 1992.

28. See, for instance, McLeod 1997, which discusses how Asian Americans were instrumental in electing two Asian American supervisors in 1996 and in passing the San Francisco 49ers' stadium project. See also Fletcher 2000.

29. The Balanced Budget Act of 1997 restored disability and health benefits to 420,000 legal immigrants who had arrived in the United States before the welfare-reform law was signed on 22 August 1996. This measure will cost an estimated $11.5 billion (White House 1999).

30. See, for instance, Gary Locke's victory in the gubernatorial race in the state of Washington (Puente 1996).

31. In fact, the incarceration of Japanese Americans during World War II may unfortunately yield a sense of justice in the minds of those Asians who suffered under Japanese military occupation that war. Indeed, most Asians do not know the history of this concentration-camp experience, nor are they aware of Asians' history of exclusion from the United States.

32. The trend here is toward providing more immigrant visas for high-tech workers to meet the demands of the computer industry.

33. As mentioned earlier, although the issue of affirmative action never took root in the national election of 1996, the seeds were in place and are now germinating across the country. Having passed anti-affirmative action related propositions in California (Proposition 209 in November of 1996), as well as the State of Washington (Initiative 200 in November of 1998), it seems affirmative action is poised to be the next divisive issue for the country.

34. The combination of well-established groups such as the Organization for Chinese Americans and the Japanese American Citizens League; newer organizations such as the National Asian Pacific American Legal Consortium, the Asian and Pacific Islander American Health Forum, the Asian Pacific American Labor Alliance, and the Asian Pacific American Institute for Congressional Studies; and recently formed organizations such as the Filipino Civil Rights Advocates, and the National Association of Korean Americans has created a stronger voice for Asians in America.

35. The campaign contribution scandal involved illegal contributions made during the 1996 presidential election by foreign Asian businesses. Politicians and the media began to call for campaign-finance reform by advocating the exclusion of contributions from legal permanent residents, even though this was permitted under the law. The characterization was that all contributions from Asians, and even Asian Americans, were from a foreign source; thus, the Democratic National Committee began to impose a "no acceptance" policy on contributions from legal permanent residents and to investigate the background of Asian American donors.

Dr. Wen Ho Lee, a nuclear scientist at Los Alamos National Laboratory, was scapegoated as a "spy" who allegedly leaked nuclear secrets to China. Although the U.S. government never formally made this charge in federal indictments, this was the insinuation that the press played out.

36. The senatorial campaign of Republican Matt Fong in California provides evidence of the potential power of the Asian American community. Although Fong eventually lost to the incumbent, Barbara Boxer, he made a strong showing in the primary election because of his ability to attract Asian Americans from both political parties (McLeod and Guara 1998).

References

AsianWeek. 1995. "Majority of APAs New Arrivals, Census Says" (1 September), 1.
———. 1996. "Asian American on the Issues" (23 August), 14–17.
———. 1997. "In the Thick of Things" (25 December), 14.
Associated Press. 1996. "Eager To Go Home." *The Record* (Bergen County, N.J.) (1 October), A16.
Ayres, B. Drummond. 1996. "After the Election: The Constituencies—The Expanding Hispanic Vote Shakes Republican Strongholds." *New York Times* (10 November), sec. 1, 1.

Bau, Ignatius. 1995. "Immigrant Rights: A Challenge to Asian Pacific American Political Influence." *Asian American Policy Review* 5: 7–44.

Cheng, Mae. 1996. "Rise in Immigrant Votes." *Newsday* (Queens, N.Y., edition) (10 November), A7.

Chung, L. A. 1992. "Asian Americans Backed Clinton." *San Francisco Chronicle* (6 November), A21.

Clymer, Adam. 1995. "G.O.P. Agrees to College Aid for Immigrants." *New York Times* (26 November), sec. 1, 1.

Ding, Ignatius. 1996. "Japanese Militarism Is Back." *AsianWeek* (27 September), 7.

Dugger, Celia. 1997. "The Budget Deal: Immigration." *New York Times* (1 August), A1.

Eljera, Bert. 1996. "Chinese Protest Japanese Land Grab." *AsianWeek* (27 September), 8.

Fletcher, Michael A. 2000. "Growing Population Confronts Bias." *Washington Post* (2 October), A3.

Gale, Susan, and Timothy Gale, eds. 1993. *Statistical Record of Asian Americans*. Detroit: Gale Research.

General Accounting Office. 1990. "Immigration Reform: Employer Sanctions and the Question of Discrimination." Washington, D.C.: U.S. Government Printing Office.

———.1995. "Higher Education: Selected Information on Student Financial Aid Received by Legal Immigrants." Washington, D.C.: U.S. Government Printing Office.

Harlan, Heather. 1997. "Elderly Brace for Immigration Reform." *AsianWeek* (4 April), 8.

Hastings, Deborah. 1998. "Reform Hits Hard Among Refugees." *AsianWeek* (19 February), 8.

Hing, Bill Ong. 1993. *Making and Remaking Asian American Through Immigration Policy, 1850–1990*. Stanford, Calif.: Stanford University Press.

Holmes, Steven. 1995. "The Strange Politics of Immigration." *New York Times* (31 December), sec. 4, 3.

Kilborn, Peter. 1997. "In Budget Deal, Clinton Keeps Welfare Pledge." *New York Times* (2 August), A1.

Kim, Hyung-Chan. 1992. *Asian Americans and the Supreme Court*. New York: Greenwood Press.

Leong, Andrew. 1995. "Welfare Reform: Effects on the Legal Permanent Immigrant." *Asian American Policy Review* 5: 63–77.

———. 1997. "The Asian Exclusion Act of 1996: Welfare Reform and Asian Pacific America." *Asian American Policy Review* 7: 88–101.

Llorente, Elizabeth. 1996. "New Citizens Swell Voting Lists; Many Cite Anti-Immigrant Backlash." *The Record* (Bergen County, N.J.) (4 October), A1.

McAllister, Karen. 1997. "No Welfare, No Hope." *Fresno Bee* (26 October), A1.

McClain, Charles. 1994. *In Search of Equality, The Chinese Struggle Against Discrimination in Nineteenth-Century America*. Berkeley and Los Angeles: University of California Press.

McLeod, Ramon, and Maria Alicia Gaura. 1998. "Crossover by Democratic Voters Helped Put Fong over the Top." *San Francisco Chronicle* (4 June), A14.

Mills, Mike. 1995. "Gates Assails Bid to Curb Immigration." *Washington Post* (29 November), F1.

Nakao, Annie. 1996. "Asian Americans Vote Big." *San Francisco Examiner* (15 December), A1.

National Immigration Law Center. 1996. "Immigrant Provisions of the Welfare Bill (H.R. 3734)." Washington, D.C.: National Immigration Law Center, 1.

New York Times. 2000. "An Overview; The Wen Ho Lee Case" (28 September), A26.

Ong, Paul, and Suzanne J. Hee. 1993. "The Growth of the Asian Pacific American Population: Twenty Million in 2020." Pp. : 11–24 in *The State of Asian Pacific America: Policy Issues to the Year 2020*. Los Angeles: LEAP Asian Pacific American Public Policy Institute and UCLA Asian American Studies Center.

Pear, Robert. 1996. "The Welfare Bill: The Overview." *New York Times* (1 August), A1.

———. 1996. "Under New Law, Nursing Homes Might Reject Legal Immigrants." *New York Times* (13 October), sec. 1, 24.

Puente, Maria. 1996. "Asians' 'Incredible' Journey in New Phase, Election of Governor a Sign of Growing Political Clout." *USA Today* (19 November), 1A.

Purdum, Todd. 1998. "Judge Nullifies Most of California's Immigrant Law." *New York Times* (19 March), A12.

Ragaza, Angelo, and Frank Wu. 1997. "Asian American Political Involvement." *New America News Service* (28 April).

Rodriguez, Gregory. 1997. "Asian Americans May Hold Key to Multiethnic Politics." *Los Angeles Times* (5 October), M1.

Schneider, William. 1998. "In California, the GOP's Scrambling." *National Journal*, vol. 30 (17 January), 138.

Schmitt, Eric. 1996a. "Author of Immigration Measure in Senate Drops Most Provisions on Foreign Workers." *New York Times* (8 March), A20.

———. 1996b. "Senate Panel Creates 2 Bills on Legal and Illegal Aliens." *New York Times* (15 March), A20.

Tamayo, William. 1992. "Asian Americans and Present U.S. Immigration Policies: A Legacy of Asian Exclusion." Pp. 1105–30 in *Asian Americans and the Supreme Court*, ed. Hyung-chan Kim. New York: Greenwood Press.

Vaitayanonta, Jack. 1997. "Asian American Political Participation, Voting Patterns and the Reshaping of American Politics, 1984–1996." *Asian American Policy Review* 7: 183–99.

Verhovek, Sam. 1996. "Immigrants' Anxieties Spur a Surge in Naturalizations." *New York Times* (13 September), A1.

Washington Post. 1998. "Food Stamp Eligibility Restored to 250,000" (24 June), A4.

White House, Office of the Vice President. 1999. "Vice President Gore Announces Administration Will Seek to Restore Additional Benefits for Legal Immigrants," press release (25 January), 1.

Wilgoren, Jodi. 1997. "Republicans Retreating on Immigration Policy." *The Globe* (Boston) (27 November), D1.

Wu, Frank, 1997. "Clinton's Honorable Decision." *AsianWeek* (18 December), 11.

Yip, Alethea. 1996a."The Asian American Mosaic." *AsianWeek* (23 August), 20.

———. 1996b. "Asian Votes Shift to the Left." *AsianWeek* (15 November), 8.

———. 1997. "Prospects for APA Unity." *AsianWeek* (11 July), 12.

About the Contributors

MARGARET ABRAHAM is an associate professor in the Department of Sociology and Anthropology at Hofstra University in Hempstead, New York. She has been involved in research and activism in the field of domestic violence in the South Asian immigrant community for a decade.

RICK BONUS is an associate professor of American Ethnic Studies at the University of Washington in Seattle. He is the author of *Locating Filipino Americans: Ethnicity and the Cultural Politics of Space* (Temple, 2000).

KAREN HAR-YEN CHOW is an assistant professor jointly in English and the Asian American Studies Institute at the University of Connecticut in Storrs. She is finishing a book on community identities in Asian American literature and vernacular publications.

MARY YU DANICO is an assistant professor in the Behavioral Science Department at California State Polytechnic University in Pomona. She is currently completing a book on 1.5-generation Korean Americans in Hawai'i.

EILEEN CHIA-CHING FUNG is an assistant professor of English at the University of San Francisco.

PENSRI HO is a visiting assistant professor and postdoctoral fellow of anthropology in the Department of Sociology and Anthropology at Gettysburg College in Gettysburg, Pennsylvania.

TARRY HUM is an assistant professor in the Department of Urban Studies at Queens College, City University of New York. Her publications include "A Protected Niche: Immigrant Ethnic Economies and Labor Market Segmentation," in *Prismatic Metropolis: Inequality in Los Angeles*, ed. Lawrence D. Bobo, Melvin L. Oliver, James H. Johnson, Jr., and Abel Valenzuela, Jr. (2000).

EMILY NOELLE IGNACIO is an assistant professor in the Department of Sociology and Anthropology at Loyola University of Chicago.

RUSSELL JEUNG teaches Race and Ethnic Relations at Foothill College in Los Altos Hills, California.

REBECCA CHIYOKO KING is an assistant professor in the Department of Sociology at the University of San Francisco.

ANDREW LEONG is an associate professor at the Law Center within the College of Public and Community Service at the University of Massachusetts in Boston.

EDWARD J. W. PARK is the director of the Asian Pacific American Studies Program at Loyola Marymount University in Los Angeles. His publications include "Competing Visions: Political Formation of Korean Americans in Los Angeles, 1992–97" (*Amerasia Journal*, 1998) and "Racial Ideology and Hiring Decisions in Silicon Valley" (*Qualitative Sociology*, 1999).

LISA SUN-HEE PARK is an assistant professor in Ethnic Studies and Women's Studies at the University of Colorado, Boulder.

JIANNBIN LEE SHIAO is an assistant professor in the Department of Sociology and a participating faculty member in the Ethnic Studies Program at the University of Oregon in Eugene.

PAUL SPICKARD is professor of History at the University of California, Santa Barbara, with affiliate appointments in Asian American Studies and Religious Studies. Among his books are *Mixed Blood: Intermarriage and Ethnic Identity in Twentieth-Century America* (1989), *Japanese Americans* (1996), the co-edited volume *We Are a People: Narrative and Multiplicity in Constructing Ethnic Identity* (Temple, 2000), and *Pacific Diaspora: Island Peoples in the United States and Across the Pacific* (in press).

LINDA TRINH VÕ is an assistant professor in the Asian American Studies Program at the University of California, Irvine. She co-edited, with Marian Sciachitano, a special issue on Asian American women for *Frontiers: A Journal of Women Studies* (2000) and is completing a book on Asian American community formation.

ERIC C. WAT is the author of *The Making of a Gay Asian Community: An Oral History of Pre-AIDS Los Angeles* (2002).

DEBBIE HIPPOLITE WRIGHT is a professional social worker and chair of the Department of Social Work at Brigham Young University–Hawai'i. She is co-editor of *Pacific Islander Americans: An Annotated Bibliography in the Social Sciences* (1995) and *Pacific Diaspora: Island Peoples in the United States and Across the Pacific* (in press).

Index